Parent-Child Play

SUNY Series, Children's Play in Society
Anthony D. Pellegrini, Editor

Parent-Child Play

Descriptions and Implications

Edited by
Kevin MacDonald

STATE UNIVERSITY OF NEW YORK PRESS

Published by
State University of New York Press, Albany

© 1993 State University of New York

For information, address State University of New York
Press, State University Plaza, Albany, N.Y., 12246

Production by Diane Ganeles
Marketing by Fran Keneston

Library of Congress Cataloging-in-Publication Data

Parent-child play : descriptions and implications / edited by Kevin
    MacDonald.
        p.   cm. — (SUNY series, children's play in society)
    Includes bibliographical references (p.   ) and index.
    ISBN 0-7914-1463-9 (CH : acid-free). — ISBN 0-7914-1464-7 (PB :
    acid-free)
    1. Play.   2. Child development.   3. Parent and child.
    I. MacDonald, Kevin B.   II. Series.
    HQ782.V35   1993
    155.4′18—dc20   92-20562
                                                              CIP
                                                              Rev.

10 9 8 7 6 5 4 3 2 1

Contents

Introduction: Parents and Children Playing

This volume brings together a varied group of researchers and theoreticians with a common interest in parent-child play. Despite considerable diversity in theoretical perspectives and research interests, the contributors share a belief that parent-child play is an important arena in which to study basic developmental processes. Indeed, the basic processes underlying parent-child play appear to be biological universals. The data presented in several chapters, especially in chapter 10 by Anne Fernald and Daniela O'Neill, show that the capacity for parent-child play is apparent in a wide range of cultures from diverse parts of the world, and the data described in chapter 5 by Jaak Panksepp and in chapter 6 by Maxine Biben and Steve Suomi indicate that at least some types of parent-child play occur among a wide range of mammalian species.

Nevertheless, despite the importance of viewing the capacity for parent-child play as a developmental universal, there is persuasive evidence that the style and amount of parent-child play varies enormously—between species, between cultures, and within cultures—and that this variation is associated with important developmental outcomes. An adequate theory of parent-child play must therefore address basic issues related to the nature and function of variation in developmental processes. On the basis of the evidence provided in this volume, I would suggest that at the very least, parent-child play is a marker variable which is associated with variation in the level of parent interest and investment in children. However, taken as a whole, the book provides convincing evidence that parent-child play is causally related to positive social and cognitive outcomes for children.

The volume begins with an introductory chapter by Brian Sutton-Smith, a pioneer in the scientific study of play. Sutton-Smith draws on his extensive experience to provide a comprehensive sum-

1

mary of the literature on parent-child play over the last fifty years. This literature supports the general importance of parent-child play, especially during the early years. Interestingly, Sutton-Smith emphasizes the social consequences of parent-child play rather than "fairly marginal academic outcomes."

However, the most intellectually provocative aspect of the chapter is the second section in which Sutton-Smith attempts to develop a wider perspective on adult attitudes toward play (including play research). Sutton-Smith argues that as children's play has come increasingly under scientific scrutiny, it has also become more supervised and controlled by adult interests. These interests have ranged from a concern to inculcate manliness (prominent from the mid to late nineteenth century) to a concern to use children's play as a means to increase academic competence (a highly salient contemporary interest). Increased knowledge of children's play has thus led to attempts to direct and control children's play, and Sutton-Smith goes on to suggest that the present emphasis on parent-child play is partly a device to justify the socialization of the lower classes according to middle-class standards.

Sutton-Smith also suggests that the increasing control of children's play in the service of adult interests has coincided with the idealization of children's play as innocent. This idealization allows adults to ignore the rather disorderly and self-indulgent aspects of adult play, so that children's play becomes elevated to the status of an ideal conscience—a politically impotent symbol of innocence. In idealizing children's play we are ignoring earlier theorists like Groos, Hall, and Freud who emphasized the idea that children's play had other baser, more "instinctual" aspects—perhaps, for example, providing a training ground for aggression.

Although some aspects of Sutton-Smith's analysis will certainly be controversial, this last point is certainly well-taken: there is no reason whatever to suppose that the only purpose of children's play is to make ideal citizens or to become academically competent. Moreover, the fact that play has been used in an effort to shape and control children in recent history emphasizes the close connection between play and developmental plasticity. Because play can have important developmental consequences, play has often been a focal point for individuals interested in influencing development, whatever their motivation.

Following this introductory chapter, the first section of the book includes three chapters which develop different theoretical perspectives on parent-child play: the dynamic interaction perspective, the organizational perspective, and an evolutionary perspective based on parental investment theory. Although these theories ultimately view parent-child play in quite different and (to some extent) incompatible ways, they share a common belief that play is intimately associated with the concept of developmental plasticity.

The dynamic interaction perspective presented by Alan Fogel, Evangeline Nwokah, and Jeanne Karns proposes that parent-infant play is not the result of systems which have evolved for the specific purpose of prescribing the form of playful interactions. Rather than consisting of a set of evolved schemas, developmental pathways involving parent-child play are underdetermined by the genetic material. Developmental plasticity is thus absolutely crucial to conceptualizing parent-child play. Parent-child play is one of a number of emergent processes "that partake of lower-level components, none of which contains explicit representations of play" (p. 45). Play consists of subtle variability and emergent creativity rather than stereotypic rules.

Because of their focus on variability and creativity as essential elements of play, Fogel and his colleagues concentrate the bulk of their chapter on reviewing cross-cultural variation in the dynamics of play as well as the influence of contextual factors on parent-infant play. Subtle changes in the physical context, changing the number of participants, or the status of the participant (other infants, older children, adults) has a profound effect on the dynamics of play. Moreover, they propose that laughter during games is the complex result of a large number of nonobligatory processes and cannot be analyzed as the consequence of a scheme or set of schemes possessed by the child. The result is certainly a powerful challenge to rigid evolutionary approaches which ignore the creativity, spontaneity, and variability of play.

The chapter by Marjorie Beeghly is also driven by a general theory of developmental processes—that of the organizational perspective on developmental psychopathology associated with several developmental theorists, including Dante Cichetti and Alan Sroufe. These theorists focus on developmental tasks which require the integration of social, emotional, and cognitive competencies that are crucial in achieving adaptation at a particular developmental level. Like the dynamic interaction theory presented by Fogel and colleagues, development is viewed as a complex dynamic process in which there are multiple transactions among parent, child, and ecological systems. Competent parent-child play thus depends on the successful accomplishment of previous developmental competencies: the reciprocal socioemotional interchanges of the two to six month period presuppose successful regulation of physiological and behavioral state occurring during the first months of life.

Moreover, the successful attainment of developmental tasks requires environmental input which is sensitive to the characteristics of the child. For example, sensitive, responsive caretaking is typical of successful socioemotional interchanges during the two to six month period in normal infants, but highly intrusive maternal styles appear to be the most effective intervention for Down's syndrome infants. In some cases, maternal behavior can even compensate for developmental abnormalities.

For Beeghly, adult-child face-to-face play provides a window on normal and abnormal developmental processes. She reviews data indicating close associations between the child's social and cognitive abilities with the structure and style of adult-child play. She then presents parent-child play data from a group of toddlers diagnosed as characterized by Intrauterine Growth Retardation (IUGR). The results indicate that the IUGR toddlers were significantly more distractible and hyperactive in the parent-child play situations. However, these effects were moderated by contextual variables, including social support and attachment status. As predicted by the organizational perspective, performance during parent-child play at two years of age was related to earlier maternal and attachment variables.

My contribution (chapter 4) develops a perspective on parent-child play based on evolutionary biology. A basic premise is that the capacity for play is a biological adaptation and thus a panhuman universal. However, like the dynamic interaction and organizational perspectives, there is a strong emphasis on developmental plasticity. Indeed, play in general is viewed as an adaptation which presupposes developmental plasticity. Children's play is viewed as an environment-engagement device which parents take advantage of in order to shape developmental outcomes. As suggested by Sutton-Smith, therefore, parents (or other interested adults) are able to achieve significant control over developmental outcomes by manipulating the context of children's play. However, consistent with the view of Panksepp in chapter 5, play is viewed as a biological adaptation with specific neurobiological underpinnings.

The principle theoretical tool used in the evolutionary analysis of parent-child play is the idea of parental investment. Parental investment in children includes providing a wide range of resources, including the stimulation available during parent-child play. As with any aspect of parental investment, there are clear costs and benefits of parent-child play. It is argued that societies with high levels of parent-child play are more likely to be characterized by monogamy, nuclear family social organization, low fertility (high age of first pregnancy, low number of offspring, high birth-spacing interval), and parent-rearing of children. On the other hand, evidence is provided that societies characterized by polygyny, extended family social organization, high fertility, and sibling rearing and/or fostering of children are low in parent-child play. This basic perspective implies that parents are able to take advantage of human developmental plasticity by programming individual development to respond adaptively to particular ecological contingencies.

The second section of the volume emphasizes the mechanisms underlying parent-child play. It begins with two discussions focusing on parent-child play (or its absence) among animals. Jaak Panksepp's contribution describes his research on the neurochemical basis of social play, especially rough and tumble (r & t) play, in animals. Panksepp takes issue with the views of many psychologists who have great difficulty in thinking in terms of fundamental brain mechanisms underlying specific behaviors with adaptive functions. Panksepp proposes just such a status for social play: "Roughhousing play is a robust central-state process of the mammalian brain" (p. 148). Panksepp argues that these mechanisms are phylogenetically ancient and are essentially shared by all mammals as a homology (i.e., a similarity which results because of evolution from a common ancestor).

As noted by Fogel and colleagues, one of the central problems for a biological theory of play is that of variability and creativity. Panksepp suggests that variability can occur in the presence of a single underlying mechanism because play is filtered and channeled through the higher information processing networks in the cortex. This neuropsychological underpinning is conceptualized as a dopamine-based reward system, closely linked to (but quite possibly separate from) exploratory activity. As reviewed in my contribution (see chapter 4), this conceptualization fits well with data and theory from personality research, and is compatible with the evolutionary conceptualization of play as involving mechanisms which result in intrinsically motivated interactions with the environment.

Panksepp concludes his contribution with the provocative idea that since play produces positive emotional states, it could be used as a reinforcer for good behavior in academic settings. Thus it may well be that a very good way to get hyperactive children to learn to play appropriately and inhibit aggression would be to make r & t play contingent on appropriate behavior in the classroom or on being able to inhibit aggression and control emotions during r & t play. Unquestionably, any highly pleasurable behavior can be used as a reinforcer, so this is an important possibility, especially for hyperactive children, since they appear to greatly enjoy r & t play.

Perhaps the most salient feature emerging from the chapter by Maxine Biben and Steve Suomi (chapter 6) is that adult-infant play is far from common among nonhuman primate species. Among squirrel monkeys adult-infant play only seems to occur if other infants are unavailable. This suggests that the primary adaptation for play in this species is for play with same-age conspecifics, but it also reminds us that the mechanisms underlying play as an environment engagement device ensure that the infant will seek playful stimulation wherever he/she can find it. Moreover, it indicates that although adults are not ordinarily play partners to younger animals, they still possess the necessary machinery for play. In fact, Biben and Suomi point out that when the living situation of rhesus macaques is altered so that adult males live in close proximity to infants, the rate of adult-infant play increases some two hundred fold.

Clearly, then, adult-infant and adult-juvenile r & t play does occur among monkeys and macaques, albeit infrequently in natural situations. When it does occur, it is sufficiently well-rehearsed and stereotyped to indicate that r & t play is a biological adaptation, even if the specific adult-offspring version merely takes advantage of this machinery. Moreover, the very rich descriptions of squirrel monkey and rhesus macaque adult-infant play could very easily be descriptions of human adult-child r & t, complete with a great deal of role reversal and self-handicapping by the adults.

Also noteworthy is Biben and Suomi's argument for delayed benefits of play among infants and juveniles. This is a difficult area, but they convincingly argue that, although immediate benefits of play presumably occur (such as exercise), these benefits do not explain the sex-differentiated patterns of play observed among the juveniles and infants. Males and females are preparing for very different ecological situations as adults, and this is reflected in their play styles.

James Carson, Virginia Burks, and Ross Parke review data on parent-child physical (r & t) play among children, highlighting the very robust age and sex differences (for both parents and children) associated with this style of play. Of particular interest are recent findings suggesting that styles of interaction across family and peer systems are "strikingly similar," providing further support for the idea that peer interactions are influenced by parent-child interactions. Measures of directive and coercive styles of parent-child play taken prior to kindergarten predicted social competence in school.

Besides expanding the research on the parent-child correlates of social competence, the authors review evidence on the mechanisms involved, with a particular emphasis on the idea that parent-child physical play provides a training ground for affect regulation and the encoding and decoding of emotional expressions. They caution, however, that while the usual assumption is that parents influence children, the results are also compatible with the view that child characteristics, such as temperament, account for the associations found thus far.

The research on the mechanisms underlying parent-child r & t play has clearly emphasized the importance of affect in conceptualizing the nature and consequences of this activity. In their contribution in chapter 8, Phyllis Levenstein and John O'Hara provide evidence for the idea that play is an affect-driven enterprise even when the playful activities are cognitively oriented. Relying on Sheldon White's classic paper, they note that children seek to master the environment and that they experience a positive feeling of efficacy when they do so. Moreover, this intrinsic motivation to master the environment is importantly influenced by the "affectively charged" presence of the parent. The teaching and learning which occur during parent-child play appear to be much more effective when they are embedded in a warm, affectively positive parent-child relationship.

Levenstein and O'Hara emphasize that interventions aimed at improving cognitive competence in young children must utilize sources of motivation which are intrinsic to the child, and this has been the guiding philosophy of Levenstein's Mother-Child Home Project from its inception. The authors report on positive results for this program, both in terms of children's cognitive competence and in terms of raising the level of the mothers' verbal interactive behavior. There was clear support for the idea that the effectiveness of parent-child play was related to the warmth of the parent-child relationship as indicated by the association between positive affective interchange in the mother-child context and a variety of cognitive measures in the child. Mother-child play must take place "in a nondidactic dyadic climate of light spontaneity and fun" (p. 234).

Moreover, the finding that mothers' verbal interactive behavior was raised is particularly important in light of some of the data provided in Tiffany Field's contribution (chapter 13; see discussion below): inadequate mother-child interactions are open to influence. Cultural and subcultural differences, while resistant to change, can be modified by reprogramming mothers to take advantage of children's intrinsic motivation to learn about their environment. Thus, even if observational studies of parent-child play suggest only "fairly marginal academic outcomes," as suggested by Brian Sutton-Smith in chapter 1, there is the suggestion that interventions based on fairly intensive parent-child play can have ecologically important consequences on children's academic potential.

In chapter 9 Jeffrey Cohn reviews data on the detailed mechanisms involved in the regulation of affect during early parent-child play. Of particular importance are the interactions of depressed mothers during interactions with their infants. These mothers may be viewed as a paradigmatically unplayful group during interaction with their infants. Infants respond to these depressed mothers with less positive affect and more negative affect, but there are marked individual differences within groups of depressed mothers. The most playful mothers were also the most affectively positive, while disengaged mothers elicited active protest in their infants, and intrusive mothers elicited avoidance in the infant. The results underscore a central finding of this volume: parent-child play is part of an affectively positive parent-child interaction. Depressed mothers are clearly not capable of interacting in a manner where there are reciprocated positive social interactions with their infants. Infant affect matches that of the mother, and this appears to have developmental consequences: over time the infants become generally more negative.

The third section of the volume focuses on studies of play viewed in cross-cultural perspective. The data presented in these chapters can be used for two quite different purposes: (1) to show that the basic forms of parent-child play are universal; or (2) to show that cross-cultural variation in patterns of parent-child play is meaningfully associated with variation in either (a) the ecological context of the different cultures, and/or (b) cross-cultural variation in child outcomes. The chapters included in this section provide evidence related to all of these points.

The work of Anne Fernald and Daniela O'Neill on peekaboo games in chapter 10 concentrates on establishing that there are universal patterns of parent-child play. They begin by noting that even though the words and melody used by mothers in South Africa are different from those used by Japanese mothers, "the rhythm, dynamics, and shared pleasure in the inevitable outcome are fundamentally similar" (p. 259). This research is in the best ethological tradition, often quite reminiscent of research on vocalizations among birds: detailed field observations are buttressed with sophisticated acoustic analysis of vocalizations to illustrate the essential commonalities of parent-child play around the world.

The results presented here reveal two different calls which are characteristic of mother-infant peekaboo games: the Alert call, used to get the baby's attention, and the Release call, which results in surprise and positive affective response in the infant. As found also by research on bird vocalization, there are subtle within-species (i.e., cross-cultural) differences which can be viewed as dialects with a central species-typical core of commonality. Interestingly, an important universal feature of peekaboo games is also the most important aspect of the game: the reappearance of the mother is "an exhilarating moment, marked by exaggerated and relatively stereotyped vocal and facial gestures" (p. 267).

Thus the universal result of this game is to produce an intensely positive affective state in the baby. The authors argue that this response depends on biological predispositions in the baby. Babies appear to be biologically programmed to respond affectively to mothers' reappearance, even though the exact routine of the mother need not be stereotyped at all. As is the case with the analysis of r & t play described in chapter 4, striking similarities seen cross-culturally in a peekaboo game presumably occur because it "exploits perceptual, attentional, and affective predispositions of the young infant, and because it both engages and accommodates the developing cognitive capabilities of the child" (p. 268).

The authors then provide a detailed account of the precise nature of these predispositions, with an emphasis on the balance between novelty and predictability as eliciting the affective response of the infant during early infancy, followed by a shift toward the infant taking pleasure also in the active orchestration of the game. Clearly, despite a variety of biological predispositions which enable babies to engage in these games, there is a pronounced lack of stereotypy. Nevertheless, the universal consequence is that the infant enjoys the games. The peekaboo game is part of a reciprocated positive affective interaction between adults and infants.

There is also considerable support for the universality of the forms of parent-child play in the work of Jaipaul Roopnarine, Frank

Hooper, Mohammed Ahmeduzzaman, and Brad Pollack in their paper on parent-child play in India (chapter 11). They begin their contribution with a summary of Indian social structure. Although nuclear families are increasing in India, the joint or extended family is still predominant. In this type of family, kinship ties are very strong, so that individuals define themselves with respect to their place in the wider kinship structure. Despite this enormous difference in social structure compared to Western norms, adult-child games are immediately comparable to games found by researchers in Western societies. These games involve visual, auditory, and tactile stimulation which is arousing and is perceived as pleasurable to the child. The authors propose that at the most general level the infant learns means-end relationships in this type of play. However, the early mother-infant games emphasize close physical contact and language in the form of songs. The physical closeness is also apparent in the practice of embedding the games in the context of massaging the infant.

Although the results reported by Roopnarine and colleagues are compatible with universal predispositions for children to enjoy certain types of stimulation, their contribution is also much concerned with variation in parent-child play along a number of dimensions. As noted also by Carson, Burks, and Parke, Roopnarine and colleagues find that the tendency for fathers to engage in rough play or highly stimulating activities is not found among several cultures from widely scattered parts of the world. Some of this variation may not be related to variation in developmental outcomes: the authors propose that similar developmental outcomes such as security of attachment can be attained by different pathways: "*Consistent* social interaction patterns involving a variety of activities which are pleasurable and intrinsically arousing to the infant probably provide the essential developmental context for much subsequent cognitive and socioemotional development" (p. 296).

Although variation in style of play may therefore not be related to variation in developmental outcomes. Roopnarine and colleagues provide evidence that variation in the amount of play is related to variation in developmental outcomes. They review the results of Indian studies which, like the comparable studies done in Western countries reviewed in chapter 1 by Brian Sutton-Smith, show an association between the amount of parent-child play and developmental status. Interestingly, while the typical social class differences in parent-child play were found, low levels of parent-child play were associated with poor developmental status in families where the home environment "appeared to be adequately furnished with objects and materials" (p. 294). Because of these patterns, there has been an effort in India to develop interventions which focus on increasing parent-child play, an effort which has met with some success.

One of the potential problems in including cross-cultural research on human development is that the research tends to be fragmented. This tendency toward fragmentation can be minimized, however, if the cross-cultural data can be categorized as representative of contrasting types of human social organization. In the present volume it is possible to contrast societies where parents perform the great majority of child rearing with societies where sibling rearing of children is the norm. Although most of the material in this volume is derived from societies where parent rearing is the norm, there are three papers describing parent-child play in cultures or subcultures where sibling rearing of children is common. These contrasting patterns of child rearing represent theoretically meaningful types for purposes of classifying parent-child play, since sibling rearing of children is strongly associated with low levels of parent-child play. Comparisons between parent-rearing and sibling-rearing societies are thus likely to shed light on the nature and functions of parent-child play.

In chapter 12 Carolyn Edwards and Beatrice Whiting describe parent-child and older sibling-child interactions in a periurban society in Kenya characterized by polygynous, extended family structure. Mothers, although very concerned about the physical needs and survival of all their children, engage in very little sociable interaction with them, while fathers have almost no contact with their children. The role of playmate devolves to the siblings, particularly the adjacent older sibling. Fully 34 percent of these sibling interactions were affectively negative, including scolding, reprimanding, insults, and physical discipline. However, the length of the age interval between the siblings was positively associated with more nurturant and less dominant-aggressive behavior, suggesting that as the sibling gets older he/she behaves more like a parent. The authors note that sibling rearing is required because the mother has an extremely heavy work load—a point that is related to the ecology of intermediate level, clan societies in the evolutionary theory presented in chapter 4.

Although her data were gathered in the United States, Tiffany Field's study in chapter 13 shows important parallels with the work of Edwards and Whiting. She finds important differences in

mother-child play among Haitian, Cuban, and American black
subcultures in Miami. These differences were found despite the
fact that all groups were of lower socioeconomic class origin. Both
the American black and the Haitian black groups lived in father
absent, extended family environments, while the Cuban group
tended to live in nuclear families and frowned on pregnancy prior to
marriage.

Field documents a low investment style of parenting among
American blacks in which girls become pregnant as teenagers, become disinterested in the baby, and leave the parenting to grandparents. Mother-infant face-to-face interactions in this group are
"significantly inferior" to Latin groups of similar socioeconomic
status. Immigrant Haitian mothers, who have a different ethnic origin than American blacks, are described as having very awkward
feeding interactions, and, although their face-to-face interactions in
the laboratory setting appeared superior to the American black
group, their behavior in the waiting room suggested that there was
little face-to-face interaction in this group. Field concludes that cultural differences are remarkably persistent among these groups—
remaining even when, as in the case of the Haitians, there is a
conscious effort to assimilate.

In chapter 14, Jo Ann Farver presents a direct comparison of
parent-child play in a rural Mexican society (characterized by extended family social organization and little parent-child play) and
lower-class American society (characterized by nuclear family social
organization and normative parent-child play). Farver finds that
American children experienced more complexity in pretend play
with their mothers, while Mexican children experienced more
complexity with their siblings. Mexican sibling-child play thus resembled American mother-child play to a considerable extent.
Farver also notes that, because the mother tends to devote her attention to the most recently born sibling and ignore the older children, sibling affectional relationships are much more important in
Mexican society.

These findings present a challenge to the parental investment
theory presented in chapter 4, since they suggest that sibling play
in societies characterized by the extended family can compensate
for the lack of parent-child play. The results presented by Farver indicate that further research is necessary on the long-term outcomes
of sibling rearing versus parent rearing. The important dependent
variables will be measures of intellectual functioning as well as
measures of the tendency to form bonded relationships later in life.

The perspective developed in chapter 4 suggests that sibling rearing is a relatively low investment style of child rearing compared to parent rearing, and will tend to result in lowered intellectual competence and less of a tendency toward pair bonding later in life. In any case, the presence of strong theoretical views in the field of parent-child play can only help to provide rigorous hypotheses regarding future research.

In the final chapter, J. Kevin Nugent, Sheila Greene, Dorit Wieczoreck-Deering, Kathleen Mazor, John Hendler, and Cynthia Bombardier compared the mother-infant play of a group of married mothers with a group of unmarried mothers in Ireland. Such comparisons again raise the issue of the role of parent-infant play in providing an optimal environment for children. The authors review literature indicating that while the mother-infant play of single mothers has been shown to be deficient, single parenthood itself may well not be the cause of the deficiency. And by comparing the play styles of single mothers in different cultures, it is possible to test the hypothesis that risk factors vary between cultures.

In the event, the authors find that indeed single parenthood does not appear to be a risk factor in the Irish sample. The mother-infant play of these Irish mothers was essentially indistinguishable from that of married mothers, and even appeared to be superior for some behaviors. The results are interpreted within what is termed a "cultural-ecological framework." The cultural-ecological perspective emphasizes two ideas: First, it emphasizes the idea that variation in cultural attitudes toward particular behaviors can affect whether the behavior is a risk factor. In the present study, the authors suggest that in Ireland the cultural disapproval of unmarried women during pregnancy is replaced by cultural acceptance of unmarried mothers and their infants. As a result, the depression characteristic of unmarried women disappears within the first three weeks of the birth of the baby, and the mother-infant play appears normal.

Secondly, the ecological-cultural perspective emphasizes the contributions of both mother and infant to early mother-infant play. While the marital status and age of the mother did not emerge as important variables in this study, mothers with higher levels of education had superior play interactions with their infants. This finding essentially replicates the findings of many investigators that parent-child play is strongly influenced by social class differences, and it reminds us that at least some maternal characteristics are important for understanding variation in mother-infant play. However, the social responsiveness of the infant was also a significant contributor to early mother-infant play, and it even appears that in the first few weeks of life the baby has a greater input into playful interactions than the mother. As emphasized also by the dynamic interaction perspective represented here by Alan Fogel and colleagues and the organizational perspective represented by Marjorie Beeghley's chapter, both the child and the mother are active agents in parent-infant play from the very beginning of life.

In concluding these introductory remarks, perhaps the most ambitious hope would be that the field of parent-child play would be able to emerge from these discussions as an identifiable field which, although obviously linked to a wide range of developmental theory and research, is distinguished by having its own set of theories and concerns. I believe that such a hope is reasonable because play is the predominant context in which children interface with the environment, whether social or nonsocial, in an affectively positive, internally driven (appetitive) manner. The present research supports the idea that parent-child play is developmentally important. The question of whether it is irreplaceable in producing optimal child functioning in a postindustrial society is a vital developmental question which can only be answered by future research.

CHAPTER 1

Dilemmas in Adult Play with Children

Brian Sutton-Smith

Introduction

In 1974 my wife and I published a book entitled *How to Play with Children: And When Not To.*[1] We did this in response to a journalist's comment that since we had been studying play for some twenty years we should by now have something to say to parents on what they should do about it. Looking back at that enterprise all these years later, I am struck with the optimism of our response. We went to print asserting that in an informational world like ours, where manual drudgery was no longer the major form of work life, there was a need for people who were both creative and flexible in symbolic ways. And since there was increasing evidence that play exercised these characteristics, then surely, we argued, we could amplify its effects by urging parents to play with children. At that time we had no indubitable evidence that parents playing with children could actually do this. But even if, in the worst possible scenario, we were wrong, we figured that our advocacy would have improved the quality of life for both parties whatever else it achieved. I now believe that our optimism was based in part on our playful experience with our own five children and in part on scientific evidence. But it was also derived from the prevailing optimism of the 1960s that it was possible to increase the humanization of modern society.

In this chapter I want to review the scholarly evidence that we had at hand to support our position at that time as well as that which has been accrued since. My major and first focus in this chapter, therefore, will be on the relationship between parental play with children and the children's subsequent growth. But in a second part of the chapter I want to raise the question of whether, despite an apparent modern concern with play and child growth, our efforts aren't also instigated by our desire to control and socialize children in terms of upper status norms. And finally I wish to ask whether these foci on children and adults as separate don't distort the reciprocal political interdependence of both in cross-generational play, which in the present context is the question whether, in advocating play with children, we are not only attempting to socialize the children but also to socialize the fairly irrational play of our irrational adult peers.

1. Adult Play and Child Growth

When the journalist asked his question about the usefulness of parents playing with children our positive response was in the first place based on approximately 150 years of accumulated doctrine about the positive values of child play from Rousseau to Piaget. In addition, during the sixties I had worked with anthropologist John M. Roberts with the cross-cultural game materials in the Human Relations Area Files. With this data we established statistically significant correlations between types of games and child rearing ranging across hundreds of human societies (Roberts and Sutton-Smith 1962; Sutton-Smith and Roberts 1981). This data made it difficult to avoid the notion that the adult child-rearing effect upon children and their play was in some way essential to children's personal development as well as to their cultural adaptation.

In addition, the period from 1940 through 1960 was one of intensive empirical study of mother-infant interaction. While much of it was instigated by wartime-associated discoveries of the effects of mother or father separation and infant deprivation, particularly in disadvantaged socioeconomic groups, the outcome was multiple discoveries of significant relationships between kinds of mother sensory and verbal stimulation and infant development. While few of these investigations were at first directly concerned with the role of mothers' play as a part of her infant stimulation, play variables were increasingly discovered to be significant. Even within behaviorist theoretical paradigms, mothers who responded contingently to the baby's initiative of coos and smiles were found to have the greatest reinforcing effects. There was recognition that if you wanted the baby's attention you had to respond to the baby by copying its behavior and then varying it in novel ways. To keep the baby's attention you had to become something of a playful mimic or fool. It was found even that mothers' stimulation was more effective during play than during their ordinary caretaking activities. It was the play, not the caretaking, which had the most positive relationships to the child's own object skill and exploratory competences. Most of this literature is summarized in the excellent 1973 monograph of the Society for Research in Child Development by K. Allison Clarke-Stewart which reviews the pioneering work of those years including the work of those such as Harriet Rheingold, Betty Caldwell, Daniel Stern, Michael Lewis, and John Watson, to mention only the ones that most influenced us personally.

The importance of these accounts of the power of mother playfulness during these years was also amplified by other research on children's play itself which appeared to show, to take one example, that it was correlated with skill on creativity tests. In the 1960s the names of Nina Lieberman, Jerome Singer, Sarah Smilanksy, and Dina Feitelson were associated with the discovery that more imaginative children were superior both on creativity tests and in ordinary schoolwork (Singer and Singer 1990). While the parallel studies on infant exploration by Berlyne (1960), Hutt (1971), and McCall (1974) occurring during these years were not typically related to mother-infant stimulation, they also served to increase interest in infant playfulness (Hutt et al. 1989). In addition Ruth Weir, in her 1962 tape recordings of her two-year-old son in his crib, had also shown how much time a child spends on solitary practice and play with language demonstrating more specifically than usual the role of language play in the child's language acquisition. Finally, as a background to all of this, there was considerable scholarly activity, both observational and experimental, on animal play which strongly suggested relationships between play and kinds of adaptation (Birch 1945; Loizos 1969; Reynolds 1972).

The excitement of the time and this congruence of animal, psychological, linguistic, and anthropological information was perhaps capped for most of us by the 1972 Jerome Bruner paper entitled "The Nature and Uses of Immaturity" where, using evidence from animal and human studies, he tied immaturity and playfulness together as essential components of human adaptation (Bruner 1976). It was a high point in the study of children's play and *How to Play with Children* fittingly symbolized our hopes at that time.

1974–1990: Mother-Infant Play

In general what has happened since 1974 has sustained and advanced the earlier findings. Our confidence in the importance of mother-child play, for example, has been assisted by the descriptive work of Daniel Stern (1977) and others showing the intricate character of that relationship. For example my own student at Columbia University, Beatrice Beebe (1973), searching for the infant origins of play, contributed to this group of studies by showing that by dual filming of the mother's and the baby's face while at play the baby could be seen to gradually learn the synchrony of looking at the mother's face while the mother was looking at the baby and looking away when the mother was looking away. It was a major accomplishment for the baby between two and three months permitting that synchronization of faces on which all later games had to be based.

I would speculate on the basis of Richard Sennett's historical account of *The Fall of Public Man* (1978) that because such face-to-face games seem to be played only in complex civilizations and not in tribal ones, they perhaps have something to do with the tremendous need for expressional diversity in complex cultures. In tribal society change in life identity is often signaled by the use of masks. Napier's thesis in *Masks, Transformations and Paradox* (1986) is that living continuously amongst familiar kin, masks are the only way to express a difference. But in the public and market world of complex societies with multiple casual acquaintances and innumberable strangers, a capacity for varied and empathic novel expressions has to be taken for granted. Hence perhaps the origin of these practices with babies. In turn, adults confronted by facial differences in their multiple adult transactions transfer these to their children in their mutual play with them. Rousseau, at a turning point in the urbanization of modern society, the late eighteenth century, lamented just this kind of diversity of public facial self that the mother inculcates with these games of silliness. He was an enemy of the inauthenticity of large societies and particularly horrified by actors with their various facial simulations of identity. He would have been horrified by these goings on in mother-infant games (Starobinksi 1988).

Bruner and Sherwood's (1976; see also Ross and Kay 1980) famous description of the phases through which the one–year-old learns how to play peekaboo through imitation and transformation is another example of the developing social synchrony of mother and infant through play. They show how the infant changes from being a more passive to becoming a more active master of the play form. Both Stern and Bruner saw the play itself as crucial to the learning of social interaction and communication between parent and child, a point of view receiving support from studies which show the parent carefully scaffolding these games with the infant, and in the present peekaboo case, the infant showing object constancy behavior in the games that is in advance of the same behavior shown outside of the games (Hodapp, Goldfield, and Boyatzis 1984). The most recent support for parental effects comes from studies showing mothers actively teaching their children how to pretend in the first years (Haight and Miller in press) although we have known for some time that mothers' speech is responsive to their children's pretending (Miller and Garvey 1984). Farer shows in this volume that such teaching of pretend can be done by siblings in other cultural settings.

Most recently Trevarthen (1989) has argued that play's contribution goes much further even than this role in supporting and inducing such external adaptations to people or things. Following Bateson, he argues that the metacommunicative nature of play implies a preexistent intrasubjectivity on the part of the child without which no such communication would be possible. Play he says is internally dialogic from the beginning because the child has already practiced internally the reflection of its own behavior and that of others in its own solitary play. When you imitate the baby's play by repeating its gurgles, etc., because the baby laughs at your imitation, then the baby must be able to discriminate the duality of its own signal from your reproduction. This is to claim much more for play as the contemplative or subjunctive system in human affairs than is usually claimed although it is not unheralded (Werner and Kaplan 1963; Sutton-Smith 1979a; Bretherton 1984).

Further support for the critical role of playfulness by the parent in the child's development can be found in a number of longitudinal studies which finally accrued in the 1980s, including particularly Levenstein's long series beginning in 1965 (1970), and her chapter in this volume entitled significantly "The Necessary Lightness of Mother-Child Play" (chapter 8), all of which show that it is the playfulness rather than the more didactic aspects of the mother's stimulation that is correlated with subsequent forms of maturity as measured by intelligence and other school-related tests. Of similar import also is the work of Andrews et al. 1982, Bornstein 1989, and Slaughter 1983. Support can be found also in the multiple studies of attachment and its correlates which supply serendipitous support for the role of play in early parent-child relationships. These studies show greater playfulness, both as exploration and as pretense in children with superior attachment to their parents (Beckwith 1986; Slade (1987a&b). Or again there are the large-scale studies listed by Gottfried and Caldwell (1986) showing that parental provision of appropriate toys in infancy is correlated with advanced maturity measures in early childhood.

In short, considerable confidence is generated by this mother-infant research that the parents' play with the child makes a difference in the child's playfulness and in the child's competence as measured both cognitively and socially. A small-scale industry in books and video tapes has now grown up around teaching the methods of such play to parents.

Parent Childhood Play

In general, as we move out of infancy into childhood, play studies tend not to deal with parental play relationships with children, but, influenced by Piaget, revolve around sequences of play structure or theories of play as representation (Garvey 1977; Fein 1981; Leslie 1987). Attempts are made to relate such play as a symbolic or representational form to developments in language, cognition, memory, literacy, narrative, etc. (Nicolich 1977; Winner and Gardner 1979; Bretherton 1984; Galda and Pellegrini 1985; Shore 1986; DiLalla and Watson 1988). In general some parallels amongst these structural phenomena are found but as in the case of similar cross-cultural parallels above, the meaning of these structural relationships is as yet quite uncertain, though an explanation is usually sought in the development of similar underlying representational stages.

Alternatively childhood studies focus on how children come to play games together, play with toys together, develop skills of playful interaction, or get access to groups and avoid being rejected or neglected, etc. (Mueller and Lucas 1975; Corsaro 1985; Dodge et al. 1986; Howes 1988; Ross and Lollis 1987). When parental interaction is added to this set of variables, in some scaffolding kind of way by looking or commenting or advising, the data typically supports Vygotsky's proximal zone of development predictions (1978) because the child acts on a more competent level than otherwise (Rubin, Fein, and Vandenberg 1983; Howes 1988; Slade 1987a&b). This means that the child's pretense activities are carried out for a longer period of time, or with more fantasy transformations than usual in place, time, action, and character; or the child is more successful in accessing entry into a peer play group. The most recent overview of this kind of material, particularly with older children four to eleven years, is to be found in the work by Jerome and Dorothy Singer (1990) entitled *Pretending: Children's Play and the Emerging Imagination*, in which they provide correlations between the imaginative life of the parents and that of their children. Parents who have more imaginative children more often tell them stories or play fantasy games with them, read to them, and restrict their television watching. If the parents are too intrusive, however, the child's playfulness tends to be restricted. In turn the Singers have also shown that imaginative children are less aggressive, more capable of delay, and in general more successful at their schoolwork than other children of similar socioeconomic standing (Singer 1979). A similar set of positive relationships between parental physical play with child and peer behavior has been found by MacDonald and Parke in a series of ongoing studies (1984; McDonald, 1988), which adds as well information on differences between the effects of mothers' versus fathers' play styles. In general fathers and mothers both engage in physical play with their children in the first two years, but only the fathers thereafter. In those first years the fathers are given to more physical play and less toy play. (See the parallel in the Indian studies of Roopnarine in chapter 11.) The authors theorize that parent-child play's major contribution towards subsequent positive social development comes through the learning of arousal and affect regulation that such play affords and they were able to show that in neglected and rejected children these emotional adjustments are not learned in their play with parents (MacDonald 1987). Although the rejected engaged in as much play as the popular they exhibited much less self control and, as shown by Pellegrini (1988), more aggression. This positive impact of moderate rather than extremes of arousal (too much or too little, overstimulation or understimulation) is intriguingly similar to older studies on the U-shaped relationship between degrees of anxiety and performance in which moderate arousal was most effective whereas high and low arousal of anxiety was not. Similar too perhaps to Rimmert van der Kooij's findings in Holland of a relationships between moderate parental warmth and the child's play intensity (1989) and also like those by Poel Rost and Bruyn (1990) also in Holland that children were more playful when parents believed children should be offered support and opportunity for play but in practice set limits on these opportunities and on their own engagement in children's play. The work on rough and tumble play by Pellegrini (1988) and Humphreys and Smith (1987) might also be taken to support the value of moderate father-induced physical play fighting (not absent, not extreme) for male social success.

One cannot help but contrast the aesthetic and culturally oriented parents of the Singers' successfully imaginative children and the physically oriented parents of the MacDonald and Parke sociometrically successful children. In both cases parent-child play is important but the nature of the parents, the type of play, and the outcomes seem to be different (redolent perhaps of an earlier distinction between the play of strategists and the play of potents in childhood in the child studies of Sutton-Smith and Roberts [1964, 1967]).

Another arena in which there has been considerable attention to mother and father effects on children's play is in gender assignment. There have been numerous investigations of the differential effects of mothers and fathers upon their children's toy choices and gender characteristics (Sutton-Smith 1979a; Liss 1983; Pitcher and Shultz 1983) and some of this has to do with the differential way in which parents play with their boys and girls, fathers in general being more differentiated in this play than are mothers who tend to play similarly with both sexes. It could be said that both fathers and boys, particularly through physical play together, seem to partially segregate themselves from the women in the family. What is most remarkable about this array of studies, however, is that wherever attempts have been made to interfere with the traditional order of gender play differences these have been only mildly effective. Children's play seems to be, as Eleanor Maccoby (1987) has said, a kind of "gender school" with its own sex role distinctions and autonomy. Similarly with play objects: it is often the toys that predict the kind of play adopted rather than the gender that plays with them (Eisenberg et al. 1985). Gender school with its female concern for affiliation (the paradox of the nasty and the nice) and its male concern for domination (the paradox of the tough and the tender) seems to reach out for some larger cultural functionalist interpretation having to do with the life roles of each gender, because each of the sexes is more differentiated in these stereotyped ways when they play with their same sex than when they are with parents alone or with the opposite sex alone or simply by themselves (Maccoby 1990).

Our final set of studies having to do with adult play effects upon children are those associated with schools. In these studies at-

tempts have been made to improve children's representational competencies through play training sessions. The key figure here has
been Sarah Smilansky (1968) who pioneered the idea of play tutoring, which has been carried out in a variety of ways by such investigators as Brainerd, Christie, P. Johnson, J. E. Johnson, Feitelson,
Golomb, Rubin, Rosen, Pepler, Saltz, and Schmukler (reviewed in
Rubin, Fein, and Vandenberg 1984). Positive effects of such training
have been observed for language development, reading, literacy,
conservation, perspective taking, memory, and decentration. In
general, the training is given to children who are considered to be
disadvantaged and is aimed to improve their school-related skills by
enhancing their imaginative capacities. Smilansky's recent view is
that the positive results of all these studies justify the induction in
all schools of required sociodramatic training (1988). Critics, however, find problems with the various studies, their discrepant
methodologies, and their reliability. One major problem, for example, has to do with the tutorial effect: whether the results of the play
training sessions were primarily due to the children playing or to
their being played with by the investigator. From our present practical point of view, however, this may be less of a handicap. If the
tutors playing with children produce important scholarly results,
this is an important finding regardless of the exact nature of the
antecedents.

To summarize, we have shown that there is a great deal of con-
vergent evidence from mother-infant play studies, mother-father
fantasy or physical play studies, peer play studies, tutorial play
studies, studies of play's relationship to other kinds of growth (linguistic, symbolic, etc), and from discoveries of play's relationship to
creativity or to exploration to suggest that play does indeed hold a
powerful if not fully explicit role in child growth. In some if not all
respects the parents seem to be able to enhance those developments.
In consequence, we have not changed our view from the time of
writing the book: *How to Play with Children: And When Not To,* although now as then we favor such occasional parent play mainly for
the way it increases the competence and vividness of family or peer
play relationships rather than for any fairly marginal academic outcomes. There is sufficient data correlating the lack of play competence with various forms of pathology to support the value of
amplifying play opportunities just for their own sake (Roff and
Ricks 1970; Fantuzzo et al. 1988).

The actual nature of how we should play with children, however, still remains a problem. The occasional participation with and

modeling of play for children seems to have a powerful influence on their own playfulness, unless it is too intrusive, overpowering, or one sided. Play's major virtue may be that when the turn taking involved is sincere it allows the child to participate on more or less equal terms with the adult, which may be the greatest motivation that the games can supply. Of course, one needs to know how to play with children, that is, in order to adjust the underlying inequity of power. As Bernard De Koven stresses in his book *The Well Played Game* (1978), there are techniques for reversing roles at critical points to ensure that the child can take over your role and inherit your accumulations or accomplishments, as when, for example, she is allowed to turn the board around in chess at any given moment. Further clarifications of the relationships and modulations of adult-child play however, seem urgently desirable as it now seems more and more authorities are looking to such intergenerational play as a solution to the problem of the alienation of parents from children in the modern family.

For example, at the 1990 meeting of the International Council for the Study of Play, a European organization concerned with play research and play therapy, play between parents and children was the central topic of the conference and was also offered as the solution for a new unity between the generations. Apart from the therapists, however, no one suggested that adults play directly with the children except through the conservative mediation of organized games, puppets, books, computers, folk toys, or fairy tales. In fact Otto and Riemann (1990) presented research from an interview study of six to twelve year-olds and their parents showing that while the parents preferred to play organized games with their children, the children contrarily wished to be allowed to role play fantasy games with their parents. The parents opted for the traditional method of playing with children which usually gives them superiority through their own more mature skill, but the children opted for using their more labile fantasy where they perhaps have superiority.

One makes some possible sense of this by attention to the recent study by my student at the University of Pennsylvania, Diana Kelly-Byrne, entitled "A Child's Play Life" (1989). She played directly with a seven–year-old girl recurrently for one year doing whatever the girl wished in fulfillment of her play fantasies. Kelly-Byrne was made a slave immediately and given the power of participation only reluctantly and gradually over that period of time. This outcome was strikingly like the power inversions that occur in the traditional festivals (Carnivale, Mardi Gras) of those countries where an underclass takes over for the festival period (Falassi 1987). And on reflection it would not be strange if children's greatest desire in a free-play situation with their parents might be to reverse the power relationships. This is obviously not what most parents or the International Council for Children's Play (ICCP) have in mind, though it may be the very issue most worthy of further research in the domain of parent-child play, particularly as the child in the Kelly-Byrne study seemed to make amazing progress in the course of the year's play. She went from enacting fantasies, to discussing scenarios for fantasies, to discussing her own personal problems, all in the course of one year—a remarkably accelerated developmental course of changes.

2. Adult Play as Control

We now move to a quite different set of questions, and ask not whether adults playing with children contributes to the children's growth, but ask what it means that adults should want to do that anyway. We question the naive scientific presupposition that underlies all of the above studies, which is that our job is simply to be investigators finding out what causes what, and interject instead the view that it is necessary also to justify why we would want to play with children in the first place.

It is after all possible to write a historical account of adult play relationships to children that provides grounds for considerable suspicion of our own motives. If we begin, for example, in history with the process by which children were segregated from community life into schools, we are struck first that this segregation from 1600 through 1900 occurred concomitantly with the segregation of other groups of irrational beings—the impoverished, the insane, and the criminal—from the larger society (Foucault 1973). Schooling appears to have been a part of this larger rationalization of life to an orderliness of space, time, and behavior by an increasingly urbanized society. We note also that the largest part (about two-thirds) of the Aries book *Centuries of Childhood* (1962), which is about the invention of modern childhood and its separation of children from adults, has to do with the flogging and hardships that children had to endure as they were inducted into these schools. This makes the process of inventing childhood appear as much about incarceration as it is about the bringing of enlightenment to the young. Aries has been accused of harboring nostalgia for the earlier more medieval and communal times of child apprenticeship and, therefore, of downgrading the humanity of the later period (Stewart 1972; Tilly 1973; Wilson 1980). DeMauss's (1974) account of the same period of industrialization and urbanization and its effects upon children is even harsher than that of Aries. And although other sources indicate that the picture is more complex even than this, the thesis that our interest in children's play has been primarily one of controlling children's violence and other irrationalities is quite sustainable (Stone 1979).

If we look at the earliest play theories of Western society, those of Comenius, Locke, Rousseau, Schiller, Wordsworth, Pestalozzi, or Froebel, they are idealized and of basically didactic import even when nature is supposed to be providing the lessons. They all make play provide some kind of rational or spiritual insight into the character of the natural world (Spariosu 1988). Modern play theory thus begins as a part of the rationalization of an irrational childhood. It is possible, for example, to find a fairly rigid intellectual barrier between the rational uses of the playful imagination as seen by Kant, John Dewey, Piaget, and most other recent play educators and play therapists, and the contrastingly cruel and violently imaginative child found in the history of children's folklore (Gomme 1894; Sutton-Smith 1981) or in the accounts of actual playground history (Cavallo 1981; Goodman 1979; Nasaw 1985; Mergen 1982; Slukin 1981).

Shifting to the mid- to late-nineteenth century the picture becomes much clearer about the exploitive way in which children's own folk and sporting play becomes organized by adults in terms of the rhetoric of sports and manliness (Mangan 1986) and the way in which this same system comes to be applied throughout the colonial world. There is both the idealization of the game phenomena and the more direct control of the players that the sports system allows, although here one might emphasize the control of play as the socialization of aggression with militaristic implications.

In the terms of this suspicious rhetoric one would want to note the increasing supervision of children's playground play in this century; the gradual substitution of sports for folk games; the introduction of physical education lessons to take the place of free play at recess; the complete abandonment or diminution of recess in many states; the contemporary attack on boys' war toys and playfighting; or the insistence that no games be organized that aren't equally accessible to both girls and boys. One would note also that this process of domesticating childhood has also been considerably advanced by the predominance of television, small families, and a retreat from street play as well as the huge substitution of solitary toy play in place of collective folk play (Sutton-Smith 1986). By turning children into consumers they have become much more amenable to domestication than was earlier the case. One is reminded that in 1695 philosopher John Locke advocated his alphabet blocks as a way of taking children off the streets and away from undesirable playmates as well as for giving them a playful amusement within the home with the parents or with their tutors. In a sense this is the first announcement of a process of child domestication that has increased ever since.

Given this historical context the research material on contemporary adult-child play relationships offered earlier takes on a new meaning. If we adopt this Foucaultian stance—that new forms of knowledge quickly become new forms of social control—then the new knowledge about play quickly becomes a ground for new ideas on how to control play. So in our own case the attempt to increase the imaginativeness of lower-class children, or the imaginativeness of any children, can also be seen as a use of play to civilize the irrational natives. By showing that parents can affect their children's play we are also showing that that is what the "best" parents already do. These are the cultured parents of the Singer's account or they are the European-derived and not the Asian-derived Jews of the Smilanksy and Feitelson accounts. We have been told that these latter Asian Jews as well as the lower socioeconomic classes (largely black) in America are deficient in the kinds of symbolic processes that pay off in school and modern society, and that teaching them how to play is one way to raise their imaginative consciousness.

Now obviously no peoples can really be deficient in imagination any more than they are deficient in language. They have survived in their own ways of life for tens of thousands of years which presumably takes considerably inventive skill. Their deployment of the imagination is what has helped them in the past to survive. It is true of course that their imaginations in oral cultures may be given more to the sustenance of the collectivites of their hierarchical existence (Sutton-Smith and Heath 1981) than they are to the development of the kind of autonomous individuality symbolized in Western society by the idiosyncratic inventiveness of artists and the logical and syncretic imagination of scientists, but they are imaginations nonetheless with their own particular logic and form.

In the Foucaultian-like view I am presenting here, the good works of Smilansky and Singer, etc., can be seen as a part of the centuries long process of domesticating the lower orders in terms of the rational and individualistic preoccupations of their upper status betters. Our sciences of play outlined in the first section are in these terms themselves rationalizations for this civilizing process (Elias 1982) of controlling children, domesticating their behavior, rationalizing their emotional processes, and decreasing the threat to be perceived in their present untutored state of culture. This doesn't necessarily make the effort irrelevant or unnecessary, but as presently constituted, it makes it an attempt to use science as an instrument for a social class control. At least this would be the Foucaultian argument, for in his terms all knowledge is also control. Through evaluation, categorization, and statistics we come to imply what is more valuable and what is less valuable and to argue both the necessary sustenance of the former and the appointment of professionals to eradicate the latter.

To entertain this suspicious rhetoric, however, is meant here only to open our minds to our own implicit practices. Knowledge and control are not always quite as conflated and as hierarchical as Foucault would have us believe. There is too much randomness in the relationship and too much idiosyncrasy throughout the systems of science and practice for his arguments to be entirely coercive. By paying more attention to the origins of our own prejudice in favor of the idiosyncratic imagination, however, we might perhaps be more sensitive in developing ways of playing with lower status children or different ethnic groups in forms which are more syntonic with their own cultural practices.

3. Cultural Play Reciprocities between Adult and Child

To this point we have been given two approaches to the adult-child play phenomenon: (a) first, research justifying adult play with children on an apparently scientific basis or: (b) second a deterministic analysis indicating the controlling socializing origins and domesticating effects of that effort by adults.

In this section we want to follow our own recommendation and enlarge the suspicions suggested in section two above. If it is possible that our adult play research has motivational underpinnings in long-term educational and child-rearing rhetorics for civilizing children through organizing and pacifying their play behavior, what other rhetorics might also be implied by this research pursuit? For example we can ask whether an implied attempt is being made to control not just children, but also those segments of adults in our own culture who seek to stimulate children to commercial forms of play, and even those more ordinary adults in our own society who like children still practice largely irrational play forms. What we imply here is that whatever we have to say about children might also implicitly say something about adults. That is, adults playing with children are not in a one-way relationship with the adults being the only ones exercising the one-way influence; that relationship also implies that the children are influencing the adults, or at least influencing their play rhetorics. This is the issue in this section of the chapter.

It is noticeable in sections one and two above that both assume a disjunction of adult and child, a disjunction which has come to be seen as inevitable and irrevocable since the work of Aries (1962) in which he contends that our own long segregated childhood is a unique Western invention. Contrary to his contention, however, about 30 percent of a scientific sample of all available contemporary and historical world cultures (in the Human Relations Area Files) have the same long childhood that we do, which implies that our invention of childhood may not be as unique as it seems to Aries. By our count approximately 50 percent of the 186 sample of world cultures described by Barry and Schlegal (1980) finish childhood at about seven years, 20 percent at about nine years, and the final 30 percent at about twelve years. For incidental interest in these samples, the areas with the greater proportion of long childhoods are Europe-Asia and North America and those with the shorter childhoods tend to be Mediterranean, Polynesian, or South American.

Secondly, Aries's case for the newly invented modern childhood is obtained only by ignoring the powerful role of youth culture in medieval Europe at which time he contends there was no childhood. Others contend on the contrary, that the childhood cum adolescence of those days lasted from about seven years of age until marriage, and this group was on many accounts a vital and functional part of social culture; its child partisans often being given the power of a moral corrective through the license and suggestion granted to them on festival occasions to attack people regarded as deviant such as idiots, adulterers, etc. (Davis 1965; Gillis 1980). There are also African counterparts, both modern and traditional, in which children and youth exercise this semiautonomous function (Cannizzo 1984).

If the medieval youth is not simply identified with adulthood (through apprenticeship as Aries does) and modern childhood not seen as an entirely new invention, it is possible to ask what the parallels in the festive role (the play role) of childhood/youth might be from medieval to modern times. We may ask if the medieval youths' playful disorders in festivals serve to control the real social aberrations of medieval adults, what does modern childhood play control?

As far as children alone are concerned we do not have any clear answer to this question. In their own peer groups and in their peer group folklore children and certainly adolescents often constitute an antithetical society with its own parodies of the adult world through rhymes, jokes, pranks, graffiti, rap, and mimicry. Furthermore children still randomly and playfully attack physically those against whom their parents hold prejudices. But, in general, child culture is more centrally concerned with its own fantasies of empowerment through games often fed by cartoons and television programs. To this extent much that happens in child culture is a persistence from earlier times.

Modern children have, however, like their tribal forbearers, begun to exercise a modern normalizing influence on deviant parents by gaining increasing decision-making power as to which sports organizations, clothes, toys, recreations, and television programs they should have access. Stimulated by entrepreneurs and their advertising they are increasingly bringing their parents into line with the requirements of the ever-changing norms of consumer culture. The advertisers become like the tribal adults who whisper to the children's groups about the deviant adults who should be attacked. The largest obvious attack that modern children carry out on adults is therefore the attack on the purse. Instigated as they are by the entrepreneurs they drag their squealing protesting parents off to the market. The parents for their part protest hysterically and continually about the meaning and importance of these new kinds of children's play for the future of their children and of civilization. Witness for example the recurrent controversies about Little League sports, playground apparatus, Barbie dolls, anatomically correct dolls, playfighting, television advertising of toys, video games, Nintendo, recess, and war toys. Much of the eagerness to discuss adult-child play at the ICCP conference mentioned above was clearly meant to be a way of counteracting this kind of power from children that members of the conference found alien to their own consideration of what childhood should be like. In this sense the movement to increase adult-child play, by its very attempt to increase parental influence on children, is a conservative movement (even if the phenomenon itself is relatively novel).

The conservative character of the movement for adult-child play becomes clearer when we look at its implication for the irrational play of adults who are not yet involved with this kind of parent-child relationship. Consider again the supposed disjunction of adult from child play. We can speculate that another meaning of this disjunction is that by truncating the child from the adult, and by idealizing the child's play, we express objection to the regressive significance of much adult play. Adult play in general and from any viewpoint is not particularly elevating. In the United States we spend $250 billion on games of chance alone and only $15 billion on children's toys, to give some sense of the disproportionate nature of our self indulgence (though we are continually lamenting the children's toy market as if it is the cause of cultural degeneration). Professional sports are estimated to cost another $50 billion. All the rest of pop culture may sum up to another $200 billion. In sum our annual expenditure on entertainments far outruns our expenditure on armaments. Although children's play is usually idealized as voluntary, of positive affect, a pretense, flexible, and given to active mastery and fun (Rubin, Fein, and Vandenberg 1983), adult play is often almost entirely the reverse. It is extraordinarily passive and obsessive (as in gambling) for most of its participants. The affect is often intense and often quite negative (ice hockey, boxing). The sense of pretense is quite minimal in these intensely pursued professional sports though they are indeed infinitely repetitive pantomimes to the glory of success.

Here it will be maintained that holding children's play up to a model of ideal growth helps us to ignore the character of these disorderly adult recreative involvements. By hallowing our children and their play we idealize our self-respect as decent parents. Children's innocence expresses our conscience just as the medieval youthful charivari exercised the conscience of their time. But this modern exercise of ideal play as a kind of conscience is like femininity as a kind of conscience or the Virgin Mary as a kind of conscience. It gives childhood play the power of an icon rather than the practical power of direct action. What childhood does is to allow us to forget the relatively irrational nature of most adult entertainment in modern civilization. Our advocacy and theory about childhood play serves to keep our own truly regressive festive character at a forgotten distance. When play is clearly defined as only what children do, we can identify both play and childhood with our ideals and our aspirations for mankind as a whole, ignoring largely our own or others irrational departures from such a path. If this makes life a little more constricted and unreal for the children who are the victims, as it was for women, that's an easier consequence than to set them free as we may be discovering with women.

But the idealization of child play earlier, and now the idealization of adult-child play goes, I think, further than this simple regression. It becomes in addition an active political force on behalf of social change for adults as well as children as I have shown earlier the members of the ICCP in Europe were hoping it could be. In sum, while the idealization of childhood play accomplished a repression of our own play, the more radical act of adults playing with children seeks to go further, and change the adult play rather than repressing it.

It is notable that the prettified view of play as intrinsic, fun, active, flexible, etc., is quite recent. Psychological theorists at the beginning of the century, such as Groos, Hall, and Freud, continued to see play as a playing out of baser instinctive life. It is only the more recent cognitive theories of Berlyne, Bruner, and Piaget that are used as a basis for the current vogue of idealized play. The emergence of these theories along with the abandonment of children's often rough play at recess times, along with newer attempts to interfere increasingly in children's play by organizing it in sports, games, or classrooms, or by having parents play with the children, has to be seen, I believe, as a fundamental shift in our attitude toward the adult-child play relationship. It means I believe not just that we are organizing children's play for their own good, but that by going further and playing with them an idealized adult-child relationship is being created as a political vehicle for the constraint of the commercial irrational play forms of both childhood and adulthood play. The new idealized play of adults with children becomes a message of restraint for older and less civilized forms. Whereas medieval elders used their youth in festivals to directly attack the deviant social members, we are using our newly defined festival enjoyments with our children to set up new patterns of family and community advocacy. We play with children thus, not just for their psychological growth, but for the rhetorical persuasion of those who are not as socialized into modern forms of gentleness as we consider ourselves to be. I would argue that the United States originated New Game movement of the 1960s, which advocated cooperative and friendly play for large groups of family members and was antagonistic to modern professional competitive sports; the Rainbow Coalition in France of the 1970s bringing in children to France from all over the world to sustain and celebrate their traditional games in the face of their extinction by Olympic competitiveness; and the attempts of OMEP [the world organization for preschool education] to organize a children's play curriculum along cooperative rather than competitive lines are all of a similar cast. We play with children for their development and for a world that might become as idealized as we have attempted to make the play of our children. Adult-child play in these terms is as much a political rhetoric as it is science, combating both ancient forms of adult play and modern forms of commercial play instigation. It would be not surprising if these strands of history, science, and politics evoke considerable ambivalence in those concerned with the destiny of play of childhood and of our idea of what it is to be "civilized."

Conclusion

Subsequent research has supported our original confidence as expressed in the book *How to Play with Children* (1974) that increased parent-child play would have a positive effect on children's playfulness as well as on their development. But we have also seen that our naïveté about the inherent funfulness and worth of doing this is complicated by many other questions worthy of careful thought. We are led to ask to what extent our enthusiasm for this activity has become in some way a technique for imposing the more gentle and imaginative play techniques of higher status, perhaps more academically inclined people, on children of other subcultures; another conservative force for strengthening parent-child relations against the alien influences of the consumer culture on children; and in yet another way a means to idealize children's play and to directly or implicitly counteract the excessively aleatic (chance) and agonistic quality of the major adult play culture. More importantly we have been forced to realize that whatever the outcomes of these possibilities, we still know very little about the central processes of adult-child play itself. At issue is the fact that generally we take for granted that in this power relationship we adults will remain in power, whereas the central issue for children may be, how they can gain sufficient power in the relationship to allow their own deep need for fantasy empowerment to take its course.

Notes

1. B. Sutton-Smith and S. Sutton-Smith. *How to Play with Children: And When Not To* (New York: Hawthorne, 1974), republished in Germany as *"Hoppe Hoppe Reiter"* (Munich: Piper, 1986); and in Hungary as *"Hogyan, Jatsszunk, Gyermekeinkkelritten,"* (Budapest: Gondolat, 1986).

References

Andrews, S. R. et al. (1982). The skills of mothering: A study of parent child development centres. *Monographs of the Society for Research in Child Development,* serial no. 196, vol. 47(6).

Aries, P. (1962). *Centuries of Childhood.* New York: Knopf.

Barry III, H., and Schlegal, A. (1980). *Cross Cultural Samples and Codes.* Pittsburgh: University of Pittsburgh Press.

Beckwith, L. (1986). Parent-infant interaction and infant's social-emotional development. In *Play Interactions. See* Gottfried and Caldwell 1986.

Beebe, B. (1973). Ontogeny of positive affect in the third and fourth months of life in one infant. Ph.D. diss. Columbia University. University microfilms.

Berlyne, D. E. (1960). *Conflict, Arousal and Curiosity.* New York: McGraw-Hill.

Birch, H. G. (1945). The relation of previous experience to insightful problem-solving. *J. Comparative Physiological Psychol.* 38:367–83.

Bloch M. N., and Pellegrini, A. D. (1989). *The Ecological Context of Children's Play.*

Bornstein, M. H. (ed.) (1989). Maternal responsiveness: Characteristics and consequences. *New Directions for Child Development,* no. 43.

Bretherton, I. (ed.) (1984). *Symbolic Play.* New York: Academic.

Bruner, J. S. (1976). The Nature and uses of immaturity. In Bruner, J. S.; Alison, J.; and Sylva K. (eds.), *Play.* New York: Basic Books, 1976.

Bruner, J. S., and Sherwood, V. (1976). Early rule structures: The case of "peekaboo." In R. Harre (ed.), *Life Sentences.* New York: Wiley.

Cannizzo, J. (1984) Play, performance and social commentary: The Alikali devils of Sierra Leone. In *The Masks of Play. See* Sutton-Smith and Kelly-Byrne 1984.

Cavallo, D. (1981) *Muscles and morals and team sports.* Philadelphia: University of Pennsylvania.

Clarke-Stewart, K. A. (1973). Interactions between mothers and their young children: Characteristics and consequences. *Monographs of the Society for Research in Child Development.* Serial no. 153, vol. 38(6–7).

Corsaro, W. A. (1985). *Friendship and Peer Culture in the Early Years.* Norwood, N.J.: Ablex.

Davis, N. (1965). *Society and Culture in Early Modern France.* Stanford: Stanford University Press.

DeKoven. B. (1978). *The Well Played Game.* New York: Dover.

DeMausse, L. (1974). *The History of Childhood.* New York: Psychohistory Press.

DiLalla, L. F., and Watson, M. W. (1988). Differentiation of fantasy and reality: Preschooler's reactions to interruptions in their play. *Developmental Psychology,* 24(2): 286–91.

Dodge, K. A.; Pettit, G. S.; McClaskey, C. L.; and Brown, M. L. (1986). Social competence in children. *Monographs of the Society for Research in Child Development,* Serial no. 212, vol. 57(2).

Eisenberg. N., et al. (1985). Parental socialization of young children's play: A short term longitudinal study. *Child Development* 56:1506–13.

Elias, N. (1982). *The Civilizing Process.* 3 vols. London: Blackwell.

Falassi, A. (1987). *Time Out of Time: Essays on the Festival.* Albuquerque: University of New Mexico Press.

Fantuzzo, J. W., et al. (1988). Effects of adult and peer social initiations on the social behavior of withdrawn, maltreated preschool children. *Journal of Consulting and Clinical Psychology* 56(1): 34–39.

Field, T. (1978). The three Rs of infant-adult interactions: Rhythms, repertoires and responsivity. *Journal of Pediatric Psychology* 3(3): 131–36.

———. (1979). Games parents play with normal and high risk infants. *Child Psychiatry and Human Development* 10(1).

Fein, G. (1981). Pretend play in childhood: An integrative review. *Child Development* 52:1095–1118.

Foucault, M. (1973). *Madness and Civilization.* New York: Vintage.

Galda, L., and Pellegrini, A. (1985). *Play, Language and Stories.* Norwood, N.J.: Ablex.

Garvey, K. (1977). *Play.* Cambridge: Harvard University Press.

Giffin, H. (1984). The coordination of meaning in the creation of a shared make believe reality. In *Symbolic Play. See* Bretherton 1984.

Gillis, J. R. (1981). *Youth and History.* New York: Academic.

Gomme, A. B. (1894). *The Traditional Games of England, Scotland and Ireland.* London: Constable.

Goodman, G. (1979). *Choosing Sides.* New York: Schocken.

Gorwitz, D. and Wohlwill, J. F. (1987). *Curiosity, Imagination and Play.* Hillsdale, New J.

Gottfried, A. W., and Caldwell, C. (eds.) (1986). *Play Interactions.* Lexington, Mass. Lexington Books, 327–33.

Haight, W. L., and Miller, P. J. (In press). The social nature of early pretend play: Middle class mother's participation in everyday pretending. *Developmental Psychology.*

Herron, R. E., and Sutton-Smith, B. (1971). *Child's Play.* New York: Wiley.

Hodapp, R. M.; Goldfield, E. C.; and Boyatzis, C. J. (1984). The use and effectiveness of maternal scaffolding in mother-infant games. *Child Development* 55:772–81.

Howes, C. (1988). Peer interaction of young children. *Monographs of the Society for Research in Child Development.* Serial no. 217, vol. 53(1).

Human Relations Area Files. P.O. Box 2015, Yale Station. New Haven, Conn. 06520.

Humphreys, A. P., and Smith, P. K. (1987). Rough and tumble, friendships, and dominance in schoolchildren: Evidence for continuity and change with age. *Child Development* 58:201–12.

Hutt, C. (1971). Exploration and play in children. In *Child's Play. See* Herron and Sutton-Smith 1971.

Hutt, St. John, et al. (1989). *Play, Exploration and Learning.* London: Routledge.

Jones, B., and Hawes, B. L. (1972). *Step It Down.* New York: Harper and Row.

Leslie, A. M. (1987). Pretense and representation: The origins of a theory of mind. *Psychological Review* 94(4): 412–26.

Levenstein, P. (1970). Cognitive growth in preschoolers through verbal interaction with their mothers. *Journal of Orthopsychiatry* 40:426–32.

Liss, M. (ed.) (1983). *Social and Cognitive Skills: Sex Roles and Children's Play.* New York: Academic.

Loizos, C. (1969). An ethological study of chimpanzee play. In Bruner et al. *Play* op. cit. pp. 345–351.

MacAloon. J. J. (1981). *The Great Symbol: Pierre de Coubertin and the Origins of the Modern Olympic Games.* Chicago: University of Chicago Press.

Maccoby, E. (1987). The varied meanings of masculine and feminine. In J. M. Reinisch (ed.), *Masculinity/Femininity.* Oxford: Oxford University Press.

Maccoby, E. (1990). Gender and relationships, a developmental account. *American Psychologist* 45(4): 513–20.

MacDonald, K. B. (1987). Parent-child physical play with rejected, neglected and popular boys. *Developmental Psychology* 23(5): 705–11.

———. (1988). *Social and Personality Development: An Evolutionary Synthesis.* New York: Plenum Press.

MacDonald, K., and Parke, R. D. (1984). Bridging the gap: Parent-child play interaction and peer interactive competence. *Child Development* 55:1265–77.

Mangan, J. A. (1986). *The Games Ethic and Imperialism.* New York: Viking Penguin.

McCall, R. B. (1974). Exploratory manipulation and play in the human infant. *Monographs of the Society for Research in Child Development.* Serial no. 155, vol. 15(2).

Mergen, B. (1982). *Play and Playthings: A Reference Guide. Westport, Conn.:* Greenwood.

Miller, P., and Garvey, K. (1984). Mother-baby role play: Its origins in social support. In I. Bretherton (ed.) *Symbolic Play.* New York: Academic.

Mueller, E., and Lucas, T. (1975). A developmental analysis of peer interaction among toddlers. In M. Lewis and L. A. Rosenblum (eds.), *Friendship and Peer Relations.* New York: Wiley.

Napier, D. (1986). *Masks, Transformations and Paradox.* Berkeley: University of California.

Nasaw, D. (1985). *Children of the City.* New York: Anchor/Doubleday.

Nicolich, L. M. (1977). Beyond sensory motor intelligence: Assessments of symbolic maturity through pretend play. *Merrill Palmer Quarterly* 23:89–101.

Otto, K., and Riemann, S. (1990). Zur specifik der besiehungen zwischen kindern und erschsenen im spiel. Paper presentation. *International Council of Children's Play,* biennial conference. Andreasburg Germany, April.

Pellegrini, A. D. (1988). Elementary school children's rough and tumble play and social competence. *Developmental Psychology* 24(6): 802–6.

Pitcher, E. G., and Schultz, L. H. (1983). *Boys and Girls at Play*. New York: Praeger.

Reynolds, P. (1972). Play, language, and human evolution. Paper presentation. American Association for the Advancement of Science. Washington, D.C.

Roberts, J. M., and Sutton-Smith, B. (1962). Child training and game involvement. *Ethnology* 2:166–85.

Roff, M., and Ricks, D. F. (1970). *Life History Research in Psychopathology*. Minneapolis: University of Minnesota.

Ross, H., and Kaye, D. A. (1980). The origins of social games. *See* Rubin 1980.

Ross, H. S., and Lollis, S. P. (1987). Communication within infant social games. *American Psychologist* 23(2): 241–48.

Rubin, K. H. (ed.) (1980). Children's play. *New Directions for Child Development*, no. 9. San Francisco: Jossey-Bass.

Rubin, K. H.; Fein, G. G.; and Vandenberg, B. (1984). Play. In E. M. Hetherington (ed.), *Socialization, Personality and Social Development*. Vol. 4, *Handbook of Child Psychology*.

Rusell, A., and Finnie, V. (1990). Preschool children's social status and maternal instructions to assist group entry. *Developmental Psychology* 25:603–11.

Schwartzman, H. (1978). *Transformations: The Anthropology of Children's Play*. New York: Plenum.

Sennet, R. (1978). *The Fall of Public Man*. New York: Vintage.

Shore, C. (1986). Combinatorial play, conceptual development and early multiword speech. *American Psychologist* 22(2): 184–90.

Singer, J. L., and Singer, D. (1990). *The House of Make-Believe*. Harvard University Press.

Slade, A. (1987a). Quality of attachment and early symbolic play. *Developmental Psychology* 23(1): 78–85.

Slade, A. (1987b). A longitudinal study of maternal involvement and symbolic play during the toddler period. *Child Development* 58:367–75.

Slaughter, D. T. (1983). Early intervention and its affects on maternal and child development. *Monographs of the Society for Research in Child Development*, Serial no. 202, vol 48(4).

Slukin, A. (1981). *Growing up in the Playground*. London: Routledge and Kegan Paul.

Smilansky, S. (1968). *The Effects of Sociodramatic Play on Disadvantaged Preschool Children*. New York: John Wiley.

Smilansky, S. (1988). How does research inform us about play. *Address at United-States Binational Science Foundation Summer Workshop:* Implications of children's sociodramatic play: learning and national policy. Wheelock College, Boston, July 18.

Smith, P. K. (ed.) (1986) *Children's Play: Research Developments and Practical Applications*. London: Gordon and Breach.

Spariosu, M. I. (1989). *Dionysius Reborn*. Ithaca, N.Y.: Cornell University Press.

Starobinski, J. (1988). *Jean Jacques Rousseau: Transparency and Obstruction*. University of Chicago Press.

Stern, D. (1977). *The First Relationship*. Cambridge: Harvard University Press.

Stewart, P. (1972). Towards a history of childhood. *History of Education Quarterly*, Summer: 198–209.

Stone, L. (1979). *The Family, Sex and Marriage in England, 1500–1800*. New York: Harper.

Sutton-Smith, B. (1975). Play as adaptive potentiation. *Sportswissenschaft* 5:103–18.

Sutton-Smith, B. (1979a). *Play and learning*. New York: Gardner.

Sutton-Smith, B. (1979b). The play of girls. In C. B. Kopp and M. Kilpatrick (eds.), *Becoming Females: Perspectives on Development*. New York: Plenum.

Sutton-Smith, B. (1981). *A History of Children's Play*. Philadelphia: University of Pennsylvania Press.

Sutton-Smith, B. (1986). *Toys as Culture*. New York: Gardner.

Sutton-Smith, B. (1989). Play as performance, rhetoric and metaphor. *Play and Culture* 2(3).

Sutton-Smith, B. (1989). The Rousseau dilemma. In Guy Bonhomme, et al. (eds.), *La Place du jeu dans l'education*. Paris: Fideps-Unesco.

Sutton-Smith, B. and Heath, S. (1981). Paradigms of pretense. *The Quarterly Newsletter of Comparative Human Cognition* 3(3): 41–45.

Sutton-Smith, B., and Kelly-Byrne, D. (eds.) (1984). *The Masks of Play*. New York: Leisure Press.

Sutton-Smith, B., and Roberts, J. M. (1964). Rubrics of competitive behavior. *Journal of Genetic Psychology* 105:13–37.

Sutton-Smith, B., and Roberts, J. M. (1967). Studies in an elementary game of strategy. *Genetic Psychological Monographs* 75:3–42.

Sutton-Smith, B., and Roberts, J. M. (1981). Play, toys games and sports. In H. C. Triandis & A. Heron (eds.), *Handbook of Cross Cultural Psychology*. Vol. 4, *Developmental Psychology*. New York: Allyn and Bacon.

Tilly, C. (1973). Population and pedagogy in France: The contribution of Phillipe Aries. *History of Education Quarterly,* Summer: 113–27.

Trevarthen, C. (1989). Origins and directions for the concept of infant intersubjectivity. *The Society for Research in Child Development Newsletter,* Autumn: 1–4.

Van der Kooij, R. (1989). Research on children's play. *Play and Culture* 2(1): 20–34.

Van der Poel, L., Rost, H. and de Bruyn, E. E. J. (1990). The relationship between parental practices and attitudes towards play and children's playfulness. Paper presented at ICCP (International Council for Children's Play). Andreasberg, Germany.

Vygtoksy, L. S. (1978). *Mind in Society.* Cambridge: Harvard University Press.

Werner, H., and B. Kaplan. (1963). *Symbol Formation.* New York: John Wiley.

Wilson, A. (1980). The infancy of early childhood: An appraisal of Phillipe Aries. *History and Theory* 19:132–53.

Wilson, S. (1984). The myth of mother a myth: A historical view of European child rearing. *Social History* 9:181–99.

Winner, E., and Gardner, H. (eds.) (1979). Fact, fiction and fantasy in childhood. *New Directions for Child Development* 6. San Francisco: Jossey-Bass.

Young, D. C. (1984). *The Olympic Myth of Greek Amateur Athletics.* Chicago: Ares Publishers.

PART I

Theoretical Perspectives

CHAPTER 2

Parent-Infant Games as Dynamic Social Systems

Alan Fogel, Evangeline Nwokah, and Jeanne Karns

By extension from the work on solitary play, parent-child social play is a form of social discourse that is distinguished by positive emotion expression, a lack of a specific task orientation, variable patterns of repetitive action, and exaggerated or incomplete communication signals. Although play has eluded formal attempts at definition and description, those who have studied play agree that it combines both structure and variation, freedom of positive expression within regularity, and lacks a recognizable purpose beyond its own boundaries (Beckoff and Byers 1981; Burghardt 1984; Smith and Vollstedt 1985).

Play is Complex and Variable

If one did a worldwide inventory of the varieties of parent-child play, there would certainly be a large number of different types of games, and an almost uncountable number of variants. Types of parent-infant games have been classified as conventional/nonconventional (Gustafson et al. 1979) having fixed/variable sequence (Duncan and Farley 1990), and with single repeated, nonsequenced and sequenced actions (Van Hoorn 1987). Yet social play is immediately recognizable compared to other, more serious, forms of mutual interaction. Social play has an ontogeny describable at least in general terms: physical motor play, object play, symbolic play, word play. Human parent-infant play has a unique

This work was supported by an NIH grant R01 HD21036 and by a grant from the University of Utah Research Council.

species-typical character of rhythm, synchrony, tempo, body contact, body orientation, and eye contact that sets it apart from the play of other species, and yet even here we can find some similarities of form and function. All primates indulge in social play and although the cross-species comparison is more apparent for peer play than for parent-child play (Burghardt 1984; Muller-Schwarze 1978), some playful primate mothers have been found to indulge in a few simple approach-withdrawal games and tickling games with their infants (Jolly 1985).

We know that play has definite characteristics, and that it has been identified with particular functions, that younger individuals play more than older ones, and that it is culture-specific. These results derive from work that, in the main, assumes play to be a dedicated system that operates in some way independently from appetitive systems of the individual. Suppose, on the contrary, that this is not true: that play is created out of other aspects of the individual, such as one's ability to communicate, to move, and to enjoy. If this is the case it is not enough to describe play, rather we have to imagine what processes account for the observed character of play. What might explain both the regularities and the variations? How does social play develop? In what ways does the social discourse interface with the individual in the act of playing? Why is play enjoyable? How does the development of social play interface with the development of its participants?

We propose that even though play is temporally patterned and repetitive, it is not guided primarily by rules for those patterns. Similarly, even though parent-child play is species- and culture-specific, it is not determined primarily by genetic predispositions, cortical connections, or cultural conventions. Finally, even though play is developmental, it cannot be explained solely on the basis of infant maturation or developmental level. Play partakes of these entities, but it is more than any one of them or any combination of them.

Our argument is similar to Gibsonian perspectives suggesting that action can be direct, context-specific, and functional, without the need for an explicit prescription for the final form of that action (Newell 1986; Reed 1982). Our view is similar also to constructivist perspectives on cognitive development that do not require the genetic material to have a foreknowledge of all the possible pathways for developmental change (Fischer and Bidell 1990; Piaget 1952). We also propose a strong sociocultural component to the development of parent-child similar to that of Vygotsky (1978). Finally, our perspective is similar to the notion that play, language, and other complex forms of human social behavior did not evolve phylogenetically as a dedicated genetic or neurological structure. Instead, play and language are emergent processes that partake of lower-level components, none of which contains explicit representations of play or language (Bates 1979; Burghardt 1984; Lock 1980).

In essence we propose that parent-child play cannot be prescribed in advance or defined as the sum of its constituent components. Rather, *parent-child play is a creative process, emergent from the dynamics of social discourse between two different individuals in a particular cultural and physical context.* This conclusion rests on theoretical developments in biological, physical, and movement sciences, in which patterned behavior can emerge spontaneously and repeatedly without any prior knowledge or prescription of the pattern (Singer 1986; Kugler, Kelso, and Turvey 1982; Prigogine and Stengers 1984; Reed 1982; Skarda and Freeman 1987).

Rules are Outcomes, Not Organizers

The term "game" has been applied to a variety of playful interactions but in addition to having the features of play, games are patterned in ways that make us think that they have *rules*. These rules seem to determine the complex interrelation of action and text (Hay et al. 1979). In most previous work on play, it has been assumed that those rules are substantiated in some representational form (genetically, neurologically, cognitively). This hypothesis is perhaps tenable when the topic of study is solitary play. Social play, however, raises the important question of where such rules might exist to regulate dyadic or group behavior. A simple solution is that representations within each individual become linked to produce synchronized dyadic actions. In attachment and psychoanalytic theory this line of reasoning is embodied in concepts such as internal working models and internalized objects, that is, in the form of internal representations of relationships with particular persons (Bowlby 1980; Bretherton 1985; Stern 1985).

Ethological perspectives have handled this issue in a number of ways. Most typically, the theoretical problem of social play is ignored entirely. Individual play is explained with recourse to phylogenetic adaptations, energy budgets, available resources, and the like, and social play is considered a special case. Most collections of work on human and animal play have little to say about the workings of social play beyond mere description (Muller-Schwarze 1978;

Smith 1984). Another approach used by ethologists is to assume that members of a species share a common repertoire that includes the movements and expressions necessary for play, common timing patterns for those movements and expressions, and also the predispositions for engaging in social discourse. All that remains to explain social play is some mechanism for mutually synchronizing these patterns (Trevarthen 1986). This approach fails to account for the creative and nonsynchronous aspects of social play, nor does it give much currency to the cultural diversity of play. Hughes (1989) has emphasized two important dimensions of all games, not adequately addressed in the literature, to date. Firstly, that by focusing on the rules of games, the ambiguity, spontaneity, and flexibility of play is neglected. Secondly, that players routinely interpret, adapt, and elaborate games to suit their own purposes, and the effect of setting and variations in the same setting has been ignored.

The fact is that the dyad or group has no higher-order executive agency that stores the rules and regulates the mutual engagement of its members. Cultures, as collections of individuals, don't publish the rules of parent-child play, and cultures, like dyads, have no consciousness or executive agencies that mandate obedience to the rules.

So if the dyad has no executive agency that stores the rules by which it behaves, we are left searching for the rules in the parent's and child's internal working models. Contrary to the phylogenetic similarity hypothesis, it is quite clear that parents and children do not have the same repertoire, goals, expectations, or senses of the rules, or of the significance of their relationship. Nor do we find evidence of parent and child explicitly setting the rules of their games beforehand. Even when this might occur with an older child, only some of the rules are discussed, with most left unspoken.

Even though parent-child play with older children could be construed as obeying a set of explicit rules, and maintained by mutual understanding of those rules, it is still not clear how one explains the variants of the game. One could argue that the rules need not be made conscious or symbolically representational, nevertheless most writings on play implicitly or explicitly assume that the rules for play are represented in some visceral form within each playing individual.

So long as we think of play in the abstract, as the ideal expression of its "rules," there can be little to contradict this notion. However, when one observes real individuals playing—in any species in which play occurs—the subtle variability and emergent creativity leap out almost in mockery of the supposed rules of the game. An entire game may contain several successive subroutines each with new elements added, or the content of a person's turn suddenly changed (Hay et al. 1979). Do we have to have rules for strategies, and rules for breaking the rules, and rules for repairing the rules that were broken? Do we have to include rules to manage the emotional and linguistic forms of communication in which play is embedded, and all the rules by which these intrapsychic factors interact with the play of the game? Try writing down all the rules that would be necessary to play a game of checkers with a ten–year-old: for the game itself, for the banter, for the friendly advice about strategy, for the one-upmanship and protecting against it, and for processing the range of emotions during and after the game. Clearly, it would be an impossible cognitive task to manage this enormous rule hierarchy, and this is precisely why computers will fail to duplicate human cognition so long as they are programmed to follow a set of decision rules prescribed in advance (Rumelhart and McClelland 1986).

A theory of social play requires a plausible explanation for both the rulelike behavior and the variations. In addition, we require that a theory of play should explain not only its mature forms, but its first appearance and developmental course. Since infants cannot abstract rules, we can't have a theory of play that requires them to do so.

We feel safe in asserting that no current theory of animal or human behavior, psychology, or development can explain even the simplest and most repetitive of games, let alone more complex games and their development. Most theories focus on the rules and their elaboration, the function of play in development, or the influence of culture. In this paper we review some currently accepted developmental theories that address the issue of play and show how they explain some, but not all the evidence. Next we propose an alternative dynamic systems perspective that, though not fully developed as a theory, offers some potentially useful insights into the process of play. Finally, we present some data from our own research that examines play as a dynamic social system.

Current Developmental Theories as Applied to Play

Most scholars interested in human development in the social context agree that developmental change arises in the process of social

interaction. Few would suggest that any single factor taken by itself—such as the maturation of the cortex, the genetic code, or the
behavior of significant adults—can explain development. In spite of
a general level of agreement about the importance of interaction,
there are theoretical differences in accounting for the precise mechanisms by which interaction may lead to developmental change.
Current theories of development can be placed into three broad categories: schematic interactionism, sociocultural interactionism,
and dynamic interactionism (Fogel 1992).

Schematic Interaction

The schematic interactionist perspective assumes that individual actions are organized by representational structures called
schemes. These schemes are believed to have a biological basis in
the neuromotor system, and they develop along genetically determined epigenetic pathways as a result of particular types of experience. In the realm of play, for example, the onset of face-to-face
play and social smiling around the age of two and a half months has
been explained schematically by a spurt of neuromotor maturation
that organizes a synchronous change in cognitive, perceptual, affective, and motor skills (Papousek and Papousek 1977; Trevarthen
1977). These coordinated changes are thought to create the conditions for the extended adult-infant eye contact, turnlike exchanges
of smiling and cooing, and mutually coordinated body movements
characteristic of face-to-face play.

Genetically based, precoded schemes are thought to underly
both the affective and cognitive features of play. Enjoyment during
play is made possible by the discrete emotion programs for positive
affect. It is argued that since newborns express what appear to be
discrete emotions, including smiling, and since the appropriate expressions are displayed during play, social play is founded upon the
mutual coordination of like schemes in adult and infant. Adults may
display similar schemes as infants during play due to empathic, intuitive processes. Expression matching, imitation, and reinforcement of these schemes account for the development of the infant
through play, as schemes are displayed, imitated, and subject to
contingent reinforcement (Izard and Malatesta 1987; Malatesta,
Culver, Tesman, and Shepard 1989; Trevarthen 1977).

A schematic developmental scenario might take the following
form. Infants display a variety of expressive and instrumental actions that are endowed genetically. Adults possess very similar ac-

tions, and because both adult and infant are biologically similar, intersubjectivity is insured. Adults are also cultural informants and the type and timing of their displays, vis-à-vis the infants' displays, can foster the acquisition of culturally appropriate display rules through play. If we further assume an operant conditioning rule, that behavior is shaped by its immediate contingencies, we have a theoretical mechanism for the mutual shaping of schemes in the social context.

Schematic thinking will apply in like fashion not only to play, but to all forms of social interactions. It is not necessary to assume a dedicated play structure. Piaget (1952), for example, viewed play as one pole of a continuum between assimilation and accommodation. Nevertheless, it is hard to deny that individual and social play routines have an integrity and structure of their own, and to be consistent, one would have to assume the development of individual schemes for social play and for all aspects of social relationships, along the lines of the internal working model derived from attachment theories. The concept of the internal working model is the creation of a representational scheme to explain the regularities in the style of a parent-child relationship across time, and between situations such as play and caregiving routines (Bretherton 1985).

The problem with the schematic interactionism perspective is that it passes the explanatory problem from observed behavior to unobserved schemes. First one assumes that observed behavior is organized by a scheme. Then behavior change can be explained by a change in the scheme. How do schemes change? By genetically based maturational processes that are regulated by environmental contingencies. These contingencies only make minor corrective adjustments to the biologically directed path of development. The ultimate explanation of development, therefore, is genetic. The genes must have precoded all the possible developmental pathways, as well as all of the behavioral input routes, such as play (e.g., Malatesta et al. 1989).

We are not the only ones to have pointed out the implicit preformationist logic underlying schematic views of development (Haroutunian 1983; Oyama 1989). The main problems with this perspective are the following (for a more detailed treatment see Fogel 1990b; Fogel 1992).

Variability. Schematic theorists have difficulty explaining variability. One could say, of course, that schemes are inherently variable, but are there encoded in each scheme the rules for behavior and the rules for all of its variation? Smiles and coos are often responded to by like actions, but they are also often responded to by rather different actions. These include head nods, touches, wide open mouths, laughs, arm movements, bouncing, etc. Do we then need to encode which behaviors might be recognized as members of a similar family of related actions? This is the suggestion proposed by Barrett and Campos (1987) in trying to account for the variety of action tendencies observed as expressions of particular affect states. While this is a step beyond traditional discrete emotion theories that locate emotion expression primarily in the face (Fogel and Reimers, 1989 commentary on Malatesta et al. 1989, and the authors' response to the commentary), there are still problems. If one recognizes variability, and still retains a schematic theory, the schemes have to carry a heavier burden. The schematic theorist has to invent a new scheme or a new part of a scheme to explain all of the rather impressive variety of variants in even simple games.

Function. Schemes, because they are presumed to be biologically rooted, are thought to exist because they subserve an important adaptive function. Smiling is functional because it leads to positive interaction and play, and play is functional because it provides opportunities for cultural learning and skill practice. The theoretical fallacy is in thinking that because we can play, we are "meant" to do so because of an evolved structure dedicated to play, deemed necessary to our species survival. There are a number of elegant arguments against this position (Bates 1979; Burghardt 1984; Gould 1977) that will not be repeated here. In brief, we share over 99 percent of our genes with the great apes who cannot, for the most part, speak, think symbolically, or play elaborate social games. These very human abilities must therefore be emergent processes based on slight variations (compared to the great apes) in the timing of expression of our genes in a rich social context over a more lengthy childhood. You don't have to assume a dedicated genetically based scheme for play, language, or symbolic thinking.

Biology. As one of us has pointed out elsewhere (Fogel 1992; Fogel and Reimers 1989; Thelen and Fogel 1989), it is ironic that the strong biologically based perspective underlying schematic interactionism is in fact biologically untenable. The notion of genes as carriers of behavioral traits and developmental predispositions, and of centrally located neurological processes having primary causal roles, is a view no modern biologist would accept.

The actions of genes are relatively nonspecific. Molecular biologists and embryologists have discovered that there is not enough information in a gene to specify more than the first few cell divisions of the developing zygote. The genes encode very simple properties such as a sensitivity to the concentrations of particular growth activators or inhibitors, but certainly not the final form of the cell or organism. The genes are just one part of a complex interactive system whose development rests on the subtle mutual timing of a hierarchy of embedded processes whose outcome is regulated by the dynamics of local interactions and not by a central executive agency (Antonelli 1985; Oyama 1985). Behavior, as we shall argue below, is regulated by analogous dynamic interactions in the absence of dedicated structures or schemes. With few exceptions (e.g., Plomin's [1990] recognition of the nondeterministic action of the genes), and with due apologies to our colleagues, most developmental psychologists persist in holding nineteenth-century views of biological processes. It's time to rethink what we mean when we invoke terms like "genetic" and "biological."

Sociocultural Interaction

The theorists that may be collected under this heading are typically silent regarding the biological constraints on behavior and development. Most assume implicitly some variant of schematic representations are the carriers of behavioral order, but explicity their energies are focused on describing the sociocultural interactions presumed to shape the development of cognition and action (cf. Bruner 1983; Kaye 1982; Rogoff 1990; Vygotsky 1978). Those who are more squarely in the schematic interaction camp (Malatesta et al. 1989; Trevarthen 1977) have relied on imitation and contingent shaping to describe social interaction. Sociocultural theorists, on the contrary, have developed a richly elaborated view of processes unique to adult-child social interaction (and by extension, to play).

Bruner (1983), for example, illustrates how complex hierarchical structures of parent-child games like peekaboo and pat-a-cake provide a structure external to the child, a scaffold, in which the child's actions are embedded. The child is not required to carry internally all the structure necessary to learn a game or acquire a cultural skill. Through the game, and by regulating carefully the child's participation in the game, the adult can guide the child's "uptake" (Bruner 1983) or "appropriation" (Rogoff 1990) of cultural skills. Thus, external-social structure eventually becomes internal-individual structure in this developmental perspective (Vygotsky 1978).

One contribution of sociocultural interaction is the recognition that social interaction has regularities and that culture is transmitted via active participation in these routines. These theorists assume that infants and children have an intrinsic interest in the life of the society around them, and some basic skill with which to participate. Sociocultural theories view children as active and motivated participants (not mere recipients of contingent reinforcements), and these theories recognize a complex role for adults that is different from that of the children. Adults are required to recognize the child's intrinsic motivation, alter the cultural activity to fit the child's level (such as by making work into a game), and gradually provide opportunities for the child to expand the scope of participation. Thus, nurture, planning, a developmental perspective, and coparticipation extend the role of adults beyond mere model or reinforcer (Rogoff 1990).

The problems of the sociocultural interactional view are similar to those of schematic interaction. There is an assumption that children have rudimentary schemes that become elaborated in the social context. Although they assume that the social context unburdens the child from having immediately to internalize complex behavior, there is nevertheless the persistent belief that social routines are represented somewhere, either in the adult or partially in the child.

Variability is still an issue. It would seem that all development must take place in highly structured, ritualistic contexts that are parts of the adult culture, that is, through conventional games and other routines. There is no place in sociocultural theory for spontaneous evolution of routines, or for nonconventional routines. So long as an assumption is made that the routines are encoded, the richness and variability of play would not be possible in any such representational system.

Functional thinking also burdens sociocultural theory. The routines described by these writers all presuppose goal-directed behavior on the part of the participants, even though sociocultural theory recognizes that the goals of the child and the adult are often dissimilar. It is difficult, therefore, to account for social interactions that are generated without plans or goals at the outset. It is often the case that a better understanding of the meaning of one's actions, or a post-hoc interpretation of meaning, arises as a result of

an otherwise spontaneous social interaction (Lock 1980). The imposition of meaning and structure at the outset of a playful interaction
may be a post-hoc representation as construed by the observer, having nothing to do with the actual process by which the interaction
emerged and was maintained.

Biological considerations cannot be ignored when discussing
cultural aspects of development. Culture and biology are often contrasted by psychologists, who persist in making artificial dichotomies between the organism and its environment. This kind of
dichotomy leads to the theoretical difficulty, faced by sociocultural
theory, of how to get the external structure of the society internalized by the child. Although we cannot quarrel with the evidence
that child-adult play acquires conventionality over time, there is no
direct evidence that the direction of developmental causation is
from parent to child. This kind of directional hypothesis is a result
of schematic thinking in which cultural schemes must be acquired
by the child.

The alternative, to which we now turn, is that social behavior
during play and other forms of interaction is not explicitly represented anywhere. Rather, the rulelike and conventional qualities of
parent-child games are outcomes of a dynamic process, not reflec-
tions of an encoded structure.

Dynamic Interaction

A dynamic interaction perspective differs fundamentally from
schematic and sociocultural interaction because dynamic interactionism does not require a schematic representation to account for
rulelike patterns of behavior. It has been demonstrated that a variety of physical and biological systems can exhibit organized patterns of behavior in the absence of an explicit representation for
that behavior, for example, lasers, crystals, and embryological morphology (Antonelli 1985; Haken 1983; Prigogine and Stengers 1984).
These patterns are not formed by underlying rules, but can be accounted for on the basis of the dynamics of interactions between
components given some simple linking properties (between mole-
cules, for example, mutual attraction, packing constraints, and molecular composition).

The patterns that result from the interaction between elements
can be said to depend on *self-organization,* emergent from the properties of the components and their linkings. Thus, rule and pattern
are not encoded, ordered regularities are the result of an interac-

tion process rather than the converse. This single assumption of self-organization, when applied to social behavior and development, has some rather far-reaching implications for our understanding of the origins and functions of play.

The problem of where and how social schemes are encoded is resolved by allowing social routines to result from the self-organizing dynamics emergent from the dynamic interaction between particular types of individuals. The notion of dynamics is crucial here. The ritualized patterns found in social play exist only as they form and dissolve over time. If participants were simply following preset rules, their actions would cease to be playful. Play is engaging precisely because it is experienced as wholly creative, made up, self-constituted.

We are not denying that individuals can cognitively represent games and their apparent rules. Anticipation based on prior expectations is certainly part of the enjoyment and engagement. The existence of such cognitions, though a component of the play, does not mean that those cognitions are constitutive of the game, any more than a coach's game plan and scorecard and each player's knowledge of the "rules" regulates the specifics of the next encounter between two opposing teams.

The rules of the game, in our view, are cultural metaphors that encapsulate the regularities of an otherwise complex and dynamic self-organizing process. More generally, schemes and rules are descriptive conveniences, they are not models for the generation of real behavior (Fogel 1992; Haroutunian 1983; Oyama 1985). Rules exist as cognitive constructions of observers, and perhaps (but not always) of the participants in social play. The reification of these constructions as central organizers for behavior and development only obscures the fundamental nature of social engagement. A theory of development through play requires, at a minimum, a recognition of both the dynamics of play and the way in which cultures infer rules from play. The inferred rules feed back into the play process, but not in any simple one-to-one predictable fashion.

Selected Review of Research on Early Parent-Infant Play

In contrast to other theories, dynamic interaction suggests that one study the constraints that give social action its particular form, without appealing to schemes that encode that form (Fogel 1990b; Thelen 1989). In a dynamic systems analysis of social play, we begin with the assumption that the sequence of play action is the emergent product of some set of simple components, none of which contains the prescription for the final form of the action. The components that enter into a play interaction may be not only the obvious cognitive and affective factors, but they may also be nonobvious components such as the mutual posturing and motor coordination of the participants.

Dynamics of Play Interactions

For example, research has shown important alterations in the interaction patterns occasioned by the introduction or removal of simple components during face-to-face play between mothers and infants at three months of age. In one experimental study, for example, the total duration of mutual gazing was doubled when the infant's seat was placed in a supine position compared to when the seat was in an upright position (Fogel 1988; Fogel, Dedo, and McEwen 1992).

Although we are still investigating why a change in postural position alters the face-to-face interaction, we know that the effect is not due to a change in the mother's behavior or style of interaction between the two postural positions, nor to an inability to hold the head upright (the youngest infants in the study were three months, and all had head control). We also found that the infant's ability to reach for objects is correlated with a reduction in gazing at mother. However, placing infants in a supine position enhances mutual gazing regardless of the infant's baseline levels of gaze at mother.

There are significant cultural differences in the dynamics of face-to-face play that seem to depend upon relatively minor variations in the types of behavior preferred by parents. Mothers in Japan, for example, respond less actively to infant vocalizations than mothers from the United States. Japanese mothers use their bodies phasically, to loom in and out, and their hands to tap the infant and create visual displays. Mothers in the United States use their hands and bodies more tonically, by staying in one position (closer, on average, to the infant's face than the Japanese mothers) and by holding and touching the infant's body for continuous periods. American mothers use their voice phasically, with many short utterances and questions, and respond more to the infant's vocalizations. The result is a very different quality of play interaction for each culture in which physical modalities are the themes and variations for the

Japanese, and vocal modalities are the themes and variations for the Americans (Fogel, Toda, and Kawai 1988). Bambara mothers from Kenya focus the themes and variations on the physical translations of the infant's body in a variety of postural-motor games (Bril, Zack, and Nkounkou-Hombessa 1989).

In a study of Chinese, Filipino, Mexican, and American parent-infant games, 80 percent were variations of traditional games passed down from parents, relatives, and friends. They always involved actions such as clapping, swinging, rocking, tickling, appearance, and disappearance (Van Hoorn 1987) and were usually accompanied by a text with the repetition of complex linguistic patterns using a culturally appropriate child-directed speech register. The existence and content, structure, and prosodic features of such game text is clearly influenced by cultural beliefs and traditions (Nwokah and Fogel in prep.). Mothers who consider it silly or unacceptable to talk to infants such as the Gusii (Kenya) (Dixon et al. 1981) or Navajo (Fajardo and Freedman 1981) would be more likely to use action in social play without the accompanying verbal text. Igbo mothers use movement to songs and lullabies and may create their own text (Nwokah 1987) and Sinhala mothers often sing poetry and nursery rhymes (Meegaskumbura 1980). British mothers have been found to engage in games with more cognitive/instructional text and American mothers in games with more socially-oriented text (Field and Pawlby 1980).

With an interactive partner other than the mother, infant social play behavior becomes radically different. When presented with a peer, three–month-olds become more intense, abrupt, active, and less facially expressive than when with their mothers (Fogel 1979). Similar intensity has also been observed during infant interactions with a doll (Legerstee, Pomerleau, Malcuit, and Feider 1987), although the specific behavior of infants with a doll is different than with a peer. Finally, infant behavior with a peer differs from that seen when the infant is presented with a mirror or with a closed-circuit TV image of self (Field 1979; Papousek and Papousek 1977).

Changing the manner in which the mother interacts also causes a reorganization of the patterns and processes of early infant social play. A sudden cessation of maternal participation while the mother continues to gaze at the baby (still-face situation) causes the baby to reduce the rate of smiling at and gazing at the mother, after initial attempts to sustain the play (Cohn and Elmore 1988; Fogel, Diamond, Langhorst, and Demos 1982; Gusella, Muir, and

Tronick 1988; Stoller and Field 1982; Tronick et al. 1978). When mothers are asked to simulate depression and reduce their affect, infants correspondingly become more sober after only a few minutes (Cohn and Tronick 1983).

Changing the number of participants in play has been found to alter the form and content of play. Weekly observations of mother-twin infant triads over the first two years shows that infants spend over half the interaction time either attending to the interaction of mother and sibling, or participating in a three-way interaction, social actions not possible in dyadic groups (Karns 1989).

The experience of observing play at close hand, though not a direct participant, is likely to be an important social experience for the developing infant. In the mother-twin interaction data, we found that when an infant was attending to one or both members of the interacting mother-infant dyad, he or she was more likely to move into interactive participation than if the infant was engaged in solitary play behavior (Karns and Fogel 1990). Similarly, preschoolers who attended to the activity of an ongoing play group were more likely to be successful in joining in the play than preschoolers who attempted to directly join an ongoing play group immediately upon entering the play area (Washington and Craig 1990).

In many of the studies cited above, different patterns of social interaction were observed following experimental changes in the mother's behavior, or by comparing interaction with mother to interaction with other partners. This is a powerful way to study interactive dynamics since even very small changes in the settings and conditions of interaction lead to very different patterns of social organization. For many of the three–month-olds we studied in the company of infant peers, for example, their mothers reported that they had never seen another baby (Fogel 1979). Yet the behavior of all the infants to peers was systematically similar across infants and significantly different from the mother. Such complex interactive-appropriate patterns were found for infants inexperienced with dolls, still faces, and maternal depression.

While a genetically based scheme seems to be the obvious explanation, consider that the existing research has found many interactive differences due to all manner of situational changes. It is hard to believe that the genes could anticipate all these possibilities and all their variants. Nor could our genes have a prescription for behavior with dolls, TVs, and mirrors, The only reasonable explanation of this interactive diversity in three–month-old infants is a dynamic interactionist perspective.

In this view the infant possesses a set of perceptual and motor faculties, each of which is attuned to specific features of the social and physical ecology. These ecologically regulated factors are also connected to each other in specific ways. Thus, for example, attention regulation is linked to perceptual ability. A baseline level of attention control is necessary to process perceptual information, but as perception becomes more acute and discriminatory, this in turn enhances attention (Ruff and Lawson 1990). Thus, perception and attention *constitute each other* in a dynamic process.

Now imagine a host of other component processes, such as posture control, emotional experience, motor skill, and cognition, each of which has specific types of connections with all the others. Although outcome behavior is determined entirely by these linkages and their interactions in a real situation, the actual outcome is dynamically constituted by the particular mutual leveraging process of all those interactions. How much a baby attends to a partner and the qualitative organization of the infant's social behavior is going to depend on a delicate dynamic balance of many factors. That balance may tip the baby into drastically different organized patterns of action even if a single factor is changed. A very happy interaction can suddenly change into a very distressed interaction for a variety of seemingly trivial reasons. A game continues when each turn or subroutine follows another fairly rapidly, but games frequently end when, for example, one partner waits too long, fails to participate, overstimulates the infant, or when the infant is suddenly distracted. If the content of turns is too varied, the partner may also cease to recognize the interaction as being a game.

It is precisely this type of sudden change in the interactive dynamics that has occupied our attention most recently. We wanted to find out the conditions under which a play episode would lead to the emergence of laughter in the mother or in the infant. It is nearly impossible to study this experimentally. Instead, we chose to select naturally occurring play episodes half of which erupted in laughter, and half of which did not. We then compared the sequence of events during each type of game to determine whether different interactive dynamics could be described for laughter versus nonlaughter games.

Onset and offset of mother's facial and vocal expressions and actions and infant gaze direction, vocalization, and facial expression were coded. We found that the only difference between games with maternal laughter and those without was a higher rate per minute of maternal vocalizations in no-laughter games and a higher rate per minute of maternal actions in laughter games (Nwokah and Fogel 1987). There was, however, often an onset of infant smiling or increase in intensity of infant smile, and gaze at mother's face prior to and at the point of laughter. This was not always the case. A mother would laugh when the infant's participation in the game involved a serious expression such as struggling to reach for mother's nose or hair, or when the infant produced a nonlaughter vocalization. A mother might still laugh at the focal point or outcome of a game, when there was only minimal involvement by the infant and no change in infant's behavior. Many different nonobligatory components seem to contribute to the occurrence of laughter within a game, including infant participation, and positive affect, anticipation of outcome, maternal emotional state, and novelty of infant behavior. Laughter is probably an emergent product of the complex interaction of a different number of components in each particular game.

Consider examples of this dynamic interactive balance as seen in two games (one with naturally occurring maternal laughter and one without). In a "gonna get you game" (infant age thirty-eight weeks), there were four repeated maternal actions/subroutines, each with mother's fingers touching infant's nose. At the onset of the game the infant was not smiling, vocalizing, or gazing at mother. The mother accompanied Action 1 with whispering and infant smiled briefly, then mother laughed. Action 2 was a repetition of Action 1 but infant did not respond this time, so Actions 3 and 4 were a change of "text" with mother whistling instead of whispering. When the infant still did not respond, the game stopped.

In a "boo" game (infant age fifty-one weeks), there were seven maternal actions/subroutines. The game commenced because the infant laughed and the mother created a spontaneous game by imitating this and looming forward with an accompanying mock laugh instead of "boo." The mother attempted four repetitive actions. Between the third and fourth, the infant imitated her mock laugh but still gazed away, and only when she changed strategies on the fifth action and bounced a doll on her knee but retained the mock laugh, did the infant look at the doll on her knee. The infant did not smile at her throughout the game until she accompanied the seventh action by moving face to face with him, he looked at her and smiled, and the game ended. Although each game described here was based on a traditional "rule-governed" game, the strategies, length, outcomes, and mutual responses of each partner were not predictable at the onset of either game.

These results suggest that social play is not a scheme that is played out by the infant in the presence of a partner. Instead, infant play engagement must be maintained as a continuous and dynamic process. Qualitative differences in the type of play interaction emerge as a function of this dynamic sequencing of events. Dynamics seem to be a more reasonable explanation for spontaneous changes in interaction (from sober to laughing), and for interactive process differences depending on situation than are schemes. In the next section we consider developmental changes in such dynamics.

Developmental Change and Social Play

In our longitudinal study described above, we observed developmental changes in object play interactions of infants and mothers observed weekly between one and six months (Fogel 1990a; West and Fogel 1990). Mothers changed their strategy depending in part on changes in the infant's reaching and object manipulation skills. So long as infants were not able to appropriately manipulate objects (squeezing a squeeze toy, or shaking a rattle) the mothers spent their time demonstrating for the infant the culturally appropriate manipulation procedure. Babies who acquired manipulation skills late, even after they could reach and grasp for objects, had mothers who ignored their bids for reaching and persisted in demonstration strategies. Once infants were able to manipulate, all mothers responded to the infant's bids for reaching by scaffolding the reach, that is, by holding the object steady and within arm's reach of the baby. Reach scaffolding replaced object demonstration as a maternal play strategy as a function of when the infants acquired culturally approved object manipulation skills.

Because our data are naturalistic, we cannot tell to what extent the infant influenced the mother's behavior, or whether the mother's behavior had a tutorial function for the infant's skill development. We can conclude that the interactive dynamics change over time, and we can begin to specify the parameters of the interaction that are most sensitive to developmental change. At this point, we are trying to extract from our data the manner in which the play process changes, rather than simply counting the weekly changes in the frequency of play or of specific types of play behavior.

Using the same infants observed in a face-to-face play situation on the mother's lap without toys, we found that mothers changed the way they held their infant's bodies as a function of the infant's gazing and affective engagement (Fogel 1992; Fogel, Nwokah, Hsu, Dedo, and Walker in press). Following a six to eight week period in which the infants prefer to gaze at mother, the same infants acquire a visual preference for inanimate, graspable objects and gaze less at mother. Mothers turned their infant's bodies away from them and toward the direction of the infant's visual interest if the infant and mother had engaged in prior weeks of mutual gazing and positive affective exchange. For infants who were developmentally late smilers (that is, they smiled in the weeks following the developmental onset of gazing away from the mother) mothers persisted in trying to attract their infant's attention to the mother until the infants began smiling leading to positive play exchanges. For those infants who never or rarely smiled, mothers did not support the infants intended gaze preference until the infant had acquired reaching. For these relatively sober babies, gaze away plus reaching was necessary to cue the mother's shift in attention management strategies.

In the triadic mother-twin situation, the interaction patterns changed as the infants acquired manipulation and locomotor skills. During the first few months, the mother played with both infants at the same time, treating them as a single unit. Both infants would be positioned identically and received identical physical manipulations from mother at the same time. These early interactions were set typically within social games, such as tickling, get 'cha, or range of motion manipulations of the infants' limbs. Mother's gaze would alternate between infants while maintaining physical action with both. The infants would maintain gaze at mother throughout the play session, but would not gaze at each other. As the infants developed motorically, there was a decreasing likelihood of this kind of symmetrical play (Karns and Fogel 1990).

In the first year, the mothers of twins tried to elicit interaction between them by turning them toward each other, which resulted in continuation of the mother-infant dyadic interaction with each infant individually, but only brief infant-infant interaction. By the beginning of the second year, the triadic play—in which all three were engaged in mutual play—become increasingly common in the form of working together on a puzzle, reading picture books, and in symbolic pretend play. These triadic encounters seemed to peak around the time that both infants were posturally stable and independently locomotor, thus allowing each partner to maintain an orientation to the group without the aid of the mother (Karns 1990).

The results of these longitudinal studies bear on the issue of how external scaffolding supports become altered by the infant over developmental time. Although we are the first to admit that the results are still tentative, the data suggests that the mother's behav-

ior—because it changes with developmental changes in the infant—
may be partially constituted by the interaction with the infant.

The mother's behavior is not caused by the infant's in any strict
or simple sense. Rather, the mother's particular actions are emergent from the process in which she is confronted with this particular infant. To say this in another way, the mother's scaffolding of an
object for reaching is constituted as much by the infant's skill as by
her own. Thus, her behavior is (in the best of circumstances) immediately "recognizable" by the infant as constitutive of his or her own
skill. The infant can and does reach in the presence of the scaffold,
and cannot reach in its absence. One of us has argued (Fogel
1990a,b) that external and internal, mother skill and infant skill,
reflect artificial dichotomies and leave us with the problem of explaining how the external scaffold becomes internalized by the
infant.

This explanatory problem vanishes if one realizes that the
mother's "external" scaffold is constituted by the form and timing of
the infant's behavior such that the infant does not usually experience the difference between inside and outside and has no reason to
suspect that his or her ability to reach is anything less than an
achievement. Although two physical bodies are interacting, their
joint action is experienced by both partners as seamless and integral (Fogel 1990b; Tamboer 1988).

This notion of dynamically constituted joint action is quite different from Vygotsky's (1978) zone of proximal development. Vygotsky's concept refers to how infants and children are most
susceptible to adult input in areas where their skills are incomplete. Vygotsky and his followers still persist, however, in conceptualizing the adult and child as separate and viewing development as
a transfer of expertise. The constitutive dynamics we have described, on the other hand, do not require a simple transfer process.
In our view, development is a continually shifting dynamic. Although from one perspective it appears as if skills are being trans-
ferred from older to younger, this could be a perceptual illusion of
the kind discussed earlier related to the artificial imposition of
function and meaning on otherwise spontaneous behavior.

Conclusions and Implications

The major topic of this chapter was to consider the complexity and
characteristics of parent-infant games in social play viewed as a dynamic social system. Current theories of development as explana-

tions of social play are presented as inadequate to deal with the spontaneity and sudden changes in behavior, variability of play routines, creativity within dyadic interaction, and the effect of onset differences in infant skill emergence on the parent's responses and scaffolding.

Interactions evolve as a result of the unique contributions of both participants. Information arises between parent and infant and vice versa, communicating messages about internal states and external actions. The flexibility and modifications that occur as a result of responses to this constant monitoring are not produced by a predetermined plan of action. Part of the complexity of the interaction is that the process of interactions with the dyad at a particular moment is affected by the expectations of the partner's responses and actions (Duncan and Farley 1990). Although the themes of many parent-infant games are based on ritualistic conventions and global mutual expectations emerge from this, our research shows that there is little predictability about the detail and development of each outcome. Expectations and anticipations are sensitively attuned and fluctuating on a moment-to-moment basis.

Spontaneity is found in the way games may emerge from ongoing or incidental activity such as an infant raspberry vocalization, laugh, pulling mother's hair, or leaning to one side. Such activities may be constantly repeated in a nonserious, nonliteral way with positive affect. In the first year these games tend to be asymmetrical in the sense that they are often initiated and managed by adults but the direction and continuation of the game is strongly dependent on the mutual engagement and contribution of the infant. Either or both members of the dyad can also spontaneously move in and out of play with quite abrupt shifts from nonliteral (playful) to literal interaction (Hay et al. 1979) especially in the second year. This is a move, for example, from simply handing the partner an object to a give-and-take game. As our data have shown, within the sequencing of game actions and text, either partner may attempt new strategies for engagement and variety and suddenly cease or prolong the social play. Expressions of positive affect also reflect this spontaneity, and the timing and frequency of smiling and laughter are not always easily predictable.

Variability can be found both between turns in one particular game and in the same game played on several different occasions. A favorite game will also be adapted as the infant increases in age. Peekaboo, for example, may change from using hands over the eyes while infant is seated on the lap, to both parent and child suddenly crawling from behind furniture at a later age. Sequences of actions change within a game such as increased exaggeration of movement, lowering or raising pitch of the voice, raising the eyebrows, or increasing physical distance. Related to variability is the presence of creativity where a game sequence could emerge through a combination of actions and skills, that the dyad or many dyads have not produced before, either by situation change or as a result of developmental changes within the infant.

We have argued that the schematic interaction perspective with genetically based precoded schemes cannot adequately account for the irregularities within regularity that produce the sheer delight, novelty, and surprise incumbent in the characteristic playfulness, smiles, and laughter of games. Neither can a sociocultural interaction perspective that is thought to elaborate, nurture, and build on already represented goal-directed behavior.

A dynamic interaction perspective offers an alternative way of conceptualizing the developmental change and unique patterns of organization of parent-infant games. In such a view, the constant shifting, changing influence of internal and external factors, and reorganization of the components in social play are not only expected but, by definition, are necessary in a continuous and dynamic process.

As a whole, the impression is often one of an ordered and cohesive game structure but further analysis is required to be able to identify the subtle and multiple adjustments, adaptations, and obvious and nonobvious components that contribute to each unique parent-infant game experience.

This view has important theoretical implications for our understanding of the functions, development, and individual differences in the emergence of social play. At the very least, parent-infant games contribute to the development of the relationship between parent and child. As further endeavors in dynamic systems approach to this type of interaction may show, games may function as an opportunity to participate in close mutually involved social interaction that has basic familiarity but is a unique dynamic and constantly reorganizing process.

References

Antonelli, P. L. (1985). *Mathematical Essays on Growth and the Emergence of Form.* Alberta, Canada: University of Alberta Press.

Barrett, K. S. and Campos, J. J. (1987). Perspectives on emotional development. In J. D. Osofsky (ed.), *Handbook of Infant Development,* 2nd ed. NY: Wiley

Bates, E. (1979). Intentions, conventions, and symbols. In E. Bates, L. Benigini, I. Bretherton, L. Camaioni, and V. Volterra (eds.), *The Emergence of Symbols: Cognition and Communication in Infancy.* New York: Academic Press.

Beckoff, M., and Byers, J. A. (1981). A critical reanalysis of the ontogeny and phylogeny of mammalian social and locomotor play: An ethologist's hornet's nest. In K. Immelman, G. W. Barlow, L. Petrinovich, and M. Main (eds.), *Behavioral Development.* Cambridge: Cambridge University Press.

Bowlby, J. (1980). *Attachment and Loss.* Vol. 3, *Loss, Sadness, and Depression.* New York: Basic Books.

Bretherton, I. (1985). Attachment theory: Retrospect and prospect. *Monographs of the Society for Research in Child Development,* serial no. 209, vol. 50:3–35.

Bril, B.; Zack, M.; and Nkounkou-Hombessa, E. (1989). Ethnotheories of development and education: A view from different cultures. *European Journal of Psychology of Education* 4:307–18.

Bruner, J. (1983). *Child's Talk: Learning to Use Language.* New York: Norton.

Burghardt, G. M. (1984). On the origins of play, 5–42. *See* Smith 1984.

Cohn, J. F., and Elmore, M. (1988). Effect of contingent changes in mothers' affective expression on the organization of behavior in 3-month-old infants. *Infant Behavior and Development* 11:493–505.

Cohn, J. F., and Tronick, E. Z. (1983). Three-month old infants' reactions to simulated maternal depression. *Child Development* 54:185–93.

Dixon, S.; Tronick, E.; Keefer, C.; and Brazelton, T. B. (1981). Mother-infant interaction among the Gusii of Kenya. In T. Field et al. (eds.), *Culture and Early Interactions.* Hillsdale, N.J.: Lawrence Erlbaum.

Duncan, S. (In press). Convention and conflict in the child's interaction with others. *Developmental Review.*

Duncan, S. D., and Farley, A. M. (1990). Achieving parent-child coordination through convention: Fixed-and variable sequence conventions. *Child Development* 61:742–53.

Fajardo, B. F., and Freedman, D. G. (1981). Maternal rhythmicity in three American cultures. In T. M. Field, A. M. Sostek, P. Vietze, and P. H.

Leiderman (eds.), *Culture and Early Interactions.* Hillsdale, N.J.: Lawrence Erlbaum.

Field, T. (1979). Infant behaviors directed toward peers and adults in the presence and absence of mother. *Infant Behavior and Development* 2:47–54.

Field, T. M., and Pawlby, S. (1980). Early face-to-face interactions of British and American working and middle-class mother-infant dyads. *Child Development* 51:250–53.

Fischer, K. W., and Bidell, T. R. (1990). Constraining nativist inferences about cognitive capacities. In S. Carey and R. Gelman (eds.), *Constraints on Knowledge in Cognitive Development.* Hillsdale, N.J.: Erlbaum.

Fogel, A. (1979). Peer vs. mother directed behavior in 1-to-3-month-old infants. *Infant Behavior and Development* 2:215–26.

Fogel, A. (1988). Cyclicity and stability in mother-infant face-to-face interaction: A comment on Cohn & Tronick (1988). *Developmental Psychology* 24:393–95.

Fogel, A. (1990a). The process of developmental change in infant communicative action: Using dynamic systems theory to study individual ontogenies. In J. Colombo and J. Fagen (eds.), *Individual Differences in Infancy: Reliability, Stability and Prediction.* Hillsdale, N.J.: Erlbaum.

Fogel, A. (1990b). Sensorimotor factors in communicative development. In H. Bloch and B. Bertenthal (eds.), *Sensorimotor Organization and Development in Infancy and Early Childhood.* NATO ASI Series. The Netherlands: Kluwer.

Fogel, A. (1992). Developmental dynamics of movement and communication in infancy. *Human Movement Science* 11:387–423.

Fogel, A.; Dedo, J. Y.; and McEwen, I. (1992). Effect of postural position and reaching on gaze during mother-infant face-to-face interaction. *Infant Behavior and Development* 15:231–44.

Fogel, A.; Diamond, G. R.; Langhorst, B. H.; and Demos, V. (1982). Affective and cognitive aspects of the two-month old's participation in face-to-face interaction with its mother. In E. Tronick (ed.), *Social Interchange in Infancy: Affect, Cognition, and Communication.* Baltimore: University Park Press.

Fogel, A.; Nwokah, E.; Hsu, H.; Dedo, J.; and Walker, H. (1990). Posture and communication in mother-infant interaction. In G. Savelsbeigh (ed.) *The Development of Coordination in Infancy.* Amsterdam: Elsevier.

Fogel, A., and Reimers, M. (1989). On the psychobiology of emotions and their development. *Monographs of the Society for Research in Child Development,* serial no. 219, vol. 54, 105–13.

Fogel, A.; Toda, S.; and Kawai, M. (1988). Mother-infant face-to-face interaction in Japan and the United States: A laboratory comparison using 3-month-old infants. *Developmental Psychology* 24:398–406.

Gould, S. J. (1977). *Ontogeny and Phylogeny.* Cambridge: Harvard University Press.

Gusella, J. L.; Muir, D.; and Tronick, E. Z. (1988). The effect of manipulating maternal behavior during an interaction on three- and six-month-olds' affect and attention. *Child Development* 59:1111–24.

Gustafson, G.; Green, J.; and West, M. (1979). The infant's changing role in mother-infant games: The growth of social skills. *Infant Behavior and Development* 2:301–8.

Haken, H. (1983). *Synergetics—An Introduction.* 3d ed. New York: Springer-Verlag.

Haroutunian, S. (1983). *Equilibrium in the Balance: A Study of Psychological Explanation.* New York: Springer-Verlag.

Hay, D.; Ross, H.; and Davis Goldman, B. (1979). *Social Games in Infancy.* In B. Sutton-Smith (ed.), *Play and Learning.* New York: Gardner Press.

Hughes, L. A. (1989). Foursquare: A glossary and "native" taxonomy of game rules. *Play and Culture* 2:103–36.

Izard, C. E., and Malatesta, C. Z. (1987). Perspectives on emotional development I: Differential emotions theory of early emotional development. In J. D. Osofky (ed.), *Handbook of Infant Development.* 2d ed. New York: John Wiley and Sons.

Jolly, A. (1985). *The Evolution of Primate Behavior.* 2d ed. New York: MacMillan.

Karns, J. (1989, April). Patterns of interaction during mother-twin infant play. Paper presented at the Society for Research in Child Development, Kansas City, Mo.

Karns, J. (1990, August). Infant age and situational differences in mother-twin infant interaction. Paper presented at the American Psychological Association, Boston.

Karns, J., and Fogel, A. (1990, April). Sequential organization of mother-twin infant interaction. Paper presented at International Conference on Infant Studies, Montreal.

Kaye, K. (1982). *The Mental and Social Life of Babies.* Chicago: University of Chicago Press.

Kugler, P. N.; Kelso, J. A. S.; and Turvey, M. T. (1982). On coordination and control in naturally development systems. In J. A. S. Kelso and J. E. Clark (eds.), *The Development of Movement Coordination and Control.* New York: Wiley.

Legerstee, M.; Pomerleau, A.; Malcuit, G.; Feider, H. (1987). The development of infants' responses to people and a doll: Implications for research in communication. *Infant Behavior and Development* 10:81–95.

Lock, A. (1980). *The Guided Reinvention of Language.* New York: Academic Press.

Malatesta, C. Z.; Culver, C.; Tesman, J. R.; and Shepard, B. (1989). The development of emotion expression during the first two years of life. *Monographs of the Society for Research in Child Development,* serial no. 219, vol. 54.

Meegaskumbura, P. B. (1980). Tondal: Sinhala baby talk. *Word* 31:287–309.

Muller-Schwarze, D. (1978). *Evolution of Play Behavior.* Stroudsberg, Pa.: Dowden, Hutchinson, and Ross.

Newell, K. M. (1986). Constraints on the development of coordination. In M. G. Wade and H. T. A. Whiting (eds.), *Motor Development in Children: Aspects of Coordination and Control.* NATO ASI Series. Dordrecht: Martinus Nijhoff.

Nwokah, E. (1987). Maidese versus motherese—is the language input of child and adult caregivers similar? *Language and Speech* 30:(3): 213–37.

Nwokah, E., and Fogel, A. (1987). *The Role of Laughter in Mother-Infant Social Games.* Presented at British Developmental Psychology Conference, Coleg Harlech, North Wales.

Nwokah, E., and Fogel, A. (In prep.). Cross-cultural differences in baby-talk to infants—the missing links.

Oyama, S. (1985). *The Ontogeny of Information: Developmental Systems and Evolution.* Cambridge, Eng.: Cambridge University Press.

Oyama, S. (1989). Ontogeny and the central dogma: Do we need the concept of genetic programming in order to have an evolutionary perspective? In M. Grunnar and E. Thelen (eds.), *Systems and Development.* The Minnesota Symposia on Child Psychology, vol. 22. Hillsdale, N.J.: Erlbaum.

Papousek, H., and Papousek, M. (1977). Mothering and cognitive headstart: Psychobiological considerations. In H. R. Schaffer (ed.), *Studies in Mother-Infant Interaction*. London: Academic Press.

Papousek, H., and Papousek, M. (1987). Intuitive parenting: A dialectic counterpart of the infant's integrative competence. In J. D. Osofsky (ed.), *Handbook of Infant Development*. 2nd ed. New York: Wiley.

Piaget, J. (1952). *The Origins of Intelligence in Children*. New York: International Universities Press.

Plomin, R. (1990). The role of inheritance in behavior. *Science* 248:183–88.

Prigogine, I., and Stengers, I. (1984). *Order Out of Chaos: Man's New Dialogue with Nature*. New York: Bantam.

Reed, E. S. (1982). An outline of a theory of actions systems. *Journal of Motor Behavior* 14:98–134.

Rogoff, B. (1990). *Apprenticeship in Thinking: Cognitive Development in Social Context*. New York: Oxford University Press.

Ruff, H. A., and Lawson, K, R. (1990). Development of sustained, focused attention in young children during free play. *Developmental Psychology* 26:85–93.

Rumelhart, D. E., and McClelland, J. L. (eds.). (1986). *Parallel distributed processing: Explorations in the Microstructure of Cognition*. Vol. 1, *Foundations*. Cambridge: Bradford Books/MIT Press.

Singer, W. (1986). The brain as a self-organizing system. *European Archives of Psychiatry and Neurological Sciences* 236:4–9.

Skarda, C., and Freeman, W. (1987). How brains make chaos in order to make sense of the world. *Behavioral and Brain Sciences* 10:161–95.

Smith, P. K. (1984). *Play in Animals and Humans*. London: Basil Blackwell.

Smith, P. K., and Vollstedt, R. (1985). On defining play: An empirical study of the relationship between play and various play criteria. *Child Development* 56:1042–50.

Stern, D. N. (1985). *The Interpersonal World of the Infant*. New York: Basic Books.

Stoller, S. A., and Field, T. (1982). Alteration of mother and infant behavior and heart rate during a still-face perturbation of face-to-face interaction. In T. Field and A. Fogel (eds.), *Emotion and Early Interaction*. Hillsdale, N.J.: Erlbaum.

Tamboer, J., (1988). Images of the body underlying concepts of action. In O. G. Meijer and K. Roth (eds.), *Complex Movement Behavior: The Motor-Action Controversy*. Amsterdam: North Holland.

Thelen, E. (1989). Self-organization in developmental processes. Can systems approaches work? In M. Gunnar and E. Thelen (eds.), *Systems in Development*. Hillsdale, N.J.: Erlbaum.

Thelen, E., and Fogel, A. (1989). Toward an action-based theory of infant development. In J. Lockman and N. Hazen (eds.), *Action in Social Context: Perspectives on Early Development*. New York: Plenum.

Trevarthen, C. (1977). Descriptive analysis of infant communicative behavior. In H. R. Schaffer (ed.), *Studies of Mother-Infant Interaction*. London: Academic Press.

Trevarthen, C. (1986). Development of intersubjective motor control in infants. In M. G. Wade and H. T. A. Whiting (eds.), *Motor Development in Children: Aspects of Coordination and Control*. NATO ASI Series. Dordrecht: Martinus Nijhoff.

Tronick, E.; Als, H.; Adamson, L.; Wise, S.; and Brazelton, T. B. (1978). The infant's response to entrapment between contradictory messages in face-to-face interaction. *Journal American Academy of Child Psychiatry* 17:1–13.

Van Hoorn, J. (1987). Games that babies and mothers play. In P. Monighan-Nourot, B. Scales, et al. (eds.), *Looking at Children's Play: A Bridge between Theory and Practice*. Teachers College Press.

Van Wieringen, P. C. W. (1986). Motor coordination: Constraints and cognition. In M. G. Wade and H. T. A. Whiting (eds.), 361–72. *Motor Development in Children: Aspects of Coordination and Control*. NATO ASI Series. Dordrecht: Martinus Nijhoff.

Vygotsky, L. S. (1978). *Mind in Society*. Cambridge: Harvard University Press.

Washington, J. A., and Craig, H. K. (1990, October). The languages of access. Paper presented at the International Conference on Pragmatics and Language Learning, Champaign, Ill.

West, L., and Fogel, A. (1990). *Maternal Guidance of Object Interaction*. Paper presented at International Conference on Infant Studies, Montreal.

CHAPTER 3

Parent-Infant Play as a Window on Infant Competence: An Organizational Approach to Assessment

Marjorie Beeghly

Introduction

Parent-infant play has long been regarded by developmentalists as an important component of children's cognitive, socioemotional, and self-regulatory development (Rubin, Fein, and Vandenberg 1983; Stern 1985; Tronick 1989). In this chapter, it is argued that parent-infant play also provides an excellent opportunity for assessing qualitative aspects of infant competence during the first two years of life. The theoretical framework guiding this approach to assessment is the organizational perspective to developmental psychopathology (Cicchetti 1984; Santostefano 1978; Sroufe and Rutter 1984). Following a brief review of this perspective, a working definition of infant competence will be provided in the context of the major developmental tasks facing infants during the first two years. With this background in place, selected parent-child play assessment paradigms which challenge infants and toddlers with respect to these stage-salient issues will then be described. Finally, parent-toddler play in an illustrative risk population—toddlers with intrauterine growth retardation (IUGR)—will be examined in order to demonstrate the usefulness of parent-child play paradigms for assessing key dimensions of competence in these children. Implications for this and similar research for play assessment with high-risk populations will also be considered.

An Organizational Perspective
on Developmental Psychopathology

The theoretical framework underlying the approach to infant assessment taken in this chapter is "the organizational perspective" as applied to developmental psychopathology (Cicchetti 1984; Cicchetti and Beeghly 1990; Kaplan 1966; Rutter 1986). A central premise of this perspective is that our understanding of the normal functioning of an organism can be enhanced and challenged by studying its pathology, and conversely, our knowledge of its pathology can be broadened and refined by studying its normal functioning. Within this approach, development is conceived as a series of qualitative reorganizations among and within behavioral and biological systems. As development proceeds, these reorganizations reflect ongoing differentiation and hierarchical integration of abilities as well as the dynamic transaction of variables at many different levels of analysis (i.e., genetic, biochemical, behavioral, psychological, environmental, psychological, and historical). Proponents of this perspective maintain that the organizational/developmental psychopathology perspective may fruitfully be applied to any unit of behavior or discipline, with all cultures, and, as in this chapter, with normally developing, high-risk, or abnormally developing populations of children (Werner 1948).

In the field of developmental psychology, investigators adopting this approach have targeted behavioral systems such as cognition, social communicative behavior, affect, and self-regulation for study. A key concern of these investigators is the organization of these behavioral systems in normal development, as well as the lack of organization or unique patterns of organization in abnormal development (Cicchetti and Schneider-Rosen 1984; Gollin 1984). Because hierarchical organization occurs both within and between each of these systems (e.g., Bishof 1975), the capacities of one behavioral system may be associated with the development or exercise of capacities of another. For this reason, proponents of this perspective are interested in examining advances and lags in one behavioral system with respect to others.

Moreover, "normal" or competent functioning at any one point of development is not defined in terms of what is "average" for a particular group, as in other approaches to child study. Rather, competence is defined as the successful negotiation of a series of interlocking cognitive, social, and affective "tasks" that the developing organism must master in ontogeny. The successful resolution of a particular developmental task broadly adapts the individual to the environment at the particular point in time. Furthermore, mastering one stage-salient task sets the stage for the formation of competence at a later developmental stage (Cicchetti and Beeghly 1990; Sroufe and Rutter 1984). Thus, according to the organizational/developmental psychopathology perspective, age-appropriate functioning results from the integration of earlier competencies into later modes of functioning.

Whereas early adaptation tends to promote later adaptation and integration, early maladaptation places the organism at risk for later maladaptation and disorganization. Accordingly, pathological development, in turn, is viewed as the *lack* of integration of the social, emotional, and cognitive competencies that are crucial in achieving adaptation at a particular developmental level (Kaplan 1966; Sroufe 1979). Importantly, transacting systems which promote either normal and pathological conditions do not occur in isolation, but rather impact upon the ontogenetic process through a hierarchy of influence (Cicchetti 1987). Because multiple transactions among parents, child, and ecology contribute to child development in a dynamic, reciprocal manner (Sameroff and Chandler 1975), development at a later point must reflect not only the quality of earlier adaptation, but also the effects of the intervening environment. Thus, a child who shows pathological development over time is presumed to have been involved in a continuous maladaptive transactional process. Moreover, the emergence of adaptive or maladaptive outcomes may be influenced by the presence of long-term protective or risk factors or by more transient buffers or challengers (Cicchetti and Rizley 1981; Cicchetti and Wagner 1990).

Taking an organizational approach to the study of parent-child play thus necessitates a multidimensional approach that considers the following: the unique characteristics of the child, the age and developmental level of his or her functioning, advances and lags among different developmental domains (cognitive, social, affective, self-regulatory), and the unique characteristics of the caregiving and the sociocultural environment (Belsky 1984), including its stability. Such an approach can provide an appropriate data set for affirming, expanding, and/or challenging current developmental theorizing about ontogenetic processes in these populations and, at the same time, for formulating a broader, more comprehensive theory of normal development (Inhelder 1966; Rutter 1986; Werner 1948).

Unfortunately, the majority of studies of atypically developing children in past decades have concentrated primarily on elucidating the cognitive deficits of these children, to the exclusion of other age-appropriate domains of functioning. While such a limited approach has informed us that many such children are indeed developmentally delayed, it has shed relatively little light on individual differences in profiles of abilities for these children or on the continuity and quality of their adaptation. Furthermore, such an approach has not addressed the "process-achievement distinction," that is, the various pathways by which children may achieve similar developmental outcomes (Werner 1948; Kaplan 1983). Yet, a more detailed understanding of the unique characteristics of these children and their caregivers, along with their developmental pathways, are crucial to obtain. Not only will this information challenge or confirm current theories of developmental processes in normally and abnormally developing children, it will also better inform clinicians and other professionals so that they may more effectively guide and time intervention efforts for these children.

In the following section, a working definition of infant competence during the first two years of life will be provided with respect to the major developmental tasks of infancy (see also Cicchetti and Beeghly 1990; Greenspan 1990; Sroufe 1979; Tronick and Beeghly 1992; Waters and Sroufe 1983). This review will provide a context within which to view the parent-infant play literature in both normally and abnormally developing populations, including the IUGR population to be discussed at the conclusion of this chapter. In addition, major paradigms for assessing infant competence surrounding these developmental tasks during parent-infant play will be described.

Infant Competence in the Context of the Major Developmental Tasks of Infancy

Proponents of the organizational perspective maintain that all infants face an epigenetic sequence of developmental issues or tasks in ontogeny that must be mastered in order to achieve and maintain adaptive functioning (Erikson 1950; Sroufe 1979). Moreover, the skill with which infants negotiate each of these tasks reflects their current level of competence. That is because infants must utilize the full range of their current cognitive, affective, social, and self-regulatory capacities in a coherent and organized fashion in order to negotiate each task successfully.

Table 3.1
Major Tasks of Development During Infancy

0–3	Months and Beyond: Physiologic and Behavioral State Regulation; Development of a Reliable Signaling System
2–6	Months and Beyond: Reciprocal Socioemotional Exchanges; Arousal Modulation and the Differentiation of Affect
5–12	Months and Beyond: Coordination of Attention to Objects and Events during Social Exchanges
6–12	Months and Beyond: Establishment of a Clear-Cut, Secure Attachment Relationship
12–30	Months and Beyond: Development of Autonomy; Self-Other Individua- tion, Mastery/Exploration of the Environment; Emergence of Symbolic Functioning

Furthermore, how well one task is resolved has implications for how well later stage-salient issues are resolved. For instance, infants' ongoing inability to regulate state in early infancy preempts their ability to engage in any other social or cognitive tasks such as parent-infant face-to-face interaction or sustained attention to objects. In turn, infants' chronic ability to regulate social exchanges compromises all later forms of social engagement (Tronick 1989; Tronick and Beeghly 1992). Moreover, because infants develop in a social context, the caregiver plays a critical role in facilitating or interfering with immature infants' inability to master these stage-salient tasks (Greenspan 1990; Tronick 1989). Finally, while the importance of these tasks may wax and wane in ontogeny, each task represents a lifelong developmental issue that requires ongoing coordination with and integration into the child's adaptation to the caregiving environment and to the stage-salient developmental issue of the period (Cicchetti and Beeghly 1990). A brief outline of the major developmental tasks of infancy is presented in Table 3.1, followed by a more detailed summary of each task and their relevance for parent-child play in different populations.

0–3 Months: Physiologic and Behavioral State Regulation.

From the moment of delivery onward, the challenge of achieving and maintaining homeostasis, state and physiologic regulation, and neurobehavioral organization confronts both the newborn infant and its caregiver (Emde, Gaensbauer, and Harmon 1976; Greenspan 1981; Sander 1962, 1975). The developmental goal of this period is the stabilization of sleep/wake cycling, patterns of feeding and elimination, and state organization. If this regulatory goal is achieved, the infant is able to interact more consistently with the environment and with the caregiver, and, as a consequence, to establish and refine a more reliable signaling system. If this goal is not achieved, the infant's ability to interact with the external environment is seriously compromised.

While normally developing infants vary in their regulatory capabilities and in neurobehavioral organization at birth (Brazelton 1984), most caregivers are able to adapt adequately to their unique characteristics and to promote healthy developmental outcomes. In contrast, parents of infants at the extremes of the "continuum of reproductive casualty" (Sameroff and Chandler 1975)—that is, infants who are biologically at risk for self-regulatory and interactive problems—may find parenting extraordinarily challenging. For example, premature infants (chapter 13), fetally growth-retarded infants (Beeghly and Cicchetti 1987), and prenatally drug-exposed infants (Tronick and Beeghly 1992) all have been reported to have marked difficulties in visual and auditory orientation to the animate and inanimate environment, immature motor responses and cogwheel-like, choreiform movements, poor autonomic and state regulation, and, in some studies, abnormal reflexes during the first month of life (Beeghly et al. 1988; Tronick and Beeghly 1992; Zuckerman and Bresnahan 1991). As a result, these infants may have exceptional difficulty with state organization and regulation, which may, in turn, compromise their mastery of the social interactive and exploratory skills that are crucial for negotiating the next developmental task successfully.

How adequately parents adapt to their newborns also plays a critical role in either facilitating or interfering with their infants' ability to resolve this developmental task. For instance, parents of infants with poor regulatory capacities may find it exhausting and unrewarding to establish effective patterns of interaction with them, resulting in either an overly stimulating, neglectful, noncontingent, or inconsistent and chaotic caregiving environment. Yet, without adequate support from the caregiving environment, these infants may not be successful in mastering the social interactive and exploratory skills that are crucial for negotiating the next developmental task (Cicchetti and Beeghly 1990; Greenspan 1990; Tronick et al. 1991).

With sustained effort and care, parents of fragile infants nonetheless may be able to adapt their behavior sensitively to their infants and thereby maximize their infants' abilities to balance inner state and attention to external stimuli. However, their ability to do this depends to a large extent on the adequacy of their own social and psychological resources. Parents at the extremes of caretaking casualty (Sameroff and Chandler 1975)—that is, those at high social or psychological risk—may have marked difficulty in meeting the regulatory needs of their vulnerable infants. Thus, fragile infants of high-risk caregiver dyads may be at double jeopardy for compromised developmental outcome.

2–6 Months: Reciprocal Socioemotional Exchanges; Arousal Modulation and the Differentiation of Affect.

With the mastery of homeostatic regulation and the establishment of more reliable signaling patterns, infants develop an increased capacity for sustained attention to the environment. Accordingly, infants begin to engage both the animate and inanimate world in a more organized manner (Sroufe and Waters 1976). This increase in interactive capacity corresponds ontogenetically with neurological brain maturation reflected both in the onset of the social smile and in recognition memory (Lamb 1984). During this phase, the infants' affective expressions become more intense and more differentiated. Moreover, expressive modalities such as facial expressions, vocalizations, gestures, and gaze become increasingly coordinated as communicative configurations and strategies (Weinberg 1989). Not only do these organized configurations help infants modulate their positive and negative arousal more effectively but they also provide clearer communicative signals for the caregiver.

In addition to infants' ability to produce coherent, clear communicative signals, caregiver sensitivity to infant cues is also critical for the successful resolution of this second developmental task. During social exchanges, for instance, when infant arousal is too high for infants to regulate on their own, parents must modulate and adjust their own affect and behavior in order to facilitate infant affective regulation from a disruptive negative state to a more regulated positive one. If these modifications are made sensitively, the result is an increase in infants' social attention, positive affect, and positive object engagement (Tronick 1989). Furthermore, these interactions mark the beginnings of differentiated emotional responses to different individuals and reflect basic structures (e.g., turn-taking) that are crucial for the coordination of more complicated interactions that occur later in development. Both the success of caregiver-infant negotiations and the sensitivity of the caregiver in response to the infant are systematically related to infants' later social and cognitive development (Tronick et al. 1991). A major goal of parent-child play at this phase is to achieve and maintain an optimal range of infant attention and positive arousal (Brazelton, Koslowski, and Main 1974; Stern 1985; Tronick 1989).

High-risk or abnormally developing infants present special challenges to caregivers with respect to affective regulation and the establishment of reciprocal socioemotional exchanges. For example, infants with Down syndrome have difficulty with arousal modulation and show delays in the appearance of affective displays such as laughter and fear (Cicchetti and Beeghly 1990). Cicchetti and Sroufe (1978) reported that these infants are slower to develop social smiles than normally developing infants and show delayed and dampened positive affect to a variety of stimuli presented by their mothers (see also Cicchetti and Beeghly 1990). Their delayed, dampened affect is thought to result from information processing delays: these infants cannot process the incongruity of the stimuli quickly enough to produce the tension necessary for laughter. Consequently, caregivers of these infants find them more difficult to read, resulting in more effortful and less positive exchanges during face-to-face interaction (Berger 1990).

Perhaps in compensation for these psychophysiological deviations, parents of infants with Down syndrome tend to exert more effort in initiating and controlling social interactions with these infants (Berger 1990; Mervis 1990). What may appear to be an overstimulating or overly intrusive caregiver style may actually facilitate the successful resolution of this developmental task in this population (Cicchetti and Beeghly 1990).

Caregivers of premature infants, IUGR infants, drug-exposed infants, and other infants at biological risk for poor state organization may also find it exceptionally difficult to initiate and maintain social play with their infants at this developmental phase. In order to achieve optimal states of attention and arousal with these infants, caregivers must adapt and fine-tune their interactive styles and become exquisitely sensitive to infant signaling for "time out" (e.g., looking away, self-comforting behaviors, loss of motor tone, perceptual inhibition [Tronick 1989]). That this is a difficult challenge is affirmed by several comparative studies of premature infants. These studies have demonstrated that parent-preterm dyads during this age period show decreased amounts of positive affect during social play (Crnic et al. 1983; Parmelee et al. 1983). Similarly, Field (1979, 1982) reported that caregiver-preterm dyads at four months (corrected-age) engaged in significantly less game playing and displayed less positive and more negative affect than caregiver-term dyads. Moreover, preterm infants were more likely to gaze avert and to cry during social play. Taken together, these findings suggest that the establishment of reciprocal socioemotional exchanges may be an especially difficult developmental task to negotiate for these biologically at-risk dyads.

Critically, the medical risk associated with biological impairments such as IUGR, prematurity, or prenatal drug exposure may be either compounded or buffered by social risks in the caregiving environment. For instance, while drug-exposed infants appear to be at physiologic risk for self-regulatory and interactive problems that may compromise their ability to negotiate the key developmental tasks of infancy (Tronick and Beeghly in press), these infants are also likely to experience a variety of environmental risks such as those associated with poverty and malnutrition (Parker et al. 1988). In addition, drug and alcohol abuse have consistently been associated with dysfunctional caregiving patterns and child maltreatment (e.g., Bays 1990; Bauman and Dougherty 1983; Belsky and Vondra 1989; Black and Mayer 1980; Rutter 1989). Moreover, drug-using women frequently have other health or psychological comorbidities (e.g., depression [Zuckerman et al. 1987]) that are likely to contribute to suboptimal caregiving environments and poor developmental outcomes. In a recent study of adolescent pregnant women (Amaro et al. 1989), for example, drug-using pregnant women were more likely to report more negative life events and to witness or experience violence than nondrug-users. Furthermore, drug-users were three times more likely to have a male partner who used marijuana or cocaine and two times more likely to have a history of venereal disease.

That the social environment can significantly impact developmental outcomes for prenatally drug-exposed children is evident in a series of studies by Hans (1989): methadone-exposed infants who had delayed motor development at four months relative to nonex-posed infants continued to show motor deficits by twelve months *only if* they were from families of high social risk. Similarly, in a study of at-risk children in Kauai, Werner (1989) reported that a combination of high perinatal risk and high family instability was a better predictor of long-term compromised developmental function-ing than high perinatal risk alone. Additionally, caregiver behavior has been demonstrated to compensate for biologically based vulner-abilities of high-risk infants (Beckwith 1986, 1990). In a longitudi-nal study of premature infants, Beckwith and Parmalee (1986) reported that eight-year IQ scores were mediated significantly by the quality of caregiving received. Specifically, among those chil-dren who had an aberrant EEG pattern (trace alternans) at one month postbirth, IQs at age eight were significantly higher if in-fants had received responsive caregiving than if they had not. Clearly, characteristics of the caregiver should be evaluated in play studies concerned with infant competence in high-risk populations.

5–12 Months: Coordination of Attention to Objects and Events during Social Exchanges.

During the latter half of the first year, infants become increas-ingly attentive to objects and sustained exploration of the external environment and, concomitantly, less interested in simple face-to-face social play. Initially, caregivers have an important and active role in facilitating object exploration by introducing objects and helping their babies regulate state and sustain attention (Trevarthen 1977; Whaley 1990). With increasing coordination of secondary action schemes (Piaget 1962), infants gradually be-come able to initiate and sustain joint attention to objects with the caregiver (Crawley et al. 1978; Crawley and Sherrod 1984). The establishment and coordination of joint attention is a major devel-opmental milestone for infants, as it marks the emergence of inten-tional communication (Bretherton and Bates 1979). At this point, objects become the topic of interaction with the caregiver, and the infant's gestures, vocalizations, and actions signal a desire for shared attention and game playing. Intentional communication is thought to be a precursor of symbolic functioning and self-other dif-ferentiation (tasks which culminate during the toddler period, as discussed below).

Infants who at previous stages manifested difficulties regulat-ing state and coordinating social schemata are at increased risk for problems in establishing and maintaining joint attention to objects with an adult partner. For instance, Olwen Jones (1977, 1980) examined object play interactions during mother-child play between infants with Down syndrome and their mothers and compared them to those of a cognitively matched group of nonhandicapped infants and mothers. Jones noted that the Down syndrome dyads engaged in shorter object-focused interactions than nonhandicapped dyads, and that infants with Down syndrome initiated fewer object interactions, had less referential eye contact, and less mutually coordinated vocal exchanges concerning objects than controls. In turn, mothers of infants with Down syndrome were more controlling and less child-centered than control mothers. Perhaps because the infants with Down syndrome offered fewer opportunities for their caregivers to reward and mark their object play behavior, mothers of infants with Down syndrome were observed to be less responsive to their infants' object play behaviors (Berger 1990). These perturbations in the organization of joint attention and social-communicative behavior during dyadic object play may have long-term ramifications for these infants' sociocognitive competence.

6–12 Months: Establishment of a Clear-Cut, Secure Attachment Relationship.

Building on developments from prior stages, a major developmental task during late infancy is the establishment of a secure attachment relationship with the caregiver (Bowlby 1982; Ainsworth et al. 1978). According to Bowlby, the attachment system is activated under the conditions of stress, fatigue, or illness. Attachment behaviors include search behaviors, proximity seeking, contact maintenance, and distal interactive behaviors. A secure infant is one who is able to coordinate his affective, communicative, motor, and cognitive systems into an adaptive and flexible goal-corrected system for using the caregiver as a secure base when under conditions of stress. Successful adaptation at this phase is marked by positive affective exchanges, resiliency to stress, and either distal or proximal relatedness. Moreover, individual differences in patterns of attachment behavior have been systematically related to maternal sensitivity and responsivity during the first year of life (Ainsworth et al. 1978) and to later developmental outcome and social competence (Bretherton 1985).

No strong evidence exists that infants at biological risk such as preterm infants are necessarily at higher risk for compromised attachment relationships with their caregivers. Instead, as for low-risk infants, the successful negotiation of this developmental task depends primarily on the quality and consistency of care received during the first year of life. An exception is a sample of full-term IUGR infants followed by Beeghly et al. (1989) (to be described in detail later in this chapter). In that study, full-term IUGR infants were more likely to have insecure-avoidant attachment relationships with their caregivers than non-IUGR infants. Moreover, the avoidant pattern was significantly and negatively related to adaptive functioning at age two (Beeghly et al. 1991b). Interestingly, these same infants showed compromised state regulation, motor organization, and social interaction difficulties during the first month of life (Beeghly et al. 1988), suggesting ongoing subtle difficulties in resolving stage-salient developmental issues throughout the infancy period.

In contrast to biologically at-risk infants, infants who fall on the extreme end of the "continuum of caretaking casualty" (Sameroff and Chandler 1975) show a different pattern. Children at high social risk such as maltreated children (Cicchetti and Carlson 1989) or infants of substance-abusing, high social-risk mothers (Rodning et al. 1989) are significantly more likely to develop an insecure pattern of attachment to the caregiver. These studies attest to the importance of the social environment in facilitating or compromising infants' ability to negotiate this stage-salient task of late infancy.

12–30 Months: Development of Autonomy, Self-Other Individuation, Mastery/Exploration of the Environment, and the Emergence of Symbolic Functioning.

During the second and third years of life, major developmental tasks include the development of an autonomous sense of self, mastery of the external environment, and the emergence of symbolic functioning. As seen at earlier phases, each of these tasks encompasses the coordination of social, affective, self-regulatory, and cognitive dimensions of functioning. Thus, with increasing cognitive and motor achievements, toddlers begin to acquire more sophisticated knowledge about self and other in different contexts (Stern 1985) and to become interested increasingly in self-management. Awareness of standards for behavior and increased motivation to explore object properties and relations are two events associated with these developments (Kagan 1981). Moreover, realizing more fully that they can have an impact on others, toddlers also begin to manifest both empathic acts and negative autonomy-seeking behavior (e.g., tantrums) around this time.

As was true for prior developmental tasks, caregiver sensitivity is critical to the successful resolution of this stage. The ability to set age-appropriate limits, while simultaneously tolerating toddler strivings for autonomy are difficult but important caregiver tasks (Cicchetti and Beeghly 1990). That caregiver sensitivity is important is evident from longitudinal research: the establishment of a secure attachment relationship with the caregiver during the first year of life is significantly related to the success with which toddlers are able to master the developmental tasks of toddlerhood (see reviews in Ainsworth et al. 1978 and Bretherton 1985). Moreover, sensitive caregiver "scaffolding" of toddler object interactions during this period is thought to be important in the development of symbolic processes (Bretherton and Bates 1979; Vygotsky 1978; Werner and Kaplan 1963).

In the next section, the value of parent-infant play paradigms as contexts for infant and toddler assessment is discussed from an organizational perspective. It will be argued that parent-infant play paradigms offer rich information about dyadic performance surrounding the major developmental tasks of infancy described above.

Parent-Child Play Paradigms and Infant Assessment

Early Parent-Infant Play as a Window on Infant Competence.

Early social parent-infant play encompasses many of the major developmental tasks of the infancy period. During face-to-face play, for instance, infants are challenged to maintain state organization, modulate arousal, regulate affect, gain control of gaze and motor movements, and sustain joint attention. As seen in the above summary, in order to sustain attention and positive affect during social exchanges, infants must have achieved control over their neurophysiological states and must be able to coordinate their communicative behaviors (e.g., gaze, facial expressions, gestures, self-regulatory behaviors) into coherent and clear behavioral-affective configurations (Weinberg and Tronick under review).

Because infants are immature and limited in their ability to coordinate behavioral states, they often fail to accomplish the task of social or inanimate engagement and state regulation during face-to-face play, resulting in negative affective states and disrupted

physiologic states (Tronick et al. in press). Therefore, adult partners
have an important role to play in helping infants sustain a positive
balance of mutual attention and positive affect. In order to accomplish this, adults first must be able to read infants' communications
accurately, since infants' success or failure during social interaction is communicated primarily through their affective displays.
Having done so, caregivers must also then respond appropriately to
these cues by adjusting the input infants are receiving and by providing additional regulatory support when warranted. The success
with which dyads engage in face-to-face play thus reflects their current level of adaptive functioning in multiple domains. Because
face-to-face parent-infant play captures these stage-salient elements of dyadic functioning, paradigms using face-to-face play as
observational contexts are excellent tools for assessing infant and
dyadic competence.

Face-to-Face Paradigm. Tronick and his colleagues (Tronick
1989; Tronick et al. 1991) as well as others have presented a valid
and reliable parent-child play assessment paradigm which taps the
major developmental tasks of infancy from three to nine months of
age. Moreover, normative data exists for this paradigm, making it
useful for comparative research with high-risk or atypical populations. In addition, this paradigm places stress on infants' current
developmental capacities, which enhances its ability to discriminate among competent and dysfunctional dyadic systems. Generally
speaking, dysfunction in an organism is clearer when the current
developmental capacities of the organism being evaluated are subjected to mild stress (see Tronick et al. 1991).

Tronick's face-to-face play paradigm consists of a sequence of
three two-minute episodes during which a normal social interaction
is followed by a perturbated interaction which, in turn, is followed
by another normal social interaction. In the normal play conditions,
caregivers are instructed to play as they normally do with their infants. The nature of the second, perturbated episode varies depending on the purpose of the study. Two commonly used perturbations
are: (1) the still-face condition, during which the caregiver watches
the infant but remains poker-faced and unresponsive; and (2) a depressed condition, in which the caregiver continues to interact with
the infant but assumes a withdrawn, depressed countenance. Additional two-minute episodes may be included in this paradigm as
well, including free play with a stranger, the infant's father, a toy/
adult interaction episode, or other variations.

In Tronick's face-to-face paradigm, the caregiver is seated facing the infant, who is strapped into an infant seat mounted on a table. Two separate cameras are used to record frontal views of the caregiver and infant during face-to-face play. Input from each camera is transmitted through a digital timer and split-screen generator to produce simultaneous views of caregiver and infant in a single video image. Once the play interchange is video recorded, stage-salient aspects of adult-infant play are then coded (typically in one-second intervals) from videotapes. In prior studies, Tronick and others have also used a less expensive and technologically simpler setup for similar effects. In this setup, a mirror is placed behind the mother, resulting in the need for only a single camera.

Objective and reliable scoring procedures for both infant and adult communicative behavior during face-to-face play are now available (e.g., Tronick 1989; Tronick & Weinberg, 1992a, b). For example, Tronick and Weinberg (1992) developed the Infant Regulatory Scoring System (IRSS) and the Maternal Regulatory Scoring System (MRSS) to code the presence or absence of a variety of discrete behaviors such as gaze and vocalizations in one-second intervals from videotapes. Other objective systems such as Izard's Maximally Discriminative Facial Movement Coding System (MAX, Izard 1971) or his System for Identifying Affect Expressions by Holistic Judgements (AFFEX, Izard et al., 1980) focus on infant facial expressions such as interest, joy, anger, and sadness, which are crucial components of the infant's communicative repertoire (Izard et al., 1980).

Affective Configurations During Face-to-Face Play. In support of the usefulness of the IRSS and AFFEX systems, Weinberg (1989) examined the relationship among the modalities of face, voice, gesture, gaze, and self-regulatory and withdrawal behaviors observed in infants during the face-to-face paradigm at six months. She reported that the first free-play episode generally elicited a wide range of emotional expressions and communicative behaviors (mostly positive), whereas the still-face condition elicited communicative bids and primarily negative affective states. In turn, the third ("reunion") free-play episode was characterized by a mix of positive and negative communicative displays. Notably, in both normal and perturbated interactions at six months, organized configurations of communicative behaviors and affects were observed. One configuration involved high levels of orientation to mother and included facial expressions of joy, infant vocalizing in a positive

manner, and gestural signals. Another was characterized primarily
by active engagement of the inanimate environment and included
facial expressions of interest and looking at inanimate objects.
Moreover, a third configuration involved a withdrawn, low activity
state, sad facial expressions, and fussing, whereas a fourth was
characterized by a high activity state, angry facial expressions, visual scanning, full-blown crying, escape/get-away and pick-me-up
gestures, and fussy vocalizations. Weinberg's study supports the assumption that low-risk, normally developing infants exhibit highly
organized communicative configurations during face-to-face play
with caregivers. Comparative play research using the face-to-face
play paradigm with high-risk or atypical populations would be valuable and informative. Such research is currently ongoing in our
laboratory.

Parent-Toddler Play Paradigms as a Window on Toddler Competence

Similarly, parent-toddler play behavior with age-appropriate
toys has also been regarded as a powerful index of toddlers'
cognitive-motivational competence (Piaget 1962; Vygotsky 1978).
According to Bruner (1964, 1972) and others, play is salient, meaningful activity for most toddlers—an important means by which
they explore the environment and form concepts about objects,
events, causality, and interpersonal relationships.

Robust and systematic changes in the structure of children's
object play behavior observed during the first two years of life have
been widely documented (Belsky and Most 1981; also see review by
Rubin, Fein, and Vandenberg 1983). For instance, although investigators differ in preferred assessment contexts (e.g., unstructured or
elicited) and coding schemes, all agree that simple sensorimotor
manipulation of objects declines linearly during this time period,
while more complex and integrated forms of play such as functional
and symbolic play rise dramatically. Moreover, these changes in
play behavior have been strongly and repeatedly associated with
children's emerging cognitive capacities as measured by standardized psychometric tests in both normally developing (see Rubin,
Fein and Vandenberg 1983, for a review) and abnormally developing
populations (e.g., Beeghly, Weiss-Perry, and Cicchetti 1990;
Kennedy et al. 1991; Sigman and Mundy 1987).

Affect and Mastery Motivation. Although emerging cognitive
abilities underlie the structure of object play, the motivating force

behind play is affective in nature (Hesse and Cicchetti 1982; Piaget 1962; Piaget and Inhelder 1969). Recent studies have documented that developmental trends in object play maturity are accompanied by concomitant changes in affective and motivational dimensions of play behavior. Thus, stylistic aspects of play such as mastery motivation, quality of exploration, and affective engagement in play have been associated with more mature forms of object play and with standardized cognitive test scores in several recent studies of normally developing children (e.g., Fein and Apfel 1979; Jennings et al. 1979) and developmentally delayed children (e.g., Beeghly, Weiss-Perry, and Cicchetti 1989; Motti, Cicchetti, and Sroufe 1983). Indeed, affective-motivational dimensions of object play have been shown to be better predictors of children's later cognitive competencies than are standard cognitive measures such as the Bayley Scales of Infant Development.

Toddler Play and Social Development. In addition, changes in children's social-communicative abilities are exhibited readily during free play with an older partner and are related to children's current cognitive functioning. During the transition from sensorimotor to representational functioning, for example, children's ability to initiate and sustain reciprocal interaction (e.g., turn-taking) and joint attention increases markedly (Beeghly 1979; Bretherton and Bates 1979; Ratner and Bruner 1978; Crawley et al. 1978; Gustafson, Green, and West 1979; Hodapp, Goldfield, and Boyatzis 1984; Ross 1982; Ross and Lollis 1987). These abilities are closely tied to children's cognitive development in early childhood.

Toddler Play and Self-Regulation. Furthermore, during unstructured free play with toys, toddlers must initiate, organize, and sustain play activities on their own, allowing a glimpse of their self-regulatory capacities. Toddlers with self-regulatory problems, such as children with IUGR or children exposed prenatally to drugs of abuse, may have particular difficulty during object play under unstructured as opposed to structured conditions. In support of this, Rodning, Beckwith, and Howard (1989) reported that children exposed to drugs of abuse in utero exhibited representational play less frequently and less coherently during unstructured free play than a control group of nonexposed preterm toddlers. Notably, these drug-exposed children performed within the normal range on standardized psychometric tests of sensorimotor development (Bayley, Gesell). In contrast, as noted below, some groups of children, particularly those with socioemotional as well as developmental delays, manifest more self-regulatory and attentional problems during focused, constrained play tasks than they do during unstructured free play (see, e.g., Kennedy et al. 1991).

In sum, because toddlers exhibit their cognitive, social-communicative, affective-motivational, and self-regulatory abilities readily during play, play assessments provide an excellent window on these age-appropriate competencies. These skills are not always directly tapped in standardized psychometric tests. For this reason, play assessments may discriminate high- and low-risk groups of children better than psychometric tests (Cicchetti and Wagner 1990).

In addition, play assessments may also be particularly fruitful for research with developmentally delayed, impaired, or other high-risk groups of children who may be difficult to test due to attentional deficits, behavior problems, or motivational problems such as pronounced passivity or learned helplessness (Yakwey and Pellegrini 1984; Zigler and Balla 1982). For example, Beeghly, Weiss-Perry, and Cicchetti (1989, 1990) reported that children with Down syndrome show both comparable and unique patterns of symbolic play behavior, social interaction, and affect during play with caregivers, as do normally developing toddlers matched for level of cognitive development. These play findings suggest that the organization of development for toddlers with Down syndrome is strikingly similar for certain aspects of play (such as the maturity of their object play) and qualitatively different in other aspects (such as in taking the initiative during social play) to that observed for normally developing children at this stage. Similarly, children with autism show markedly different patterns of social interaction and affect during parent-infant play than do cognitively matched controls, but they also exhibit similar developmental trends for certain aspects of object play (Cicchetti, Beeghly, and Weiss-Perry, in press). Critically, these similar and unique patterns are not always readily apparent during standard psychometric testing. In addition, because high-risk and abnormally developing children vary in how they perform in unstructured and structured situations, it is recommended that parent-toddler play paradigms include a combination of both for maximal discriminatory power.

Parent-Toddler Play Paradigms. Parent-child play paradigms for toddlers are popular and numerous (Rubin et al. 1983). A commonly used paradigm is one in which the examiner seats the mother-child dyad on the floor of a laboratory playroom alongside a box of standard, age-appropriate toys, invites the dyad to play with the toys, and leaves the room. In general, mothers are instructed to play with the child "as you normally would at home." Other studies request the caregiver not to direct the child's play, but to participate in play and be responsive to any requests for help or social interaction from the child. Still others request the mother to occupy herself with a magazine or questionnaire and to refrain from active participation in play. The dyad's play behavior is videotaped from behind one-way mirrors, typically for fifteen to thirty minutes. Stage-salient aspects of toddler adaptive functioning (cognitive, social-communicative, affective, self-regulatory) are readily coded from these video recordings.

Because contextual issues have been demonstrated to affect children's play performance and affective involvement in systematic ways, these concerns need to be addressed in the design of play assessment paradigms. For example, Slade (1987) demonstrated that toddlers exhibit more enthusiasm and higher object play maturity when interacting with an actively involved adult partner, as opposed to a passive partner. Moreover, modeling paradigms are thought to elicit higher levels of object play than unstructured free-play procedures in normally developing children (see McCune-Nicolich and Fenson 1984, for a review). For example, Sigman and her colleagues (e.g., Sigman and Mundy 1987) have designed and successfully implemented an elicited play assessment tool that has proved to be valid and reliable in both normal and abnormal samples: symbolic play as measured in their paradigm has been significantly associated with separate, concurrent measures of receptive language and nonverbal communicative skills.

In addition, structured play paradigms may be particularly suited to the assessment of particular stage-salient skills, such as social communicative skills. For example, using a structured social play paradigm, Hildy Ross and her colleagues (e.g., Ross and Lollis 1987) demonstrated significant age-related changes in toddlers' ability to participate actively in social games with adults from nine to eighteen months. In their paradigm, Ross and Lollis used a structured turn-taking procedure with two phases: (1) establishment of reciprocal turn-taking games with standard objects and (2) an interruption period involving a pause in adult behavior analogous to Tronick's still-face condition in his face-to-face mother-infant interaction procedure (Tronick 1989; Tronick et al. in press). Ross and Lollis reported that children's ability to initiate and sustain turn-taking increased dramatically during late infancy.

However, not all children respond to increased structure with improved performance. In a recent study developmentally delayed preschoolers of varying etiology (Kennedy et al. 1991), children with attentional or socioemotional delays as well as developmental delays did not perform more optimally during structured tasks. Rather, during structured play, their play maturity deteriorated relative to that observed during unstructured free play. For these children, unstructured free play proved to be a better observational context for observing optimal levels of adaptive functioning (see also Rodning et al. 1989, as described above).

The usefulness of parent-child play observations for assessing toddler competence and for discriminating between high- and low-risk toddlers will be illustrated next in a sample of mothers and toddlers with IUGR.

Illustration of the Value of Parent-Toddler Play Assessment in a Population of Toddlers with Intrauterine Growth Retardation (IUGR)

What Is IUGR?

Generally speaking, IUGR is thought to result from prenatal malnutrition of heterogeneous etiology (Villar et al. 1984), including maternal factors (e.g., toxemia, chronic hypertension, substance abuse, smoking, abnormal uterine structures), placental factors (e.g., vascular and inflammatory lesions, placental infarction, abnormal cord insertion, twinning), and/or fetal factors (e.g., intrauterine infections, chromosomal anomalies, other major fetal anomalies such as those involving the gastrointestinal tract and cardiovascular system). Typically, IUGR status is assigned to newborns in research studies if their birth weight is low for their gestational age (e.g., below the tenth percentile).

Developmental Sequelae Following IUGR

Despite its heterogeneity, IUGR has been repeatedly associated with both short- and long-term negative developmental sequelae (Smeriglio 1989; Villar et al. 1984). In multiple independent studies, children with IUGR tend to exhibit mildly compromised postnatal behavior and development relative to normally grown children. For example, during the newborn period, researchers have documented that IUGR results in poor state organization, hypotonia, decreased motor maturity, and an increased number of abnormal reflexes (Als et al. 1976; Beeghly et al., 1988; Lester and Zeskind 1978). Moreover, IUGR has been associated with longterm sequelae, including neurobehavioral deficits (Beeghly et al. 1989, 1991a; Vohr et al. 1979), social dysfunction in infancy (Beeghly et al. 1989, 1990b, 1991b), preschool cognitive deficits (Walther and Ramaekers 1982), language delays (Walthers and Ramaekers 1982), and poor academic performance (Henricksen et al. 1986).

Unfortunately, many of these studies suffer from confounds due to overly heterogeneous samples of IUGR infants (e.g., preterms, infants with chromosomal anomalies, infants with other medical comorbidities), making generalization of results difficult. Moreover, many investigators have not distinguished different types of IUGR that may be associated with differential developmental outcome. For instance, two types of IUGR have been identified which are thought to differ in the timing of prenatal insult (Villar et al. 1984), with consequences for postnatal outcome. "Symmetrical" IUGR infants are small for gestational age (i.e., below the tenth percentile) in both birth weight and birth length and are hypothesized to have suffered from chronic malnutrition in utero. In contrast, "asymmetrical" infants are small in birth weight relative to birth length, as calculated by "ponderal index" ([birth weight/birth length^3] × 100). These asymmetrical IUGR infants are thought to have experienced prenatal insult only after the growth peak for length has occurred (after the twenty-seventh to the thirtieth week of gestation). Villar et al. (1984) and others have hypothesized that, because symmetrical IUGR have been exposed to chronic prenatal insult, their developmental outcome should be more severely compromised than that of asymmetrical IUGR infants.

The Present Study

Results from a longitudinal study of both symmetrical and asymmetrical IUGR infants will be reported here, with special attention to developmental and behavioral outcomes at twenty-four months observed during parent-child play. To avoid common sampling confounds that plague the IUGR literature, a sample of full-term IUGR infants who were healthy, clinically normal, and at low demographic risk were selected.

Summary of Prior Research. Our prior research with this sample attests to the developmental risk status of full-term IUGR infants. To summarize, both types of IUGR infants had more signs of fetal distress during labor and delivery than did control infants, and had mothers who used tobacco more frequently during pregnancy (McKenzie, et al. 1988). At delivery, both symmetrical and asymmetrical infants showed deficits in behavioral organization and attentional capacity relative to controls as assessed by the Brazelton Neonatal Behavior Assessment Scale (NBAS) (Brazelton 1984; see Beeghly et al. 1988). Parental attitudes were also affected by their IUGR infants: both mothers and fathers reported feeling more concern for these infants at the time of delivery (Beeghly et al. 1988).

By four months, mothers of IUGR mothers also differed in interactive behavior with their infants during face-to-face interaction with toys. Compared to controls, mothers of symmetrical IUGR infants showed less positive affect during face-to-face playful interactions with toys, whereas mothers of asymmetrical IUGR infants had a more active teaching style, with more gestures, toy demonstrations, and descriptive language. Moreover, mothers of both types of IUGR infants reported feeling more confined and closed in than control mothers at four months (Beeghly et al. 1988).

In addition, symmetrical and asymmetrical IUGR infants showed different patterns of compromised cognitive and socioemotional development during the first two years. Whereas asymmetrical IUGR infants had significantly lower developmental quotients on the Bayley Scales of Infant Development at four months relative to symmetrical IUGR infants and control infants, a different pattern emerged from four to twenty-four months. As expected, symmetrical IUGR infants deteriorated by twenty-four months in aspects of their sensorimotor and psychosocial development, relative to controls, while asymmetrical infants improved and no longer differed from controls.

Specifically, by twenty-four months, symmetrical IUGR toddlers manifested less mature motor development and poorer fine motor skills than either controls of asymmetrical IUGR toddlers. In addition, qualitative ratings of infant performance during the Bayley examination (Beeghly, Vo, Burrows, and Brazelton 1990) revealed that symmetrical IUGR infants were less socially responsive to the examiner, more squirmy and fidgety during testing, showed more signs of physiological and behavorial "cost" of paying attention to the task (e.g., negative mood changes, yawning, hiccupping, distractibility) and required greater examiner effort and persistence to complete the exam than control infants.

That these seemingly direct effects of birth status were mediated by the social environment is evident from their attachment behavior during Ainsworth's Strange Situation at twelve months (Ainsworth et al. 1978). Symmetrical IUGR infants were significantly more likely to be classified as "insecure-avoidant" in this paradigm than control infants, confirming our data that these infant-caregiver dyads have experienced compromised social and affective interactions throughout infancy. In contrast, asymmetrical IUGR infants showed a reverse trend, decreasing in vulnerability in both cognitive and psychosocial domains by twenty-four months.

Results attest to the usefulness of distinguishing these two types of IUGR infants in longitudinal outcome studies. Moreover, findings suggest that full-term, healthy infants showing a symmetrical pattern of growth retardation in utero are at greater risk for developmental delays and for difficult infant-caregiver relations than asymmetrical IUGR infants.

IUGR and Parent Toddler Play. Because parent-child play offers a naturalistic look at the organization and coherence of toddlers' cognitive, social, affective, and self-regulatory functioning surrounding the major tasks of toddlerhood, it was hypothesized the IUGR infants would best be discriminated from non-IUGR infants during play than during standard psychometric testing (i.e., Bayley Scales of Infant Development). Following the theoretical guidelines of the organizational perspective (Cicchetti 1984; Santostefano 1978; Sroufe and Rutter 1984), two parent-child play contexts were therefore included in the twenty-four–month outcome assessments conducted in this sample (Beeghly et al. 1990b). Results from these play observations will be presented in detail in the following sections.

Method.

Subjects. Seventy-five full-term, clinically normal toddlers and their middle-class mothers comprised the twenty-four month sample. Thirty-two toddlers had been of normal weight at birth, with birth weights and lengths falling between the tenth and ninetieth percentiles for gestational age, and served as controls. Forty-three were IUGR, with birth measurements falling below the tenth percentile. Of these IUGR toddlers, twenty-two had a symmetrical pattern of IUGR, and twenty-one were asymmetrically growth retarded. Mothers in each group experienced one of two short-term perinatal interventions during the first month post birth. Subject characteristics are presented in Table 3.2. (categorical variables) and Table 3.3 (continuous variables).

Table 3.2.
Subject Characteristics: Categorical Variables

Variable	Controls (N = 32)	IUGR Asymmetrical (N = 21)	Symmetrical (N = 22)
Intervention Type			
1 (55%)	14	10	10
2 (45%)	18	11	12
Infant Gender			
Males (43%)	15	9	8
Females (57%)	17	12	14
Socio-economic Status (Hollingshead)			
1 (41%)	12	11	8
2 (45%)	15	9	10
3 (14%)	5	1	4
Marital Status			
Single (7%)	2	1	2
Married (93%)	30	20	20
Ethnicity			
White (81%)	28	16	17
Black (19%)	4	5	5
Parity			
1 (62%)	18	14	0
2 (35%)	13	6	2
3 (3%)	16	6	0
Delivery Status			
Vaginal (71%)	26	13	14
C-section (29%)	6	8	8

Note: There were no significant differences for these variables for infant IUGR status or intervention group status, nor were there any significant interactions of infant IUGR status group by intervention interactions.

Table 3.3
Subject Characteristics: Continuous Variables

| Variable | Controls (N = 32) | IUGR | |
		Asymmetrical (N = 21)	Symmetrical (N = 22)
Birth Weight[a] (kg)	3.6 (1.3)	2.6 (3.0)	2.8 (2.2)
Birth Length[b] (cm)	51.5 (1.3)	48.9 (1.6)	47.5 (1.5)
Birth Head Circumference[c] (cm)	34.2 (.9)	32.9 (1.2)	32.9 (.9)
Ponderal Index[d]	2.6 (.1)	2.2 (.1)	2.6 (.1)
Maternal Age	30.3 (4.3)	30.4 (3.4)	30.3 (4.4)

Note: Group differences were tested with intervention (2) by infant group (3) ANOVAs, with Tukey post hoc tests. No significant main effects of intervention or interactions of infant IUGR status with intervention status were observed. Moreover, maternal age did not differ significantly by infant IUGR status. Significant differences in infant IUGR status are listed below:

a. $F(2,69) = 122.8$; $p = .0001$; controls > both IUGR groups.

b. $F(2,69) = 50.9$; $p = .0001$; controls > both IUGR groups, and IUGR-symmetrical > IUGR-symmetrical.

c. $F(2,59) = 22.9$; $p = .0001$; controls > both IUGR groups.

d. $F(2,69) = 75.7$; $p = .0001$; controls, IUGR-symmetrical > IUGR symmetrical.

Procedure. Toddlers were videotaped in two laboratory contexts varying in task demands: unstructured free play and a mother-child object play context involving maternal teaching. During the free-play context, mothers were present but occupied with completing a questionnaire at a table in the corner of the room. Mothers were instructed to be responsive to any toddler social bids, but not to initiate social interaction or direct toddler activity. Thus, toddlers were required to structure their own play interactions with toys and to initiate any social bids with mother. In contrast, during the teaching context, mothers were asked to teach their toddlers the concepts of color and size during two successive block sorting tasks. Mothers were instructed to use any method they preferred to teach their toddlers.

Measures. Measures were selected that tapped the major domains of stage-salient functioning during toddlerhood. Coders, blind to infant group status and intervention history, independently rated maturity of object play, quality of object exploration, mastery pride, attention to task, social attunement, clarity of communication, mood, activity level, and general well-being in each context using Likert-type scales. Repeated measures were averaged across contexts to create composite variables, in order to increase reliability and because preliminary analyses revealed significant cross-context correlations and no significant group by context interactions. Ratings unique to a particular context were also included. Average interrater reliability for ratings was .82 based on independent coding by two raters of seventeen (23 percent) of the videotapes.

Data Analyses. Group differences were tested with intervention status (2) by IUGR group (3) analyses of variance, followed by Tukey post hoc tests. Pearson correlations of dependent variables with continuous variables of birth weight, birth length, birth head circumference, and ponderal index were also performed. Means, standard deviations, and results of ANOVAs are presented in Tables 3.4, 3.5, and 3.6. Correlation coefficients are listed in Table 3.7.

Results. Although toddler groups did not differ significantly on developmental quotients from the Bayley Scales of Infant Development, IUGR and non-IUGR groups were discriminated using qualitative measures of adult-child play behavior, as predicted. Notably, the context of mother-toddler play proved important in distinguishing IUGR from non-IUGR toddlers in this study. During structured teaching interactions with objects, symmetrical IUGR infants were more distractible, remained seated for less time, and showed more physiological and behavioral signs of disregulation ("cost of attention") than their controls. In contrast, during unstructured free play groups did not differ significantly in quality of toy exploration, mastery pleasure, or interest in the environment.

Similar findings were seen for aspects of social and communicative behavior during structured mother-child interactions. During the mother-toddler teaching task, symmetrical IUGR infants were significantly harder to engage in tasks, had less mutually attuned interactions, and were less cooperative than controls. Moreover, symmetrical IUGR infants exhibited less positive affect and pleasure during interaction than controls. Coders also rated these dyads as being more unpleasant/uncomfortable to watch than con-

Table 3.4
Means and Standard Deviations: Object Interaction Variables

Variable	Controls	IUGR	
		Asymmetrical	Symmetrical
Interest/Involvement	5.0 (.9)	5.0 (.7)	4.7 (1.1)
Mastery/Self-Awareness	3.0 (1.5)	2.4 (1.4)	2.4 (1.4)
Quality of Toy Exploration	4.9 (.9)	4.3 (.8)	4.5 (1.1)
Goal-Directedness	4.7 (.9)	4.2 (.8)	4.1 (1.1)
Disengagement	1.4 (.5)	1.5 (.5)	1.7 (.9)
Distractibility[a]	2.4 (1.6)	3.5 (1.7)	3.7 (1.4)
Cost of Attention[b]	6.7 (1.8)	5.5 (1.9)	5.0 (1.8)
Sits at Table[c]	4.9 (1.3)	4.1 (1.4)	3.8 (1.2)

Note: 6-point Likert-type scales except as noted.

a. $F(2,66) = 5.45$; $p = .006$; controls < IUGR-symmetrical.

b. 9-point Likert-type scale; high scores are optimal; $F(2,69) = 5.32$; $p = .007$; controls > IUGR-symmetrical.

c. $F(2,67) = 5.86$; $p = .004$; controls > IUGR-symmetrical.

trol dyads. Notably, mothers did not differ by group in sensitivity or in quality of teaching behavior.

Similarly, symmetrical IUGR toddlers were more active than controls and were rated lower in general well-being and attractiveness during structured (but not unstructured) interactions, relative to their counterparts.

Notably, only one significant difference emerged for IUGR and non-IUGR groups during unstructured free play: symmetrical IUGR infants spent less time in close proximity to their mothers than controls. This finding is consistent with the insecure-avoidant attachment histories of IUGR-symmetrical infants (Beeghly et al. 1989a; Beeghly et al. 1991b).

Moreover, continuous variables of birth weight and length in this full-term, healthy IUGR sample were significant correlated with toddler behavior ratings. These findings suggest that individual differences in birth characteristics are associated with social

Table 3.5
Means and Standard Deviations: Social Interaction Variables

Variable	Controls	IUGR Asymmetrical	IUGR Symmetrical
Ease of Engagement[a]	5.0 (.9)	4.3 (1.3)	3.8 (1.4)
Mutuality of Interaction[b]	4.5 (1.0)	3.7 (1.2)	3.4 (1.5)
Resistance[c]	2.7 (1.0)	3.1 (1.4)	3.8 (1.2)
Dyadic Pleasure[d]	4.8 (.8)	4.1 (1.3)	4.1 (2.6)
Coder Pleasure[e]	4.6 (.9)	3.6 (1.4)	3.7 (1.5)
Social Referencing	2.9 (1.3)	3.0 (1.4)	2.6 (1.0)
Demands Mother's Attention	1.9 (1.6)	1.4 (.7)	1.8 (1.7)
Clarity of Maternal Teaching	4.3 (1.3)	3.7 (1.2)	3.6 (1.3)

Note: 6-point Likert-type scales.

a. $F(2,69) = 7.09$; $p = .002$; controls > symmetrical IUGR.

b. $F(2,69) = 5.52$; $p = .006$; controls > symmetrical IUGR.

c. $F(2,69) = 5.25$; $p = .008$; controls < symmetrical IUGR.

d. $F(2,69) = 4.31$; $p = .02$; controls > symmetrical IUGR.

e. $F(2,69) = 5.17$; $p = .008$; controls > symmetrical IUGR.

and attentional dimensions of toddler behavior during challenging interactive situations at two years.

Subsequent analyses examined the role of moderating social variables such as maternal social support (Beeghly et al. 1991a) and attachment history (Beeghly et al. 1991b) in determining toddler outcome. As predicted by an organizational perspective, results indicated that maternal and attachment variables significantly mediated dimensions of social and object play at two years. Mothers at higher psychosocial risk (i.e., those with less social support and lower life satisfaction) had toddlers who exhibited less optimal patterns of behavior during adult-toddler play. In addition, toddlers with an avoidant style of attachment behavior toward mother at twelve months—whether IUGR or not—displayed more compromised and less cooperative interactive behavior at twenty-four

Table 3.6
Means and Standard Deviations: Other Toddler
Behavior Variables

| Variable | Controls | IUGR | |
		Asymmetrical	Symmetrical
Disengagement	1.4 (.5)	1.5 (.5)	1.7 (.9)
Productive Language Maturity[a]	4.3 (.9)	4.0 (1.1)	3.9 (1.1)
Productive Language Frequency	3.8 (1.1)	3.7 (1.3)	4.3 (1.4)
Proximity to Mother[b]	4.0 (1.5)	3.0 (1.7)	2.4 (1.7)
Activity Level FP	3.2 (1.1)	4.1 (1.2)	4.1 (1.2)
Activity Level T[c]	3.2 (1.1)	3.9 (1.2)	4.1 (1.1)
Positive Mood	4.6 (.9)	4.4 (1.0)	4.5 (1.2)
General Well Being[d]	5.0 (.8)	4.4 (1.3)	4.2 (1.3)
Attractiveness[e]	7.6 (1.2)	6.8 (1.8)	6.3 (2.5)

Note: Ratings were based on 6-point Likert-type scales, except as noted.

a. 5-point Likert-type scale.

b. $F(2,67) = 6.39$; $p = .003$; controls > IUGR-symmetrical.

c. $F(2,69) = 4.67$; $p = .01$; controls < IUGR-symmetrical.

d. $F(2,69) = 3.83$; $p = .03$; controls > IUGR-symmetrical.

e. 9-point Likert-type scale; $F(2,69) = 3.38$; $p = .04$; controls > IUGR-symmetrical.

months. Nevertheless, symmetrical IUGR status continued to predict certain dimensions of toddler functioning—particularly attentional and social interactive behavior—affirming the risk status of this group.

In sum, results suggest that full-term, healthy infants with a symmetrical pattern of fetal growth retardation showed subtle deficits in attention, self-regulation, and social interaction that may place them at risk for later developmental delays and for continuing problematic parent-child relationships. Further follow-up and replication of this sample are warranted.

Table 3.7
Correlations of Infant Birth Characteristics
with Toddler Behavior

Variable	BWT[a]	BLN[b]	BHC[c]	PI[d]
Interaction with Objects				
Distractibility	−.26**	−.21+	−.14	−.15
Cost of Attention	.31**	.26**	.18	.18
Remains Seated	.27**	.25*	.20+	.10
Social Interaction				
Ease of Engagement	.34***	.31**	.20+	.15
Mutuality of Interaction	.30**	.30**	.13	.08
Resistance	−.27**	−.24*	−.14	−.13
Dyadic Pleasure	.41***	.38***	.17	.19
Coder Pleasure	.38***	.34***	.09	.19
Clarity of Maternal Teaching	.24*	.30**	.12	.01
Other Toddler Behavior Variables				
Proximity to Mother	.34***	.38***	.36***	.06
Activity-T	−.24*	−.20+	.15	.13
General Well-Being	.30**	.31**	.18	.10
Attractiveness	.22*	.22*	.13	.07

Note: Only toddler behavior variables for which significant correlations with birth variables were found are listed. Twenty-eight percent of toddler play behavior variables were significantly correlated with infant birth variables.

a. BWT = birth weight

b. BLN = birth length

c. BHC = birth head circumference

d. PI = ponderal index: [birth weight/birth length $(cm)^3$] × 100

***p <.001 **p <.01 *p <.05 +p <.10

Implications. Results attest to the value of including adult-child play paradigms (particularly structured object play) in addition to standard psychometric testing as an observational context in developmental outcome studies of high-risk infants and toddlers. Results of the twenty-four–month observations of parent-toddler play interactions confirmed and extended prior findings of compromised cognitive and psychosocial development in full-term, symmetrical IUGR infants. Notably, these deficits were not apparent on standard psychometric tests of infant cognitive development (i.e., the Bayley Mental Scale). At age two, these IUGR toddlers showed subtle deficits in social and attentional behavior during challenging interactive tasks with mother. Compared to controls, symmetrical IUGR toddlers were more distractible, more active, and showed greater behavioral and physiological signs of disregulation ("cost of attention") during mother-toddler teaching tasks characterized by high-task demands. Moreover, these infants required greater persistence on the part of adults to maintain interaction.

Notably, IUGR infants were discriminated best during structured rather than unstructured object play contexts, suggesting that challenging social situations may be powerful assessment contexts for these high-risk infants. However, because other studies have reported that unstructured play contexts may prove equally challenging for other types of high-risk infants (e.g., those exposed prenatally to drugs, see Rodning et al. 1989), a combination of both structured and unstructured components should be included in play assessment paradigms for maximum discriminatory power, as noted above.

Moreover, results of supplementary analyses suggested that the behavioral and developmental outcome of biologically vulnerable infants is determined by a complex and dynamic interplay between aspects of the social environment and biological risk, rather than as a simple main effect of IUGR. Our data suggest that long-term or transitory aspects of the caregiving environment may act either to compensate for or to exacerbate biologic vulnerabilities caused by IUGR.

Conclusion

In this chapter, the usefulness of parent-infant play paradigms as age-appropriate contexts for assessing qualitative aspects of infants' adaptive functioning has been examined. Taking an organizational perspective, it was hypothesized that the quality and coherence of a child's stage-salient functioning may be readily observed during playful interactions with an adult partner. Moreover, it was argued that parent-infant play paradigms are especially valuable assessment contexts for these dimensions of behavior if they stress the infant's current developmental capacities. Evidence from both the parent-infant interaction literature and our own study of parent-toddler play in an IUGR sample supports these theoretical contentions: infant competence in cognitive, social, affective, and self-regulatory domains can fruitfully be measured during parent-child play both in infancy and in toddlerhood. In our IUGR sample, infant group differences were discriminated better during a challenging structured object play task with mother than during unstructured play with objects when mother was preoccupied and nonparticipant.

Several reliable parent-child play assessment paradigms that tap stage-salient aspects of child functioning were presented that incorporate both structured and unstructured contexts. For assessments during early infancy, face-to-face paradigm for studying parent-infant play was presented for which normative data is available. In addition to unstructured play episodes, this paradigm includes a perturbated play episode (e.g., the still-face condition). For assessing older infants and toddlers during parent-child play with objects, various parent-toddler play paradigms were presented as alternatives or supplements to standard psychometric assessments of toddler competence. Again, the inclusion of both structured and unstructured components proved important, as evident in the results from our study of parent-child play in a full-term IUGR sample.

Although the focus of this chapter has been on parent-child play as a window on infant competence during early childhood, it is also recommended that investigators observe parent-child interactive behavior in multiple settings for maximum reliability and discriminatory power. This is especially important for research with high-risk dyads who may be especially likely to manifest unstable patterns of behavior over time and setting (see, e.g., Kennedy et al. 1991). As alternatives or supplements to traditional psychometric assessments of infants, multidomain, multicontextual observations of parent-child play can offer increased information and precision about infant development in a social context. This rich information can then be used to extend and challenge current theories of development. Moreover, insights obtained from observations in these social settings can be used by professionals in service-related fields to facilitate the creation, guidance, and timing of more effective, age-appropriate intervention strategies for mothers and infants at risk.

Acknowledgments

Partial support during preparation of this chapter was provided by NIMH grant R01 MH 37234, by a grant from the Hearst Foundation, and by a grant from the Mailman Family Foundation to T. B. Brazelton, M.D. (PI); by grants R01MH43398 and R01MH5547 to E. Z. Tronick (P.I.); by NIDA grant R01-DA06532 to Debbie Frank (P.I.), and by grant R18-DA06365 to Elizabeth Brown (P.I.). My thinking about assessment has been influenced by a number of people. I am indebted to Dante Cicchetti for his theoretical guidance concerning the organizational perspective and atypical development and for his ongoing support and friendship, to Berry Brazelton for his challenging clinical insights and his valuable and central role in our ongoing research with children at risk, and to Ed Tronick and Katherine Weinberg for their thoughtful contributions concerning infant socioemotional development and the face-to-face paradigm. In addition, I am grateful to the families who participated in the research project described here and to the myriad staff at the Child Development Unit who unfailingly assisted with data collection and/or data reduction during the tenure of this longitudinal project. Correspondence should be addressed to Marjorie Beeghly, Ph.D., Child Development Unit, The Children's Hospital, 300 Longwood Avenue, Boston, Mass. 02115.

References

Ainsworth, M. D. S.; Blehar, M.; Waters, E.; and Wall, S. (1978). *Patterns of Attachment: A Psychological Study of the Strange Situation.* Hillsdale, N.J.: Erlbaum.

Als, H.; Tronick, E.; Adamson, L.; and Brazelton T. B. (1976). The behavior of the fullterm yet underweight newborn infant. *Developmental Medicine and Child Neurology* 18:590–602.

Amaro, H.; Zuckerman, B.; and Cabral, H. (1989). Drug use among adolescent mothers: Profiles of risk. *Pediatrics* 84:144–51.

Bauman, P., and Dougherty, F. (1983). Drug-addicted mothers: Parenting and their children's development. *International Journal of Addiction* 18:291–302.

Bays, J. (1990). Substance abuse and child abuse: Impact of addiction on the child. *Pediatric Clinics of North America* 37:881.

Beckwith, L. (1986). Parent-infant interaction and infants' socioemotional development. In A. Gottfried and C. Brown (eds.), *Play Interactions: The Contribution of Play Materials and Parental Involvement to Children's Development.* Lexington, Mass.: Lexington Books.

Beckwith, L. (1990). Adaptive and maladaptive parenting: Implications for intervention. In S. Meisels and J. Shonkoff (eds.), *Handbook of Early Intervention*. New York: Cambridge University Press.

Beckwith, L., and Parmalee, A. H. (1986). EEG patterns in preterm infants: Home environment and later IQ. *Child Development* 57:777–89.

Beeghly, M. (1979). Adult style and infant characteristics in adult-infant interaction from 12 to 24 months. Unpublished master's thesis, University of Colorado, Boulder.

Beeghly, M., and Cicchetti, D. (1987). An organizational approach to symbolic development in children with Down syndrome. *New Directions in Child Development* 36:5–29.

Beeghly, M.; Weiss-Perry, B.; and Cicchetti, D. (1990). Beyond sensorimotor functioning: Early communicative and play development of children with Down syndrome. In D. Cicchetti and M. Beeghly (eds.), *Down Syndrome: A Developmental Perspective*. New York: Cambridge University Press.

Beeghly, M; Nugent, J. K; Burrows E.; and Brazelton, T. B. (1988). Effects of intrauterine growth retardation (IUGR) on infant behavior and development in the family. *Infant Behavior and Development* (special ICIS issue) 11:21.

Beeghly, M.; Flannery, K.; Birss, S.; Jernberg, E.; Turiano, D.; and Barrett, D. (1989a). Cognitive and psychosocial development of small-for-gestational-age (SGA) infants: A follow-up study. *Society for Research in Child Development Abstracts* 6:189.

Beeghly, M.; Weiss-Perry, B.; And Cicchetti, D. (1989b). Structural and affective dimensions of play development in young children with Down syndrome. *International Journal of Behavioral Development* 12:257–77.

Beeghly, M.; Vo, D.; Burrows, E.; and Brazelton, T. B. (1990a). The qualifier coding system for toddlers (QCS-T). Unpublished manuscript, Child Development Unit, the Children's Hospital, Boston.

Beeghly, M.; Vo, D.; Burrows, E.; and Brazelton, T. B. (1990b). Social and task-related behavior of fullterm small-for-gestational-age infants at two years. *Infant Behavior and Development* (special ICIS issue) 13:266.

Beeghly, M.; Nugent J. K.; and Flannery, K. (1991a). Predicting two-year behavior and development of full term SGA infants from the perinatal period. *Society for Research in Child Development Abstracts* 8:170.

Beeghly, M.; Birss, S.; and Vo, D. (1991b). Social and task-related behavior of secure and avoidant SGA infants at two years. *Society for Research in Child Development Abstracts* 8:170.

Belsky, J. (1984). The determinants of parenting: A process model. *Child Development* 55:83–96.

Belsky, J, and Most, R. (1981). From exploration to play: A cross-sectional study of infant free play behavior. *Developmental Psychology* 17:630–37.

Belsky, J., and Vondra, J. (1989). Lessons from child abuse: The determinants of parenting. In *Child Maltreatment*, 153–202. *See* Cicchetti and Carlson 1989.

Berger, J. (1990). Interactions between parents and their infants with Down syndrome. In D. Cicchetti and M. Beeghly (eds.), *Children with Down Syndrome: A Developmental Perspective.* New York: Cambridge University Press.

Bischof, N. (1975). A systems approach toward the functional connections of attachment and fear. *Child Development* 46:801–17.

Black, R., and Mayer, J. (1980). Parents with special problems: Alcoholism and opiate addiction. *Child Abuse and Neglect* 4:45.

Bowlby, J. (1982). Attachment and loss (vol. 1). New York: Basic.

Brazelton, T. B. (1984). *Neonatal Behavioral Assessment Scale.* 2d ed. Philadelphia: J. B. Lippincott.

Brazelton, T. B.; Koslowski, B.; and Main, M. (1974). The origins of reciprocity: The early mother-infant interaction. In M. Lewis and L. A. Rosenblum (eds.), *The Effect of the Infant on its Caregiver.* New York: Wiley.

Bretherton, I. (1984). *Symbolic Play.* New York: Academic.

Bretherton, I. (1985). Attachment theory: Retrospect and prospect. In I. Bretherton and E. Waters (eds.), Growing points of attachment theory and research. *Monographs of the Society for Research in Child Development,* serial no. 209, vol. 50.

Bretherton, I., and Bates, E. (1979). The emergence of intentional communication. *New Directions for Child Development:* 81–100.

Bruner, J. (1964). The course of cognitive growth. *American Psychologist* 19:115.

Bruner, J. (1972). Nature and uses of immaturity. *American Psychologist* 27:687–708.

Cicchetti, D. (1984). The emergence of developmental psychopathology. *Child Development* 55:1–7.

Cicchetti, D. (1987). Developmental psychopathology in infancy: Illustration from the study of maltreated youngsters. *Journal of Consulting and Clinical Psychology* 55:837–45.

Cicchetti, D., and Beeghly, M. (1990). An organizational approach to the study of Down syndrome: Contributions to an integrative theory of development. In D. Cicchetti and M. Beeghly (eds.), *Down syndrome: A developmental perspective.* New York: Cambridge University Press.

Cicchetti, D.; Beeghly, M.; and Weiss-Perry, B. (In press). Symbolic development in children with Down syndrome and in children with autism: An organizational, developmental psychopathology perspective. In A. Slade and D. Wolf (eds.), *Modes of Meaning.* New York: Oxford University Press.

Cicchetti, D., and Carlson, V. (1989). *Child Maltreatment: Theory and Research on the Causes and Consequences of Child Abuse and Neglect.* New York: Cambridge University Press.

Cicchetti, D., and Rizley, R. (1981). Developmental Perspectives on the etiology, intergenerational transmission and sequelae of child maltreatment. *New Directions for Child Development* 11:31–55.

Cicchetti, D., and Schneider-Rosen, K. (1984). Theoretical and empirical considerations in the investigation of the relationship between affect and cognition in atypical populations of infants: Contributions to the formulation of an integrative theory of development. In C. Izard, J. Kagan, and R. Zajonc, (Eds.), *Emotions, Cognition, Behavior.* New York: Cambridge University Press.

Cicchetti, D., and Sroufe, L. A. (1978). An organizational view of affect: Illustration from the study of Down's syndrome infants. In M. Lewis and L. Rosenblum (eds.), *The development of affect.* NY: Wiley.

Cicchetti, D., and Wagner, S. (1990). Alternative assessment strategies for the evaluation of infants and toddlers: An organizational perspective. In S. Meisels and J. Shonkoff (eds.), *Handbook of Early Childhood Intervention.* New York: Cambridge University Press.

Coster, W.; Gersten, M.; Beeghly M.; and Cicchetti, D. (1989). Communicative functioning in maltreated toddlers. *Developmental Psychology* 25:1020–29.

Crawley, S. B.; Rogers, P. P.; Friedman, S.; Iacabbo, M.; Criticos, A.; Richardson, L.; and Thompson, M. (1978). Developmental changes in the structure of mother-infant play. *Developmental Psychology* 14:30–36.

Crawley, S.; and Sherrod, K. (1984) Parent-infant play during the first year of life. *Infant Behavior and Development* 7:65–75.

Crnic, K.; Ragozin, A.; Greenberg, M.; Robinson, N.; and Bashaw, R. (1983). Social interaction and developmental competence of preterm and fullterm infants during the first year of life. *Child Development* 54:1199–1210.

Emde, R.; Gaensbauer, T.; and Harmon, R. (1976). *Emotional Expression in Infancy: A Biobehavioral Study*. New York: International Universities Press.

Erikson, E. (1950). *Childhood and Society*. New York: Norton.

Fein, G., and Apfel, N. (1979). The development of play: Style, structure, and imitation. *Genetic Monographs* 99:231–50.

Fenson, L. (1984). Developmental trends for actions and speech in pretend play. *See* Bretherton 1984.

Field, T. (1979). Games parents play with normal and high-risk infants. *Child Psychiatry and Human Development* 10:41–48.

Field, T. (1982). Affective displays of high-risk infants during early interactions. In T. Field and A. Fogel, (eds.), *Emotion and Early Interaction*. Hillsdale, N.J.: Erlbaum.

Garvey, C. (1977). *Play*. Cambridge: Harvard University Press.

Greenspan, S. (1981). *Psychopathology and Adaptation in Infancy and Early Childhood*. New York: International Universities Press.

Greenspan, S. (1990). Comprehensive clinical approaches to infants and their families: Psychodynamic and developmental perspectives. In S. Meisels and J. Shonkoff (eds.), *Handbook of Early Intervention*. New York: Cambridge University Press.

Gollin, E. (1984). *Malformations of Development*. New York: Academic.

Gustafson, G.; Green, J.; and West, M.; (1979). The infant's changing role in mother-infant games. The growth of social skills. *Infant Behavior and Development* 2:301–8.

Hans, S. (1989). Developmental consequences of prenatal exposure of methadone. *Prenatal Abuse of Licit and Illicit Drugs, Annals of the New York Academy of Sciences* 562:195–207.

Henricksen, L.; Skinhoj, K.; and Anderson, G. (1986). Delayed growth and reduced intelligence in 9–17 year-old intrauterine growth retarded children compared with their monozygous co-twins. *Acta Paediatrika Scandinavia*. 75:31.

Hesse, P., and Cicchetti, D. (1982). Toward an integrative theory of emotional development. *New Directions for Child Development* 16:3–48.

Hodapp, R.; Goldfield, E.; and Boyatzis, C. (1984). The use and effectiveness of maternal scaffolding in mother-infant games. *Child Development* 55:772–81.

Inhelder, B. (1966). Cognitive development and its contribution to the diagnosis of some phenomena of mental deficiency. *Merrill-Palmer Quarterly* 11:299–319.

Izard, C. E. (1971). *The face of emotion.* New York: Appleton-Century-Croft.

Izard, C. E., Dougherty, L. M., and Hembree, E. A. (1980). *A system for identifying affect expressions by holistic judgements (AFFEX).* Newark, DE: University of Delaware, Instructional Resources Center.

Jennings, K.; Harmon, R.; Morgan, G.; Gaiter, J.; and Yarrow, L. (1979). Exploratory play as an index of mastery motivation: Relationships to persistence, cognitive functioning, and environmental measures. *Developmental Psychology* 15:386–94.

Jones, O. H. M. (1977). Mother-child communication with prelinguistic Down syndrome and normal infants. In H. H. Schaffer (ed.), *Studies in Mother-Infant Interaction.* London: Academic Press.

Jones, O. H. M. (1980). Prelinguistic communication skills in Down syndrome and normal infants. In T. Field, D. Goldberg, D. Stern, and A. Sostek (eds.), *High-Risk Infants and Children: Interactions with Adults and Peers.* New York: Academic Press.

Kagan, J. (1981). *The second year.* Cambridge: Harvard University Press.

Kaplan, B. (1966). The study of language in psychiatry. The comparative-developmental approach and its application to symbolization and language in psychopathology. In S. Arieti (ed.), *American Handbook of Psychiatry.* New York: Basic.

Kaplan, E. (1983). Process and achievement revisited. In S. Wapner and B. Kaplan (eds.), *Toward a Holistic Developmental Psychology.* Hillsdale: Erlbaum.

Kennedy, M.; Sheridan, M. K.; Radlinski, S.; and Beeghly, M. (1991). Play-language relationships in young children with developmental delays: Implications for assessment. *Journal of Speech and Hearing Research* 34:112–22.

Lamb, M. (1984). Social and emotional development in infancy. In M. Bornstein and M. Lamb (eds.), *Developmental Psychology.* Hillsdale, N.J.: Erlbaum.

McCune-Nicolich, L. and Fenson, L. (1984). Methodological issues in studying early pretend play. In T. Yawkey and D. Pelligrini (eds.), *Child's play: Developmental and applied*. Hillsdale, NJ: Erlbaum.

McKenzie, L.; McKenzie, M.; Johnson, C.; Jordan, T.; Grimanis, M.; and Brazelton, T. B. (1988). The effects of maternal health variables on fetal growth. *Infant Behavior and Development* (special ICIS issue) 11:214.

Mervis, C. B. (1990). Early conceptual development of children with Down syndrome. In D. Cicchetti and M. Beeghly (Eds.), *Children with Down syndrome: A developmental perspective*. New York: Cambridge U Press.

Motti, F.; Cicchetti, D.; and Sroufe, L. A. (1983). From infant affect expression to symbolic play: The coherence of development in Down syndrome children. *Child Development* 54:1168–75.

Parker, S.; Greer, S.; and Zuckerman, B. (1988). Double jeopardy: The impact of poverty on early child development. *Pediatric Clinics of North America* 35:1227–40.

Parmelee, A. H.; Beckwith, L.; Cohen, S.; and Sigman, M. (1983). Social influences on infants at medical risk for behavioral difficulties. In J. D. Call, E. Galenson, and R. Tyson (eds.), *Frontiers of Infant Psychiatry*. New York: Basic.

Piaget, J. (1962). *Play, Dreams, and Imitation in Childhood*. New York: Norton.

Piaget, J.; and Inhelder, B. (1969). *The Psychology of the Child*. (H. Weaver, trans.) London: Routledge and Kegan Paul.

Ratner, N., and Bruner, J. (1978). Games, social exchange, and the acquisition of language. *Journal of Child Language* 5:391–401.

Rodning, C.; Beckwith, L.; and Howard, J. (1989). Characteristics of attachment organization and play organization in prenatally drug-exposed toddlers. *Development and Psychopathology* 1:277–89.

Ross, H. S. (1982). The establishment of social games among toddlers. *Developmental Psychology* 18:509–18.

Ross, H. S., and Lollis, S. P. (1987). Communication within social games. *Developmental Psychology,* 23:241–48.

Rubin, K.; Fein, G.; and Vandenberg, B. (1983). Play. In E. M. Hetherington (ed.), *Carmichael's Manual of Child Psychology*. Vol. 4, *Social Development*. New York: Wiley.

Rutter, M. (1986). The developmental psychopathology of depression: Issues and perspectives. In M. Rutter, C. Izard, and P. Read (eds.), *Depres-*

sion in Young People: Clinical and Developmental Perspectives. New York: Guilford.

Rutter, M. (1989). Intergenerational continuities and discontinuities in serious parenting difficulties. *See* Cicchetti and Carlson 1989.

Sameroff, A., and Chandler, M. (1975). Reproductive risk and the continuum of caretaking casualty. In F. Horowitz (ed.), *Review of Child Development Research*. vol. 4. Chicago: University of Chicago Press.

Sander, L. (1962). Issues in early mother-child interaction. *Journal of the American Academy of Child Psychiatry* 1:141–66.

Sander, L. (1975). Infant and caretaking environment: Investigation and conceptualization of adaptive behavior in systems of increasing complexity. In E. J. Anthony (ed.), *Explorations in Child Psychiatry*. New York: Plenum.

Santostefano, S. (1978). *A Bio-Developmental Approach to Clinical Child Psychology*. New York: Wiley.

Sigman, M., and Mundy, P. (1987). Symbolic processes in young autistic children. *New Directions for Child Development* 36:31–46.

Slade, A. (1987). A longitudinal study of maternal involvement and symbolic play during the toddler period. *Child Development* 58:367–75.

Smeriglio, V. (1989). Developmental sequelae following intrauterine growth retardation. In T. L. Gross and R. J. Sokol (eds.), *Intrauterine Growth Retardation: A Practical Approach*. Chicago: Year Book Medical Publishers, Inc.

Sroufe, L. A. (1983). Infant-caregiver attachment and patterns of adaptation in preschool: The roots of maladaptation and competence. In M. Perlmutter (Ed.), *Minnesota Symposium on Child Psychology (Vol 16)*.

Sroufe, L. A. (1979). The coherence of individual development. *American Psychologist* 34:834–41.

Sroufe, L. A., and Rutter, M. (1984). The domain of developmental psychopathology. *Child Development* 55:1184–99.

Sroufe, L. A., and Waters, E. (1976). The ontogenesis of smiling and laughter: A perspective on the organization of development in infancy. *Psychological Review* 83:173–89.

Stern, D. (1985). *The Interpersonal World of the Infant: A View from Psychoanalysis and Developmental Psychology*. New York: Basic.

Thompson, R.; Cicchetti, D.; Lamb, M.; and Malkin, C. (1985). The emotional responses of Down syndrome and normal infants in the

Strange Situation: The organization of affective behavior in infants. *Developmental Psychology* 21:828–41.

Trevarthen, C. (1977). Descriptive analysis of infant communicative behavior. In H. R. Schaffer (ed.), *Studies in Mother-Infant Interaction.* New York: Academic.

Tronick, E. Z. (1989). Emotions and emotional communication in infants. *American Psychologist* 44:112–19.

Tronick, E. Z., and Beeghly, M. (1992). Effects of prenatal exposure to cocaine on newborn behavior and development: A critical review. *OSAP Prevention Monograph, 11,* 25–48.

Tronick, E. Z.; Beeghly, M.; Fetters, L.; and Weinberg, K. (1991). New methodologies for evaluating residual brain damage in infants exposed to drugs of abuse: Objective methods for describing movement, facial expressions, and communicative behaviors. *NIDA Monograph Series, "Methodological Issues in Controlled Studies on the Effects of Prenatal Exposure to Drug Abuse," 114,* 262–290.

Tronick, E. Z. and Weinberg, M. K. (1992a). The Infant Regulatory Scoring System (IRSS). Unpublished manuscript, Children's Hospital, Boston, 1992a.

Tronick, E. Z. and Weinberg, M. K. (1992b). The Maternal Regulatory Scoring System (MRSS). Unpublished manuscript, Children's Hospital, Boston, 1992a.

Ungerer, J., and Sigman, M. (1983). Developmental lags in preterm infants from one to three years of age. *Child Development* 54:1217–28.

Villar, J.; Smeriglio, V.; Martorell, R.; Brown, C.; and Klein, R. (1984). Heterogeneous growth and mental developmental of intrauterine growth-retarded infants during the first three years of life. *Pediatrics* 74:783–91.

Vohr, B.; Oh, W.; Rosenfield, A. G.; and Cowett, R. M. (1979). The preterm small-for-gestational-age infant: A two-year follow-up study. *American Journal of Obstetrics and Gynecology* 133:425.

Vygotsky, L. (1978). *Mind in Society.* Cambridge: Harvard University Press.

Walthers, F. J., and Ramaekers, L. H. J. (1982). Language development at the age of 3 years of infants malnourished in utero. *Neuropediatrics* 13:77.

Waters, E., and Sroufe, L. A. (1983). Competence as a developmental construct. *Developmental Review, 3,* 79–97.

Watson, M., and Fisher, K. (1977). A developmental sequence of agent use in late infancy. *Child Development* 48:828–36.

Weinberg, M. K. (1989). Infant emotion and behavior: The relation between facial emotional expressions and behavior at 6 months. Unpublished master's thesis, University of Massachusetts, Amherst.

Weinberg, M. K., and Tronick, E. Z. (Under review). Affective-behavioral configurations in the young infant. Manuscript under review.

Werner, E. (1989). Children of the Garden Island. *Scientific American* 106:111.

Werner, H. (1948). *Comparative Psychology of Mental Development.* New York: International Universities Press.

Werner, H., and Kaplan, B. (1963). *Symbol Formation.* New York: Wiley.

Whaley, K. K. (1990). The emergence of social play in infancy: A proposed developmental sequence of infant-adult social play. *Early Childhood Research Quarterly* 5:347–58.

Yawkey, T., and Pelligrini, A., (eds.), (1984). *Child's Play: Developmental and Applied.* Hillsdale, N.J.: Erlbaum.

Zigler, E., and Balla, D. (1982). *Mental Retardation: The Developmental-Difference Controversy.* Hillsdale, N.J.: Erlbaum.

Zuckerman, B.; Amaro, H.; and Beardslee, W. (1987). Mental health of adolescent mothers: The implications of depression and drug use. *Developmental and Behavioral Pediatrics* 8:111–16.

Zuckerman, B., and Bresnahan, K. (1991). Developmental and behavioral consequences of prenatal drug and alcohol exposure. *Pediatric Clinics of North America, 38,* 1387–1398.

CHAPTER 4

Parent-Child Play: An Evolutionary Perspective

Kevin MacDonald

The purpose of this chapter is to develop an evolutionary perspective on parent-child play. Such a perspective of necessity must involve different levels of analysis and incorporate a disparate array of data. Evolutionary biologists distinguish between ultimate and proximal levels of analysis. Ultimate level analysis asks the question of why a certain behavior evolved in a particular species. Ultimate level questions are essentially questions regarding the evolved function of the behavior. Thus many birds migrate south in the winter because that is where the food is. In the case of parent-child play, however, the answer does not appear to be as straightforward, and is further complicated by the finding that parent-child play is far from universal among humans (see chapters 12 and 14). An adequate ultimate level explanation of parent-child play must then also be part of a theory of human behavioral variation at the cultural level; that is, it must be part of a theory of human behavioral ecology.

Besides ultimate level analysis, a second level of analysis is that of proximal mechanisms. Proximal mechanisms are the actual biological and psychological mechanisms which underlie behavior. In the case of bird migration these mechanisms may include hormones which are triggered by changing light periods, whereas in the case of parent-child play the mechanisms may include the brain processes proposed by Panksepp (see chapter 5) as underlying social

I would like to acknowledge the helpful comments of Peter K. Smith on an earlier draft of this paper.

play, as well as learning processes or other environmental influences directed at the specific biological systems involved. Because parent-child play is far from universal in humans, the issues of plasticity and possible genetic variation are particularly relevant. Given that specific biological systems are involved in parent-child play, how can individual and cross-cultural differences be conceptualized?

I. The Ultimate Evolutionary Context of Parent-Child Play

A. *Plasticity and the Training Function of Play*

Modern evolutionary theory fundamentally concerns the costs and benefits of behavior or morphology to individuals or other units of natural selection. In the case of play both the costs and benefits are problematic and raise important questions. The basic logic of evolutionary theory implies that a behavior as ubiquitous as play must have an evolutionary function—that it must benefit organisms. The following propositions are relevant to the benefits of play and are derived from Robert Fagen's (1981) encyclopedic work on play in animals as well as the work of Peter K. Smith (1982; see also Smith and Boulton 1990).

First, play is ubiquitous among mammals and clear cases occur among many bird groups. Play occurs among the marsupial as well as the placental mammals and even among the monotremes. This indicates that play is phylogenetically ancient and most likely that it evolved independently in several different lineages. This also suggests that whatever function(s) play has, it represents a very important adaptation. Moreover, it also indicates that functional explanations of play must propose that play solves some very general problems of adaptation rather than problems peculiar to, for example, social species.

Secondly, increased levels of play are associated with increased brain size, and particularly increased cortical size. For example, the bird species with the highest level of cortical development (macaw, raven, and many raptors) are also the species with the highest levels of play, and the differences among mammals reflects this generalization. This trend toward increased levels of play apparently reaches its pinnacle in humans, and indeed Barnett (1988) has termed humans *homo ludens* because of the central role of playfulness in human life.

There is good evidence for the training hypothesis of the function of play. This hypothesis goes back at least to Plato, and it is the only one which is strongly supported my modern investigations. By engaging in playful versions of adult behaviors (e.g., fighting or predatory behavior) the animal is able to learn the subtleties of the adult behaviors without incurring the risks and dangers which may be present in the adult activity. Moreover, it will be argued below that the association between play and large brain size is due to the fact that play allows these animals to learn about their world—to develop the skills necessary for adult life. Smith (1982) summarizes evidence that play facilitates a wide range of social and cognitive abilities which are essential for adult adaptation, including social communication and social skills (see chapters 7 and 1), and generalized cognitive skills. Fagen finds that play and exploration are the only behaviors known to mediate the differential patterns of dendritic growth and branching in animals subjected to enriched versus deprived environmental rearing experiences (see also chapter 5). These experiments have effectively ruled out a variety of nonplay experiences as explaining these results, including observational learning, nonplayful training, operant conditioning, and group living.

Further supporting the training hypothesis, the types of play animals engage in seem related to the types of activities the animal will engage in as an adult. Among species such as carnivores where adults engage in fighting or predation, there are high levels of play fighting and few sex differences in play. On the other hand, in species where males fight and females do not, quite often the play of males is focused on fighting while that of females appears to be training for predator avoidance. In our own species as well as many other primates the play of males is more vigorous and oriented toward fighting than that of females, differences which reflect adult differences in aggression and physical capacity.

The training function of play suggests that play should be particularly useful during development and indeed, although adult play is known in a number of species, including humans, play is generally much more frequent among young animals. The general trend is for play to decrease as animals get older and to be replaced by behavior which is of immediate functional value for survival.

The training function of play implies that plasticity is a central human adaptation. In a very real sense, without plasticity there would be no purpose for play, since animals could not benefit from its presence. In other words, the training hypothesis logically presupposes plasticity. Several writers have noted a trend in evolution toward the development of flexible response capabilities which can be programmed by immediate environmental contingencies rather than by rigid, genetically controlled responses to a few highly salient environmental cues (see Lerner 1984 for a review.)

The primitive, stereotypical programs of the lower animals have obviously been a successful route to adaptation but they are minimally sensitive to subtle variation in environmental contingencies. Because of these limitations, the trend in the evolution of some groups has been toward increased plasticity and flexibility in coping with environmental contingencies. This requires a much larger brain—one capable of the rapid learning and sophisticated information processing required in order to make adaptive decisions and prevent mistakes. Play is thus a sort of environment-engagement device, a device ideally suited to a large-brained, plastic species. During play an animal places itself in a position to learn about a large array of environmental contingencies and commits physiological and neural resources to particular adaptive demands: rather than attempting to design an animal which will be able to make an increasing number of stereotypical responses to an increasing number of recurring environmental contingencies, the animal is programmed to seek out information from the environment about contingencies, and many of these contingencies could not possibly have been recurring events in the environment of evolutionary adaptedness. Rather than genetically determining the structure of the brain in advance, there is important plasticity such that via play the brain can be programmed to prepare itself for the types of stimulation it will encounter later in life.

The organism is programmed, as Piaget recognized, to actively seek out information. This active seeking out of environmental stimulation is the very essence of many types of play. Play with objects involves exploration and manipulation with a view to understanding what the objects can do. Animals and children eventually get bored with simply exploring a new object unless it has some other source of rewards besides simply being new. The same is also the case with play fighting: Rather than rigidly program the enormous number of subtle feints, holds, and bites which are the optimum responses to the stimuli provided by the other animal, the animal is programmed to seek out rough and tumble play and during this play it is able to learn what works best. The fighting behavior of advanced animals like carnivores is thus likely to be far more subtle and complex than is typical of, for example, fish or insects, and this is indeed the case. The purpose of the second section of this chapter will be to describe the proximal mechanisms underlying both the rulelike and synchronized nature of play as well as the enormous range of variation occurring within particular play bouts and between different parent-child dyads.

As a further point related to the interplay of plasticity and play, development is also a time when the animal's brain can be selectively programmed to respond to differing requirements in the animal's environment. The early experience literature indicates that experience during times of plasticity can effectively alter the structure of the brain so that resources are devoted more to one competence than another (Greenough, Black, and Wallace 1987; Lerner 1984). As an extreme example, cats reared in chambers with vertical stripes become specialized for vertical perception and even lose some of the ability to observe horizontal bars (Hirsch and Spinelli 1971; see Lerner 1984 for further examples). These processes result in increased specialization, since environments which are particularly salient during development are more influential in producing the structure of the brain. By programming the animal to seek out a large variety of environmental stimulation (i.e., by programming the animal to play) the animal will develop neural structures which are maximally responsive to the salient features of its environment.

Play and plasticity are thus intimately connected to each other. If there were no plasticity, there would be no reason to engage in play, and the decline in play during adulthood is an important prediction of this perspective. Development is a time when the organism is able to learn the way the world works, while in adulthood the animal reaches a point of diminishing returns and increased cost as play behavior results in resources being diverted from efforts at reproduction and other vital activities.

Within this perspective, parent-child play is conceptualized as an environment-engagement device, the primary purpose of which is to provide stimulation for the child. Although it is conceivable that parents benefit directly from playing with their children, the usual assumption of parental investment theory (Trivers 1986) is that children are a net resource drain on their parents and thus net beneficiaries of parental resources. Moreover, the above logic suggests that play will be most useful early in life when the training function of play is important and plasticity relatively high. In a biological sense, the parent presumably benefits from parent-child play in the same manner as for any other aspect of parental investment—that is, because it contributes to the adaptiveness of his/her offspring. However, there is no reason to suppose that play represents anything more than a cost for parents.

One obvious suggestion from this line of reasoning is that parent-child play represents an elaboration of play as an environment-engagement device such that more complex and/or more intense environmental stimulation can be provided to the developing individual than would occur if the mechanisms were restricted to the solitary individual. The parent is a potentially far more powerful source of environmental stimulation than are inanimate objects. Parents can direct the attention of children to things in their environment, engage in fantasy or argumentative discourse with them, or provide high levels of physical stimulation. Moreover, the parent is at a much higher level of cognitive and physical development than is the child and is thus able to structure and control the complexity of stimulation so that it is challenging and interesting to the child.

Moreover, although peers care certainly able to provide high levels of stimulation and joint play later in childhood, this is not the case early in development. Peer relationships are rudimentary at best during infancy, although the complexity and quantity of infant play increases with increased contact (Becker 1977).

In the present volume Farver (see chapter 14) shows that sibling play after infancy can actually mimic parent-child play in complexity. This is an important finding which raises a number of theoretical questions. In the following section a principal point will be that parent-child play is an important aspect of parental investment and that sibling rearing tends to be characteristic of societies with low investment parenting and lower quality offspring. Future research must address the issue of whether the outcomes of sibling play versus parent-child play are identical. One would wonder, for example, how oldest children could be provided with the highly stimulating environment represented by parent-child play in such families and whether the level of stimulation they in turn provide to younger siblings is indeed equivalent to that provided by parents.

The general tenor of the following section suggests that it would not. If indeed one supposes that play is an important source of environmental programming for the child and if postinfancy children are systematically neglected by their parents in sibling-rearing societies, one would suppose that these eldest children would be relatively poor sources of stimulation for their younger siblings, and that, in any case, a competent, energetic adult would be able to provide very high-levels of stimulation compared to older children.

Significantly the parent-rearing families in Farver's study came from economically depressed areas, and many studies have shown that parent-child play is far less common in economically depressed circumstances (see chapter 1). Moreover, even though sibling play in the extended family culture was more complex than sibling play in the nuclear family culture, at both twenty-four and thirty-six months of age the mother-child play in the nuclear family was more complex than the sibling play in the extended family culture. In addition, shared positive affect was more characteristic of mother-child than sibling play in both cultures. Farver's findings are thus highly compatible with the hypothesis that parent-child rearing among middle- and upper middle-class families represents a higher level of stimulation than is available in families were sibling rearing occurs.

B. The Costs of Play: Play as Parental Investment

Play and the Theory of Parental Investment. Modern evolutionary theory fundamentally concerns the costs and benefits of behavior, and for our purposes Brian Sutton-Smith has provided an excellent summary of the benefits of this type of play for children (see chapter 1). However, the cost of the ledger is of equal interest, and can perhaps provide a theoretical framework for understanding the cross-cultural distribution of parent-child play.

One might begin by noting that, however one views the state of the empirical evidence that parent-child play has evolved functions, from a theoretical perspective the best evidence that play must have benefits is the very clear evidence that it has costs. Theoretically it is difficult to conceive of a behavior with clear costs remaining in a population without some overcompensating benefits. Play requires high amounts of energy (10 percent of the time budget of the stumptail macaque), and field observations on a wide range of animals have often shown that play can result in injury or even death. Even more telling is the finding that play drops off when animals are sick or hungry: Fagen (1981) provides evidence that play tends to occur in the absence of factors which threaten the animal's immediate well-being.

Smith (1982) notes that high levels of play are expected to be an aspect of a K-style reproductive pattern. K-selected species tend to have a relatively long period of development, a long life span, and require a relatively large investment on the part of parents. The opposite style of reproduction is termed r-selected. Although K- and r-selection define two poles of parenting styles, high investment parenting can occur as a result of other selective pressures besides K-selection (e.g., adversity selection [Southwood 1981]). As a result, the following discussion will use the terminology of high and low investment parenting without the implication that this necessarily results from r/K continuum of natural selection.

As indicated above, plasticity and play are strongly associated, and high investment parenting is generally associated with larger brain size and a greater role of plasticity and learning in development. There is no question that humans are at the extreme end of the parental investment continuum. Compared to other primates, humans are relatively long-lived and require a large parental investment over many years. The requirement of a large parental investment is expected to be particularly salient in the most primitive human societies; that is, hunger-gatherer societies whose economic base must reflect the human environment of evolutionary adaptedness. Reflecting the high level of parental investment required in these societies, monogamy tends to be the typical pattern of marriage in hunter-gatherer societies (e.g., van den Berghe 1979). Monogamy is a common correlate of high investment parenting styles and is associated with high levels of paternal investment in offspring (Kleiman 1981).

Smith (1982) and Fagen (1981) argue that play should be associated with high investment reproductive practices because, since play has no immediate benefits, the benefits must accrue later in life. There would be little point therefore in engaging in play toward the end of the life span. Moreover, a large brain size and a prolonged period of development are virtually defining characteristics of high investment reproductive styles and are also associated with high levels of plasticity during development. The implication is that play is one of a complex set of interdependent life-history traits: a large brain which is able to learn a large number of nongenetically pre-programmed contingencies related to social and cognitive development; a prolonged period of development in which to learn them; a high level of plasticity during development so that the brain can be fine-tuned by experience during this period; and a high level of parental investment required by the prolonged period of development and which provides a source of stimulation which shapes developmental outcomes.

It is an important thesis that parent-child play is an aspect of this high investment reproductive pattern. Parent-child play is thus conceptualized as a cost of parenting with benefits for offspring. In the case of parent-child play, one of the costs is simply the time and energy of the parent. As in the case of basic care and feeding of children, play involves a commitment of resources.

Parent-Child Play and Cross-Cultural Variation in Parental Investment. While the theory of parent-child play as investment correctly predicts that such play will be more common among species at the high end of the parental investment continuum, it further predicts that any variation in parental investment within a species will also be correlated with variation in the extent of parent-child play. For humans, it is possible to test this hypothesis because there is considerable variation within human groups in reproductive strategy which is interpretable in a parental investment framework (Belsky, Steinberg, and Draper 1991; MacDonald 1988; Rushton 1985, 1988). Societies which for other reasons can be viewed as engaging in relatively low investment style reproductive strategies are expected to be relatively low in parent-child play.

In particular, human societies characterized by monogamy, low fertility (high age of first pregnancy, low number of offspring, high birth-spacing interval), and parent rearing of children (high investment characteristics) are expected to be relatively high in parent-child play, whereas societies characterized by polygyny, high fertility, and sibling rearing and/or fostering of children (low investment characteristics) are expected to be low in parent-child play. Although societies can often be generally characterized by the existence of relatively high or low investment parenting styles, the continuum of parental investment can also be conceptualized as an individual differences dimension within human societies.

The present perspective would predict that parent-child play would be very low or absent in sub-Saharan African societies beyond the foraging level of economic base. These societies tend to be characterized by intensive polygyny (high levels of sexual competition among males), sibling rearing of children, and/or fostering of children away from the natal family (Draper 1989). In these societies the fundamental basis of marriage is economic and there is no expectation of intimacy or affection as the basis of marriage. There is a very strong pressure toward having large numbers of children and fathers have little contact with children. Girls are valued because they can bring bridewealth to their family, while sons are valued because they increase the power of one's faction in clan rivalries (e.g., LeVine and LeVine 1966). In this context sibling rearing and fostering out children relieve parents of some of the burdens of child rearing. For example, the data of Pennington (1991) suggest that fostering functions as an adaptive behavior by increasing the reproductive success of women in a polygynous African society (see also Draper and Harpending 1987).

Children from an early age are recruited into the family economic chores, so that play in general is less common. Sutton-Smith (1985) notes that in societies where children have a heavy load of chores there is less peer play (see also Feitelson 1977). As expected, and as Edwards and Whiting note (see chapter 12), adult-child play is generally absent. Draper and Harpending (1987) note that "descriptions of peer group cultures often describe how the mother is less accessible to young children than any other adult of the village. The mother seems to make a conscious attempt to avoid the child's presence . . . " (p. 216). Indeed, parent-child relationships tend to be distant and hostile in these societies. For example, Ainsworth (1967) found that Ugandan mothers never engaged in positive reciprocal interactions with their babies. Moreover, in two independent studies of the Gusii of Kenya, LeVine and LeVine (1966) found mother-child interactions characterized by lack of warmth and affection, and Dixon, Tronick, Keefer, and Brazelton (1981) found that these mothers looked away from their infants more and had less investment in affectively charged episodes. Their interactions were affectively flat. The interactions of American mother-infant dyads were much more intense, and American mothers would appear to intentionally attempt to intensify the affective response of the infant.

In striking contrast Western societies are characterized by socially imposed monogamy resulting in the nuclear family and lowered levels of sexual competition among males, a relative emphasis on conjugal affection as the basis of marriage (as opposed to male control of resources), and high levels of parental investment in offspring (MacDonald 1988, 1990, in press). Within Western samples parent-child play is characterized by positive affect and affection (Beckwith 1985; Stern 1977; Tronick 1982). Clarke-Stewart (1973) found that social play loaded on an optimal maternal factor, and Pettit and Bates (1984) reported that it was associated with intensive maternal involvement. Slade (1987) found that the level and duration of play was highest when mothers were actively interacting with their infants, suggesting that mothers provide a scaffolding effect such that children are able to play more cognitively advanced games in the presence of the mother. The research on rough and tumble (r & t) play between parents and their children is also interpretable within this framework (MacDonald and Parke 1984; MacDonald 1987; see chapter 7): high levels of parent-child r & t play characterized by positive affect and lack of overstimulation are associated with social competence in children.

Similar relationships are quite probable in hunter-gatherer societies viewed by anthropologists as the prototype of human evolution (e.g., Lee 1979). These societies are characterized by a strong tendency toward monogamy, relatively low levels of male sexual competition, warm familial relationships, a high degree of paternal investment characterized by paternal involvement in the family (Katz and Konner 1981), and long birth intervals (Lee 1979). Draper (1990) finds that parent-child relations among the !Kung are characterized by warmth and affection, and that adults often play the sort of mother-infant games of affect regulation described by Tronick (1982) and Stern (1977) in Western societies. Adults loom in close and make incongruous facial expressions as well as talk in baby talk with the infant. In contrast to the agricultural and pastorally based African societies such as the Gusii described above, there is a high level of emotional expressiveness and a very positive affective tone to these interactions.

To summarize, in evolutionary terms the data reviewed here are highly compatible with the idea that parent-child play is an aspect of parental investment in high quality of offspring. Moreover, the data suggest that there is a close linkage between the general affective tone of the parent-child relationship and the existence of parent-child play. In families where affection is lacking therefore we expect to find low levels of parent-child play.

Parent-Child Play and Variation in Parental Investment Within Western Society. It should also be noted that individual differences in parent-child play within Western societies may also reflect this continuum of parental investment. An evolutionary model proposes that these differences are interpretable as reflecting differences in parental investment. Low levels of parental investment within Western societies, associated, for example, with single parenting, social class, or ethnic differences may then be analyzed from this perspective. For example, there is evidence that single parenting and neglectful parenting are associated with a wide range of less than optimal functioning—for example, lower school functioning, higher rates of delinquency, and psychiatric dysfunction (see review in MacDonald 1988[1]), and Sutton-Smith (chapter 1) notes the commonly found social class differences in social play which is associated with similar developmental outcomes.

The data of Field (chapter 13) are particularly interesting in this regard since they indicate a pattern of low parental involvement among American black mothers with their infants, including low levels of parent-child play and low levels of positive affect. Teenage mothers are reported to quickly lose interest in their babies, so that care is typically provided by the maternal grandmother. Field notes that the population is also characterized by very high levels of single parenthood and teenage motherhood as well as dependence on public assistance. Interestingly, the parent-infant interaction styles and the high levels of fostering children reflect the patterns found in the African societies described above; that is, fostering of children and low levels of parent-child involvement, especially interaction of a playful, affectively positive nature.

Field also describes ethnic differences within the lower social class, so that social class *per se* does not appear to be the crucial variable. Similarly Nugent and colleagues (see chapter 15) have found that single parenthood in an Irish sample does not predict dysfunctional early mother-infant interactions, although other studies using different samples have noted this result (see review in chapter 15). Whether these differences in parental functioning within the lower socio-economic status and within groups of single mothers are due in part to genetic variation (as would be compatible with the theory of Rushton 1985, 1988) or due to some other cause is an important scientific hypothesis. Indeed, I would suggest that the question of whether this and similar issues can be objectively judged is really the same question as whether developmental psychology can claim to be a science of human behavior or an arm of various political causes.

Some General Comments on the Relationship between Resources and Low Investment Parenting. Recently Belsky, Steinberg, and Draper (1991) have noted the co-occurrence of low investment parenting, early reproductive competence and behavior, low re-

---

1. The data of Nugent and colleagues in chapter 15 are compatible with the hypothesis that single parenthood represents a low investment style of reproduction even though early mother-infant interactions in their Irish sample of single mothers are not noticeably different from the interactions of married mothers. One would have to follow these children through adolescence at least in order to determine if there were any deficits associated with the marital status of their mothers.

sources available to the family, a stressful early environment, and weak affectional bonding within the family. High investment parenting and delayed reproductive competence and behavior, on the other hand, tend to be associated with an affectively positive, nonstressful environment, and adequate resources. The model can be framed either as a path model in which low investment parenting, weak pair-bonding, etc., are an ecological response to low resource availability, or it may be framed in terms of cumulative-conditional probabilities, in which case there is no necessary implication that inadequate resources are causally related to low investment parenting. Belsky et al. (1991) prefer the latter interpretation, and I would agree for the following reasons.

First, the data of Field (see chapter 13) indicate important variation in parental investment within the lower SES. Thus low availability of resources does not necessarily lead to low investment parenting. Such data are similar to other data indicating important variation within SES in parenting styles and other traits. For example, McQueen (1979) found variation in a variety of characteristics related to parenting among urban black families. In addition, further evidence that lower social status does not inevitably lead to low investment parenting comes from data on infant mortality. High rates of infant mortality are expected to be associated with low investment parenting (Barash 1977). Guttentag and Secord (1983) found that lower-class Jewish families living in Baltimore in 1915 had a much lower rate of infant mortality than other lower-class ethnic groups (and most middle-class groups). This was the case despite the general finding that lower social class was associated with higher rates of infant mortality for all ethnic groups. These results suggest that inadequate resources at best explain only part of the variance in low investment parenting, but there are theoretical reasons why even this is unlikely.

From the standpoint of ecological theory, there is no reason to suppose that inadequate resources would result in low investment parenting. K-selected (i.e., high investment) species are selected to adjust their reproduction to current resource environments (e.g., Southwood 1981). Rather than respond to current adversity with a low investment strategy, they cut back and delay reproduction. On the other hand, r-selected species are expected to always reproduce to the maximum of available resources, independent of level of current resources. Thus from the standpoint of ecological theory there is no expectation that inadequate resources would result in low investment parenting for any species. The causal theory, however, must suppose that the ecologically appropriate response to inadequate resources is to engage in low investment reproduction.

We have already seen that there is good reason to suppose that humans are a relatively K-selected species. This would imply that humans should respond to resource inadequacy by delaying reproduction, and there is excellent evidence that this is indeed the case. For example, during the Great Depression of the 1930s as well as during the depression of the 1890s there was a decline in fertility and postponement of marriage among the middle-class people most affected by the poor economy (Caldwell 1982; Elder 1974). The decline in fertility in the 1930s occurred despite an increase in negative affective tone in family relationships consequent to the economic hardship of the times (Elder 1974). Moreover, this response to the Great Depression was also typical of preindustrial European populations: when resources became scarce there was a tendency for delayed marriage, a higher proportion of never-married adults, and fewer children within marriage—trends that were reversed in times of resource abundance (Wrigley and Schofield 1981). The general theory that low investment/high fertility parenting is a facultative response to a resource-poor, stressful environment is not well founded on ecological theory and is not compatible with the data of historical demography.

These considerations go beyond merely dissociating variation in parental investment from immediate resource availability, since there is also the suggestion that negative familial interactions are not incompatible with high investment parenting. The data of Elder (1974) suggests that even though the Great Depression resulted in negative familial interactions, there was no tendency for early reproduction and low investment parenting. This is particularly interesting because it would appear that the most likely evolutionary function of the human affectional system is to facilitate close family relationships and high levels of parental (and especially paternal) investment (MacDonald 1988, in press).

I would interpret these results to indicate the need for a discrete systems perspective in which high investment parenting is not a unitary set of biological systems, but rather consists of several discrete systems which do not necessarily co-occur, even though empirically they are often found together. Within this perspective, high investment parenting may consist of providing economic resources, playful cognitive stimulation, affection, and moderate discipline, as well as monitoring children's school performance, and engaging in social and cognitive play with children. Although the ideal high investment parent may indeed perform all of those activities, actual parents may perform only a subset of them, or they may emphasize certain aspects of high investment parenting. Such a perspective fits quite well with factor analytic studies of parenting: the warmth-hostility dimension is independent of the control dimension (Baldwin 1955; Baumrind 1971; Maccoby and Martin 1983; Schaefer 1959).

This multidimensional perspective on parental investment focuses attention on individual variation in traits related to high and low investment parenting and the relation of this variation to variation in resource adequacy. Individuals who are on the high investment end of the parental investment continuum respond to resource inadequacy with delayed reproduction (a K-style ecological response), while those on the low end do not view resource inadequacy as a cue that they should delay reproduction (a relatively r-style ecological response). From this perspective, lowered resource adequacy does not cause low investment parenting for such individuals, but it does not prevent low investment parenting in this group either. The result is that the correlation between low resource availability and low investment parenting is real and not at all unexpected. But it is a correlation, not a cause. The conclusion is that inadequate resources are expected to be a marker variable for low investment parenting and can function as part of a cumulative probability model. The causal model, however, must be rejected.

A Concluding Comment on Play and Plasticity. Within the perspective developed here there is an emphasis on the interrelationship of play and plasticity. Elsewhere (MacDonald 1988) I have argued that heritability studies are often very misleading indexes of environmental influence. For example, behavior genetic studies done among the Gusii and in an American middle-class sample may both find high heritability of characteristics related to parental investment because of relatively low environmental variance within these societies. However, this is compatible with very large between-society environmental differences, reflected, for example, in the types of stimulation received by infants in these societies.

From reading the study of Dixon et al. (1981), there is some indication that Gusii infants are very open to environmental stimulation but that mothers consistently cut off interactions before any peaks of positive affect are achieved. From the standpoint of the following section where proximal mechanisms underlying play are discussed, it makes excellent sense to suppose that the capacity for many types of parent-child play is a biological universal: Parent-child play, such as r & t play, as well as many mother-infant games, involves affective responses to basic aspects of stimulation. There is no indication from the Gusii data that infants are unresponsive to sudden changes in stimulation provided during many types of parent-child play, or to the incongruities and novelties of the typical types of stimulation parents provide when playing with children such as the affective arousal which occurs during vestibular stimulation and tickling.

This would suggest that reprogramming of Gusii mother-infant interaction might have large consequences on behavior. However, there is now overwhelming evidence for genetic variation in high and low investment characteristics of parenting (Rushton 1985, 1988; see also Belsky et al. 1991), and this must be part of any complete theory. Nevertheless, it is theoretically sound to expect that an important aspect of the high investment style of reproductive behavior will involve a high level of environmental stimulation and other nongenetically programmed aspects of development. A high investment style of reproductive behavior can involve morphological traits, such as a delayed age of reproductive competence, as well as more commitment of resources to children during the child's life. Parent-child play is clearly a member of the latter class. This environmental aspect of parental investment encompasses a large set of behaviors, including providing economic resources for children (including dowry and bridewealth in many traditional societies), providing environmental stimulation, as well as physical protection.

This is not to deny that traits such as age of menarche are influenceable by the environment or that tendencies to provide environmental stimulation to children are influenced by the genes. It only states that some aspects of investment are intrinsically environmental, and the basic logic of this chapter is that these aspects of stimulation make no evolutionary sense unless the organism is able to benefit from them in some way (i.e., the organism must have the plasticity required to benefit from the stimulation).

In any case, it makes excellent sense to view low levels of parent-child play as a marker of low investment parenting generally which can be grouped conceptually with single parenting, the consequences of divorce, neglectful parenting, and teenage parenthood (Belsky et al. 1991; MacDonald 1988). From the present perspective the movement to encourage higher levels of parent-child play among lower class families (e.g., Smilansky 1968) is far more than an upper-class bias toward controlling the lower classes, as maintained by Sutton-Smith (see chapter 1). It is rather an attempt to modify parenting practices toward a high involvement, high investment parenting style which is ideally suited to life in an advanced postindustrial society. The low investment style of parenting is much more likely to lead to low educational outcomes, low level jobs, high levels of reliance on public assistance, and increased levels of criminality compared to the high investment style of parenting reliably associated with high levels of social play.

II. An Evolutionary Perspective on the Proximal Mechanisms Involved in Parent-Child Play

The above adaptationist account of parent-child play prompts an interest in possible evolved mechanisms which may underlie these phenomena. Any proposed account must be compatible with high levels of both cross-cultural and intrasocietal variation in parent-child play. Moreover, the chapters in the present volume indicate that parent-child play is a diverse phenomenon encompassing a wide variety of systems. Parent-child play ranges from the cognitively oriented styles of play described in chapter 8 by Levenstein, to peekaboo games described in chapter 10 by Anne Fernald, to the r & t play reviewed in chapter 7 by James Carson, Virginia Burke, and Ross Parke.

This wide variety of play interactions suggests an equally wide array of proximal mechanisms underlying parent-child play. Despite this variety, it is likely that these mechanisms conform to a general pattern of providing intrinsic, affective motivation to engage in playful interaction. Rubin, Fein, and Vandenberg (1983) note that play is widely regarded as intrinsically motivated, a view that is highly compatible with the idea that evolved affective responses to expected environmental stimulation are the great shapers of human motivation (MacDonald 1988, 1991). When Flavell (1985) states that Piaget developed a theory of cognitive development which proposes that children are optimally designed to obtain information from the environment, he is essentially stating that Piaget held a modern evolutionary perspective. For Piaget, children are designed to find their environments interesting and to find learning about their environments rewarding.

This evolutionary perspective is well-represented by the work of Panksepp (see chapter 5), who provides evidence for evolved reward systems underlying social play in mammals. Panksepp (1989), along with Zuckerman (1983); Gray, Owen, Davis, and Tsaltas, (1983); and MacDonald (1988, 1991) have similarly proposed evolved reward systems as underlying other human appetitive traits, including sensation seeking, sexual and foraging behavior, and the human affectional system.

In previous work (MacDonald 1988), I have proposed that the reward systems underlying parent-child r & t play are phenotypically and genetically correlated with the personality trait of sensation-seeking/impulsivity. Individuals high on this trait seek high levels of environmental stimulation. Briefly, the children least likely to engage in parent-child r & t are neglected children, while parent-child r & t is common among popular as well as rejected children (MacDonald 1987). Similarly Pellegrini (1988) and Coie and Kupersmidt (1983) found that neglected children engage in less r & t with peers than popular or rejected children. Descriptions of neglected children clearly indicate that they tend to be shy and socially withdrawn (see Berndt and Ladd 1989; and Coie, Dodge, and Kupersmidt 1990).

Many popular and rejected children, on the other hand, tend to be highly extraverted and engage in high levels of r & t with their peers (Pellegrini 1988) as well as with their parents (MacDonald 1987). These categories of children can be differentiated, however, by the findings that the r & t of rejected children with their peers tends to lead to aggression (Pellegrini 1988), while r & t parents is characterized by high levels of withdrawal, overstimulation, negative affect, and aggression (MacDonald 1987). While rejected children tend to engage in high levels of r & t leading to aggression and social rejection, dominant children tend to use r & t play to maintain and improve dominance status (Smith and Boulton 1990).

The trait of sensation-seeking/impulsivity is higher in males generally (Zuckerman 1979), and this corresponds to much higher levels of r & t among boys than among girls both among peers and between parents and children (e.g., Blurton Jones 1972; MacDonald and Parke 1986). At the extreme end of this dimension are hyperactive children, the vast majority of whom are boys. These children tend to be rejected by their peers, seek very high levels of environmental stimulation, and are impulsive and aggressive with peers. Like subclinical rejected children, they tend to overarousal and aggression during parent-child r & t (see MacDonald 1988).

The conclusion of this line of reasoning is that parent-child r & t is part of an evolved reward system which results in children being attracted to particular types of environmental stimulation. This does not imply that cognitive processes are irrelevant to r & t play generally, and in the case of parent-child r & t these processes are particularly salient (MacDonald 1988). Parent-child r & t is often "framed" within a playful context and often includes pretense, as when a parent pretends to be a monster who is going to eat the child. The child knows that nothing worse than a little tickling is in the offing, but the pretense heightens the tension and drama of the encounter. Smith and Boulton (1990) note that peer r & t requires a variety of scripts necessary to interpret cues of aggression versus play-fighting.

I would also like to suggest that the gentler parent-child games of infancy involve a different evolved reward system—the reward system underlying the human affectional system. Early parent-child games involve a dance of affective modulation whose goal is "to be with and enjoy someone else" (Stern 1977, p. 71) or to "maintain a relational state that is evaluated positively" (Tronick 1982, p. 3) (see also chapter 3, this volume). This stream of affective modulation is clearly highly pleasurable to infants, and there is abundant evidence that pleasurable, rewarding interactions are characteristic of warm parent-child relations and secure attachment. We have already noted the association between play and "optimal parenting" and parent-child warmth. In addition, Malatesta, Culver, Tesman, and Shepard (1989) found that mothers of secure infants showed more positive expression during play, and that the insecure infants appeared to be "angry, vigilant, and emotionally controlled" (p. 52). Bates, Maslin, and Frankel (1985) found that securely attached infants had more "positive mutuality in play and maternal interest in initiating play bouts" (p. 174). These findings are also compatible with the findings, described above, that in societies with cold, hostile parent-child interactions, parent-child play tends to be absent.

It is perhaps an exaggeration, however, to suggest that parent-child r & t involves completely different systems than the affectional systems. Parent-child play is typically highly pleasurable to the child, so that the source of that stimulation is expected to be highly valued by the child. Moreover, the early social games of infancy oftentimes rely on similar properties of stimuli for their affective consequences. A mother playing peekaboo with an infant is using many of the same stimulus properties apparent in parent-child r & t: stimuli are surprising, fact-paced, and often achieve their affective salience by mimicking stimulation which is threatening. For example, a mother looming in quickly toward an infant is highly arousing and fear inducing, but in the context of play this behavior provokes laughter. The overall goal of the interaction, however, is pleasurable engagement, and we have seen that these activities are strongly associated with optimal parenting and warm parent-child relationships generally.

These findings indicate that parent-child play is an integral part of the evolved machinery of parent-child interaction. Both the sensation-seeking/extraversion traits as well as the human affectional system are influenced by genetic variation (Fulker 1981; Cloninger 1987; MacDonald 1988). Moreover, the findings are highly compatible with the idea that discrete systems have evolved which underlie parent-child play. Such a view is implicit in the perspective developed in Section I: parent-child play is a typical aspect of human adaptation in societies characterized by high parental investment in children. The human affectional system and the sensation-seeking/extraversion system are two such evolved systems, and there are presumably other systems underlying different types of parent-child play.

Nevertheless, we have seen that parent-child play is far from universal. The lack of universality in behaviors is commonly assumed to indicate that there are no biological systems underlying behavior—that the human mind is a blank slate that is infinitely malleable by cultural processes. A blank slate perspective cannot account for the wide cross-cultural distribution of both r & t as well as mother-infant games tied to the affectional systems. For example, warm parent-child relationships occur in both modern, industrialized societies as well as in the most economically primitive of human societies—hunter-gatherer societies (Bacon, Child, and Berry 1963; Katz and Konner 1981; MacDonald 1988), and r & t play has a similarly wide distribution among human groups and is well-known among many animal species.

Thus the blank slate perspective cannot account for the very wide distribution of a well-defined cluster of behaviors we recognize as human parent-child play. The fact that it is possible to set up standard laboratory procedures which result in producing positive affect in infants (e.g., Cichetti and Sroufe 1978) further indicates the species-typical nature of the stimuli which elicit positive affect in human infants: parent-child play in its widest sense is the production of a nonrandom set of parental behaviors which reliably elicit positive affect in children.

In theoretical terms, these stimuli which reliably result in particular affective responses are examples of Bowlby's (1969) "natural clues": that is, stimuli which result in affective responses as a result of biologically mediated (unlearned) connections. With respect to play, Berlyne (1966) has proposed that intensity of stimulation as well as the collative variables such as novelty, suddenness of change, surprise, incongruity, complexity, and uncertainty are aspects of stimuli which tend to result in emotional response. Moreover, other stimuli, such as gentle tickling and the vestibular stimulation often occurring during parent-child play, as well as the stimuli sought after by a Piagetian "optimal learning device" (Flavell 1985), may well be intrinsically rewarding.

The fact that this style of play is not present in all human societies invites two possible explanations: First, there could be genetic variation such that some groups, whether through natural selection or genetic drift, do not have this capacity. Thus one might suppose that in the African groups described above there has been natural selection away from high investment parenting in favor of high levels of sexual competition among males and mechanisms to place some of the costs of parenting, such as play, onto nonparents. Since warm, affectionate relationships are not at all essential to marriage, the biological basis for this type of relationship is gradually lost. There is in fact some evidence for ethnic differences in basic temperament traits: Orientals have been consistently found to be more behaviorally inhibited than Caucasian populations (Freedman and Freedman 1969; Kagan, Kearsley, and Zelazo 1978).

This is a possible scenario, but it is not necessitated by the data at the present time. In addition to the arguments made above with respect to the heritability of characteristics related to high investment parenting, rapid historical shifts in parent-child affective relationships indicate that profound historical shifts in behavior affected by these systems can occur too quickly to be due to natural selection (MacDonald, 1984 1988). These rapid shifts suggest that cultures are able to take advantage of human plasticity by selectively facilitating and suppressing specific systems.

In the case of play this plasticity is facilitated by the fact that the proximal mechanisms underlying parent-child play are fundamentally environment-expectant; that is, they program for the affective response to expected environmental stimulation. The child may be biologically predisposed to find certain types of stimulation pleasurable, but parents can manipulate whether in fact the stimulation actually occurs. If cultures strongly discourage such stimulation, these reward systems are minimally elaborated and parent-child play as well as parent-child relations characterized by warmth and affection are lacking.

This perspective thus requires a robust notion of human plasticity but is not at all compatible with a blank slate perspective. Cultures are able to manipulate environments and, by means of human plasticity, they are able to meet immediate environmental challenges. Nevertheless, the possible endpoints of human development are sharply delimited: we can easily imagine cultures where parent-child play is absent, but, when parent-child play does occur, it is "of a type," and this is the case in a wide range of human cultures. It is recognizably human, and recognizably play.

Finally, it should be noted that it is something of a paradox that the interrelated extraversion, impulsivity, and sensation-seeking traits are often utilized during parent-child play but that these traits, especially impulsivity, tend to be linked with a relatively low investment style reproductive pattern (Belsky et al. 1991; Rushton 1985, 1988). These traits may be conceptualized generally as involving, at one extreme, a heightened sensitivity to rewards generally (Gray et al. 1983), so that, for example, hyperactive children are highly prone to immediate gratification as well as highly prone to engage in r & t play bouts with their parents (see MacDonald 1988, for a discussion).

Perhaps the key is to utilize the multidimension concept of parental investment described above. High investment parents do not *only* engage in r & t play with their children, but they also set limits and encourage the child to be able to delay gratification when necessary; they make sure that the child does not get out of control or overly aggressive during the play session; they stimulate the child cognitively; they have a good affectional relationship with the child; and they monitor school performance and pay for college. Indeed, if r & t were the only type of parent-child interaction, the parent-child relationship would be a strange one indeed. High investment parenting must be multidimensional because the child and the world he/she is adapting to are multidimensional.

III. Play as an Adaptation Versus Play as a Dynamic Social System

Finally, I would like to compare this perspective with the perspective developed by Fogel, Nwokah, and Karns in chapter 2. They propose that play is not a "dedicated genetic or neurological structure" (p. 45), but rather is "a creative process, emergent from the dynamics of social discourse between two different individuals in a particular cultural and physical context" (p. 45).

Fogel et al. correctly criticize some ethologically derived theories of play for inattention to developmental processes and for a tendency to propose genetically determined rules underlying play. As they note, it is difficult to conceptualize the creativity and variability of play in these terms.

However, unlike the ethologically oriented theories discussed by Fogel et al., the perspective described above does not emphasize genetically determined rules of play. A reward system theory of play (see also MacDonald 1988) is consistent with the idea that there are many different movements as well as culturally specific and even idiosyncratic methods by which the these reward centers can be stimulated. The aspects of stimulation suggested by Berlyne (1966) as affecting arousal can be utilized in a wide variety of ways. Play can thus be highly creative as well as synchronous or nonsynchronous. Thus the finding that laughter in mother-infant games was associated with higher rates of maternal actions could be due to the fact that mothers' actions tend to be stimulating and affectively arousing. Mothers make silly faces (incongruity), loom quickly towards the infant (suddenness), provide vestibular stimulation (e.g., turning quickly in a circle while holding the infant and gazing into its eyes), and gentle tickling. All these activities are arousing to the child and, within an optimal level of arousal, they are pleasant. They certainly need not be stereotyped. Panksepp also suggests that variability can result in the presence of a single underlying mechanism because play is filtered and channeled through cortical information processing mechanisms. These mechanisms would result in many different forms of play while still relying on a central process involving the pleasantness of certain types of stimulation.

At the same time, the theory developed here is consistent (perhaps identical) with what Fogel et al. term the Schematic Interaction theory of play, except that it provides a meaningful way to incorporate variability and creativity into play. Such a theory proposes that neurological maturation underlies some abilities related to play, such as the ability to smile and laugh. However, the main emphasis is on specific, discrete emotion systems, and in the present theoretical perspective these emotions include the subjective feelings related to the sensation-seeking/extraversion system which result in strong affective response to particular types of environmental stimulation, as well as the human affectional system.

While the present theory proposes that play depends on specifically evolved systems involving the affective response to environmental stimulation, Fogel et al. deny that in general evolution results in specific, dedicated structures which have evolved with specific adaptive function. I believe that the argument for the general importance of specific, evolved structures involves the following considerations: (1) There are traits which can be measured in personality and temperament questionnaires, such as the dimensions of sensation-seeking and the tendency toward affection emphasized here; (2) There are specific brain structures which underlie these traits (see chapter 5); (3) Individual differences on these traits are influenced by genetic variation (see Fulker 1981). Although genetic variation is not essential for an adaptationist argument, its presence indicates that there are genes which affect variation in the trait.

(4) Some aspects of the phenotypic distribution of the trait can be predicted by broad theoretical considerations. For example, in the case of sensation-seeking underlying r & t play, the sex difference between males and females is predicted from the general theory of sex: males are expected to be the high risk, aggressive sex, while females, because they are the high investment sex, are expected to adopt a more conservative strategy (see MacDonald 1988).

(5) The presence of the trait makes adaptive sense. If any trends at all are noticeable in recent evolutionary theorizing about behavior, it is that evolutionary design for specific structures is becoming more rather than less emphasized (e.g., Symons 1989; Tooby and Cosmides 1989), and my own work has emphasized the evolution of specific evolved structures which are nevertheless highly manipulable and plastic (MacDonald 1984, 1988, 1989, 1991). In the case of sensation-seeking, there is a clear evolutionary rationale for developing systems which make the individual have a psychological interest in engaging the environment. Panksepp's foraging systems are another case in point. The organism seeks food, sex, and other environmental necessities because of specific reward centers in the brain which make appetitive behaviors psychologically compelling.

The contrary view suggests that genes code only for very general properties of the organism and that structure evolves as a result of complex organism/environment interplay. Such a view is conceivable, but to the extent that it is compatible with even a minimal evolutionary approach, it must suppose that natural selection has the opportunity to act on genes which result in delimiting possible developmental outcomes and channeling developmental outcomes so that adaptive systems and very complexly elaborated structures result. Indeed this is precisely the contemporary view emerging from developmental genetics (Endler and McLellan 1988). I doubt that any one is proposing a theory in which the genetic constraints on play are so weak that any conceivable outcome is possible. If the genes are an element in a set of processes which result in the emergent structures of play and indeed affect variation in those structures, I am not clear on what is gained by denying that the genes are dedicated structures underlying specific evolved systems.

Finally, there is another question which has not thus far been addressed. Given that the proximal mechanisms underlying play involve affective response to environmental stimulation, is it possible that play itself is not an adaptation but is rather an evolutionary by-product which takes advantage of these characteristic responses to stimulation? According to this scenario, the fact that infants react with affective arousal at new and interesting stimuli is a result of natural selection for a Piagetian optimal learning device, but this would not imply that parent-child play which utilizes this evolved function is similarly an adaptation. Such a scenario would be consistent with the idea of Fogel et al. that parent-child play is not the result of "dedicated genetic structures" designed specifically for parent-child play.

The argument against such a perspective is essentially contained in the first sections of this chapter. If indeed play is an integral aspect of high investment parenting, as appears to be the case, it is in that sense an adaptation. It is an adaptation to a highly competitive environment with uncertain structure in which optimal programming of individual development requires high levels of stimulation and in which parents are best able to perform this function. It is an adaptation, but, like so many human adaptations, it is a manipulable adaptation. Its very presence offers considerable hope that development can be optimally programmed for life in a very complicated civilization.

References

Ainsworth, M. D. S. (1967). *Infancy in Uganda*. Baltimore: Johns Hopkins University Press.

Bacon, M. K.; Child, I. L.; and Berry, K. (1963). A cross-cultural study of the correlates of crime. *Journal of Abnormal and Social Psychology* 56: 291–300.

Baldwin, A. L. (1955). *Behavior and Development in Childhood.* New York: Dryden.

Barash, D. (1977). *Sociobiology and Behavior.* New York: Elsevier.

Barnett, S. A. (1988). *Biology and Freedom.* Cambridge, Eng.: Cambridge University Press, 1988.

Bates, J.; Maslin, C. A.; and Frankel, K. A. (1985). Attachment security, mother-child interaction, and temperament as predictors of behavior-problem ratings at age three years. In I. Bretherton and E. Waters (eds.), Growing points of attachment theory and research. *Monographs of the Society for Research in Child Development,* serial no. 209, vol. 50 (1–2).

Baumrind, D. (1971) Current patterns of parental authority. *Developmental Psychology Monograph* 4 (1, Pt. 2).

Becker, J. T. M. (1977). A learning analysis of the development of peer-oriented behavior in 9-month old infants. *Developmental Psychology* 13:481–91.

Beckwith, L. (1985). Parent-child interaction and social-emotional development. In C. C. Brown and A. Gottfried (eds.), *Play Interactions: The Role of Toys and Parental Involvement* in *Children's Development.* Skillman, N.J.: Johnson and Johnson Baby Products Co.

Belsky, J.; Steinberg, L.; and Draper, P. (1991). Childhood experiences, interpersonal development, and reproductive strategy: An evolutionary theory of socialization. *Child Development* 62:647–70.

Berlyne, D. (1966). Curiosity and exploration. *Science* 153:25–33.

Berndt, T., and Ladd, G. (eds.) (1989). *Peer Relationships in Child Development.* New York: Wiley, 1989.

Blurton Jones, N. (1972). *Ethological Studies of Child Behavior.* Cambridge: Cambridge University Press.

Bowlby, J. (1969). *Attachment and Loss.* Vol. 1, *Attachment.* New York: Basic Books.

Caldwell, J. C. (1982). *The Theory of Fertility Decline.* New York: Academic Press.

Cichetti, D., and Sroufe, L. A. (1978). An organizational view of affect: Illustration from a study of Down's syndrome infants. In M. Lewis and L. Rosenblum (eds.), *The Development of Affect.* New York: Plenum Press.

Clarke-Stewart, A. (1973). Interactions between mothers and their young children: Characteristics and consequences. *Monographs for the Society for Research in Child Development*, serial no. 153, vol. 38 (6–7).

Cloninger, R. C. (1987). A systematic method for clinical description and classification of personality variants. *Archives of General Psychiatry* 44:573–88.

Coie, J; Dodge, J.; and Kupersmidt, J. (1990). Peer group behavior and social status. In S. Asher and J. D. Coie (eds.), *Peer Rejection in Childhood*. Cambridge, Eng.: Cambridge University Press.

Daly, M., and Wilson, M. (1983). *Sex, Evolution, and Behavior,* 2d ed. Boston, Mass.: Willard Grant.

Dixon, S.; Tronick, E.; Keefer, C.; and Brazelton, T. B. (1981). Mother-infant interaction among the Gusii of Kenya. In T. Field, A. M. Sostek, P. Vietze, and P. H. Leiferman (eds.), *Culture and Early Interactions*. Hillsdale, N.J.: Lawrence Erlbaum Associates.

Draper, P. (1989). African marriage systems: Perspectives from evolutionary biology. *Ethology and Sociobiology* 10:145–70.

Draper, P. (1990, October 1). Department of Individual and Family Studies, The Pennsylvania State University. Personal communication.

Draper, P., and Harpending, H. (1987). Parent investment and the child's environment. In J. Lancaster, A. S. Rossi, and L. Sherrod (eds.), *Parenting across the Life-Span: Biosocial Perspectives*. New York: Aldine de Gruyter.

Elder, G. (1974). *Children of the Great Depression*. Chicago: University of Chicago Press.

Endler, J. A., and McLellan, T. (1988). The processes of evolution: Toward a newer synthesis. *Annual Review of Ecology and Systematics* 19: 395–422.

Fagen, R. (1981). *Animal Play Behavior.* New York: Oxford University Press.

Feitelson, D. (1977). Cross-cultural studies of representational play. In B. Tizard and D. Harvey (eds.), *Biology of Play*. Philadelphia: Lippincott.

Flavell, J. (1985). *Cognitive Development*. 2d ed.. Englewood-Cliffs, N.J.: Prentice-Hall.

Freedman, D. G., and Freedman, N. A. (1969). Differences in behavior between Chinese-American and European-American newborns. *Nature* 224:1227.

Fulker, D. (1981). The genetic and environmental architecture of psychoticism, extraversion, and neuroticism. In H. Eysenck (ed.), *A Model for Personality*. Munich: Springer-Verlag.

Gray, J.; Owen, S.; Davis, N.; and Tsaltas, E. (1983). Psychological and physiological relations between anxiety and impulsivity. In M. Zuckerman (ed.), *Biological Bases of Sensation Seeking, Impulsivity, and Anxiety*. Hillsdale, N.J.: Erlbaum.

Greenough, W. T.; Black, J. E.; and Wallace, C. S. (1987). Experience and brain development. *Child Development* 58:539–59.

Groos, K. (1901). *The Play of Man*. London: Heinemann.

Guttentag, M., and Secord, P. F. (1983). *Too Many Women? The Sex Ratio Question*. Beverly Hills: Sage Publications.

Hirsch, H. V. B., and Spinelli, D. N. (1971). Modification of the distribution of receptive field orientation in cats by selective visual exposure during development. *Experimental Brain Research* 13:509–27.

Jolly, A. (1985). *The Evolution of Primate Behavior*. 2d ed. New York: Macmillan.

Kagan, J.; Kearsley, R.; and Zelazo, P. R. (1978). *Infancy: Its Place in Child Development*. Cambridge: Harvard University Press.

Katz, M. M., and Konner, M. J. (1981). The role of the father: An anthropological perspective. In M. E. Lamb (ed.), *The Role of the Father in Child Development*. 2d ed. New York: Wiley.

Kleiman, D. G. (1981). Correlations among life history characteristics of mammalian species exhibiting two extreme forms of monogamy. In R. D. Alexander and D. W. Tinkle (eds.), *Natural Selection and Social Behavior*. New York: Chiron Press.

Lee, R. B. (1979). *The !Kung-San: Men, Women and Work in a Foraging Society*. Cambridge: Cambridge University Press.

Lerner, R. M. (1984). *On Human Plasticity*. New York: Cambridge University Press.

LeVine, R. A., and LeVine, B. B. (1966). *Nyansongo: A Gusii Community in Kenya*. New York: Wiley.

Maccoby, E., and Martin, J. (1983). Socialization in the context of the family. In E. M. Hetherington (eds.), *Handbook of Child Psychology*. Vol. 4, *Socialization, Personality, and Social Development*. New York: Wiley.

MacDonald, K. B. (1984). An ethological-social learning theory of the development of altruism: Implications for human sociobiology. *Ethology and Sociobiology* 5:97–109.

MacDonald, K. B. (1987). Parent-child physical play with rejected, neglected and popular boys. *Developmental Psychology* 23:705–11.

MacDonald, K. B. (1988). *Social and Personality Development: An Evolutionary Synthesis*. New York: Plenum.

MacDonald, K. B. (1989). The plasticity of human social organization and behavior: Contextual variables and proximal mechanisms. *Ethology and Sociobiology* 10:171–94.

MacDonald, K. B. (1990). Mechanisms of sexual egalitarianism in Western Europe. *Ethology and Sociobiology* 11:195–38.

MacDonald, K. B. (1991). A perspective on Darwinian psychology: The importance of domain-general mechanisms, plasticity, and individual differences. *Ethology and Sociobiology* 12, In press.

MacDonald, K. B. (In press). Warmth as a developmental construct: An evolutionary analysis. *Child Development*.

MacDonald, K. B., and Parke, R. D. (1984). Bridging the gap: Parent-child play interactions and peer interactive competence. *Child Development* 55:1265–77.

MacDonald, K. B., and Parke, R. D. (1986). Parent-child physical play: The effects of sex and age of children and parents. *Sex Roles* 15:367–78.

Malatesta, C. Z.; Culver, C.; Tesman, J. R.; and Shepard, B. (1989). The development of emotion expression during the first two years of life. *Monographs of the Society for Research in Child Development*, serial no. 219, vol. 54 (1–2).

McQueen, A. J. (1979). The adaptation of urban black families: Trends, problems, and issues. In D. Riess and H. A. Hoffman (eds.), *The American Family: Dying or Developing?* New York: Basic Books.

Panksepp. J. (1989). The psychobiology of the emotions. In H. Wagner and A. Manstead (eds.), *Handbook of Social Psychophysiology*. Chichester, Eng.: Wiley.

Pellegrini, A. D. (1988). Elementary-school children's rough and tumble play and social competence. *Developmental Psychology* 24:802–6.

Pennington, R. (1991). Child fostering as a reproductive strategy among Southern African pastoralists. *Ethology and Sociobiology* 12:83–104.

Pettit, G. S., and Bates, J. E. (1984). Continuity of individual differences in the mother-infant relationship from six to thirteen months. *Child Development* 55:729–39.

Rubin, K. H.; Fein, G.; and Vandenberg, B. (1983). Play. In E. M. Hetherington and P. Mussen (eds.), *Handbook of Child Psychology*. Vol. 4, *Social and Personality Development*. New York: Wiley.

Rushton, J. P. (1985). Differential K theory: The sociobiology of individual and group differences. *Personality and Individual Differences* 6: 411–42.

Rushton, J. P. (1988). Race differences in behavior: A review and evolutionary analysis. *Personality and Individual Differences* 9:1009–24.

Schaefer, E. S. (1959). A circumplex model for maternal behavior. *Journal of Abnormal and Social Psychology* 59:226–35.

Slade, A. (1987). A longitudinal study of maternal involvement and symbolic play during the toddler period. *Child Development* 58:367–75.

Smilansky, S. (1968). *The Effects of Sociodramatic Play on Disadvantaged Preschool Children.* New York: Wiley.

Smith, P. K. (1982). Does play matter? Functional and evolutionary aspects of animal and human play. *Behavioral and Brain Sciences* 5:135–84.

Smith, P. K., and Boulton, M. (1990). Rough-and-tumble play, aggression and dominance: Perception and behaviour in children's encounters. *Human Development* 33:271–82.

Southwood, T. R. E. (1981). Bionomic strategies and population parameters. In R. M. May (ed.), *Theoretical Ecology: Principles and Applications.* Sunderland, Mass.: Sinauer Associates.

Stern, D. (1977). *The First Relationship.* Cambridge: Harvard University Press.

Sutton-Smith, B. (1985). Origins and developmental processes of play. In C. C. Brown and A. W. Gottfried (eds.), *Play Interactions: The Role of Toys and Parental Involvement in Children's Development.* Skillman, N.J.: Johnson and Johnson, Inc.

Symons, D. (1989). A critique of Darwinian anthropology. *Ethology and Sociobiology* 10:131–44.

Tooby, J., and Cosmides, L. (1989). Evolutionary psychology and the generation of culture, Part I: Theoretical considerations. *Ethology and Sociobiology* 10:29–50.

Trivers, R. (1986). *Social Evolution.* Menlo Park, Calif.: Benjamin Cummings.

Tronick, E. Z. (1982). Affectivity and sharing. In E. Z. Tronick (ed.), *Social Interchange in Infancy.* Baltimore: University Park Press.

Van den Berghe, P. (1979). *Human Family Systems.* New York: Elsevier.

Van Lawick, J. (1981). *In the Shadow of Man.* Boston: Houghton-Mifflin.

Wrigley, E. A., and Schofield, R. (1981). *The Population History of England, 1541–1871.* Cambridge: Harvard University Press.

Zuckerman, M. (1979). *Sensation Seeking: Beyond the Optimal Level of Arousal.* Hillsdale, N.J.: Erlbaum.

Zuckerman, M. (1983). A biological theory of sensation seeking. In M. Zuckerman (ed.), *Biological Bases of Sensation Seeking, Impulsivity, and Anxiety.* Hillsdale, N.J.: Erlbaum.

PART II

Mechanisms of Parent-Child Play

CHAPTER 5

Rough and Tumble Play:
A Fundamental Brain Process

Jaak Panksepp

Our empirical work on the neuropsychological mechanisms which control rough and tumble social play was precipitated by our interest in understanding the intrinsic brain mechanisms which mediate social emotions and social bonding. One of our initial findings was that brain opioids are very powerful in quelling the intensity of separation distress (Panksepp, Herman, Bishop, Conner, and Scott 1978; Panksepp, Siviy, and Normansell 1986) and we became interested in determining how this neurochemical system modulates a host of other social behaviors, including aggression, sexuality, parental behavior, dominance and especially, social play (Panksepp 1981a, 1986a; Panksepp, Jalowiec, Bishop, and DeEskinazi 1985). At the outset of the work, the systematic psychobiological analysis of play was nonexistent in behavioral neuroscience. Although there were abundant descriptions of social play in various species in the ethological literature (see Fagen 1981; Smith 1978; Symons 1978), no useful model systems had been developed which could be deployed in the laboratory to systematically analyze the neural underpinnings of this seemingly robust brain process. The empirical neglect was based largely on the assumption that play was a flimsy construct which did not reflect any intrinsic psychoneural reality in the brain. Most behaviorists deemed it to be a verbal-social construction reflecting little more than the richness of human imagination. It was also commonly believed that play was a highly variable behavior and hence difficult to bring under experimental control. In fact, these assumptions are woefully incorrect, and we now have a preliminary knowledge of how ludic processes are controlled within the brain.

We, and others, have found that play is remarkably easy to study in various species including juvenile rats (Panksepp, Siviy, and Normansell 1984; Thor and Holloway 1984), cats (Barrett and Bateson 1978; Caro 1981; Martin and Caro 1985), and primates (see chapter 6, this volume). However, obvious forms of play are not clearly evident in some species, most notably in various strains of laboratory mice and guinea pigs (perhaps because we do not have innate feature detectors for their forms of play, or perhaps those creatures do not, in fact, play very much). In any event, rough and tumble activity is a robust phenomenon in rats, and most people readily recognize it as play, even though it has the outward trappings of fighting. In several tests of this proposition, undergraduates have identified the target behaviors as play more than 75 percent of the time, children (four to nine years of age) 100 percent of the time, yet visiting behavioral scientists, when first exposed to the phenomenon are tempted to label it as a form of aggression! I am confident that the sceptical scientists are wrong, since low doses of antiaggressive drugs like fluprazine (4 mg/kg) can increase the behavior (Jalowiec, Panksepp, and Nelson unpublished data 1989) while aggression facilitating agents such as testosterone can decrease it (Panksepp unpublished data 1985). Also, the roughhousing interaction is a positive incentive for both participants (Humphreys and Einon 1981; Normansell and Panksepp 1990).

Social play in laboratory rats exhibits as little variance as other genetically ordained regulatory systems of the organism such as feeding and drinking (Panksepp and Beatty 1980), and we can now feel confident that roughhousing play is a robust central-state process of the mammalian brain. When we eventually understand the neurobiological underpinnings of this form of play in some detail, we may be able to understand how behavioral competence emerges spontaneously from the innate potentials of our genetic libraries. At present we have excellent operational definitions for the concept of *play,* but we remain remote from adequate conceptual definitions. However, we need not worry about that: primary brain processes cannot be usefully defined in words prior to the pertinent brain work; an adequate conceptual definition can only come at the end of our neurobehavioral inquiries. The aim of this chapter is to provide an overview of what little we know about the mechanisms and functions of social play in the mammalian brain. Since there is very little systematic work on the role of parental interactions in the governance of animal play, I also proceeded to gather some preliminary data on that topic to share in this chapter.

Affective Neuroscience—An Excursion into Some Conceptual Dilemmas and New Frameworks

At the outset, I would briefly make some remarks concerning the scientific *zeitgeist* which has delayed progress in understanding the nature of some fundamental brain mechanisms which arise from the genome as hereditary birthrights of organisms. For a more extensive recent discussion of such issues see Bunge (1990) and commentaries on that article as well (Panksepp 1988, 1989, 1991). Because of the intellectual traditions of logical positivism and radical behaviorism, psychobiology has never learned to deal effectively with the intrinsic operating systems (central-state processes) of the brain. In a sense, such "heirlooms" of brain evolution are neurodynamic processes which symbolize (in terms of unconditional neural circuit properties) the major psychobehavioral adaptations of each species. These "hidden" functions, genetically woven into the neuronal architecture of the brain, can only be observed indirectly via the analysis of behavior. They must be theoretically inferred from careful behavioral observations coupled with brain research and a cautious anthropomorphic analysis of the evolutionarily shared functions of the mammalian brain. This is not a comfortable recipe for the discipline of behavioral neuroscience which prides itself on observational objectivity and rigorous logic. Unfortunately, such *hubris* of perceived rigor has, in addition to its many empirical successes, all too often delayed scientific understanding by discouraging investigators (via funding, publication policies, and long-established educational biases) from studying hidden brain function which can only be approached via theoretically guided brain research. For instance, we initially encountered great difficulty in publishing our research on rough and tumble ludic activities because we used the word "play" which could not be adequately defined. With some bemusement, we entertained relabeling the complex social phenomena as PLAY (i.e., Prominent Ludic Activity of Youth) so as to give it more traditional (albeit *ludicrous*) trappings of scientific respectibility. But perhaps even that would not be safe, and we should call play the Social Action Facilitation Effect (SAFE). However, we persisted in using the vernacular terminology, and now it seems to be much more acceptable to use the word *play*

in behavioral brain research. In short, we must properly conceptualize functional brain systems before we can analyze them. The
choice of words should facilitate rather than hinder that.

Conversely, it could be noted that progress may also have been
delayed by those interested in human behavior because they
commonly despise the anthropomorphism which animal models
necessarily imply. Thus, investigators of human psychobehavioral
functions often fail to recognize the relevance of animal data. This is
unfortunate, since animal models are typically the only way we can
obtain a mechanistic understanding of how certain primal psychobehavioral functions emerge from the human brain. In any
event, the underlying premise of our work is that brain mechanisms
of rough and tumble play (and other basic emotive systems [Pank-
sepp 1982, 1988, 1989, 1990, 1991]) are ancient psychobehavioral
control systems which most mammals still share in essentially homologous fashion. Hence, neurobiological clarification of the executive infrastructure of the mechanisms in the animal brain will yield
a preliminary understanding of the same executive mechanisms in
the human brain. In the case of play, this belief is empirically premised on the observation that the basic impulse to indulge in rough
and tumble play survives radical neodecortication in several species
(Murphy, MacLean, and Hamilton 1981; Normansell and Panksepp
1984), which suggests that the essential brain mechanisms were
laid down before the divergence of the human line from the rodent-
like species whose descendants we commonly study in the behavioral brain research laboratory. Although the species-typical
expressions of play may differ quite markedly among existing mammalian species, the core mechanisms have probably been conserved
in a highly homologous fashion. Subsequent evolutionary divergence has probably operated much more on the surface details—the
species-specific expressions—rather than on the executive circuitry
which instigates animals to play. Accordingly, the fundamental issue that must be clarified is the nature of the neuronal infrastruc-
tures (including chemical, anatomical, and electro-informational)
that trigger ludic states in the nervous system. We presently remain remote from that goal, but the intent of this chapter is to summarize how far we have come and where we may be going.

On the Varieties of Play

Human play has been divided into a large number of categories, including exploratory/sensorimotor play, relational/functional play,

constructive play, dramatic/symbolic play, games-with-rules play, and rough and tumble play. Probably this last form, roughhousing play, is presently easiest to study in animal models, but except for a few outstanding pieces of work (Humphrey and Smith 1984) it has received the least attention in human research. This is understandable, for roughhousing is boisterous and often viewed as disruptive and potentially dangerous by adults. Of course kids love it (it brings them "joy"), and animals readily learn instrumental responses to indulge in it (Normansell and Panksepp 1990). This is the main form of play that other mammals exhibit (and includes, I suspect, the relatively solitary motor play—running, jumping, prancing— play of many herbiverous animals). Although human play has been extensively taxonomized, it is still worth contemplating to what extent the various forms are merely higher elaborations (culturally derived as well as higher neuro-evolutionary variants) on a single primal theme. Are there multiple executive circuits for play in the human brain, or do they ultimately reflect multiple manifestations of a single underlying mechanism shared by all mammals? Until demonstrated otherwise, I am tempted to believe the latter alternative. For instance, just as each of the basic human emotions can be expressed in many ways, including dance, drama, music, and art, a basic neuronal form of ludic activity (which can add "fun" to many activities) may be filtered and channeled through the higher information processing networks of the human cortex and result in seemingly distinct forms of play. The common denominator for all forms of human play may still be the neuronal activities of brain systems which were originally designed to generate rough and tumble ludicity.

Perhaps this source "energy" can be channeled voluntarily into a large variety of distinct activities. Indeed, at times humans simulate playfulness and thereby attempt to evoke ludic feelings in a reafferent way via pretenses. Do such playful expressions remain hollow until the ancient circuits of playfulness—which appear to be affectively characterized by "lightness," "joy," and "flow"—are recruited? By attempting to voluntarily activate the natural ludic mechanisms of the brain, humans may achieve totally new forms of playfulness (including various games, toys, and dramatic and linguistic devices). It should be remembered that a single higher brain system can energize a number of distinct behavioral options. Indeed, the other basic emotional command circuits of the mammalian brain appear to operate in this way (Panksepp 1982, 1986b, 1989). Of course at present such ideas must remain controversial. We will not be able to characterize the source "energies" for the other forms of play until the neurobiology of the most ubiquitous form of mammalian play—roughhousing—is better clarified.

By attempting to voluntarily and formally recruit playfulness for educational ends, humans probably exercise many cortical potentials independently of play-related functions, and one is led to wonder to what extent the extensive literature, which has sought to evaluate the role of play in facilitating learning and development of social competencies, has simply evaluated the power of positive social interactions to facilitate desired educational goals (e.g., Christie and Johnsen 1983; Rubin 1980; Saltz and Brodie 1982). It does seem that many of the supposed benefits of play that have been revealed by formal investigation simply reflect the beneficial effects of intense social interactions and supplemental tutoring effects on learning (e.g., Simon and Smith 1983; Smith, Dalgleish, and Herzmark 1981; Smith and Syddall 1978). There is presently no assurance that the many play interventions that have been studied in laboratory settings do in fact arouse primary process play circuits intensely. Of course, it remains very attractive to assume that the consequences of playful activities are adaptive in many ways, but there are no robust and credible demonstrations of that in either humans or animals (Fagen 1981; Smith 1982). Once we have a clear understanding of basic play circuits in the mammalian brain, it may be possible to monitor the development of behavioral and social competence in animals deprived of normal activity in those circuits.

One psychobehavioral dimension that will deserve special attention in future work is the role of foraging-curiosity-investigatory circuits (e.g., Panksepp 1981b, 1986b) in playful activities. It has been quite common in the human literature to combine play and exploratory activities under the same general category (e.g., Weisler and McCall 1976; Welker 1971). This may be more problematic than is commonly realized. The mammalian brain probably contains distinct circuits for arousal of roughhousing types of social interaction and for arousal of exploratory/investigatory activities. These circuits may not always operate in synergistic ways. For instance, one highly effective way to reduce rough and tumble play in animals as well as humans (as indicated by the observation of "hyperkinetic" children) is to administer psychostimulants such as amphetamines which increase attention and investigatory activities, yet markedly diminish playfulness (Beatty, Dodge, Dodge, White, and Panksepp 1982). Although a definitive conclusion cannot yet be reached, such data raise the possibility that activities in the two systems are often antagonistic rather than synergistic. However, it should also be noted that certain manipulations, such as blockade of the alpha-2 noradrenergic receptor systems with idazoxan can increase both rough and tumble play and exploratory activities (Siviy, Atrens, and Menendez 1990). Since the exploratory urge seems to be triggered to a substantial extent by brain dopamine activity (which could be one of the sources of locomotor and manipulative/object play, Panksepp 1986b), it is of some interest to determine whether dopamine systems are aroused during the course of rough and tumble social play. To evaluate this, several years ago in my lab James Cox (1986) placed small amounts of the dopamine neurotoxin 6-hydroxydopamine into the nucleus accumbens at doses that did not debilitate the animal, but he did not observe any clear effect on play. In more recent work, Cox and I (unpublished data 1987) measured the levels of forebrain dopamine and DOPAC (the metabolite that is commonly taken to reflect impulse flow in dopamine systems of the brain, especially when it is related to levels of dopamine—i.e., the DOPAC/DA ratio). As can be seen in Figure 5.1, twenty minutes of rough and tumble play led to an apparent increase of utilization of dopamine in the brain (as indicated by dopamine levels, the DOPAC/DA ratio, but not DOPAC alone). This suggests that certain dopamine neurons may be especially active during play, which is not surprising from the perspective that brain dopamine controls psychomotor arousal and positive hedonic states (DePue and Iacono 1989; Panksepp 1986b; Wise and Rompre 1989). Of course, whether the same populations of dopamine neurons are active during the various forms of play and exploration will require a finer analysis of neural changes than has yet been conducted.

At present, it seems most reasonable to assume that basic exploratory and play circuits in the brain are distinct, and that they can operate both antagonistically and synergistically depending upon circumstances. However, there should be considerable concern in equating exploratory activities with play, even though both may yield positive hedonic tone in the nervous system. Perhaps vigorous activity of the exploratory/investigatory systems (e.g., the Behavioral Activation System of Gray [1990] and the "Expectancy System" of Panksepp [1982]) is the source process for what is typically called object or manipulative play. In any event, because of such concerns, it will be difficult to determine to what extent the massive child development literature on the effects of "play" reflects the functions of brain systems which actually control rough and tumble activities, as opposed to simply other desired activities, such as exploration. Surely these distinct processes should not be placed un-

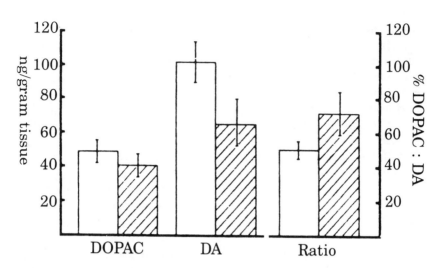

Figure 5.1. Frontal cortex (tissue anterior to the striatum) dopamine (DA) and dihydroxyphenylacetic acid (DOPAC) levels following twenty minutes of rough and tumble play in thirty–day old rats (Cox and Panksepp unpublished data). The levels of DOPAC were not different between groups, but DA was reliably reduces (t(12) = 2.10, p < .05), as was the traditional measure of DA utilization, the DOPAC/DA ratio (t(12) = 1.83, p < .05).

der the same construct of "play," especially since the exploratory system was probably designed to generate certain powerful forms of learning (Panksepp 1981b, 1986; Renner 1990). In sum, the position of this chapter is that there is presently an urgent need to determine what contributions to child development are in fact exerted by the rough and tumble play circuits of the brain. Since roughhousing play cannot be studied in a long-term and controlled fashion in human children, the use of animal models should be deemed invaluable in adjudicating this issue. It presently seems likely that in the existing play literature for human children, several distinct types of behavioral processes are included under an excessively broad conceptual umbrella. Perhaps this potential overgeneralization has resulted from the mystic appeal of the play concept for the post–World War II "cult-of-childhood" era of developmental psychology (Bettelheim 1987). In any event, I suspect that we cannot critically and definitively answer the question—what is the function of play?—without more intensive use of the available animal models in the behavioral brain research laboratory.

The Study of Ludic Processes in the Brains of Rodents

Despite the misgivings of behaviorism with central-state concepts such as play, it turns out that rough and tumble play is remarkably easy to operationalize and measure in animals (see Panksepp, Siviy, and Normansell 1984). When one puts several young rats together who have not been given an opportunity to play for several hours (by either individual housing or housing with a nonplayful adult), they promptly begin to exhibit vigorous chasing, pouncing, and wrestling with frequent rapid shifts in positions and "roles."

A remarkable amount of behavioral activity is exhibited during these play bouts, and a fine-grained analysis of the motor movements would be a herculean task. We have chosen to index the overall amount, intensity, and duration of play by utilization of various indicator variables, and after years of observation we have settled on the following: (1) The counting of the frequency of times that one animal touches the other animal on the dorsal surface with its two paws (play pouncing). We assume this measure reflects play solicitation and hence the appetitive phase of play. It is noteworthy that while the frequency of pinning can be markedly reduced by application of xylocaine subcutaneously to the anterior surface of a rat's back, such animals exhibit normal play motivation as indexed by dorsal contacts (Siviy and Panksepp 1987b). (2) The counting of the frequency and duration of pinning behavior where one animal ends up on its back (at least three limbs off the ground) with the other animal on top; we assume this measure to reflect some consummatory aspect of play (reflecting play dominance), because apparent play bouts are typically terminated by prolonged pins. It should be noted that we always include the very brief pins that occur in the midst of wrestling. We suspect that these short pins and the longer pins that tend to terminate play bouts can be usefully distinguished, but that would make any analysis substantially more difficult. (3) Finally, we measure the total amount of activity that is generated during play using a stabilimeter movement platform upon which the play chamber is situated. This measure yields on overall estimate of the amount of rough and tumble energy expended. In addition, there are many forms of chasing and pursuit that occur during play, which could be quantified, but those behaviors are more difficult to score accurately during on-line observation, and we are not formally evaluating those aspects of play. Although "playful" activity is assertive (and, as indicated before, some have even suggested it is juvenile aggression), we know from learning tests that both animals of a play pair find the activity to be a positive experience as indicated by their willingness to work for opportunities to indulge in such activities (Normansell and Panksepp 1990). If true aggression were involved, we would expect the "loser" to avoid situations in which such punishment occurs, and we would also expect the resident to typically prevail over the intruder. Neither prediction holds. Also, a recent formal analysis of the behavior sequences seen during aggression and play indicate that they are in fact quite distinct (Pellis and Pellis 1987). This does not mean that play cannot end up in some serious fighting, but whenever such a rare event transpires (at an increasing rate as animals, especially males, mature), playful social interactions promptly diminish.

How do we find where the ludic circuits are situated in the brain, and how can we most efficiently study their activity? Let me address the latter question first. Can we completely automate the measurement of play? I think we can objectively monitor the amount of play simply by measuring the total amount of kinetic energy expended during rough and tumble activities. Indeed, for the past few years we have done most of our observations of play on stabilimeter platforms, where the floor of the play arena is situated on a bar magnet located inside a coil, and the induced current can be used to drive counters which yield a direct measure of rough and tumble activity which correlates highly with the ethological measures of play described above. Alternatively, one could simply amplify the acoustic energy generated by animals bounding around the play chamber and probably get an equally efficacious automated measure of play. Of course, it would be ideal to actually get a measurement which could be translated directly into a measure of actual energy expended, but we have yet to implement that precise a measurement system. It is noteworthy that direct calorimetry in playing cats suggest that only about 4–9 percent of daily food energy consumption is expended in play (Martin 1982, 1984), and that hunger can markedly reduce play (Siviy and Panksepp 1985a).

Although we do not advocate that ethological measures should ever be neglected, let me summarize some of the data we have obtained with the automated inductance platforms which highlights the type of energy expenditure that is generated during play. Figure 5.2 summarizes minute by minute activity counts of pairs of animals on the play platform in fifteen pairs of thirty-eight–to forty–day-old juvenile rats who had been weaned and individually housed at twenty–three days of age and had been permitted five ten–minute play session in the boxes prior to the data which is summarized. The animals were tested in a counterbalanced manner under three conditions: (1) free play where both animals could do as they pleased with each other; (2) animals were on the same platform but physically separated by a solid partition placed diagonally across the 30 × 30 cm play area; and (3) animals were separated by the same type of partition that had a 17 × 13 cm wire mesh window separating the animals so they could detect each other better but could not physically interact. As is evident from the data (Figure 5.2), the testing condition had a very marked effect on activity, with a reliable effect of treatment (F (2,28) = 135.9, p < .0001) and time (F (9,126) = 4.13, p < .001) which reflect the decline in play as the session proceeded, as well as a time by groups interaction (F (18.252) = 6.04, p < .0001) which indicates that activity increased slightly during the session in which animals were not allowed to play while decreasing slightly in animals permitted free social interaction. The data highlight how powerful the effect of free social interaction is on an overall measure of ludic activity, and suggests that the play impulse is aborted almost completely in animals that are not allowed free physical interaction, although a marginal behavioral energization (an eagerness to interact?) is apparent if animals are permitted some sensory contact through a screen that precludes direct physical interaction.

In a follow-up experiment, one or both animals of each test pair were treated with 5 mg/kg of scopolamine hydrobromide, a drug which does not attenutate general activity when animals are tested alone but which totally eliminates playfulness as measured by pins and measures of play solicitation (Thor and Holloway 1984). As summarized in Figure 5.3, overall activity again distinguished groups clearly. When both animals had received scopolamine, rough and tumble activity was totally absent. When only one animal had the drug, playful activity was substantially elevated (reflecting the play solicitations of the normal animal) but it was not close to the activity generated by two playful animals. Since each animal of a play pair was treated on separate occasions, the data are summarized with the more active animals of each pair (High Ss) and the less active animals (Low Ss) presented separately. When one animal is scopolamine treated, there is no pinning at all. The undrugged animal continues to solicit play (accounting for practically all of the activity), but the drugged animal does not reciprocate. Thus, the motor activity under those conditions reflects play solicitations. It is

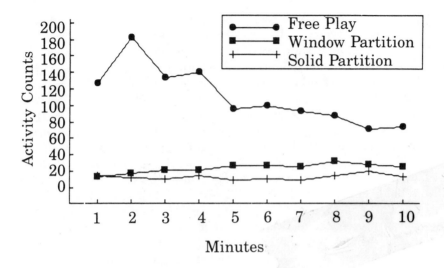

Figure 5.2. Minute-by-minute activity levels in pairs of animals allowed free play, or when they are separated either by solid partitions or ones with a screen window separating the animals. The partitions were placed diagonally across the square play chamber, with one animal on each side of the partition (Panksepp unpublished data 1986).

noteworthy that the amount of activity generated by "Low Ss" and "High Ss" combined was just about the same as the activity generated by two undrugged animals indulging in free play: Specifically, during the ten-minute play session, the average activity of controls was 99.5 counts / minute, while the High Ss were 51.1 and the Low Ss 30.9, yielding a sum of 82.0 for the pair. Apparently the animals of a play pair only potentiate each other's overall motor energization by approximately 20 percent when allowed full intraction. This pattern suggests that the overall amount of rough and tumble activity is essentially an additive reflection of the playful tendencies of the individual animals. This finding can be used as justification for analyzing the data of each animal separately during play periods as opposed to combining data from animals in each dyadic encounter.

However, since scopolamine-treated animals do show considerable locomotor activity, which could contribute to the overall activity counts, in a subsequent experiment on the same animals we evaluated playful activity of each animal in the presence of a totally immobile partner. Rigid immobility of target animals was achieved

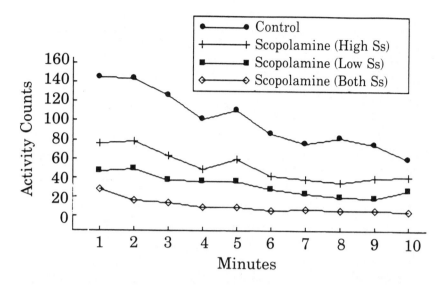

Figure 5.3. Minute-by-minute play activity levels in vehicle treated animals and when either one or both animals had been treated with 5 mg/kg of scopolamine twenty minutes before testing. Scopolamine animals are active but they do not reciprocate in response to play solicitations. "High" and "low" scores are for the single animal drug tests, with the more and less active animals of each pair averaged separately (Panksepp unpublished data 1986).

by administration of the powerful opiate oxymorphone given at 10 mg/kg to yield a state of catatonic waxy-flexibility. Animals treated in this way will remain immobile in most any posture in which they are placed for hours on end (as is verified by the zero stabilimeter activity counts when both subjects were drug treated, Figure 5.4). Using this approach, the results were less additive. During the first half of the session the individual play solicitation scores summed to only about half the activity levels observed when both animals were exhibiting free reciprocal play. Only during the second half of the session did the scores approach additivity. This suggests that the mere presence of nonplayful locomotor activity (as is present in scopolamine animals) yields some social infectiousness in the free-play situation. In any event, it seems clear from the above results that playful tendencies can be readily monitored using automated procedures, and such activity scores correlate highly (greater than 0.8) with pinning and play solicitation measures. Although dissociations between the measures can also be produced (e.g., xylocaine treated

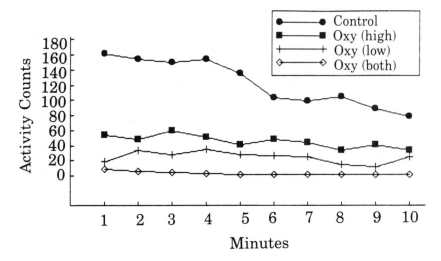

Figure 5.4. Minute-by-minute play activity levels in vehicle treated animals and those treated with 10 mg/kg oxymorphone. Data were handled as described in Figure 5.3 (Panksepp unpublished data 1986).

animals solicit a lot but exhibit markedly diminished pinning—Siviy and Panksepp 1987b) we suspect that those dissociations do not reflect anything profound about the underlying executive systems (e.g., play consummation may be aborted because the efficacy of a critical input system has been inhibited).

Now to the other question posed above: How shall we determine where play circuits are located in the brain? How are we to implement the abundant neuroscience technologies when animals are in the midst of such robust physical activities? It is hard to imagine that recording of electrical activity of the brain can be conducted accurately when animals are exhibiting flurries of intense ludic activity. We have tried radioactive 2-deoxyglucose functional mapping studies, but nothing clear has emerged. Subtractive autoradiography studies suggest brain opioid activity is enhanced throughout the brain, with perhaps the greatest activity in the preoptic area which is known to participate in sexual and other social behaviors (Panksepp and Bishop 1981; Panksepp 1981c). Pharmacological approaches could be used (as reviewed elsewhere—Panksepp, Siviy and Normansell 1984, Panksepp, Normansell, Cox, Crepeau and Sacks 1987; Thor and Holloway 1984a) but those maneuvers cannot be used to localize circuits. Perhaps the brain lesion approach, problematic as it is for unambiguous interpretations, may be the most workable way to approach the issue of circuit localization.

We have pursued the lesion approach in conjunction with an analysis of the sensory systems which control play. Past work has indicated rats play essentially normally even though they can't see or smell. Although hearing may have some modest facilitating effect (Hagemeyer and Panksepp 1988), our most comprehensive analysis suggests that normal touch is especially important for the normal elaboration of play (Siviy and Panksepp 1987a,b). Sensations from the anterior dorsal surface of the animal appear to be critical for elaboration of pinning, which has led us to believe that mammals may have specific play-skin trigger zones on their bodies (which, may be homologous to the "tickling-skin" around the thoracic cage in humans). In any event, we have systematically lesioned various areas of the somatosensory system, and the data suggest that the nonspecific somatosensory projection areas of posterior thalamus and parafascicular area may be important for receiving playful signals (Siviy and Panksepp 1985, 1987). Various behavioral control studies suggest the observed play deficits are behaviorally specific. Having identified one area of the brain which may contain true play circuitry makes the further analysis of the system a bit easier. By analyzing the anterograde and retrograde connectivities of the parafascicular area we should be able to generate a set of candidates for some of the major relay stations of play circuitry. Finally, it is worth indicating that recent functional neuroanatomical techniques such as those which can visualize oncogene expression in the brain (e.g., *c-fos*, see Sudol 1988) may be capable of highlighting play-related activity changes in the brain. Once the broad anatomical and neurochemical outlines of play circuits have been identified, we will be in a better position to ask definitive questions concerning the functions of play.

On the Short- and Long-Term Regulation of Play

Although there is not sufficient space here to discuss the relevant data in detail, the evidence indicates that play is a regulated process, both in the short-term, as well as the life span (Panksepp et al. 1984). Namely, the amount of play generated within short sessions can be markedly increased by social deprivation (as well as specific play deprivation, where juveniles are housed with nonludic adults) and diminished by prior social interaction. Indeed, play satiation can be induced manually by the experimenter if they simulate playful activities—dorsal contacts with some pins (Panksepp and Normansell unpublished data 1984). Also, there is evidence for long-term regulation of play. Animals exhibit more play later in life if they have been deprived of play during early life. Finally, there is every indication that roughhousing play is an instinctual process that requires no apparent learning on the part of the animal (Panksepp 1981a). Indeed in our most recent test of the proposition that play is almost totally instinctive, animals which were weaned very early in life when their eyes are just opening and the first glimmers of roughhousing play are evident (fifteen days), exhibited higher levels of play than animals housed socially until later weaning at twenty-four days of age (Ikemoto 1990).

Is there a natural time to play during the life span and during the day? Developmentally, the answer is evident: There are clear ontogenetic patterns in various species, with play peaking during the midjuvenile phase of development (Barrett and Bateson 1978; Panksepp 1981; Thor and Holloway 1984b; Welker 1971). However, circadian variability has been less well studied. In socially deprived animals tested for brief periods, there does not appear to be a clear circadian effect (Panksepp et al. 1984). However, animals in the wild have been observed to exhibit two distinct periods of high play—early morning and during the evening prior to retiring (e.g., see Strum 1987 for baboon observations and MacDonald 1980 for wolves). Also, it is a common experience that human children are often hard to put to bed because of elevated playfulness before retiring (a phenomenon which may have helped give arise to many a bedtime ritual). Since visual observation of animals around the clock is tedious, we decided to monitor the circadian changes in play using the activity platforms described previously. Figure 5.5 summarizes twenty-four-hour activity data in pair-housed rats, and it was evident that rats also exhibit two distinct periods of high play near the light transitions.

Sex Differences in Play

It is commonly believed that males exhibit more rough and tumble play than females, and this has been documented using a variety of observational procedures in a variety of species (for review see Meaney, Stewart, and Beatty 1985). Indeed, Meaney (1988) has summarized the possible hormonal mechanisms which mediate the

Circadian Cycles of Juvenile Rat Play

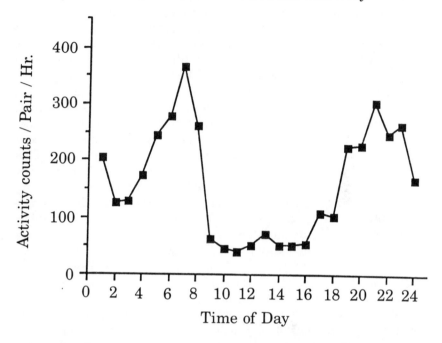

Figure 5.5. Twenty-four successive hourly activity recording in pairs of juvenile rats. The peaks correspond to high play phases during the day. The animals were tested in continuous light, but the peaks correspond to the approximate times for transitions of the lighting cycle from the previous housing conditions, with the first peak corresponding to the shift from night to day, and the second from day to night (Crepeau and Panksepp unpublished data 1988).

apparent differences between the social play of males and females in various mammals, especially rats. Because of the abundance of published evidence, I am loathe to challenge the credibility of the reported effect. However, I must say that in ten years of rather intensive and systematic study of social play in rats (of several thousand pairs of rats), we have never observed a robust difference in the amount of play between male and female rats. Hence, I suspect that the reported effect is more apparent than real—the heightened play in males may be due to some sex difference other than the vigor and character of neuronal activity within the play circuits of the brain.

Why are there such inconsistencies in the literature? Part of the problem may be in the two distinct methodologies that are presently used to study rodent play. At the start of the modern era of systematic research into rodent play about a dozen years ago, two approaches were taken to the question. One uses more naturalistic circumstances where animals are studied in their normal home cage social environments and one of the main dependent measures is the frequency and duration of "play bouts." Using observational techniques employed by ethologists studying animals in the wild, the investigators typically focus their attention successively on specific target animals to the exclusion of the others who are simultaneously present on the playing field (Poole and Fish 1975). This so-called "focal-observation" procedure is the one which Meaney and Stewart have routinely employed in their work documenting sex differences in rodent play. The other approach, the "paired-encounter" technique, which we developed and routinely employ, was premised on the supposition that it would be experimentally ideal to minimize as many potential confounding variables as possible within the testing procedures (Panksepp and Beatty 1980; Panksepp 1981a). In this approach, pairs of animals are observed continuously in a neutral test arena for relatively short measurement periods. This procedure was facilitated by our early observation that emission of play behavior is intensified markedly by prior social as well as specific play deprivation. As indicated before, instead of measuring "play bouts" we routinely use three well-operationalized indices of play activity—pins, dorsal contacts, and the automated measure of rough and tumble activity. To minimize extraneous influences, the play chamber is situated inside a sound-dampened outer chamber (observations being made on-line via a porthole); background masking sound is provided by a circulation fan; and typically animals have nothing else in the test chamber except for some bedding on the floor. In the more ethological "focal-observation" situation that Meaney and Stewart employ, not only are there many other animals in the immediate test chamber (males mixed with females) but there are also the potential distractions of ever-present food and water, minor noises and odors from the attending experimenter, and animals in nearby cages. Hence there are more sources for potential variance, and systematic bias could yield behavioral differences which do not reflect real sex differences in play temperament.

While sex differences in play are observed with the "focal-observation" procedure, none have yet been reported with the "paired-encounter" procedure. Why? Although the issue remains experimentally unresolved, it is noteworthy that in different experiments from a single lab, sex differences have been found with the "focal-observation" procedure (Thor and Holloway 1983), but not with the "paired-encounter" procedure (1984c). Accordingly, the reported sex difference may be due more to situational variables which characterize the focal-observation procedure rather than to intrinsic sex differences in play circuits. For instance, female rats, as a population, weigh less than males (Nance 1976), and hence they may simply play less in social housing situations because they have failed to prevail over the heavier males in past encounters. Their lower play could be due to learned wariness. Even with body weight equated, differential social-reinforcement histories may arise from differential strength, speed, motor skills, and other subtle attributes (e.g., nonplayful, emotional tendencies) which dictate who does what to whom in social encounters. Beside the obvious differential social-reinforcement histories which are bound to emerge when animals are allowed to live in complex social environments, the focal-observation testing procedure also increases the potential influence of other intrusive variables. Females may be more responsive and distractible to the various auditory stimuli which are normally present in animal colony rooms. Indeed, only in classroom laboratory situations where there are many extraneous noises during behavioral observations have I ever found male rats to play more than females. Alternatively, the experimenter observing animals in a colony room may be viewed as a potential threat. Recent work has raised the issue that observational studies may be influenced by a "human-predator" effect (Renner, Prierre, and Schilcher 1990), and it is possible that females are more emotionally affected by this. Females rats may be more prone to fear, as indicated by their faster acquisition of conditioned shock-avoidance behaviors (Beatty 1979). Indeed, a remarkable number of sex differences in nonplayful behavioral tendencies have been documented in rats (Beatty 1979). Thus, we must at least entertain the possibility that the reported sex effects in play are secondary consequences of nonludic sex differences. Although real sex differences in playfulness may well exist, in my estimation, the existence of such an effect remains to be demonstrated in a credible manner, and hence it is premature to argue that real sex differences exist in the brain circuitries of play.

Conversely, perhaps the fault is with the "paired-encounter" methodology. It is possible that a "real" sex difference in play disappears only because of the extremely high play levels typically evoked by prior social deprivation. This possibility is not very likely since we have observed no sex effect under milder deprivation conditions where there is plenty of room for increments to be observed. Indeed, I would note that under certain circumstances, females appear to play somewhat more than males. In unpublished work we have observed that during the weeks following puberty, play declines more in males than females, perhaps because the heightened levels of testosterone in males eventually tend to counteract playful impulses. Indeed, in our experience, high doses of testosterone (1 mg/day) reliably reduced play in both male and female rats, apparently because of heightened irritability.

In sum, our best guess is that the sex differences that have been observed with the focal-observation procedure are due to the biasing effects of differential social-reinforcement histories, especially the potential effect of heavy body weights in males leading to more social punishment of females housed continuously in social circumstances. In affirmation of this possibility, in unpublished work, we have observed that sex effects in play dominance (males prevailing) are quite evident when males and females are housed together (permitting social reinforcement confoundings to emerge) but is not evident when animals are weight-matched and housed in isolation except for the daily play periods. In this context, it is noteworthy that early neonatal androgenization, which has been reported to increase play in females with the focal observation procedure (Beatty, Dodge, Traylor, and Meaney 1981), also increases body weights (Nance 1976). In our experience, such manipulations do not facilitate play in the paired-encounter procedure. Although the organizational and activational role of hormones in controlling play behavior remains an intriguing question, there is presently no credible evidence that sex hormones have a specific organizational effect on play circuitry of rats. Indeed, it should be noted that the supposedly robust sex difference in human play is practically nonexistent when observations are conducted in circumstances where pressures for stereotyped sex role identification are minimal (Hamer and Missakian 1978).

Maternal Factors and Play

Although we have not conducted a formal analysis of the issue, our impression from years of research is that after puberty, females tend to remain more playful than males. This would be reasonable if mothers eventually exert an important facilitory influence on the play activities of their offspring, while males, who make a comparatively small contribution to parenting in most mammals, do not. Indeed, our preliminary work suggests that high titers of estrogen are compatible with (and may even facilitate) the emission of play, although progesterone reduces play (Birke and Sadler 1983) perhaps because of its sedative effects. Indeed, it is noteworthy that aspects of female sexual proceptivity resemble playfulness—including hopping and darting movements which resemble those seen in play.

Although there are occasional descriptions of mother-child play in the animal ethology literature (for review see Fagen 1981, pp. 442–45), there is only modest systematic work on the role of maternal influences on play. One curious finding is that pharmacological inhibition of lactation in a mother cat can increase object play in the kittens (Bateson, Martin, and Young 1981). The classic primate work is that social and maternal isolation produces despair and thereby reduces social play dramatically (Harlow, Dodsworth, and Harlow 1965). Janus (1987) has recently reported a similar effect, in that rats prematurely separated from their mothers (day fifteen) exhibited deficient dominance (as measured by being pinned longer) when compared to animals weaned at a later age (thirty days). Unfortunately, in that work the maternal influence was confounded with the social presence of other pups. Also, fast pins which occur in the midst of wrestling were not counted, which may preclude any definitive conclusions concerning the overall level of playfulness of the early-weaned animals. In my lab, Ikemoto (1990) has reanalyzed the effects of early weaning (fifteen days). Contrary to the trends reported by Janus using long pins, Ikemoto, who measured all pins, long as well as short, found that early-weaned animals are more playful than either peer housed or family housed animals. There was no difference between peer and family reared animals suggesting no major maternal influence that was carried over from preweaning housing conditions.

Since so little experimental evaluation of maternal influence has been conducted so far, I decided to do a series of preliminary studies to determine if cohabitation with the mother affects play dominance in male offspring. In this "mama's boy" series of experiments, two basic questions were asked. In the first, I simply determined whether a male allowed to continue living with the mother at normal weaning age (twenty-one to twenty-three days of age) exhibited any differences in play when paired with a weight-matched brother who was rehoused alone in a cage of similar construction. Animals were tested for seven successive days, starting twenty-four hours following the rehousing experience.

As summarized in Figure 5.6, in the eight pairs tested, the isolated pups exhibited essentially identical levels of pinning behavior as brothers kept with their mothers $(F\ (1,42) = .44)$. However, across the week of testing, the animals housed with the mothers did exhibit longer pin durations $(F\ (1,42) = 19.57,\ p < .005)$, even though on several days this effect was not evident. The most striking trend was in the number of dorsal contacts (i.e., play solicitations), with socially isolated animals exhibiting more than twice as many instances as the "mama's boys." This effect lasted for the duration of testing. Considering that both types of animals exhibited essentially the same level of pinning, this pattern of results could be taken to suggest that the presence of mothers made animals more effective players (i.e., they exhibited more consummatory aspects of play [pins] per solication [dorsal contacts]). However, it should also be noted that the above effects need not be a maternal effect at all but simply a generalized consequence of social housing. Indeed, in follow-up control experiments, we have found very similar patterns of decreased solicitations in animals housed with a littermate companion playing with isolate-housed animals.

In any event, after the above phase, I isolated the mama's boy's (as well as the mothers), and when the pups were fifty-four days of age, I evaluated the amount of play animals directed toward the mothers or toward nulliparous strange females of the same age (which had comparable prior social histories, including sexual and juvenile playful encounters, but without impregnation). The results were provocative: the juveniles exhibited the same number of dorsal contacts toward both females (while the females exhibited practically no solications), but the mothers allowed themselves to be pinned more than twice as frequently $(\overline{X} = 5.7)$ than the strange females $(\overline{X} = 2.3)$ $(t(22) = 2.06\ p < .05)$. All this is even more remarkable since at the age of testing the females were twice as heavy as the juveniles. The mothers pinned their pups fewer times $(\overline{X} = 2.6)$ than did the strangers $(\overline{X} = 4.7)$, but this trend was not statistically reliable $(t(22) = 1.53)$. There were no such differences

Figure 5.6. Play behaviors between weight-matched male littermates. One animal was housed with the mother throughout testing (mama's boy). The other was housed alone. All play tests were five minutes in duration (Panksepp unpublished data 1990).

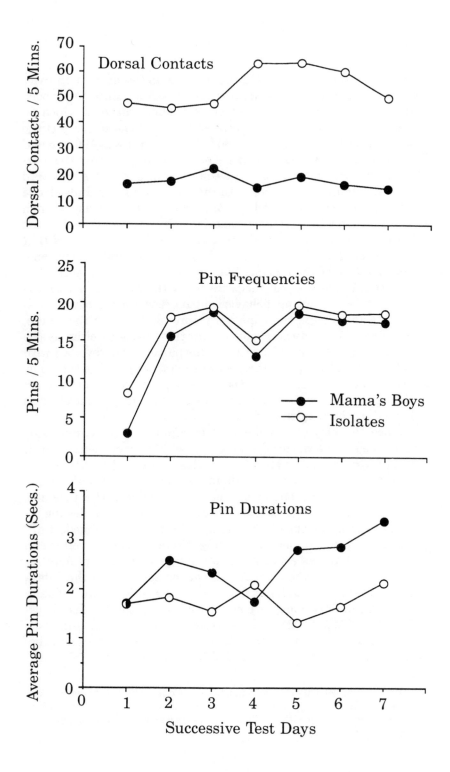

in dorsal contacts, but overall, the pups exhibited more than twice as many soliciations as the mature females. Also, since the experiment was run blind—the observers not being informed which females were the mothers—I evaluated how well the identity of the mother could be accurately guessed. The hit rate was 100 percent! The judgment appeared to be based on the perception that the overall type of social interaction between pups and mothers appeared "friendlier" than interactions with the strange females. Indeed, one incidental observation which needs to be quantified was the high frequency with which females (especially the strangers) pushed the soliciting juveniles away with their hind legs. It also seemed that the pups recognized their mothers, since they exhibited more anogenital sniffing of their moms than of the strangers—a gesture of recognition which was not reciprocated by the mothers. There was practically no mounting behavior during the course of the five-minute tests. In sum, the pups were more playful than the adults, and the pups pinned their moms more than twice as often as the moms pinned the pups. If anything, this pattern was reversed with the strangers. Thus, while there was no evidence that the rat moms actively solicited social interaction, they were more receptive when it did occur, and were apparently willing to handicap themselves as indicated by the incidence of pins.

Since the play effects depicted in Figure 5.6 appeared to be largely due to general social effects, in a second experiment we evaluated play differences between juveniles housed with their mothers, and weight-matched brothers housed with a nulliparous strangers of comparable nonmaternal experience. The juveniles were tested for ten consecutive days starting two days following rehousing. As summarized in Figure 5.7, there were only modest differences between groups. For pinning, there was no overall group effect, but there was a marginal ($p = .06$) elevation of pinning by the "mama's boys" when the data from the second and third days were combined ($p < .05$), but not when the days were individually compared. Pin durations were slightly higher in the "mama's boys" ($F(1,54) = 2.53$, $p < .02$), and the reliable days by groups interaction ($F(9,54) = 2.77$, $p < .01$) was due to reliable differences between groups on the second and third days of testing (p's $< .01$,

Figure 5.7.   Play behaviors between weight-matched male littermates for ten successive days. One pup was housed with the mother throughout testing (mama's boy) and the other was housed with a nulliparous strange female (Panksepp unpublished data 1990).

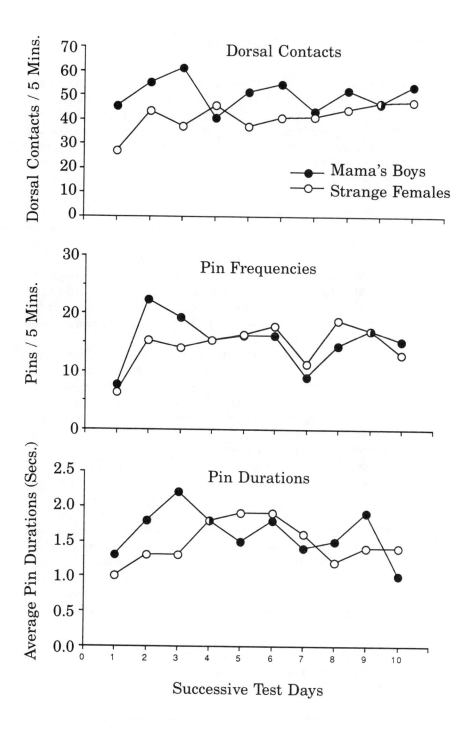

Dorsal Contacts

● Mama's Boys
○ Strange Females

Pin Frequencies

Pin Durations

Successive Test Days

Newman Keuls test). Analysis of dorsal contacts indicated a slight
elevation in the "mama's boys," but the overall effect was not reliable (F(1.54) = 2.04) nor was the days by groups interaction, even
though a suggestive trend was evident during the first three days of
testing. Following the initial ten days of testing, animals were continued for another three days with conditions reversed (i.e., the mama's boys were housed with the strange females, and their brothers
were rehoused with their mothers). On observation, this yielded a
slight elevation of pinning by the pups reunited with their mothers,
a decrease in pin durations of the pups placed with the strange females, and no reliable change in dorsal contacts. At the end of these
initial tests, each pup was also tested with the mother and the
strange female during separate five-minute tests. Although the
pups did not exhibit different levels of dorsal contacts directed to
the moms ($\bar{X} = 43$) than to the strangers ($\bar{X} = 39$), the mothers
again were pinned more (3.6 times) than were the strange females
(1.3 times / 5 min., F(1,15) = 4.92, p < .05).

In sum, these experiments suggest that male rats living with
their mother have a marginal play dominance advantage over
brothers living in isolation or those living with strange females. The
former effect is largely due to the effect of social presence rather
than a true maternal effect, while the latter seems to be due to maternal presence. These effects may reflect the willingness of mothers to respond to the playful overtures of their offspring, but from
the present data we do not know whether mothers will exert this
effect only on their own pups or whether they would also exert similar influences on strange pups. The effect, albeit small, was present
in both experiments, and it could be important in the acquisition of
future social dominance by the offspring. That maternal dominance
can be conferred to offspring has been observed in primate societies
(Goodall 1986), and presumably this effect could be conferred to offspring not only by the mother's direct interaction with others in the
social group, but also by the quality and quantity of play interaction
directed at the offspring. These issues will have to be resolved by
future research.

That primate mothers do have an input into the playful inter-
actions of their offspring has been noted by others (e.g., Strum 1987;
Symons 1978). For instance, in her analysis of chimpanzee societies,
Goodall (1986, p. 369) noted that:

> A chimpanzee infant has his first experience of social play from his
> mother as, very gently, she tickles him with her fingers or with lit-

tle nibbling, nuzzling movements of her jaws. Initially these bouts are brief, but by the time the infant is six months old and begins to respond to her with play face and laughing, the bouts become longer. Mother-offspring play is common throughout infancy, and some females frequently play with juveniles, adolescents, or even adult offspring.

To determine whether these maternal effects have some decisive influence over the future competence of the child, effective laboratory models of maternal influence will need to be developed. The rodent model described above exhibits some promise, but more work is needed before its utility and overall reliability will be established. Also, before we can evaluate the role of maternal play on the development of behavioral competence, we need to know more about the basic role of rough and tumble play in the genesis of adaptive behavioral competence. At present there are many theories, but few definitive facts.

Functions of Brain Play Circuits

The possible functions of play have been extensively discussed, and the major types of benefits that have been suggested include increased physical fitness, the learning of competitive social skills, the learning of predatory and predator-avoidance skills, the learning of various noncompetitive social skills (including facilitation of social bonding, establishment of social rank, learning of social communication, and other complex social skills), and the learning of cognitive skills (including tool use, generalized cognitive skills, and innovative skills) (see Fagen 1981; Smith 1982; Symons 1978). Perhaps the collective wisdom has been best summarized in a quote to be found on the instruction sheet to Lego [R] toys:

> When children play, they exercise their sense, their intellect, their emotions, their imagination—keenly and energetically . . . to play is to explore, to discover and to experiment. Playing helps children develop ideas and gain experience. It gives them a wealth of knowledge and information about the world in which they live—and about themselves. So to play is also to learn. Play is fun for children. But it's much more than that—it's good for them, and it's necessary . . . play gives children the opportunity to develop and use the many talents they were born with.

The most straightforward perspective is that during play natural (unconditional) behavioral potentials of the brain are exercised. However, in addition to the relatively obvious functional hypotheses that have been generated, all of which remain without substantive empirical support, it is to be expected that play may have some coherent function which is congruent with only certain aspects of brain organization. One possibility is that play may serve to exercise and extend the range of behavioral options which are under the executive control of inborn emotional systems of the brain (Panksepp 1986). It is obvious how such a function may be further enhanced by parental influences. In this view, play may serve an orthogonal function to REM sleep: Namely, REM may exercise the affective information organizing potentials of emotional circuits while play exercises the emotive behavioral potentials of these circuits in the relative emotional safety of a positive affective state. Thus, there could be as many subtypes of play as there are primary emotional systems in the brain.

From this perspective, it would seem probable that play may have direct trophic effects on neuronal and synaptic growth in many systems of the brain. Although the evidence is modest, environmental enrichment, including social dimensions, has been well studied (see Greenough and Bailey 1988; Sirevaag and Greenough 1988), and there is some evidence that the observed social effects are due to rough and tumble play. Neuronal effects of social enrichment (increased brain RNA and heavier cortices) can be observed after as little as ten minutes of exposure for four days during sensitive periods of juvenile development (Ferchmin and Eterović 1986). Other basic hypotheses concerning play which deserve more experimental attention are the possibilities that play is a "neuro-tonic" which can have antistress, health-promoting effects. Recently, Loring Crepeau (1989) evaluated this possibility in his doctoral disseration (via analysis of corticosterone secrection to mild stress in play versus nonplay experienced animals). Unfortunately he found no evidence to support that hypothesis. One could also generate a variety of more specific fitness-promoting effects that may be enhanced by rough and tumble play, such as innoculation against social stress in future adult competitive encounters or perhaps the facilitation of social attractiveness so that reproductive potential is enhanced. It almost goes without saying that play must increase reproductive fitness in some way, but it should be noted that sexual-type behaviors are very infrequent during the course of rough and tumble play. Indeed, in unpublished work, we have been unable to find any evidence that male rats which had been socially deprived during the whole juvenile period exhibited any deficiency at maturity in the latency and onset of sexual behaviors toward hormone primed females. The only reasonably well-documented beneficial effects from the rodent behavioral literature are mild increases in problem-solving ability in rats (Einon, Morgan, and Kibbler 1978), but we have not been able to replicate that effect. Although systematic work in the area is still in its infancy, there seems to be a growing consensus that play is not superfluous, and that some distinct adaptive function should be capable of being demonstrated in a reasonably rigorous fashion. If play proves to be more than just a brain mechanism for generating fun, then it will be important to try to neuropharmacologically unlock the door to increased playfulness for various beneficial, therapeutic, and growth effects. At present, playfulness can only be induced by appropriate types of social interactions, but if play circuits do exist in the brain, then they should be capable of being aroused pharmacologically.

In Search of the Ludic Cocktail

Clearly, the neuronal impulse to play increases during early childhood, and diminishes markedly as children pass through puberty into early adulthood. Since the period of childhood is greatly extended in humans compared to other mammals including the other great apes (perhaps via genetic regulatory influences which have promoted "neoteny"), the play impulse of adult humans may also remain somewhat stronger throughout the life span than it does in other mammals. Presumably, the intensity of playfulness can change as a function of some aspect of parenthood, especially one would think, motherhood. Generally, parents seem to be more playful than nonparents, and it is reasonable to suppose that this tendency is promoted by neurobiological vectors. It is noteworthy that motherhood does arouse certain neurochemical systems of the brain (e.g., oxytocin gene expression is increased) which promote parenting behavior (Jirikowski et al. 1989; Pedersen, Asher, Monroe, and Prange 1985; Wamboldt and Insel 1987). It is also worth considering whether similar types of neurochemical changes might occur in play circuits as a function of certain stages of parenthood. Within the present context, I would only note that in preliminary work on the effects of intraventricular injections of oxytocin on play, we have observed only reductions, and no increases at any dose tested (1.0 −0.01 ug administered to the third ventricle region).

Unfortunately, we cannot yet speculate what the nature of such sensitization might look like. At present, we really do not know anything substantive about the executive infrastructure of the basic roughhousing circuits of the mammalian brain. All we presently have is an abundance of neuropharmacological data which suggest a variety of modulatory influences on play circuitry (Panksepp et al. 1987) and some types of brain lesions that tend to reduce play in a specific way (e.g., damage to the parafascicular area, Siviy and Panksepp 1987a). About a decade ago, we took some of the more suggestive items from the list of available pharmacological manipulations (i.e., those that seemed to mildly promote play) to see if we could generate some combinations that would facilitate play in a vigorous fashion. Namely, we were hoping to find a "ludic cocktail" that might resurrect high levels of juvenile playfulness in older animals. The items selected were three pharmacological manipulations which appeared to promote play (albeit, to a very mild degree). They were opiate receptor agonists (e.g., morphine), serotonin antagonists (e.g., methysergide), and a dopamine agonist (apomorphine, given at a very low dose which may activate postsynaptic as opposed to presynaptic auto-receptors). These drugs were given in all possible permuatations (two to three drugs concurrently), using various levels of social deprivation that should have allowed one to see both increases and decreases in play. This initial effort was eminently unsuccessful. No combination of drugs seemed to uniquely potentiate play, and each of the agents alone was at best, marginally effective. Parenthetically, in recent work we have found that the ability of morphine to increase play (Panksepp et al., Jalowiec, DeEskinazi and Bishop 1985) is only clear when baseline levels are reduced by external threat (e.g., cat smell or cues which signal shock). We still hold out the hope that eventually a neurochemical manipulation will be found which can free ludic activity from the inhibitory influences which accompany adulthood, but that may be a vain hope. It is possible that age-related decrements in play emerge from a diminished vigor of the underlying play circuits rather than a diminished availability of "play transmitters." If that is the case, then it will be unlikely that a "ludic cocktail" can ever be generated.

In Summary

At present we know little about the primal nature of the underlying neural circuits which induce animals to play. We assume the behavior is driven by endogenous pacemaker circuits which generate intense "ludic impulses" in the brain which lead young animals and children to "jump with joy and excitement" yielding infectious playful states in nearby conspecifics. The central states aroused in this way recruit a variety of sensory, motor, and emotional systems in the brain, allowing organisms to exercise and experience the potentials of the innate circuit functions with which they were born. A great deal of research remains to be done in this underdeveloped area of behavioral neuroscience before we can say anything definitive about the functions of play. To achieve this goal, more basic research on animal models will be essential. Only when we have established a solid foundation of knowledge about the basic aspects of play will we be able to evaluate the role of parental influences on the various expressions of the underlying systems in a definitive fashion.

Perhaps excessive expectations have been generated concerning the possible long-term functions of play. It is worth considering that the main adaptive function of play may simply be the generation of positive emotional states. In such states, animals may be more willing and more likely to behave in flexible and creative ways. If this is so, then one application of play interventions in educational settings should not simply be attempts to facilitate more efficient acquisition of new information, but also as a reinforcement for good behavior. One of the most definitive psychological aspects of rough and tumble play is that it is great fun for all participants. To what extent would children be willing to discipline themselves with educational tasks, if the availability of roughhousing play were made contingent on good academic performance. I suspect the benefits, both for classroom discipline and educational progress, might be substantial. But this would require us to begin viewing this ancient evolutionary function of the brain as a potentially desirable ingredient for facilitating educational goals, rather than a disruptive force whose energies need to be dissipated on the playground before the earnest business of education can proceed.

References

Barrett, P., and Bateson, P. (1978). The development of play in cats. *Behaviour* 66:105–20.

Bateson, P.; Martin, P.; and Young, M. (1981). Effects of interrupting cat mothers' lactation with bromocriptine on the subsequent play of their kittens. *Physiology and Behavior* 27:841–45.

Beatty, W. W. (1979). Gonadal hormones and sex differences in nonreproductive behaviors in rodents: Organizational and activational influences. *Hormones and Behavior* 12:112–63.

Beatty, W. W.; Dodge, A. M.; Traylor, K. L.; and Meaney, M. J. (1981). Temporal boundary of the sensitive period for hormonal organization of social play in juvenile rats. *Physiology and Behavior* 26:241–43.

Beatty, W. W.; Dodge, A. M.; Dodge, L. J.; White, K.; and Panksepp, J. (1982). Psychomotor stimulants, social deprivation and play in juvenile rats. *Pharmacology Biochemistry and Behavior,* 16:417–422.

Bettelheim, B. (1987, March). The importance of play. *The Atlantic Monthly:*35–46.

Birke, L. I. A., and Sadler, D. (1983). Progestin-induced changes in play behaviour of the prepubertal rats. *Physiology and Behavior* 30:341–47.

Bunge, M. (1990). What kind of discipline is psychology: autonomous or dependent, humanistic or scientific, biological or sociological? *New Ideas in Psychology* 8, In Press.

Caro, T. M. (1985) Sex differences in the termination of social play in cats. *Animal Behavior* 29:271–79.

Christie, J. F., and Johnsen, E. P. (1983). The role of play in social-intellectual development. *Review of Educational Research* 53: 93–115.

Cox, J. and Panksepp, J. (1987). Brain dopamine levels and metabolites following bouts of rough-and-tumble play. Unpublished data.

Cox, J. F. (1986). Catecholamine control of social play: Mechanisms of amphetamine suppression of play. Unpublished Master's Thesis, Bowling Green State University, Bowling Green, Ohio.

Crepeau, L. J. (1989) The interactive influences of early handling, prior play exposure, acute stress, and sex on play behavior, exploration, and H-P-A reactivity in juvenile rats. Unpublished doctoral dissertation, Bowling Green State University.

Depue, R. A., and Iacono, W. G. (1989). Neurobehavioral aspects of affective disorders. *Annual Review of Psychology* 40:457–92.

Einon, F. D.; Morgan, J. M.; and Kibbler, C. C. (1978). Brief periods of socialization and later behavior in the rat. *Developmental Psychobiology* 11:213–25.

Fagen, R. (1981). *Animal Play Behavior.* New York: Oxford University Press.

Ferchmin, P. A., and Eterović, V. A. (1986). Forty minutes of experience increases the weight and RNA content of cerebral cortex in periadolescent rats. *Developmental Psychobiology* 19:1–19.

Goodall, J. (1986). *The Chimpanzees of Gombe, Patterns of Behavior.* Cambridge: Harvard University Press.

Gray, J. A. (1987). *The Psychology of Fear and Stress.* Cambridge: Cambridge University Press.

Gray, J. A. (1990). Brain systems that mediate both emotion and cognition. In *Cognition and Emotion,* in press.

Greenough, W. T., and Bailey, C. H. (1988). The anatomy of a memory: Convergence of results across a diversity of tests. *Trends in Neuroscience* 11:142–47.

Hagemeyer, J. A., and Panksepp, J. (1988). An attempt to evaluate the role of hearing in the social play of juvenile rats. *Bulletin of the Psychonomic Society* 26:455–58.

Hamer, K. H., and Missakian, E. (1978). A longitudinal study of social play in synanon/peer-reared children. In E.O. Smith (ed.) *Social Play in Primates.* New York: Academic Press.

Harlow, H. F.; Dodsworth, R. O.; and Harlow, M. K. (1985). Total social isolation in monkeys. *Proceedings of the National Academy of Sciences* 54:90–96.

Humphreys, A. P., and Einon, D. F. (1981). Play as a reinforcer for maze-learning in juvenile rats. *Animal Behavior* 29:259–70.

Humphreys, A. P. and Smith, P. K. (1984). Rough-and-tumble in preschool and playground. In P. K. Smith (Ed.), *Play in Animals and Humans,* Oxford: Blackwell.

Ikemoto, S. (1990). The effects of early social isolation on play behavior in juvenile rats. Unpublished Master's Thesis, Bowling Green State University, Bowling Green, Ohio.

Jalowiec, J.; Panksepp, J.; and Nelson, E. (1989). Effects of fluprazine and eltroprazine on rough-and-tumble play in juvenile rats. Unpublished data.

Janus, K. (1987). Early separation of young rats from the mother and the development of play fighting. *Physiology and Behavior* 39:471–76.

Jirikowski, G. F.; Caldwell, J. D.; Pilgrim, C.; Stumpf, W. E.; and Pedersen, C. A. (1989). Changes in immunostaining for oxytocin in the forebrain of the female rat during late pregnancy, parturition and early lactation. *Cell and Tissue Research* 256:411–17.

Johnson, E. E.; Christie, J. F.; and Yawkey, T. D. (1987). *Play and Early Childhood Development.* Glenview, Ill.: Scott Foresman.

MacDonald, K. B. (1980). Activity patterns in a captive wolf pack. *Carnivore,* 2:62–64.

Martin, P. (1982). The energy cost of play: Definition and estimation. *Animal Behavior* 30:294–95.

Martin, P. (1984). The time and energy costs of play behaviour in the cat. *Z Tierpsychol.* 64:298–312.

Martin, P., and Caro, T. M. (1985). On the functions of play and its role in behavioral developments. *Advances in the Study of Behavior* 15: 59–103.

Meaney, M. J. (1988). The sexual differentiation of social play. *Trends in Neurosciences* 11:54–58.

Meaney, M. J.; Stewart, J.; and Beatty, W. W. (1985). Sex differences in social play: The socialization of sex roles. *Advances in the Study of Behavior* 15:1–58.

Murphy, M. R.; MacLean, P. D.; and Hamilton, S. C. (1981). Species-typical behavior of hamsters deprived from birth of the neocortex. *Science* 213:459–61.

Nance, D. M. (1976). Sex differences in the hypothalamic regulation of feeding behavior in the rat. In A. H. Riesen and R. F. Thompson (eds.), *Advances in Psychobiology, Vol. 3.* New York: John Wiley and Sons.

Normansell, L. A., and Panksepp, J. (1984). Play in decorticate rats. *Society for Neuroscience Abstracts* 10:612.

Normansell, L., and Panksepp, J. (1990). Effects of morphine and naloxone on play-rewarded spatial discrimination in juvenile rats. *Developmental Psychobiology* 23:75–83.

Panksepp, J. (1981a). The ontogeny of play in rats. *Developmental Psychobiology* 14:327–32.

Panksepp, J. (1981b). Hypothalamic integration of behavior: Rewards punishments, and related psychobiological processes. In P. J. Morgane and J. Panksepp (eds.), *Handbook of the Hypothalamus, Vol. 3, Part A. Behavioral Studies of the Hypothalamus.* New York: Marcel Dekker.

Panksepp, J. (1981c). Brain opioids: A neurochemical substrate for narcotic and social dependence. In S. Cooper (ed.), *Progress in Theory in Psychopharmacology.* London: Academic Press.

Panksepp, J. (1982). Toward a general psychobiological theory of emotions. *The Behavioral and Brain Sciences* 5:407–67.

Panksepp, J. (1985). Effects of chronic high-dose testosterone injections on rough-and-tumble play in juvenile rats. Unpublished data.

Panksepp, J. (1986a). The psychobiology of prosocial behaviors: Separation distress, play, and altruism. In C. Zahn-Waxler, E.M. Cummings, and R. Iannotti (eds.), *Altruism and Aggression: Biological and Social Origins*. Cambridge: Cambridge University Press.

Panksepp, J. (1986b). The anatomy of emotions. In R. Plutchik (ed.), *Emotion: Theory, Research and Experience*. Vol. 3, *Biological Foundations of Emotions*.

Panksepp, J. (1988). Brain emotional circuits and psychopathologies. In M. Clynes and J. Panksepp (eds.), *Emotions and Psychopathology*. New York: Plenum Press.

Panksepp, J. (1989). The psychobiology of emotions: The animal side of human feelings. In G. Gaionotti and C. Caltagirone (eds.), *Experimental Brain Research, Series 18, Emotions and the Dual Brain*, Heidelberg, Germany: Springer-Verlag.

Panksepp, J. (1990). Psychology's search of identity: Can "mind" and behavior be understood without understanding the brain? *New Ideas in Psychology*, 8:139–149.

Panksepp, J. (1991). Affective Neuroscience: A conceptual framework for the neurobiological study of emotions. In. K. Strongman (ed.), *International Reviews of Emotional Research, Vol. 1*. John Wiley and Sons.

Panksepp, J., and Beatty, W. W. (1980). Social deprivation and play in rats. *Behavioral and Neural Biology* 30:197–206.

Panksepp, J., and Bishop, P. (1981). An autoradiographic map of the (^{3}H) diprenorphine bidning in rat brain: Effects of social interaction. *Brain Research Bulletin* 7:405–10.

Panksepp, J.; Herman, B.; Conner, R.; Bishop, P.; and Scott, J. P. (1978). The biology of social attachments: Opiates alleviate separation distress. *Biological Psychiatry* 13:607–18.

Panksepp, J.; Herman, B. H.; Villberg, T.; Bishop, P.; and DeEskinazi, F. G. (1980). Endogenous opioids and social behavior. *Neuroscience and Biobehavioral Reviews* 4:473–87.

Panksepp, J.; Jalowiec, J.; DeEskinazi, F. G.; and Bishop, P. (1985). Opiates and play dominance in juvenile rats. *Behavioral Neuroscience* 99: 441–53.

Panksepp, J. and Normansell, L. (1984). Effects of simulated play with a human hand on subsequent expression of rough-and-tumble social play between juvenile rats. Unpublished data.

Panksepp, J.; Normansell, L.; Cox, J. F.; Crepeau, L. J.; and Sacks, D. S. (1987). Psychopharmacology of social play. In J. Mos (ed.), *Ethnopharmacology of Social Behavior.* Holland: Duphar.

Panksepp, J.; Normansell, L.; Herman, B.; Bishop, P.; and Crepeau, L. (1988). Neural and neurochemical control of the separation distress call. In. J.D. Newman (ed.), *The Physiological Control of Mammalian Vocalizations.* New York: Plenum Press.

Panksepp, J.; Siviy, S.; and Normansell, L. (1984). The psychobiology of play: Theoretical and methodological perspectives. *Neuroscience and Biobehavioral Reviews* 8:465–92.

Panksepp, J.; Siviy, S. M.; and Normansell, L. A. (1985). Brain opioids and social emotions. In M. Reite and T. Fields (eds.), *The Psychobiology of Attachment and Separation.* New York: Academic press, 1985.

Pedersen, C. A.; Asher, J. A.; Monroe, Y. L.; and Prange, A. J., Jr. (1985). Oxytocin induces maternal behavior in virgin female rats. *Science* 216: 648–49.

Pellis, S. M., and Pellis, V. C. (1987). Play-fighting differs from serious fighting in both target of attack and tactics of fighting in the laboratory rat *Rattus norvegicus. Aggressive Behavior* 13:227–42.

Poole, T. B., and Fish, J. (1975). An investigation of playful behavior in *ratus norvegicus* and *mus musculus* (mammalia). *Journal of Zoology,* 175: 61–71.

Renner, M. J. (1990). Neglected aspects of exploratory and investigatory behavior. *Psychobiology* 18: 16–22.

Renner, M. J.; Prierre, P. J.; and Schilcher, P. J. (1990). Contrast-based digital tracking versus human observers in studies of animal locomotion. *Bulletin of the Psychonomic Society* 28:77–79.

Rubin, K. H. (1980). Fantasy play: Its role in the development of social skills and social cognition. In. K. H. Rubin (ed.), *New Directions for Childhood Development, No. 9, Children's Play.* San Francisco: Jossey Bass.

Saltz, E., and Brodie, J. (1982). Pretend-Play training in childhood: A review and critique. *Control of Human Development* 6:97–113.

Simon, T., and Smith, P. K. (1983). The study of play and problem solving in preschool children: Have experimenter effects been responsible for previous results? *British Journal of Developmental Psychology* 1: 289–97.

Sirevaag, A. M., and Greenough, W. T. (1988). A multivariate statistical summary of synaptic plasticity measures in rats exposed to complex, social and individual environments. *Brain Research* 441:386–92.

Siviy, S. M.; Atrens, D. M.; and Menendez, J. A. (1990). Idazoxan increases rough-and-tumble play, activity and exploration in juvenile rats. *Psychopharmacology* 100:119–23.

Siviy, S. M., and Panksepp, J. (1985a). Energy balance and play in juvenile rats. *Physiology and Behavior* 35:435–41.

Siviy, S. M., and Panksepp, J. (1985b). Dorsomedial diencephalic involvement in the juvenile play of rats. *Behavioral Neuroscience* 99: 1103–13.

Siviy, S. M., and Panksepp, J. (1987a). Juvenile play in the rat: Thalamic and brain stem involvement. *Physiology and Behavior* 41:103–14.

Siviy, S., and Panksepp, J. (1987b). Sensory modulation of juvenile play in rats. *Developmental Psychobiology* 20:39–55.

Smith, E. O. (ed.) (1978). *Social Play in Primates*. New York: Academic Press.

Smith, P. K. (1982). Does play matter? Functional and evolutionary aspects of animal and human play. *Behavioral and Brain Sciences* 5:139–84.

Smith, P. K.; Dalgleish, M.; and Herzmark, G. (1981). A comparison of the effects of fantasy play tutoring and skills tutoring in nursery classes. *International Journal of Behavioral Development* 4:421–41.

Smith, P. K.; and Syddall, S. (1978). Play and non-play tutoring in preschool children: Is it play or tutoring which matters? *British Journal of Educational Psychology* 48:315–25.

Strum, S. C. (1987). *Almost Human: A Journey into the World of Baboons*. New York: Random House.

Sudol, M. (1988). Expression of proto-oncogenes in neural tissues. *Brain Research Reviews* 13:391–403.

Symons, D. (1978). *Play and Aggression: A Study of Rhesus Monkeys*. New York: Columbia University Press.

Thor, D. H., and Holloway, W. R., Jr. (1983). Play-solicitation behavior in juvenile male and female rats. *Animal Learning and Behavior* 11: 173–78.

Thor, D. H., and Holloway, W. R., Jr. (1984a). Social play in juvenile rats: A decade of methodological and experimental research. *Neuroscience and Biobehavioral Reviews* 8:455–64.

Thor, D. H., and Holloway, W. R., Jr. (1984b). Developmental analyses of social play behavior in juvenile rats. *Bulletin of the Psychonomic Society* 22:587–90.

Thor, D. H., and Holloway, W. R., Jr. (1984c). Sex and social play in juvenile rats *(R. norvegicus)*. *Journal of Comparative Psychology* 98:276–84.

Wamboldt, M. Z, and Insel, T. R. (1987). The ability of oxytocin to induce short latency maternal behavior is dependent on peripheral anosmia. *Behavioral Neuroscience* 101:439–41.

Weisler, A., and McCall, R. B. (1976). Exploration and play, resume and re-direction. *American Psychologist,* 31:492–508.

Welker, W. I. (1971). Ontogeny of play and exploratory behaviors: A defini-tion of problems and a search for new conceptual solutions. In H. Moltz (ed.), *The Ontogeny of Behavior.* New York: Academic Press.

Wise, R. A., and Rompre, P. P. (1989). Brain dopamine and reward. *Annual Review of Psychology* 40:191–225.

CHAPTER 6

Lessons from Primate Play

Maxeen Biben and Stephen J. Suomi

Female primates are usually considered to be exemplary mothers, carrying, protecting, and feeding their infant offspring for relatively extended periods of developmental time. So it is perhaps surprising to learn that nonhuman primate mothers do not, in general, play with their young. Monkeys (and apes) are certainly playful, but in most species, playful interactions between youngsters and adults are greatly overshadowed by the frequency and importance of youngsters playing together. Great ape mothers, especially chimpanzees and gorillas, are the only ones so far known to take a regular role in playing with their offspring (Goodall 1967, 1971; Fossey 1979). Great ape mothers are their infants' first playmates (Plooij 1979; Goodall 1990) but mother-infant play is soon overshadowed by solitary play and then by social play between youngsters (Fossey 1979; Hoff, Nadler, and Maple 1981). While play with one's mother is a typical activity for infant gorillas, we have never seen (or seen reported) a squirrel monkey mother play with a youngster less than sixteen months old, even when a mother-infant pair was housed alone (an impoverished and abnormal social condition for squirrel monkeys which we try to avoid). This is not to say that adult monkeys do not play with youngsters—in our own squirrel monkey colony we often observe fathers wrestling with their infant or juvenile offspring, or play bouts involving an adult female and a youngster (but rarely a mother and her own youngster).

Social demography, and the subsequent availability of different age and sex classes, are a major determinant of an infant primate's play partners. Where a species is solitary or lives in small family groups, or where mothers forage alone for extended periods, infants

185

tend to play with any available partner, or by themselves (Walters 1987). However, where more options are available, preferences become clear. It seems to be a general rule that in any monkey species living in a social group and demonstrating a limited breeding season (thus producing a large birth cohort), most play will occur between youngsters. Young monkeys prefer partners of about the same age or size, and play with them most often and most successfully, with fewer breakdowns (Baldwin 1969; Baldwin and Baldwin 1977; Cheney 1978; Suomi and Harlow 1972; Symons 1978). But here again, the great apes may be different, in that Fossey (1979) described infant mountain gorillas as preferring juvenile play partners even when other infants were available.

By far the most frequent occurrence of adult-infant play in our squirrel monkey colony has been in the social groups having the fewest infants. Those with only a single infant had a 100 percent certainty of adult-infant play, but this diminished precipitously as the number of infants in the group increased. Because it appears that adult-infant play is secondary to, and probably a substitute for, primate youngsters' play with each other, it is important to understand both the nature of youngsters' play and the purposes for which it is evolved/designed.

The first tentative play interactions of squirrel monkeys occur at about five weeks of age, when infants begin to venture off their mothers' backs for a few moments at a time. Infants grab at and wrestle with each other but nervous mothers retrieve them quickly. Within a few weeks, vigorous and noisy play becomes a common daily event, and remains an important (if not the most important) peer activity for another year or so for females, two or more years for males. Male-male play persists longest between individuals who have been housed together for years without females, and in fact it is likely that adult male-male and female-female play is much more common in the benign no-threat, no-sweat environment of captivity than in the cold cruel world of the forest.

Play between squirrel monkey adults and youngsters may also be enhanced by some conditions of captivity. Yet no one who has seen it could say that it was an artifact of captivity, primitive, or poorly developed. The most common scenario, an adult male with his infant or juvenile offspring, is also the most striking: a fully adult male weighing over 1000 grams lies supine on a perch, limbs flailing, and fully adult canine teeth exposed in an exaggerated open mouthed grin, while a 300 gram youngster repeatedly leaps upon and attacks him playfully. Normally aloof, squirrel monkey males rarely interact directly with the females and youngsters in their troop outside of breeding season. Yet, when they do play, their gentle tolerance of youngsters seems well-rehearsed, almost stereotyped. In fact it features prominently two universal (in the animal world) stereotyped signals of harmless and playful intent: the grin or "play face," and lying on the back to expose the belly. The normally forbidding adult male is sending the message that he will not retaliate against the attacks of the infant and that their interaction is all in fun.

The form and patterning of an adult male's play with youngsters has its roots in the play wrestling that occurs dozens of times a day over the course of many months in the lives of young monkeys. Bouts generally begin with one of three specific behaviors that lead to play: leaping toward a chosen partner, rolling onto one's back, or performing acrobatic antics while hanging from a perch in front of him or her. If the partner's interest is successfully engaged, the interactants proceed to wrestling and chasing, punctuated with pulling and grabbing and more of the initiation behaviors, and accompanied by abundant and noisy vocalizing. Two kinds of wrestling can be discerned: (1) Directional wrestling occurs on flat surfaces, with one animal "pinning" the other by straddling and holding him down or otherwise restricting his movements; (2) In nondirectional wrestling, both animals hang from a perch with legs clasped about one another. Unlike in directional wrestling, neither partner appears to be dominant during nondirectional wrestling.

Performance of directional versus nondirectional wrestling is not a random event in squirrel monkeys. It can easily be seen that males do more of the former and females do more of the latter, especially when playing with partners of the same sex (the preferred condition in most primates, including humans).

A general pattern of gender differences is apparent in many aspects of play, throughout the primates (again, including humans). Males play more often, more roughly, and for a longer developmental period than females. Squirrel monkeys also show some further, more subtle, differences. If one examines the directional wrestling of males and of females, using slow motion replay of videotaped play bouts, one is struck by as rhythm that occurs in males' wrestling but not in females'. Specifically, males alternate between the dominant and subordinate roles, each being in the on top position, and then on bottom. The males' behavior is referred to as role reversal and it is one of the most important and obvious characteristics distinguishing play fighting from the real thing, where an animal presses his advantage until his opponent is defeated or retreats. This is not to say that males' directional wrestling is a polite or genteel event. On the contrary, they vie aggressively to be on top, maintaining the position through what certainly looks like force, and then relinquishing it to the partner, who struggles just as aggressively to be on top, and so forth. Females, on the other hand, tend to assume one position or the other and maintain it throughout a bout and even from one bout to the next.

While dominance is not as definitive a feature of squirrel monkey society as it is to, say, baboons, having the opportunity to be dominant seems to be important to squirrel monkeys. Youngsters are always subordinate to the juvenile and adult members of their troop and, within their own age group, dominance relations are also apparent. These can remain stable for many months and are significant predictors both of who youngsters prefer to play with and how they play with them. Simply, everyone prefers to wrestle with a partner he or she can dominate, and most attempts to solicit play are made by a more dominant animal to a subordinate. Unfortunately (for dominant animals) this is not a particularly attractive offer for the subordinate and, with a limited pool of play partners, play activity could easily grind to a halt as animals refused to play with anyone dominant to themselves, and those subordinate refused to play with *them*. Role reversal is a solution. Subordinate youngsters get enough opportunities to be dominant to keep them interested while dominant ones generally retain just enough of an edge. Role reversal is a strategy used by dominant animals of many different species to keep subordinate individuals interested in play (Bekoff 1978).

Female youngsters do reverse roles during directional wrestling, but not to the same extent as males, who usually share no worse than about 55–45. Females' directional wrestling is significantly more egalitarian than their very skewed dominance relationships outside of play, but their sharing of the dominant role is closer to 70–30. This does not mean that equality or give and take is unimportant in females' play. They simply achieve it in another way— by spending most of their play time engaged in nondirectional wrestling, where neither partner is clearly dominant. Males usually do not reverse roles in play with females, and male-female directional wrestling is accordingly uncommon, as is female-female directional wrestling. Directional wrestling between males is by far the most common play activity.

Why do gender differences like these occur? The benefits of play are often divided into "immediate," that is, enjoyed during infancy, and "delayed," only appreciated during a later developmental period. Immediate benefits of play probably include exercise and possibly include psychological well-being or "fun" (Ghiselin 1982; Burghardt 1984; Fagen 1992), general socialization and signaling to adults that youngsters are healthy (Cummins and Suomi 1976; Fagen 1981, p. 361; 1992). While these may explain, in part, why play occurs at all, they are not sufficient to explain why play takes the forms it does, or why males and females play differently.

These are most easily accounted for by delayed benefit explanations which see play as practice or preparation for adulthood, specifically as indirect practice for certain skills when more direct practice might be unsafe (Smith 1982). The key role played by dominance may be a clue.

An adult squirrel monkey society presents quite structured and predictable roles for females, more variable ones for males. Most females probably remain with their mothers and sisters in the troop where they were born. Their affiliations are likely to remain stable over time, and dominance relationships within these affiliations tend to be stable. Differences among females with respect to access to resources and reproductive output are minimal.

Males' experiences are quite different. A male leaves his natal troop at some point before reproductive maturity and must compete with other more established males in his new troop. Competition may involve both bluff and actual combat, with the survivors of numerous such encounters achieving greater reproductive output over their lifetimes. Survive is the operative word here, as it may take several years for a male to achieve such a high rank. No male can be dominant to all others throughout his life, and young males in particular must recognize the point in a social interaction when it is wise to communicate one's subordinate status.

Role reversal in play encounters may provide cognitive and motor experience in taking both dominant and subordinate roles, thereby reducing stress and uncertainty in serious encounters over status. Wrestling play allows youngsters to experience the close physical contact and feeling of being more powerful when in the dominant role (and less powerful when in the subordinate role) without the stress that would accompany these roles in a nonplayful context. It teaches youngsters how to be flexible in social interactions and how to "read" others' behavior—important lessons for socially living primates. Such experience is less available in nonplay social interactions, where dominance behavior is performed according to actual status. Gaining experience in the subordinate role without actual loss of status is an important reason why a dominant youngster will take the subordinate role in play, and may explain the differential expression of role reversal in young male and female squirrel monkeys.

The foregoing paragraphs describe the normative play situation in a fair-sized group of age-matched youngsters of both sexes (the study described [Biben 1986] is based on ten animals), such as might be found in a typical squirrel monkey troop in the wild. But what happens when appropriate playmates are not available, as might happen in a very small birth cohort?

Under captive conditions in the lab, it sometimes happens that a youngster becomes the only nonadult member of a social group. While such a circumstance would be rare in the wild, the ability of adults to step in and act as playmates for a lone youngster is obviously there, as is illustrated by the following descriptions of typical adult-infant play behavior for two six–month-old infants who were the only youngsters in their respective groups.

11B, a female, was left without playmates when the only other infant in her group died before 11B was a month old. 11B played regularly with adult female Blue, who also acted as her aunt and wet nurse. No genetic relationship existed between Blue and 11B, but allomaternal care such as carrying, protecting, and socializing is not uncommon between unrelated females in the highly social *Saimiri sciureus* and *Saimiri boliviensis* species.

Adults do not solicit play in an active manner, as do youngsters, but they often position themselves in ways that seem to passively invite play. For example, youngsters swing acrobatically from a perch to initiate play, while adults merely hang there; youngsters rolled over but adults often just semireclined. Still, the less energetic adult behaviors were quite effective in that youngsters responded by leaping at and grabbing the obliging adult, and wrestling soon developed. Many other play bouts were initiated by a youngster leaping at and landing upon an adult who was resting, eating, or simply moving about.

All the play observed between these two was of the nondirectional wrestling type. Most bouts lasted less than a minute, with frequent interruptions as one or the other seemed to lose interest, only to return a few seconds later and resume when Blue again hung from the perch and 11B leaped at her (or these two events might happen in reverse order). Nondirectional wrestling between 11B and Blue looked very similar to that which might occur between female youngsters. Both hung by the digits of either the fore- or hindlimbs, changing position often and grabbing at each others' upper body. 11B made repeated soft, short peeps as she played, and Blue cackled. Both are play vocalizations typical of youngsters as well (Biben and Symmes 1986). During much of the time the two were playing, Blue displayed a prominent open-mouth play face, the universal mammalian signal that no harm is intended, it's all in fun.

P8A, a six–month-old male, was the only surviving infant in a social group that included five adult females and one adult male. He spent much of his day leaping at adults and performing acrobatics in front of them. However, he elicited play from only two of the six, his father Y3 and an aunt P1, whose genetic relationship to P8A was unknown. Male infants in our facility have all played only with males who were their fathers. However, it is unclear whether the genetic relationship is relevant because the breeding male is the only male over the age of one year that is kept with a group of females in our facility.

P8A solicited play from P1 by repeatedly grabbing at her and rolling over, peeping and displaying the play face. The word "pester" comes easily to mind when we observe young squirrel monkeys behaving in this way and when they follow adults about, leaping at them from every angle. Infant males are much more persistent than females. Sometimes the adults respond with a reprimand (cackling and a firm head grab), but often they will play. If an adult stood still, P8A might tug at its upper upper body, peeping all the while, trying to pull the adult over onto himself. Infants usually initiated a play session, or at least were the first to perform the behaviors that indicate readiness to play.

P8A's play interactions with P1 were similar to those described for 11B and Blue. With the male Y3, however, almost all wrestling was clearly directional. The adult lay on his back on a shelf, often displaying the play face. P8A leaped upon Y1 and the two grabbed and gently bit each other. Adult males spend most of their time in the supine, subordinate position when playing with infants, but they also do some role reversing by rolling over wholly or partially onto the infant or by grabbing and restraining an infant lying atop them. Infants responded to these usually very brief shows of dominance by copious play peeping. Adult males remained in a play-ready position for anywhere from a few seconds to a minute or two, during which the youngster might retreat and then leap back into action several times. P8A and other infants playing with adults seemed to be in control of the play bout most of the time.

One year later, P8A was first observed playing with his mother (P8), who seemed a reluctant participant. P8A pestered her relentlessly, leaping and grabbing at her, or swinging vigorously in front of her, until she finally gave in. While P8 gamely showed a play face and did some chasing and acrobatic swinging herself, P8A was clearly in charge of the play bouts. P8A and P8 wrestled nondirectionally (mostly side by side) 20 percent of the time, but the remaining 80 percent of bouts found P8A pinning his mother down in a typical male-male play style. Y1 and some of the adult females joined in, too, usually on the side of P8A, although he hardly needed the help.

It thus appears through both incidence and form that squirrel monkey adults act as surrogate playmates for youngsters who are deprived of normal opportunities to play with peers. The most obvious difference between adult-infant and infant-infant play is the tendency for adult males to assume and maintain the subordinate, on-bottom, position during directional wrestling. It is most striking because of the great inequalities of age, size, and skill of the players; while the adult male is clearly capable of being dominant most or all of the time, he allows the youngster this opportunity. By placing himself in the subordinate role, the adult male both encourages the younger male to play and provides him with what may be his only chance to gain early experience in the dominant role.

Female youngsters seem to get similar play experiences whether they play with adults or other youngsters: mostly nondirectional wrestling and some directional wrestling with limited opportunities for role reversal.

Even juvenile squirrel monkeys can alter their play styles to promote more play activity between mismatched partners, as we found when we paired year-old male subjects with play partners who were either the same age and the same or opposite sex, or one year older (juveniles) and of the same or different sex as our subjects. In large social groups, youngsters usually avoid play with partners who are older, larger, more vigorous, or more skilled because such partners tend to take advantage of them in play. In this study, we found that play partners compensated, through increases in role reversal and nondirectional wrestling, for playmates who were younger or of the opposite sex. Play occurred at about normal rates despite the fact that, given a larger choice of playmates, these same animals would be unlikely to play together.

Similar observations have been made for rhesus macaques, the Old World species for which the most play data are available. The overwhelming majority of rhesus youngsters' play interactions are with other youngsters, preferably of similar age and size. Very little of their play in a typically sized social group is with adults of either sex (Symons 1978). Adult male rhesus, like most nonhuman primate males, have little contact with youngsters and are usually avoided by them in the wild. To see whether males could express a more affiliative parental response if the need arose, Redican and Mitchell (1974) experimentally confined two male and two female infants, each with a different adult male (not the fathers) for the second through the eighth month of life.

All of the males responded admirably, playing with their infant charges, particularly the two male infants, at a rate approximately 200 times greater than that reported for adult males in the wild. Redican and Mitchell's description of play between adult males and male infants is very similar to that for a similar play pairing in squirrel monkeys. Most play was initiated by vigorous swinging or leaping about, jumping at or swatting at the adult while hanging from the ceiling, or oral and manual manipulation of the adult by the infant. Wrestling play between the adult and infant males was described as more reciprocal than that between adult males and infant females, with mutual clasping and play biting. Infant females seemed less at ease, froze when clasped, and broke off play sooner, while infant males broke away from the adults repeatedly, only to return for more. Towards the end of long play sessions, the adult males became more passive, allowing the young males to continue unopposed in their biting and grabbing.

In contrast, a similar control population kept only with the mothers, experienced a much lower incidence of play. Infants may have been trying to solicit play when they leaped at the mother, but they were generally unsuccessful in getting a positive or playful response. While, in squirrel monkeys, aunts play more often than mothers, Symons (1978) reported an equally poor showing by rhesus mothers and other females in a large free-ranging social group.

Conclusions

While the function or functions of play in primate development are far from clear, most researchers believe that it has a determinative role. The normative situation for young monkeys is peer play with abundant role reversal. When peers are not available, adult-infant wrestling play provides these smallest and most subordinate troop members with the cognitive and physical experiences of being dominant. It is interesting to speculate on the long-term consequences of not getting this experience. Youngsters who lack adequate experience in being dominant may lack assertiveness in their later social interactions, or may avoid interactions. For instance, Baldwin (1969) observed that a last-born squirrel monkey infant, born three months after the first, was constantly dominated by his older peers, and at four months of age was spending considerably less time than is usual in play. Youngsters who, for one reason or another, had too little experience in the subordinate role may be at a disadvantage too. This could occur if a youngster had only younger or much smaller playmates or if a male had only females to play with (Symons 1978; Biben 1989). Such an individual might develop an inflated sense of his own abilities. Bullies and sissies may exist in animals' play, as they do in humans'.

The behavior of adult monkeys playing with infants should sound familiar to many. Any parent who has played with young children has done the same as these other primates. Adults mock wrestle with babies, protesting cheerfully while being tugged and pulled, but never retaliating with full strength. In board games or athletic games with rules, adults and older siblings routinely offer younger children an extra turn, more time, or simplified criteria for success. This puts all participants on a more equal footing and gives a child the opportunity to win, when he could not possibly do so otherwise. Adults who graciously "allow" youngsters to win most of the time, whether the game be wrestling or checkers, are not teaching them to cheat, but are giving them lessons in success and self-confidence, as well as assuring the youngster will want to play that game again, eventually as a full participant.

References

Baldwin, J. D. (1969). The ontogeny of social behaviour of squirrel monkeys (*Saimiri sciureus*) in a seminatural environment. *Folia Primatologica* 11:35–79.

Baldwin, J. D., and Baldwin, J. I. (1977). The role of learning phenomena in the ontogeny of exploration and play. In S. Chevalier-Skolnikoff and F. E. Poirier (eds.), *Primate Bio-Social Development: Biological, Social, and Ecological Determinants*. New York: Garland.

Bekoff, M. (1978). Social play: Structure, function, and the evolution of a cooperative social behavior. In G. Burghardt and M. Bekoff (eds.), *Comparative and Evolutionary Aspects of Behavioral Development.*

Biben, M. (1986). Individual- and sex-related strategies of wrestling play in captive squirrel monkeys. *Ethology* 71:229–41.

Biben, M. (1989). Effects of social environment on play in squirrel monkeys: Resolving Harlequin's Dilemma. *Ethology* 81:72–82.

Biben, M., and Symmes, D. (1986). Play vocalizations of squirrel monkeys (*Saimiri sciureus*). *Folia Primatologica* 46:173–82.

Burghardt, G. (1984). On the origins of play. In P. K. Smith (ed.), *Play in Animals and Humans.* Oxford: Basil Blackwell.

Cheney, D. (1978). The play partners of immature baboons. *Animal Behaviour* 26:1038–50.

Cummins, M., and Suomi, S. (1976). Long-term effects of social rehabilitation in rhesus monkeys. *Primates* 17:43–51.

Fagen, R. (1981). *Animal Play Behavior.* New York: Oxford University Press.

Fagen, R. (1992). Play, fun, and communication of well-being. *Play and Culture* 5: 40–58.

Fossey, D. (1979). Development of the mountain gorilla (*Gorilla gorilla beringei*) through the first thirty-six months. In D. A. Hamburg and E. R. McCown (eds.), 139–86. *The Great Apes.* Menlo Park, Calif.: Benjamin-Cummings.

Ghiselin, M. (1982). On the evolution of play by means of artificial selection. *The Behavioral and Brain Sciences* 5:165.

Goodall, J. (1967). Mother-offspring relations in chimpanzees. In D. Morris. Weidenfield, and Nicolson (eds.), 287–346. *Primate Ethology.* London.

Goodall, J. (1971). *In the Shadow of Man.* Boston: Houghton Mifflin Co.

Goodall, J. (1990). *Through a Window.* Boston: Houghton Mifflin Co.

Hoff, M.; Nadler, R.; and Maple, T. (1981). The developmental infant play in a captive group of lowland gorillas (*Gorilla gorilla gorilla*). *American Journal of Primatology* 1:65–72.

Plooij. F. (1979). How wild chimpanzee babies trigger the onset of mother-infant play—and what the mother makes of it. In M. Bullowa (ed.), *Before Speech.* Cambridge: Cambridge University Press.

Redican, W. K., and Mitchell, G. (1974). Play between adult male and infant rhesus monkeys. *American Zoologist* 14:295–302.

Smith, P. K. 1982. Does play matter? Functional and evolutionary aspects of animal and human play. *The Behavioral and Brain Sciences* 5: 139–184.

Suomi, S., and Harlow, H. F. (1972). Social rehabilitation of isolate- reared monkeys. *Developmental Psychology* 6:487–96.

Symons, D. (1978). *Play and Aggression: A Study of Rhesus Monkeys.* New York: Columbia University Press.

Walters, J. (1987). Transition to adulthood. In B. Smuts, D. Cheney, R. Seyfarth, R. Wrangham, and T. Struhsaker (eds.), *Primate Societies.* Chicago: University of Chicago Press.

CHAPTER 7

Parent-Child Physical Play: Determinants and Consequences

James Carson, Virginia Burks, and Ross D. Parke

"Father picks up 7 month old Zachary, tosses him up in the air, and then throws his head back so that he and Zachary are face to face. As Zachary giggles and chortles, father lowers him, shakes him, and tosses him up in the air again."

This example illustrates a common form of parent-child play that is pervasive throughout infancy and early childhood. In recent years, researchers have made significant progress in describing the nature and determinants of this type of playful interchange between parents and their offspring.

The research in this area can be conveniently divided into two phases. In the first phase of research, the focus was on description of the nature of the play partners, and the frequency and developmental course of this type of play. Issues such as the impact of the sex of the child and sex of the parent were of interest as well as the influence of developmental shifts in both the child and the parent on the occurrence of this type of play.

In a second, and more recent phase, the implications of this type of parent-child play for children's development has been the focus. Specifically, is children's development altered by variations in opportunities for participation in this type of play between parent and child, especially children's social interaction skills?

Preparation of this chapter was supported by National Science Foundation Grant BNS 89 1939 1 (Parke, PI). Thanks to Chris Strand for her assistance in the preparation of the manuscript.

197

The goal of this chapter is to review and evaluate the two phases of this research.

The Developmental Course of Parent-Child Physical Play

Age of Child

A variety of studies indicate that parent-child physical play begins in the early months of infancy and continues throughout the preschool years as an important form of interchange between infants, children, and their parents.

The most detailed profile of the developmental changes comes from a survey study by MacDonald and Parke (1986). In their study, 390 families with a total of 746 children ranging in age from under one year of age to ten years were contacted by telephone and questioned about the frequency of physical play interactions with their children. A curvilinear developmental effect was found, with comparatively low levels of physical play prior to age one, a peak in the preschool years (1–4), and a decline after to very low levels of parent-child physical play after ten years of age.

Age of Parent

Not only does the age of the child determine the frequency of physical play between parent and child, recent evidence suggests that the age of the parent may be an important determinant as well. MacDonald and Parke (1986), in their survey study, found that age of parent is negatively related to the frequency of physical play. Even after controlling for the age of the child, the size of the relationship is reduced but generally reveals the same pattern. However, this relationship appears stronger for some categories of play than for others. Some physical activities, such as bounce, tickle, chase, and piggyback, which show strong negative relationships with the age of parent, are also activities that tend to require more physical energy on the part of the play partner. This assumption of the energy expenditure required by different types of play activity is based on an independent survey of adults who rated the categories of play according to their energy requirements. These findings underscore the importance of considering the age of the parent in studies of physical play. The negative correlation between age of parent and physical play may be due to either the unwillingness or inability of older parents to engage in high-energy affectively arousing activities, such as physical play. Alternatively, children may elicit less physical activity from older parents. Observational analyses of parents at different ages with their children revealed that younger fathers (25 years or younger) displayed more physically arousing and stimulating play than older fathers (30 yrs. or older) who, in turn, verbalized more (Nevelle and Parke 1992). This issue is of particular importance in view of the trends toward delayed childbearing among American couples (Parke 1988; Parke and Tinsley 1984).

Not only is age per se of importance, but the timing of entry into familial roles may be another determinant of parent-child physical play. In their study of thirty grandfathers who were observed in interaction with their seven–month-old infants, Tinsley and Parke (1988) found that grandfather age was related to the level of stimulating play. Grandfathers were divided into three categories: younger (36–49), middle (50–56), and older (57–68). Grandfathers in the middle age group were rated significantly higher on competence (e.g., confident, smooth, accepting), affect (e.g., warm, interested, affectionate, attentive), and play style (e.g., playful, responsive, stimulatory). From a life span developmental perspective, the middle group of grandfathers could be viewed as having been optimally ready for grandparenthood, both physically and psychologically. Unlike the oldest group of grandfathers, they were less likely to be chronically tired, or to have been ill with age-linked diseases. And, unlike the youngest grandfathers, they had completed the career-building position of their lives and were prepared to devote more of their time to family-related endeavors. Moreover, the age of the middle group of grandfathers fits the normative age at which grandparenthood is most often achieved; thus, for these men, the role of grandfather was more age-appropriate than it was for the youngest and oldest groups of grandfathers.

Sex of Parent and Sex of Child as Determinants of Parent-Child Physical Play

Sex of Parent

A wide range of studies indicate that mothers and fathers differ in the extent to which they engage in physical play with their infants and children. From the first weeks of life, this sex of parent difference is apparent. Yogman (1981) studied the interaction patterns of mothers, fathers, and strangers in infants from two weeks to six months. The most common type of father-infant games were tactile and limb movement games. Limb movement games, which were associated with increases in infant arousal, represented 70 percent of all father-infant games and only 4 percent of mother-infant games. In contrast to this type of physically arousing game used by fathers, mothers played physically by utilizing more conventional motor games such as "pat-a-cake," "peekaboo," or waving. "The visual games more often played by mothers represent a more distal attention-maintaining form of interactive play than the more proximal, idiosyncratic limb movement games played more often by fathers" (Yogman 1980, p. 39).

Stylistic differences in mothers' and fathers' play are not restricted to very young infants. In a series of studies by Power and Parke (1982), mothers and fathers were videotaped while playing with their firstborn, eight–month-old infants in a laboratory playroom. Fathers played more bouncing and lifting games than mothers. In contrast, mothers played more watching games in which a toy is presented and made salient by moving or shaking it. The mother-father difference in lifting games was qualified by sex of the infant; the game was played primarily by fathers of boys. In addition to examining the amount of time that mothers and fathers devoted to different types of play, Power and Parke examined the sequencing of various types of play for mothers and fathers. Two further ways in which mothers and fathers differ in interaction style are illustrated by this type of analysis. First, fathers were more likely than mothers to engage in extended physical no-toy play interaction; even if they were engaged in toy-mediated play they were generally less successful than mothers in successfully maintaining play of this type. When fathers failed to elicit their infants' attention in toy play, they often shifted to physical no-toy play. In contrast, mothers were better able to maintain infant attention during toy play, and a loss in infant attention led to continued toy play as opposed to a shift to the physical mode as in the case of fathers. In short, there is a general tendency for parents to rely on familiar and predominant modes of play, particularly when infant interest lessens: for mothers this involves prolonging toy play, while for fathers this involves shifting to physical play.

Observations of father- and mother-infant interaction in unstructured home contexts with older infants indicate mother-father differences in style of play. Lamb (1977a), in an observational study of infants at seven to eight months and again at twelve to thirteen months in their homes, found that fathers engage in more physical (i.e., rough and tumble) and unusual play activities than mothers. Similar findings emerged from home observations of the infants at fifteen, eighteen, twenty-one, and twenty-four months of age (Lamb 1977b). Again, fathers played more physical games and engaged in more parallel play with their infants. Mothers, in contrast, engaged in more conventional play activities (e.g., "peekaboo," "pat-a-cake"), stimulus toy play (where a toy was jiggled or operated to stimulate the child directly), and reading than fathers. Power and Parke (1982) found that fathers engaged in more physical play than mothers in home observations of seven-and-a-half and ten-and-a-half–month-old infants. Similar differences in the style of play patterns were found by Clarke-Stewart (1980) in a study of infants fifteen to thirty-months old and their parents: "Fathers' play was relatively more likely to be physical and arousing rather than intellectual, didactic, or mediated by objects—as in the case of mothers" (Clarke-Stewart 1980, p. 37).

Nor are these effects evident only in infancy. MacDonald and Parke (1984), in a study of the play interaction patterns between mothers and fathers and their three– and four–year-olds, found that fathers engaged in more physical play with their children than mothers. In contrast, mothers engaged in more object-mediated play with their children than fathers.

In all studies reviewed, a reasonably consistent pattern emerges: fathers are tactile and physical while mothers tend to be verbal. Clearly, infants and young children experience not more stimulation from their fathers, but a qualitatively different stimulatory pattern.

There is evidence of some cross-cultural generality to this pattern of mother-father differences in play style. Parents in England show similar sex differences (Smith and Daglish 1977); fathers in New Delhi, India, again show more rough physical play (tossing, roughhousing) and minor physical play (tickling, bouncing on lap) with infants than mothers, although rough and minor physical play forms were relatively infrequent (chapter 11, this volume; Roopnarine, Talukder, Jain, Joshi, and Srivastav 1990).

However, other evidence suggests that this pattern of mother-father differences in play style may be in part culture bound. Specifically, neither in Sweden (Lamb, Frodi, Hwang, Frodi, and Steinberg 1982) nor among Israeli kibbutz families (Sagi, Lamb, Shoham, Dvir, & Lewkowicz, 1985) were there clear sex-of-parent differences in the tendency to engage in play or in the types of play initiated.

Perhaps this reflects the more egalitarian arrangements effective (at least during observation periods) in Sweden and Israel than in the United States. This would suggest that at least in regard to Sweden and Israel, sex differences in maternal and paternal behavior, are influenced by the concrete competing demands on the parents' time, as well as by their socialization and biogenetic tendencies (Sagi et al. 1985, p. 283).

Clearly, more research is needed to determine the features of different cultural niches that promote different forms of playful interaction between mothers, fathers, and their offspring.

Sex of Child

A number of studies have documented that boys and girls experience different types of play with boys being the recipients of physical play more than girls. In the newborn period, Parke and O'Leary (1976) found that fathers touched (and vocalized to) their boys, especially firstborns, more than their girls, regardless of their ordinal position. This pattern is clearly evident by eight months, with fathers of boys engaging in lifting and tossing bouts more often than fathers of girls (Power and Parke 1982).

A similar sex difference is evident in three–to four–year-olds with boys receiving more parental physical play than girls (Mac-Donald and Parke 1984). A related sex difference is evident from the MacDonald and Parke (1986) survey of parent-child play: boys were more likely to be engaged in wrestling and ball playing than girls, while girls participated more often in nonstrenuous physical games with their parents, such as patty-cake and being bounced on the parents' knee. Jacklin, DiPietro and Maccoby (1984) found that four–year-old boys played more rough and tumble games and more arousing games with their parents than girls.

Although these findings are evident in some other cultures (e.g., England; Smith and Daglish 1977), other evidence suggests that sex of child differences in parent-child play are not always present. In their recent study of families in New Delhi, India, Roopnarine et al. (1990) failed to find any gender of infant differences on any types of play measures, including physical play. In spite of the fact that sex of infant differences are evident in play patterns of nonhuman primates that are similar to human findings (Parke & Suomi 1981), the cross-cultural evidence suggests that caution is needed before any firm conclusions about the universality of these patterns can be drawn.

On the other hand, there are clear sex differences in physical play between peers. Across a range of cultures, there is evidence that boys engage in more physical play with their peers than girls. For example, this pattern is evident in the United States (DePietro 1981), the United Kingdom (Smith and Lewis 1985), and Italy (Attili, 1989). (See Smith 1989 for a review.)

Parent-Child Physical Play and Children's Peer Competence

In spite of the interest in descriptions of parent-child physical play, it is only recently that we have entered the second phase of research. In this phase, the implications of this type of parent-child interaction for children's social development have been examined.

The work of this phase of our research was based on our earlier descriptive studies of parent-infant physical play, earlier studies of primates, and evidence of the importance of physical play in peer-peer interactions.

On the basis of our descriptive analysis of parent-child physical play bouts, it was noted that

> these bouts often serve as contexts for a wide range of communicative and affectively charged social interactions between parents and their infants. Therefore, through such interactions fathers may play an important role in facilitating the development of communicative skills and the formation of social relationships (Power and Parke 1982, p. 160).

Another implication of the physical play between parents and their infants, especially fathers, is suggested by the earlier work of Harlow and his colleagues (Suomi and Harlow 1971). In this research, infant monkeys who were deprived of opportunities for physical interaction with either peer or adult monkeys showed serious deficits in their ability to regulate physical social exchanges, particularly aggression. "Therefore we might expect that early physical play may be important both as an antecedent of later peer-peer play and in the regulation of agonistic and aggressive interactions" (Power and Parke 1982, p. 160).

Some recent evidence suggests that the ability to engage successfully in rough and tumble play with peers is more common among popular than rejected children, which supports the argument that the ability to play physically may be a social skill that is important for peer-peer interaction (Pellegrini 1988; see Smith 1989 for a review of this work).

Together, these arguments suggest that it is worthwhile to examine the proposition that parent-child physical play may be an important antecedent of variations in children's social adaptation to peers. In the next section, evidence pertinent to this hypothesis will be reviewed and evaluated.

Relationships between Parent-Child Physical Play and Children's Social Competence

Several studies have addressed the question of the link between parent-child physical play and children's social competence. In an early study, MacDonald and Parke (1984) examined the physical play of three– to five–year–olds and their parents; in turn, teachers rated the children in terms of their popularity with their peers. Although the pattern differed for boys and girls, their findings showed that popular boys have mothers and fathers who are engaging, mothers who are verbally stimulating, and fathers who are low in directiveness but physically playful. Girls whose teachers rated them as popular have physically playful and affective eliciting but nondirective fathers and directive mothers. In short, physical play, especially father physical play, was an important correlate of popularity for both boys and girls.

Further work (Burks, Carson, and Parke 1987) confirms our earlier findings. To secure a more accurate measure of the duration of sustained play between children and their parents, the dyadic play session was divided into molar units called "bouts." A bout was defined as a play activity with a common theme and structure (e.g., chasing, tumbling). The amount of time that the dyad was engaged in play was determined by totaling the length of all play bouts. This provided a more precise measure of the duration of play than was available in the earlier study which relied upon a time-sampling strategy (MacDonald and Parke 1984).

To complement this molar level of analysis (bouts), a molecular coding strategy was employed involving second-by-second analysis that allowed the determination of differences in initiations to engage in a play bout, as well as responses to these initiatives and the success of these attempts as assessed by whether or not the dyad engaged in the activity. This allowed us to assess behavior at both molar and molecular levels. Second, in this work we utilized a current measure of sociometric status instead of the reliance on teacher ratings. This assessment is derived from earlier research that supports the value of a two-dimensional conceptualization of sociometric status, including the independent dimensions of being liked by peers and being disliked by peers (Coie, Dodge, and Coppotelli 1982). Within this framework rejected children are considered to be highly disliked by their peers and score low on being liked by peers, while popular children are highly liked by their peers and are not actively disliked by them. One of the main advantages of using sociometric status is the fact that there has been previous research concerning the behavioral correlates of these status categories. Specifically, it has been found that peer interactions with popular children generally involve more engaged activities which are of longer duration than interactions involving rejected children (Dodge 1983). Similarly, popular children tend to be less controlling and more willing to adapt to the activities of the group, while rejected children tend to be assertive and directive when they interact with peers (Coie and Dodge 1983; Coie and Kupersmidt 1983). One of our goals was to determine whether similar styles of interaction between children of different sociometric status and their peers are evident in their interactions with their parents as well. A second advantage of the use of an extreme group design is the heightened probability of detecting differences across groups of parent-child dyads.

Popular and rejected three—to five—year-old boys and girls participated (seven popular boys and seven popular girls; eight rejected boys and five rejected girls) in a laboratory playroom and were observed interacting with their mothers and fathers on separate occasions for a five-minute warmup free-play period as well as a twenty-minute physical play session. Separate groups of sociometrically average boys and girls are being added to the design, but this phase is not yet completed.

Results indicated that dyads involving popular children and their parents engaged in play bouts for a longer period than dyads involving the rejected children and their parents, particularly when the popular children were with their fathers. Moreover the average length of a play bout tended to be longer for dyads involving popular children than for dyads involving rejected children. These results for the molar level of analysis are complemented by the molecular findings. The interaction strategies used varied by status of the child. As found in our earlier study, the degree of coerciveness of initiation tactics differed across the two groups. In this study, initiation tactics were assumed to vary in terms of their degree of control. Questions were least controlling, suggestions more controlling followed by directives; physical initiations were most controlling. This latter tactic occurs when one member of the dyad begins an activity without any verbal warning. Separate analyses were conducted for the initiation tactics of popular and rejected children, mothers and fathers of popular and rejected children, and the dyad (mother-child and father-child combined).

In their use of the low-control tactic of questions, popular children with their fathers and dyads involving popular children tended to be higher than either rejected children with their fathers or dyads involving rejected children. In the case of the more controlling initiating tactics, such as suggesting, fathers of rejected children and rejected dyads were higher than popular fathers or dyads. In the case of directiveness, rejected children were more likely to use this initiating strategy than popular children, especially with their fathers. Finally, for the tactic of initiating an activity in a physical manner, rejected children, especially boys as well as rejected dyads, were more likely to use physical initiations than popular boys. Similarly, responses to initiations differed across the status groups. Dyads involving a rejected child were more likely to respond negatively—verbally or physically—than popular dyads.

Of particular interest was the finding that in spite of the fact that rejected dyads respond negatively to their partners' initiations, the rate of success of popular and rejected dyads in engaging their partners in the activity did not differ. This suggests that even though there was initially a negative response, the rejected children and their parents eventually engaged in the activity—an indication that coercive tactics were successful in achieving their interactional goals. Many of these patterns of coercive interchanges that were found in families of rejected children are similar to patterns of interactions between rejected children and their peers. This is clear confirmation of our hypothesis that styles of interaction across the family and peer systems are strikingly similar in many ways. In turn, this provides further support for the argument that these styles may possibly have their origins in family interactional experiences.

Other evidence suggests that directive and coercive patterns of parent-child interaction during physical play is not only a concurrent correlate of children's social competence but may, in fact, be an *antecedent* of variations in social adaptation. In one of the few longitudinal studies in this area, Barth and Parke (in press) secured a measure of parent-child physical play just before children entered kindergarten. Mother-child and father-child sessions were conducted separately in the home. As in our earlier study, the amount of time spent in bouts of physical play was a significant predictor of the child's social behavior. In this case, the longer the maternal-child play bouts, the higher the teachers' ratings of a child's consideration of others and the lower the ratings of depending at both two weeks after school entry and again at the end of the semester. Moreover, longer play bouts were negatively related to teacher ratings of hostility at the end of the semester. Father-child play bouts were favorably related to more favorable ratings of their behaviors at home (e.g., how well the child gets along with others in the family; physical signs of stress; and appetite and sleep patterns).

In addition, style of interaction was an important correlate of children's social adjustment. In contrast to earlier studies, a dyadic measure of parent-child interaction was obtained by use of a principal components analysis for mother-child and father-child interactions.

Mother-child dyads, in which the child was highly directive and was unwilling to accept maternal input, were related to poor social adjustment as indexed by high hostility and low consideration ratings from teachers. In addition, these children reported higher levels of loneliness after the initial onset of school. A mother-child dyad characterized by a dominant mother and uncooperative, resistant child was related to teacher ratings of dependency after the onset of school and higher ratings of hostility at the end of the semester. Similarly, father-child dyads characterized by a pattern of parent control and child resistance were also correlated with poor social adjustment in both home and school settings. Immediately after school entrance, this interaction style was associated with children's reports of loneliness and parents' reports of behavior problems at home. By the end of the semester, this style was negatively correlated with teachers' reports of consideration.

Finally, nondirective dyads in which fathers use an indirect style of interaction (e.g., high reliance on questions and low reliance on directives) was consistently related to favorable home behaviors at the onset of school and at the end of the semester and with reports of low hostility from the teacher at the end of the semester.

Taken together, these results support past research that shows controlling and directive parenting styles and noncompliant demanding child behaviors are negatively related to social adjustment in school settings (Campbell, Breaux, Ewing, and Szumoski 1985) and peer sociometric assessments (MacDonald 1987; MacDonald and Parke 1984; Putallaz 1987). Most importantly, these data suggest that earlier observed parent-child interaction patterns have value in predicting later social adjustment in school and peer contexts. While this study does not imply a causal relationship between parent-child interaction and later behavior in peer contexts, it suggests the plausibility of this direction of effect.

Social learning processes of observational learning as well as cognitive working models which are used to form expectations concerning the ways in which people behave in social situations and in turn how one ought to behave are both viable explanatory candidates for explaining these findings (Main, Kaplan, and Cassidy 1985; Parke, MacDonald, Burks, Carson, Bhavnagri, Barth, and Beitel 1989). A third explanatory candidate is available which flows more explicitly from our focus on physical play as an interaction context. In the following section we turn to an analysis of how a variety of emotional processes may contribute to explaining the linkage between family and peer systems.

Lessons from Parent-Child Physical Play

In this section, possible processes that may serve as mediators between parent-child interaction and peer competence are outlined. These mediating processes—affect regulation, emotional decoding, and emotional encoding—are discussed below. A guiding model is presented in Figure 7.1.

Learning to Regulate Emotional Arousal

Throughout our work the focus has been primarily on the context of parent-child physical play; this choice was made, in part, because successful parent-child physical play involves the regulation of affectively arousing stimulation—a process thought to be central to social competence in infancy as well as among older children (Sroufe, Schork, Motti, Lawroski, and LaFreniere 1984; Stern 1977, 1985). Parent-child physical play requires complex and subtle ability on the part of the parent to help keep stimulation within an optimal range. Overstimulation of the child by the parent and approach-withdrawal behaviors of the part of the child are common and both parent and child may be seen as regulating the child's affective display during these bouts.

To evaluate directly the ways in which these arousal regulatory strategies are utilized in the case of parent-child play by parents of

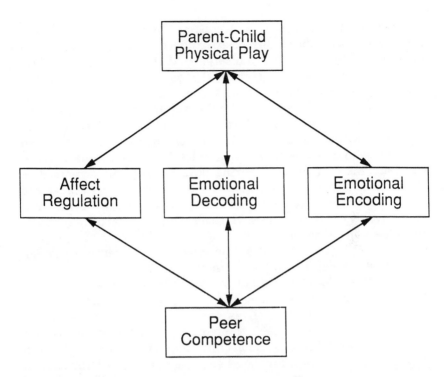

Figure 7.1. Model of relationship between parent-child physical play and peer competence.

children of different sociometric statuses was the goal of the recent study by MacDonald (1987). As in our other studies three–to five–year-olds were subjects, but in this investigation only boys were included. Children were selected on the basis of their sociometric status using the Coie et al. (1982) method and twelve rejected, twelve popular, and in this case, twelve neglected children were included as well. Twenty-minute videotaped observations of parent-child interaction were made in the home (ten minutes of free play and ten minutes of physical play). Mother-son and father-son sessions were conducted on separate home visits. The results indicated that popular children engage in higher levels of physical play and express more positive affect than rejected children especially during the physical play sessions. Moreover, parents tend to be more directive with rejected children. These findings are consistent with earlier investigations (Barth and Parke in press; Burks et al. 1987; MacDonald and Parke 1984; Putallaz 1987).

Despite the indication that popular children engage in more physical play and show more positive affective expressiveness than rejected children, the data indicated that the play sessions of rejected children are characterized by more overstimulation and avoidance of stimulation than is the case of popular children and their parents. The interactions of the rejected children were characterized by alternatively approaching the source of stimulation and then withdrawing from stimulation. Moreover, the rejected children were characterized by higher levels of overstimulation (i.e., child became over aroused during physical play and screamed or showed a negative affective response to stimulation). Because the rejected children were characterized by higher levels of overstimulation over the other groups and because withdrawal from stimulation often coincided with expressions of overstimulation on the part of the child, it suggests that withdrawal from stimulation was motivated by the child being overstimulated. This, in turn, may account for the reduced amount of positive affect in the sessions of the rejected children in comparison to their popular counterparts observed in this study as well as earlier studies (MacDonald and Parke 1984; Burks et al. 1987). Moreover this pattern could account for other recent findings. Carson (1991) found that popular children showed more happiness and laugher while rejected children showed more neutral affect, and the fathers of rejected children showed more anger and more neutral expressions than fathers of popular children. Boyum (1991) has found similar findings based on home observations. Specifically, she reported negative correlations between father negative affective displays (e.g., anger, disgust, and anxiety) and their kindergarten children's sociometric status.

These findings underscore the regulation of affectively arousing stimulation as an important social process. Moreover, the differences that were found in the regulation of arousal in the dyads of parents with popular and rejected children may, in fact, be evident in peer-peer interactions as well. If this hypothesis is correct, deficits in arousal-regulating ability may be another factor associated with the lowered acceptance of rejected children. While the current work cannot confirm that this skill is learned in parent-child interactive contexts, it is a viable possibility and provides a further clue concerning potential ways that parents may contribute to children's differing social competence with their peers. Next, we turn to a further refinement of the arousal regulatory hypotheses by exploring the possible role that the ability to encode and decode emotional signals may play in this regulatory process.

Decoding and Encoding Others' Emotions

One set of possible skills that are of relevance to successful peer-peer interaction and may, in part, be acquired in the context of parent-child play, especially affectively arousing physical play, is the ability to decode others' emotional states and to clearly encode their own emotional signals. In other words, through physically playful interaction with their parents, especially fathers, children may be learning the social communicative value of their own affective displays as well as how to use these emotional signals to regulate the social behavior of others. In addition, they may learn to accurately decode the social and affective signals of other social partners.

In the next section, two studies are described that provide evaluations of these hypotheses, namely that decoding and encoding skills are related to peer competence. A preliminary evaluation of the relationship between these skills and parent-child play is then presented.

The Decoding Hypothesis

To determine the role that the ability to decode affective cues may play in mediating peer relationships, we conducted a further study (Bietel and Parke 1985). Children were asked to correctly identify facial expressions depicting the following emotional states: happy, sad, scared, angry, or neutral. To determine the relationship between emotional decoding ability and children's peer relationships, the teacher popularity rating (Connolly and Doyle 1981) was secured as well as two measures of sociometric status. One hundred fifty-eight three– and four–year-olds were shown pictures of their classmates. In one procedure, they were asked to indicate their degree of liking on a three-point scale using pictures of happy (like a lot) to said (don't like) schematic faces (Asher, Singleton, Tinsley, and Hymel 1979). In a second approach, they were asked to choose the classmate they like best using a paired comparison procedure (Cohen and Van Tassel 1978).

The results indicate that there are significant relationships between emotional decoding ability and various measures of children's sociometric status as well as teacher ratings of popularity. For boys, these relationships are evident even after age of child, a strong correlate of emotional decoding ability is controlled; in contrast, for girls the effect is less evident after controlling for age. This finding of a link between emotional decoding and social status is consistent with other investigators (Edwards, Manstead, and Mac-Donald 1984; Field and Walden 1982), who found evidence that pre-schoolers' sociometric status was positively related to children's ability to correctly identify facial expressions of emotion. Together this evidence suggests that one component of peer acceptance may be a child's ability to correctly identify the emotional states, as indexed by their facial expressions, of other children. It is assumed that this emotional identification skill would permit a child to more adequately and sensitively regulate his social interactions with other children; in turn, this could contribute to his greater acceptance by his peers.

The Encoding Hypothesis

Evidence suggests that not only is emotional decoding linked with children's social status with their peers, but emotional encoding ability is a correlate as well. A number of investigators (Buck 1975, 1977; Filed and Walden 1982) have found positive relationships between children's ability to accurately encode specific emotional expressions and children's popularity with peers.

Carson, Burks, and Parke (1987) extended earlier work by examining how sociometric status is related to emotional production and recognition skills within the family. In our paradigm, parents and children were asked to identify each other's facial expressions (happy, sad, mad, scared, surprised, neutral, and disgusted). There were no sociometric status-related differences in parents' ability to recognize the faces of their children or in children's abilities to recognize their parents' faces. This suggests that within the family, children and parents, regardless of sociometric status, can recognize each other's facial expressions.

However, emotional expressions exchanged within the family might not be clear to individuals outside of the family. Some families may utilize idiosyncratic affect cues that are not recognizable in interactions outside of the family. Their communications may reflect a "familycentric" bias. In support of this possibility, we found that there was a significant sociometric status difference in undergraduates' ability to accurately decode the children's facial expressions. The undergraduates were better able to recognize the facial expressions of the popular children than those of the rejected children. There were no status differences in the recognition of the facial expressions of parents. This suggests that the emotional production skills of popular children are greater than those of rejected children, since rejected children's facial expressions are not as well recognized outside the family. These studies provide support of the links between children's emotional encoding and decoding skills and children's sociometric status.

Parent-child play as the Context for Learning Decoding and Encoding Skills

The next step is to examine the relationship between these abilities and parent-child play. While some evidence suggests that variations in encoding and decoding ability may be related to parent-child physical play (see Parke et al. 1988), other evidence shows only modest support for this hypothesis. However, it remains a viable assumption that children may acquire and refine encoding and decoding skills in the context of parent-child play. Further support for a link between parent-child interaction and children's ability to encode and decode emotional expressions comes from recent studies of abusive families: there is evidence of parental deficiencies in both emotional encoding and decoding skills among abusive parents. When abusive mothers and control mothers were shown slides of babies producing pain, surprise, joy, interest, fear, and anger expressions, Kropp and Haynes (1987) found that abusive mothers had fewer correct identifications overall and were more likely to identify negative emotional signals as positive. Other evidence (Camras, Ribordy, Hill, Martino, Spaccarelli, and Stefoni 1988) suggests that abusive mothers of preschoolers exhibited encoding deficits. Their facial expressions were less easily identified by objective observers than those of control mothers.

Among abused children, similar evidence of emotional encoding and decoding deficits is available. Camras and her colleagues (Camras, Grow, and Ribordy 1983; Camras et al. 1988) found that abused children perform more poorly on affect identification tasks and also produce less clear facial expressions than control children. The potential influence of parents in accounting for these child deficits in encoding and decoding skills is further supported by the finding of a positive relationship between children's ability to identify facial expressions and mothers' ability to pose facial expressions (Camras et al. 1988).

To complete our argument it is necessary to briefly examine differences in social competence between abused and nonabused children. Several investigators have found marked differences in the social skills and peer acceptance of abused children in comparison to their nonabused counterparts. In general, abused children are rated by peers (Cicchetti, Lynch, Shonk and Manly 1992), teachers (Camras et al. 1983), and observers (Cicchetti et al, 1992; George and Main 1979; Main and George 1985) as less socially skilled.

A plausible interpretation of this pattern of findings would be that parental deficits in encoding and decoding skills, in turn, promote similar deficiencies among their children. One consequence of these skill deficits may be an inability to function well in social interactions with peers.

Remaining Issues

Several issues require more attention in future studies in this area.

First, we must be careful not to overemphasize the importance of parent-child physical play as a context for acquiring important social and cognitive skills. Other types of play, such as parent-child pretend play, may provide important opportunities for learning to negotiate successfully in the social environment beyond the family. Moreover, other types of skills, especially verbally based social strategies, such as persuasion and role taking, may be learned in these contexts. Currently, comparative studies of physical and non-physical pretend play are underway to assess the impact of experience in these different types of play on children's emerging social competence (Haight and Parke 1991; Haight 1991).

Second, the direction of effects remains an important unresolved issue in the studies in this area. While it is assumed that the causal arrows flow from family to peers, it remains a plausible alternative that child characteristics may account for the consistencies observed across settings. More detailed examination of the impact of child characteristics, such as temperamental variations on both parent-child play patterns and on subsequent peer-peer interactions, is required. Obviously, longitudinal and experimental studies are needed strategies as well if we are to untangle the direction of effects dilemma.

Third, continued effort to uncover the mechanisms that mediate the effects of parent-child play on later peer competence is necessary. While encoding and decoding skills are important candidates, more data on self-regulation of emotion arousal (Gottman and Katz 1990) and emotional understanding (Cassidy and Parke

1991; Cassidy, Parke, Butovsky and Braungart, 1992) as possible mediators are needed.

Fourth, the implications of the developmental trends in parent-child physical play need to be examined more closely. What other forms of interaction between parents and children replace physical play as children develop? Are the same or different lessons learned in alternative forms of interaction at later ages?

Finally, the cross-cultural boundaries of this form of play need to be examined more closely. This search will not only inform us about the limitations of our largely Western-based research, but more importantly provide insights concerning different pathways by which families and children acquire skills that are important for successful adaptation to extrafamilial social contexts.

As this chapter has shown, parent-child play is an important interactive context. By gaining a better understanding of its role in socialization relative to other forms of influence, its unique contributions to children's development will be more clearly understood.

References

Asher, S. R.; Singleton; L. C.; Tinsley, B. R.; and Hymel, S. (1979) A reliable sociometric measure for preschool children. *Developmental Psychology* 15:443–44.

Attili, G. (1989) Social competence versus emotional security: The link between home relationships and behavior problems in preschool. In B. H. Schneider, G. Attili, J. Nadel, & R. P. Weissberg (Eds.) *Social competence in developmental perspective* Boston: Kluwer Academic Publishers.

Barth, J. M., and Parke, R. D. (in press). Parent-child relationship influences on children's transition to school. *Marrill-Palmer Quarterly.*

Beitel, A., and Parke, R. D. (1985). Relationship between preschoolers' sociometric status, parent interaction and emotional decoding ability. Unpublished manuscript, University of Illinois.

Boyum, L. (1991) Family emotional expressiveness: A possible antecedent of children's social competence. Poster presented at the *Biennial Meeting of the Society for Research in Child Development* Seattle, WA.

Buck, R. (1975). Nonverbal communication of affect in children. *Journal of Personality and Social Psychology* 31:644–53.

Buck, R. (1977). Nonverbal communication of affect in preschool children: Relationships with personality and skin conductance. *Journal of Personality and Social Psychology* 35:225–36.

Burks, V.; Carson, J.; and Parke, R. D. (1987). Parent-Child Interactional Styles of Popular and Rejected Children. Unpublished manuscript, University of Illinois.

Campbell, S. B.; Breaux, A. M.; Ewing, L. J.; and Szumoski, E. K. (1985). A one-year follow-up study of parent-referred hyperactive preschool-children. *Journal of the American Academy of Child and Adolescent Psychiatry, 23*(3), 243–249.

Camras, L.; Grow, G.; and Ribordy, S. (1983). Recognition of emotional expressions by abused children. *Journal of Clinical Child Psychology* 12:325–28.

Camras, L.; Ribordy, S.; Hill, J.; Martino, S.; Spaccarelli, S., and Stefani, R. (1988). Recognition and posing of emotional expressions by abused children and their mothers. *Developmental Psychology* 24:776–81.

Carson, J. (April 1991). In search of mediating processes: Emotional cues as links between family and peer systems. Poster presented at the Biennial Meeting for the Society for Research in Child Development, Seattle, WA.

Carson, J.; Burks, V.; and Parke, R. D. (1987). Emotional encoding and decoding skills of parents and children of varying sociometric status. Unpublished manuscript, University of Illinois.

Cassidy, J., and Parke, R. D. (1991). Family-peer connections: The roles of parental emotional expressiveness and children's understanding of emotions. Paper presented at the biennial meeting of the Society for Research in Child Development, Seattle, Wash.

Cassidy, J.; Parke, R. D.; Butovsky, L.; and Braungart, J. (1992). Family-peer connections: The role of emotional expressiveness within the family and children's understanding of emotions *Child Development, 63*, 603–618.

Cicchetti, D.; Lynch, Shonk, S.; and Manly, J. T. (1992). An organizational perspective on peer relations in maltreated children. In R. D. Parke and G. W Ladd (eds.). *Family-Peer Relationships: Modes of Linkage.* Hillsdale, N.J.: Erlbaum.

Clarke-Stewart, K. A. (1978). And daddy makes three: The father's impact on mother and young child. *Child Development* 49:466–78.

Clarke-Stewart, K. A. (1980). The father's contribution to children's cognitive and social development in early childhood. In F. Pedersen (ed.), *The Father-Infant Relationship.* New York: Praeger.

Cohen, A. S., and Van Tassel, E. (1978). Comparison of partial and complete paired comparisons in sociometric measurement of preschool groups. *Applied Psychological Measurement* 2 (1):31–40.

Coie, J. D.; Dodge, K. A.; and Coppotelli, H. (1982). Dimensions and types of social status: A cross-age perspective. *Developmental Psychology, 18,* 557–570.

Coie, J. D., and Dodge, K. A. (1983). Continuities and changes in children's social status: A five-year longitudinal study. *Merrill-Palmer Quarterly, 29,* 261–282.

Coie, J. D., and Kupersmidt, J. B. (1983). A behavioral analysis of emerging social status in boys' groups. *Child Development, 54,* 1400–1416.

Connolly, J., and Doyle, A. (1981). Assessment of social competence in preschoolers: Teachers versus peers. *Developmental Psychology* 17:50–58.

DiPietro, J. A. (1981). Rough and tumble play: A function of gender. *Developmental Psychology* 17:50–58.

Dodge, K. A. (1983). Behavioral antecedents of peer social status. *Child Development* 54:1386–99.

Edwards, R.; Manstead, A. S. R.; and MacDonald, C. J. (1984). The relationship between children's sociometric status and ability to recognize facial expressions of emotion. *European Journal of Social Psychology* 14:235–38.

Field, T. M., and Walden, T. A. (1982). Production and discrimination of facial expressions by preschool children. *Child Development* 53:1299–1311.

George, C., and Main, M. (1979). Social interactions of young abused children: Approach, avoidance and aggression. *Child Development* 50:306–18.

Gottman, J. M., and Katz, L. F. (1989). Effects of marital discord on young children's peer interaction and health. *Developmental Psychology* 25:373–81.

Haight, W., and Parke, R. D. (1991). Longitudinal comparison of pretend and physical parent-child play. Unpublished manuscript, University of Utah.

Haight, W. (1991, April). Belief systems that frame and inform middle class parents' participation in their young children's pretend play. Paper presented at the Society for Research on Child Development, Seattle, Wash.

Jacklin, C. N.; DePietro, J. A.; and Maccoby, E. E. (1984). Sex-typing behavior and sex-typing pressure in child-parent interaction. *Archives of Sexual Behavior* 13:413–25.

Kropp, J., and Haynes, O. M. (1987). Abusive and non-abusive mother's ability to identify general and specific emotion signals of infants. *Child Development* 58:187–90.

Lamb, M. E. (1977a). The development of mother-infant and father-infant attachments in the second year of life. *Developmental Psychology, 13,* 639–647.

Lamb, M. E. (1977b). Father-infant and mother-infant interaction in the first year of life. *Child Development, 48,* 167–181.

Lamb, M E.; Frodi, A.; Hwang, P.; Frodi, M.; and Steinberg, J. (1982). Mother and father-infant interaction involving playing and holding in traditional and non-traditional Swedish families. *Developmental Psychology* 18:215–22.

MacDonald, K. B. (1987). Parent-child physical play with rejected, neglected and popular boys. *Developmental Psychology* 23:705–11.

MacDonald, D. B., and Parke, R. D. (1984). Bridging the gap: Parent-child play interaction and peer interactive competence. *Child Development* 55:1265–77.

MacDonald, K. B., and Parke, R. D. (1986). Parent-child physical play: The effects of sex and age of children and parents. *Sex Roles* 7–15:367–78.

Main, M., and George, C. (1985). Response of abused and disadvantaged toddlers to distress in agemates: A study in a daycare setting. *Developmental Psychology* 21:407–12.

Main, M.; Kaplan, N.; and Cassidy, J. C. (1985). Security in infancy, childhood, and adulthood: A move to the level of representation. In I. Bretherton and E. Waters (Eds.), *Growing points of attachment theory and research. Monographs of the Society for Research in Child Development, 50*(1, 2, Serial No. 209).

Nevelle, B., and Parke, R. D. (1991). Parent age and patterns of play: An observational analysis. Unpublished study, University of Illinois.

Parke, R. D. (1988). Families in life-span perspective: A multi-level developmental approach. In E. M. Hetherington, R. M. Lerner, and M. Perlmutter (eds.), *Child Development in Life Span Perspective.* Hillsdale, N.J.: Lawrence Erlbaum Associates.

Parke, R. D.; MacDonald, K. D.; Beitel, A.; and Bhavnagri, N. (1988). The role of the family in the development of peer relationships. In R. Peters and R. McMahon (eds.), *Social Learning and Systems Approaches to Marriage and the Family*. New York: Bruner-Mazel.

Parke, R. D.; MacDonald, K. D.; Burks, V.; Carson, J.; Bhavnagri, N.; Barth, J. M.; and Beitel, A. (1989). Family and peer systems: In search of the linkages. In K. Kreppner and R. M. Lerner (eds.), *Family Systems and Life-Span Development*. Hillsdale, N.J.: Lawrence Erlbaum Associates.

Parke, R. D., and O'Leary, S. E. (1976). Father-mother-infant interaction in the newborn period: Some findings, some observations and some unresolved issues. In K. Riegel and J. Meacham (eds.), *The Developing Individual in a Changing World. Vol. 2, Social and Environmental Issues*. The Hague: Mouton.

Parke, R. D. & Suomi, S. (1981) Adult male-infant relationships: Human and non-human primate evidence. In K. Immelmann, G. W. Barlow, L. Petrinovitch and M. Main (Eds.) *Behavioral Development* Cambridge: Cambridge University Press.

Parke, R. D., and Tinsley, B. R. (1984). Fatherhood: Historical and contemporary perspectives: In K. McCluskey and H. Reese (eds.), *Life Span Development: Historical and Generational Effects*. New York: Academic.

Pelligrini, A. D. (1988). Elementary school children's rough & tumble play and social competence. *Developmental Psychology, 24*, 802–806.

Power, T. G., and Parke, R. D. (1982). Play as a context for early learning: Lab & home analyses. In L. M. Laosa and I. E. Sigel. (Eds.) *Families as learning environments for children*. New York: Plenum

Putallaz, M. (1987). Maternal behavior and children's sociometric status. *Child Development* 58:32–340.

Roopnarine, J. L.; Talukder, E.; Jain, D.; Joshi, P.; and Srivastav, P. (1990). Characteristics of holding patterns of play and social behaviors between parents and infants in New Delhi, India. *Developmental Psychology* 26:667–673.

Sagi, A.; Lamb, M. E.; Shoham, R.; Dvir, R.; and Lewkowicz, K. (1985). Parent-infant interaction in families on Israeli Kibbutzim. *International Journal of Behavioral Development* 8:273–84.

Smith, P. K. (1989). The role of rough and tumble play in the development of social competence: Theoretical perspectives and empirical evidence. In B. H. Schneider, G. Attili, J. Nadel, and R. Weissberg (eds.), *Social Competence in Developmental Perspective*. Dordrecht, Holland: Kluwer.

Smith, P. K., and Daglish (1977). Sex differences in parent and infant behavior in the home. *Child Development* 48:1250–54.

Smith, P. K., and Lewis, K. (1985). Rough and tumble play, fighting and chasing in nursery school children. *Ethology & Sociobiology* 6:175–81.

Sroufe, L. A.; Schork, E.; Motti, F.; Lawroski, N.; and LaFreniere, P. (1984). The role of affect in social competence. In C. Izard, J. Kagan, and R. Zajonc (eds.), *Affect, Cognition and Behavior.* New York: Plenum.

Stern, D. N. (1977). *The first relationship.* Cambridge, MA: Harvard University Press.

Stern, D. N. (1985). *The interpersonal world of the infant.* New York: Basic Books.

Suomi, S. J., and Harlow, H. F. (1971). Abnormal social behavior is young monkeys. In J. Helmuth (ed.), *The Exceptional Infant: Studies in Abnormality.* Vol. 2. New York: Bruner Mazel.

Tinsley, B. J., and Parke, R. D. (1988). The contemporary role of grandfathers in young families. In P. Bronstein and C. P. Cowan (eds.), *Fatherhood Today: Men's Changing Role in the Family.* New York: Wiley.

Yogman, M. W. (1980). Child development and pediatrics: An evolving relationship. *Infant Mental Health Journal,* 1:89–95.

Yogman, M. W. (1981). The development of the father-infant relationship. In H. Fitzgerald, B. Lester, and M. W. Yogman. *Theory and Research in Behavioral Pediatrics.* Vol. 1. New York: Plenum.

CHAPTER 8

The Necessary Lightness of Mother-Child Play

Phyllis Levenstein and John O'Hara

It is now a well-worn truism that play is the work of a child's early years. When the child's mother joins the "work" of her very young child, its effect can be significantly productive for the child's cognitive and social-emotional development. Many investigators have found that interactive play between mother and child in early childhood, including their reading together, is related to the child's intellectual and/or social-emotional growth (e.g., Clarke-Stewart 1973; Bradley 1986; MacDonald 1988; Whitehurst et al. 1988) and even predicts his or her later competence in these areas (Bradley and Caldwell 1984; Levenstein 1988). Robert W. White has credibly demonstrated, in his seminal essays based on a comprehensive review of widely varied research (1959, 1963), that a child's competence is achieved through his being able to master the environment ("effectance") and his joy at such mastery ("efficacy"). Other reported research strongly hints at the power of the attachment between mother and child to strengthen the links among effectance, efficacy, and competence, although these may go by different names (e.g., Bronfenbrenner 1968, 1974). What has not been so clear is the recognition that play, although it may be the important work of little children, must be real play if it is to have deep and lasting consequences, regardless of whether an adult coplayer has a hidden pedagogical agenda.

When the Verbal Interaction Project's Mother-Child Home Program (MCHP) for two– to four–year-olds and their mothers (U.S. DHEW, Office of Education, 1972; U.S. DHEW, National Institute of Mental Health, 1978) was conceived in 1965 as a preventive educational and mental health intervention, it seemed clear from the work of a variety of theorists and investigators, with Jerome Bruner (1964, 1966) and Lev Vygotsky (1962) foremost among them, that its main method must rest on fostering verbal interaction between mothers and their young children. Formative research in the MCHP's 1965 pilot program affirmed that this could best occur within a play context (Levenstein and Sunley 1968).

Moreover, observers have noted (e.g., Bowlby 1952; Ainsworth 1973; Sroufe et al. 1985) that beginning in their earliest years and perhaps especially evident between the ages of two and four years, children have a strong attachment to their mothers as their primary caregivers. Harlow's work with monkeys (Harlow and Zimmerman 1959) suggested that young children also regard their mothers as a safe base from which to explore the world around them. The strength of a child's bond to his or her mother probably exceeds any other in those early years. The mother's attachment to her child is usually at least as great, with added elements of nurture and protection. When the child's innate drive toward effectance, and the resulting feeling of efficacy achieved through play with self-motivating materials, are combined with the mother's play partnership, the child's effectance and subsequent feelings of efficacy are powerfully reinforced by the mother's affectively charged presence.

Many studies tended to confirm these consequences for mother-child play, independent of White's schema (e.g., Clarke-Stewart et al. 1979; Beckwith 1986; Denham 1989). Gottfried, however, explicitly elaborated on White's concepts in discussing the intrinsic motivational aspects of play experiences and materials (Gottfried 1986).

Designers of the MCHP reasoned, and the program's pilot study confirmed, that for maximum motivation the MCHP's play must be developmentally suited to the children and as acceptable to the mothers as to the children. In fact, the MCHP's philosophy of play contained a paradox: play is children's work, but it should not be perceived as work by the child—and no doubt it never is so perceived in the real world. However, in some departure from real world play experience because formative research in the MCHP's 1965 pilot project indicated that play in the MCHP must be at least minimally planned, the method was designed to give the interveners (and the mothers) a one-page curriculum and a modicum of structure.

Ideas for the kind of play and for the play materials finally chosen for the program drew from sources going back to the beginning of the century (Groos, 1901) and to a few decades later (Moyer and Gilmer 1955; Piaget 1962; Held 1965; Bruner 1976) but fit mainly into the framework provided by Robert White. For these very young children the fantasy and games aspects of play made familiar through the widely known work of Brian Sutton-Smith (e.g., 1971) were secondary to White's conception of play as instinctually motivated attempts to explore and master the environment with the consequence to the child of "joy in being a cause," as Groos phrased it. Piaget adapted Groos's phrase to his own conception of the relation of play to intellect. However, White coined "efficacy" as a special word for this kind of satisfaction, the feeling that comes from having had an effect ("effectance") on the environment. Both effectance and efficacy were antecedent to the feelings of competence crucial to the continuing mastery of increasingly sophisticated skills, including school-related proficiencies.

The MCHP's method was based on the assumption that the elements of effectance, efficacy, and mother-child attachment are vitally linked to the verbally oriented mother-child play interaction which fosters children's intellectual and social-emotional competencies. The method incorporated what many investigators have demonstrated, giving further empirical support to the theories of Bruner and Vygotsky, that a preschool child needs language exchange with significant others for optimum cognitive development (Brown 1958; Irwin 1960; Deutsch 1965; Freeberg and Payne 1967; Moore 1968; Nelson 1973). Overall, it was an attempt to put into practice a method to utilize language stimulation in optimum quality, quantity, and circumstance to prevent the school and mental health problems of children at risk because of poverty. To activate the method it was essential to win the cooperation of their often problem-ridden, mainly single-parent mothers, many of whom had themselves dropped out of high school.

The MCHP's approach was nondidactic and also discouraged the mothers from having a didactic attitude toward their children as the latters' first teachers. Responding to the families' poverty, to White's formulations, and to its own 1965 formative research experience, another of the MCHP's premises was that mother and child needed not loans but gifts of materials intrinsically motivating to both, to stimulate verbal interaction between them. The mother also needed someone to demonstrate, but not directly teach her, how to use those materials to be responsive to her child and to keep the conversation going between them. The most obvious materials attractive to both children and mothers were colorful picture books and toys. They were chosen from commercially available play materials to be capable of stimulating verbal interaction and of sparking White's benign chain of motivation: effectance, efficacy, competence. Their program-fostered use by a mother with her child was intended to provide a foundation for the child's future school-age skills, both literacy and social-emotional development (e.g., task orientation, social responsibility and, self-confidence).

The MCHP was built around twice-weekly half hour home sessions with mother and child for two school years (a total of ninety-two or fewer, the number tailored to the mother's needs) starting when the child was two years old. A home visitor called a "Toy Demonstrator" involved the mother in play with her child while modeling for the mother a curriculum of verbal interaction techniques focused around the "verbal interaction stimulus materials" usually called by the acronym "VISM." These, of course, were the gifts of picture books and toys permanently assigned to the child as "curriculum materials." The curriculum consisted, for each VISM, of a guide sheet containing core conceptual language illustrated by the book or toy (colors, numbers, matching, reasoning, etc.). Every guide sheet was in the same basic format and always ended with the reminder to have fun with the child, the mother, and the VISM. The guide sheets were intended for the Toy Demonstrators but were also given to the mothers. The Toy Demonstrators kept them in a cumulative notebook and referred to them for discussion and guidance at their weekly Toy Demonstrator conferences (group supervision by their MCHP's coordinator).

The method appeared to succeed in its aims (Madden, Levenstein, and Levenstein 1976). From 1967 through 1972 six yearly cohorts in "quasi-experimental" research (families in each of three housing projects agreed to participate in either the MCHP, placebo, or evaluation-only treatments, whichever had been randomly assigned to their own low-income housing project) yielded for the MCHP treatment group not only significant short-term IQ superiority to similar comparison children but also intellectual and academic scores which met national norms in first, third, and fifth grade. Economically disadvantaged graduates of a MCHP replication followed through eighth grade in Pittsfield, Massachusetts, were found to be academically superior to a similar comparison group and actually equal to their nondisadvantaged classmates (DeVito and Karon 1984). Anecdotal data showing positive changes in maternal attitudes came from the original program and from its many replications (all trained and monitored to be valid copies of the original).

A detailed description of the MCHP's method and research findings with both research designs, as well as the program's social background and rationale, may be found elsewhere (Levenstein 1988). However, Figures 8.1, 8.2, and 8.3 (from Levenstein and Madden 1976) summarize in graphic form the intellectual, social-emotional, and academic scores at first and third grades of the quasi-experimental treatment groups (children in the now standard two-year MCHP, in an obsolete one-year MCHP, and in a no-treatment group).

Outside evaluator's outcome data may be seen in Table 14 of Lazar and Darlington 1982, which shows MCHP graduates' IQ as normal and significantly superior at fifth grade to that of a comparison group; and in the numerous data tables of follow-up outcomes through eighth grade for the Pittsfield MCHP graduates and their comparison group in the DeVito and Karon 1984 report.

The MCHP's in-house investigators surmised that a mother's wish to help her child's development and her perception of having been the agent of visibly increasing the child's maturing competence increased her own feelings of efficacy and thus offset some of the dysfunctional "parenting determinants" from her own life posited by Belsky 1984. In the MCHP she had, at least in her own view, promoted her child's development and readiness for school. The attachment between them seemed to have been both utilized and strengthened by the program. Further, to enter into and continue the play with her child, the mother also must have been intrinsically motivated and rewarded by the dyadic play.

No instruments except mothers' self-report measures (of dubious value because of their "demand characteristics") could be found to demonstrate the presence of a mother's program-fostered feeling of efficacy. But perhaps the best indication of its presence were unobtrusive measures: the high percentage of mothers who stayed with the MCHP for its full two years (75 percent in spite of many mothers having to relocate away from the MCHP's geographical reach) and the low percentage of mothers' cancellation of home sessions shown in Figure 8.4 (from Levenstein and Madden 1976). In Figure 8.4, Program 1 refers to the first year of the MCHP and Program 2 to its second year.

However, a "true experimental" (subject-randomized) research design, that was attempted, with variations, in four yearly cohorts

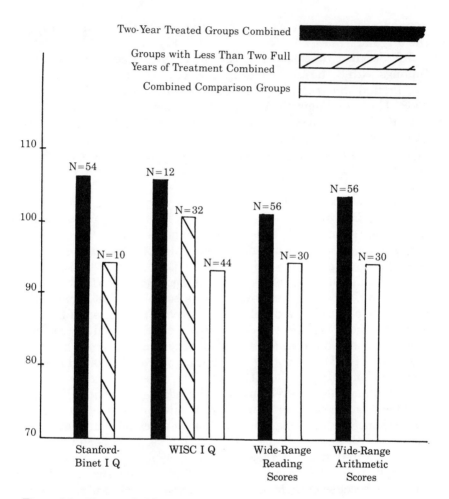

Figure 8.1. First-grade IQ, reading, and arithmetic achievement scores for combined groups receiving two full years of treatment, less than two full years of treatment, and no treatment.

from 1973 to 1976, yielded an opportunity to measure the MCHP's effects on the mother's verbal interactive behavior although, because of sample-bias (Rosenthal and Rosnow 1975), it had resulted in ambiguous IQ outcomes for the children (Madden, O'Hara, and Levenstein 1984; Levenstein 1988). The frequencies of maternal interactive behaviors video-demonstrated by both MCHP and control mothers enabled the investigators not only to measure program

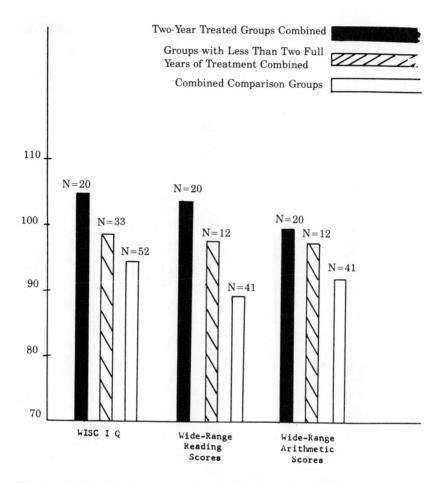

Figure 8.2. Third-grade IQ, reading, and arithmetic achievement scores for combined groups receiving two full years of treatment, less than two full years of treatment, and no treatment.

effects on mothers but also to study, through a relatively sophisticated statistical analysis, the links between mothers' specific interactive behaviors and their children's school-age competencies. The study's aim was to trace relationships that had been previously demonstrated only partially and through simple correlations (Levenstein 1979).

The study of Maternal Interactive Behaviors (MIB) focused on one cohort of "true experiment" mothers and children enrolled as

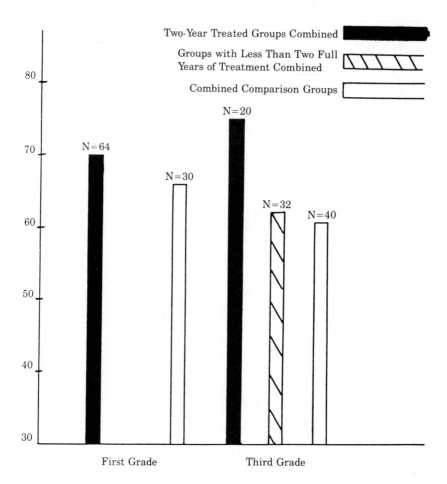

Figure 8.3. First- and third-grade classroom teacher's ratings of socioemotional competence for combined groups receiving two full years of treatment, less than two full years of treatment, and no treatment.

either MCHP or control dyads in 1976. Both groups of mothers showed their verbal interactive behavior in ten minutes of video-taped play at the end of the MCHP in 1978 (when the children were three-and-a-half years old) and two years later in 1980, when the children were in kindergarten. At both times the mothers were scored on the Maternal Interactive Behavior or "MIB" instrument which contained ten items from the MCHP's curriculum which could be demonstrated in a ten-minute videotape segment, as follows:

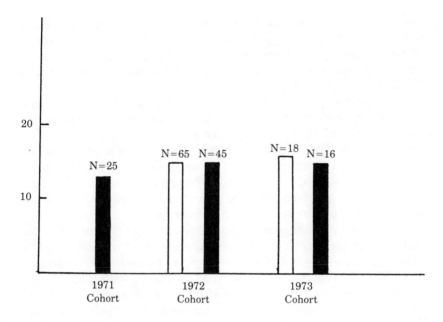

Figure 8.4. Percentage of mothers' home session cancellations in Program 1 and Program 2 for three cohorts.

Item 1. Gives label information: "This is a circle."

Item 2. Gives color information: "Blue circle."

Item 3. Verbalizes actions: "We make the train go."

Item 4. Gives number or shape information: "Four wheels."

Item 5. Solicits information, not "yes" or "no": "What is this shape?"

Item 6. Vocalizes praise: "Good!" "Uh-huh!"

Item 7. Stimulates divergence, fantasy: "Roll the round puzzle piece."

Item 8. Smiles or other positive gesture: Hugs or pats child.

Item 9. Replies to child's vocalization within three seconds.

Item 10. No reply to child's vocalization within three seconds.

The videotaping was planned to give both groups exactly the same experience in a situation which was equally strange to all of the mothers and children. Each program and nonprogram mother was requested, as part of the arrangements for postprogram or follow-up testing, to allow us to videotape her and her child playing with some toys, as well as being offered the opportunity to view the film later herself. Almost all agreed.

The person (a staff member unfamiliar to both program and nonprogram mothers) who drove the mothers and children to the MIB site showed them to the "video play room." It was actually a stripped-down office furnished mainly with a child's table and two chairs for mother and child. Two attractive toys anticipated to be new to all of the dyads were arranged on the table, and a video camera was on a tripod in one corner. A cable connected it with a video recorder and monitor screen in the next room.

The two toys were prearranged on the table in the same way for each mother-child pair: (1) two cars and a locomotive that could be linked by hook-eye connections to form a stylized, colorful freight train; and (2) an unassembled form board puzzle with multicolored recesses for eight forms, surrounded by the eight forms of differing shapes and of contrasting colors, designed to fit into the recesses.

The car driver explained: "This is the play room and toys we talked about. Here's a chair for (Child) and one for you. (Child) may play with the toys after I leave you and of course you may help in any way you like. That video camera will take the pictures. I'll turn it on just before I leave you and (child), and I'll turn it off when I come back. I'll be back in ten minutes." She answered the mother's questions, if any, by saying pleasantly, "That's up to you."

The car driver then turned on the camera and left, shutting the door behind her. After ten minutes, she returned to shut off the camera and to escort the mother and child to the next testing "station" (the MIB measurement was the first station of postprogram and follow-up subject evaluations.)

Some time later the videotape was viewed and scored by a trained rater who did not know whether or not the mother and child on the videotape had been in the program. She watched the tape four times in order to be able to count the exact number of times a mother showed the interactive behaviors contained in the ten MIB items. Nine maternal behaviors were types of interactions encouraged by the program (items 1–9), and one was discouraged by the program (Item 10).

The rater tallied the count for each item on mothers' MIB instruments, which contained the ten interactive behavior items and space to record how often they occurred. The total count for all the

MIB items except for item 10 became the "Total Positive Score." The score for item 10 was subtracted from that score to get the final "Total MIB Score."

The MIB scores for the 1976 cohort, that was evaluated in both 1978 and in 1980, strongly suggested that program mothers had learned, practiced, and retained the program's verbal interaction techniques. In the 1978 after-program rating of all 1976 mothers in videotaped play with their children, the program mothers scored markedly above nonprogram mothers in their total MIB behavior with their children, an average of 50 percent higher. Moreover, the program mothers maintained their superiority when videotaped again in play with their children in 1980 when the youngsters were five and a half years old and in kindergarten. The 1980 MIB item scores, the total positive score and the total MIB score for all of the 1976 mothers were reported in Table 6.10 of Levenstein 1988.

The program mothers had learned from their home sessions, and had retained at least through their children's kindergarten year, the specific, program-related interactive behavior which they showed before the video camera. The nonprogram mothers had had no opportunity to learn these specific techniques and therefore could not demonstrate them in the MIB situation.

However, of wider interest, when the two treatment groups were combined (N = 37) for a 1980 stepwise multiple regression data analysis, relating MIB item scores to child competency measures, the results indicated that some of the program-promoted maternal behaviors (MIB items 1, 2, 3, and 6) were negatively related to school connected competencies, summarized in Table 8.1, "Multiple Regressions of MIB Items[a] (Follow-Up 1980) on Children's Behavior (Follow-Up 1980) Combined MCHP-Control Groups" (from Levenstein and O'Hara 1983).

Nonetheless, as Table 8.1 shows, the mother's verbal responsiveness on the MIB (item 9: "Replies to child's vocalization within three seconds") predicted consistently and significantly their children's kindergarten competencies. Specifically, this maternal interactive behavior predicted the children's:

- Stanford-Binet IQ;
- Reading ability;
- arithmetic ability;
- general social-emotional competence (CBT or "Child's Behavior Traits" [Levenstein and Verbal Interaction Project Staff 1976] Total Score);

Table 8.1
Multiple Regressions of MIB Items [a](Follow-Up 1980) on Children's Behavior (Follow-Up 1980) Combined MCHP- Control Groups

Children's Variables

MIB Item	Stanford-Binet IQ	WRAT Reading	WRAT Arithmetic	CBT Total Score	CBT Social Responsibility	CBT Task Orientation	CBT Self-confidence	CBT Psy-chologist Rating
1-Gives label information	−.62	−.45	−.75					
2-Gives color information	−.52	−.46	−.38	−.24		−.48	−.32	−.19
3-Verbalizes actions		−.85	−.42	−.32		−.52		−.54
4-Gives number and shape info.	+.53	+.50	+.35					
5-Questions Policits info.								
6-Vocalizes praise	−.51			−.45	− .30	−.20	−.55	−.47
7-Stimulates divergent use	+.20	+.68	+.61			+.29		
8-Smiles/ Positive Gesture	+.68	+.33	+.54				+.28	+.24
9-Replies	+.59	+.72	+.36	+.74	+.45	+.60	+.45	+.68
10-Does not reply				−.22		−.26		
R	.83	.70	.73	.56	.38	.65	.64	.70
R^2	.69	.48	.53	.32	.15	.42	.41	.49
F	7.74	3.29	3.92	2.34	1.91	2.99	4.26	4.75
df	8,28	8,28	8,28	6,30	3.33	7.29	5.31	6,30
P	.001	.01	.01	NS	NS	.05	.01	.01
Adjusted R^2	.60	.37	.39	.18	.07	.28	.31	.38

Notes: Values across MIB item rows are standardized beta weights. A value is given for only those items which entered into the predictions of children's variables prior to a preselected cutoff point. The regression summary statistics are presented for the prediction including only the variables for which beta weights are given (not for all MIB items). $N = 37$.

a. Treatment effects were partialled out prior to entering MIB items into the prediction. This procedure used 1 *df*. The independent treatment variable R^2s were .01 for IQ, .07 for WRAT Arithmetic, .02 for CBT Task Orientation and CBT Psychologist, and .00 for all other variables. The R^2s presented in the table include the treatment effect.

- social responsibility;
- task orientation;
- self-confidence.

Moreover, the mothers' warmth toward their children as expressed in MIB item 8 ("Smiles or makes other positive gesture") also significantly predicted the children's:

- Stanford-Binet IQ;
- reading ability;
- arithmetic ability;
- self-confidence.

Similarly, mothers' stimulation of creativity ("divergence"), MIB item 7, significantly predicted the children's:

- Stanford-Binet IQ;
- reading ability;
- arithmetic ability;
- task orientation.

Consistent with these correlations, item 10 ("No reply to child's vocalization within three seconds") was either not related at all or was negatively related to all of the children's skills included in Table 8.1.

However, inconsistent with the positive correlations between mothers' warmth/creativity stimulation and children's skills were negative correlations between the children's skills and MIB item 6 ("Vocalizes praise"). One could speculate that mothers' vocalized praise, rather than the mere giving of nonvocalized emotional support (the warmth seen in item 8, "Smiles or other positive gesture"), may have been used most with children whom the mothers had already identified as needing extra support, an identification predictive of children's future weaknesses. The negative correlations between children's competencies and three information-giving maternal behaviors which were part of the MCHP curriculum may have a similar explanation, that mothers tended to provide more information to children whose noticeable developmental lags had already predicted weaknesses in school-related skills.

In any case, one important program-related conclusion seems very clear: mothers' bombardment of their children with a relentless barrage of information is dysfunctional for the children's development of school-related cognitive and social-emotional skills. Pedagogically driven mother-child play must negotiate a thin line between feeding information to the child and simply responding quickly to the child with lighthearted conversation around play materials. It is the verbal responsiveness of the mother which is the important element in mother-child play and indeed in all mother-child transactions (Bradley 1989; Clarke-Stewart 1973; Clarke-Stewart et al. 1979).

Thus Table 8.1's correlations not only revealed a network supportive of children's school-related skills apparently formed by mothers' warmth, stimulation of creativity and, most of all, by their verbal responsiveness, it also issued a sharp warning that early childhood learning in the MCHP can function best in a nondidactic dyadic climate of light spontaneity and fun. It showed that even the minimal emphasis on the MCHP's curriculum contained in the VISM guide sheets was actually less important than the nondidactic maternal verbal responsiveness made possible by the play elements of the program.

Lightness in mother-child play appears to be a necessary condition if children's optimal cognitive and social-emotional development is to result from the dyadic interaction.

References

Ainsworth, M. D. (1973). The development of infant-mother attachment. In B. M. Caldwell and H. N. Ricciuti (eds.), *Review of Child Development research.* Vol. 3, *Child Development and Social Policy.* Chicago: University of Chicago Press.

Beckwith, L. (1986). Parent-infant interaction and infants' social-emotional development. In A. W. Gottfried and C. C. Brown (eds.), *Play Interactions.* Lexington, Mass.: Lexington.

Belsky, J. (1984). The determinants of parenting: A process model. *Child Development* 55:81–96.

Bowlby, J. (1952). *Maternal Care and Mental Health.* Geneva: World Health Organization.

Bradley, R. H. (1986). Play materials and intellectual development. In Gottfried and Brown, *Play Interactions.*

Bradley, R. H. (1989). HOME measurement of maternal responsiveness. In M. H. Bornstein (ed.), *Maternal Responsiveness.* San Francisco: Jossey-Bass.

Bradley, R., and Caldwell, B. (1984). The relation of infants' home environment to achievement test performance in first grade: A follow-up study. *Child Development* 55:803–9.

Bronfenbrenner, U. (1968). Early deprivation: A cross-species analysis. In G. Newton and S. Levine (eds.) *Early Experience and Behavior.* Springfield, Ill. C. Thomas.

Bronfenbrenner, U. (1974). *Is Early Intervention Effective? A Report on Longitudinal Evaluations of Preschool Programs* (Vol. II). U.S. Department of Health, Education and Welfare, Office of Human Development, OHD 74-25. Washington, D.C.: Government Printing Office, 1974.

Brown, R. (1958). *Words and Things.* Glencoe, Ill.: The Free Press.

Bruner, J. S. (1964). The course of cognitive growth. *American Psychologist* 19:1–15.

Bruner, J. S; Olver, R.; and Greenfield, P. (1966). *Studies in Cognitive Growth.* New York: John Wiley and Sons.

Bruner, J. S. (1976). Nature and uses of immaturity. In J. S. Bruner, A. Jolly, and K. Sylva (eds.), *Play.* New York: Basic Books.

Clarke-Stewart, K. A. (1973). Interactions between mothers and their young children: Characteristics and consequences. *Monographs of the Society for Research in Child Development* 38 (6–7).

Clarke-Stewart, K. A.; Vanderstoep, L.; and Killim, G. (1979). Analysis and replication of mother-child relations at two years of age. *Child Development* 50:777–93.

Denham, S. A. (1989). Maternal affect and toddlers' social-emotional competence. *American Journal of Orthopsychiatry* 59:368–76.

Devito, P. J., and Karon, J. P. (1984). Final Report, Parent-Child Home Program, Chapter I, ECIA, Pittsfield Public Schools, September 1, 1984.

Deutsch, M. (1965). The role of social class in language development and cognition. *American Journal of Orthopsychiatry* 35:78–88.

Freeberg, N. E., and Payne, D. T. (1967). Parental influence on cognitive development in early childhood: A review. *Child Development* 38: 66–87.

Golden, M., and Birns, B. (1968). Social class and cognitive development in infancy. *Merrill-Palmer Quarterly* 14:139–49.

Gottfried, A. E. (1986). Intrinsic motivational aspects of play experiences and materials. In Gottfried and Brown, *Play Interactions.*

Groos, K. (1901). The play of man. In Bruner, Jolly, and Sylva, *Play,* 1976.

Harlow, H. F., and Zimmerman, R. R. (1959). Affectional response of the infant monkey. *Science* 130:421–32.

Held, R. (1965). Plasticity in sensory-motor systems. *Scientific American,* 213:84–94.

Irwin, O. C. (1960). Infant speech: Effect of systematic reading of stories. *Journal of Speech and Hearing Research* 3:187–90.

Lazar, I., and Darlington, R. (1982). Lasting effects of early education: A report from the Consortium for Longitudinal Studies. *Monographs of the Society for Research in Child Development,* serial no. 195, vol. 47 (2–3).

Levenstein, P. (1970). Cognitive growth in preschoolers through verbal interaction with mothers. *American Journal of Orthopsychiatry* 40: 426–32.

Levenstein, P. (1979). The parent-child network. In A. Simmons-Martin and D. R. Calvert (eds.), *Parent-Child Intervention.* New York: Grune and Stratton, Inc.

Levenstein, P. (1988). *Messages from Home.* Columbus, Ohio: Ohio State University Press.

Levenstein, P., and Madden, J. (1976). *Progress Report to the Carnegie Corporation of New York, 1973–1976.* Freeport, N.Y.: Verbal Interaction Project. Mimeographed.

Levenstein, P., and O'Hara, J. M. (1983). *Tracing the Parent-Child Network: Final Report, 9/1/79–8/31/82.* Grant No. NIE G 8000042, National Institute of Education, U.S. Department of Education.

Levenstein, P., and Staff, Verbal Interaction Project. (1976). Child's Behavior Traits. In O. Johnson (ed.), *Tests and Measurements in Child Development, Handbook II.* San Francisco: Jossey-Bass.

Levenstein, P., and Sunley, R. (1968). Stimulation of verbal interaction between disadvantaged mothers and children. *American Journal of Orthopsychiatry* 38:116–21.

MacDonald, K. B. (1988). *Social and Personality Development.* New York: Plenum.

Madden, J.; Levenstein, P.; and Levenstein, S. (1976). Longitudinal IQ outcomes of the Mother-Child Home Program. *Child Development* 47: 1015–25.

Madden, J.; O'Hara, J. M.; and Levenstein, P. (1984). Home again. *Child Development* 55:636–47.

Moore, T. (1968). Language and intelligence: A longitudinal study of the first eight years. *Human Development* 11:2–24.

Moyer, K. N., and Gilmer, B. V. (1955). Attention span for children for experimentally designed toys. *Journal of Genetic Psychology* 87: 187–201.

Nelson, K. (1973). Structure and strategy in learning to talk. *Monographs of the Society for Research in Child Development,* serial no. 149 (1–2).

Piaget, J. (1962). *Play, Dreams and Imitation in Childhood.* New York: W. W. Norton.

Rosenthal, R., and Rosnow, R. L. (1975). *The Volunteer Subject.* New York: Wiley-Interscience.

Sroufe, L. A.; Jacobvitz, D.; Mangelsdorf, S.; DeAngelo, E.; and Ward, M. J. (1985). Generational boundary dissolution between mothers and their preschool children. *Child Development* 56:317–85.

Sutton-Smith, B. A. (1971). A syntax for play and games. In R. E. Herman and B. Sutton-Smith (eds.), *Child's Play.* New York: John Wiley and Sons.

U.S. Department of Health, Education, and Welfare, National Institute of Mental Health. (1978). *Parent-Child Program Series, Report No. I: Mother-Child Home Program, Freeport, New York.* Publication No. 78-659. Washington, D.C.: Government Printing Office.

U.S. Department of Health, Education, and Welfare, Office of Education. (1972). *Model Programs, Compensatory Education: Mother-Child Home Program, Freeport, New York:* Office of Education, 72-84. Washington, D.C.: Government Printing Office.

Vygotsky, L. S. (1962). *Thought and Language.* Boston: Massachusetts Institute of Technology.

White, R. W. (1959). Motivation reconsidered: The concept of competence. *Psychological Review* 66:297–333.

White, R. W. (1963). *Ego and Reality in Psychoanalytic Theory.* Psychological Issues, 3, Monograph 11. New York: International Universities Press.

Whitehurst, G. J.; Falco, F. L.; Lonigan, E. J.; Fischel, J. E.; DeBaryshe, B. D.; Valdez-Menchaca, M. C.; and Caulfield, M. (1988). Accelerating language development through book reading. *Developmental Psychology* 24:552–59.

CHAPTER 9

Mother-Infant Play and Maternal Depression

Jeffrey F. Cohn

During the first six weeks of life, babies are inwardly directed. Their developmental task is learning to regulate internal states, such as arousal. Beginning at about eight to ten weeks, they change dramatically. With greater control of their internal states and increased visual acuity, tracking, and information processing, babies come to participate in truly social interactions. Two achievements mark this transition: the abilities to make eye contact and to smile in response to external stimulation.

For the next six to seven months the central developmental task becomes learning to regulate dyadic interactions, and especially social play. Sustained mutual gaze and the sharing of positive affect become key features of parent-infant interactions. Individual differences in parent-infant play set the stage for social and emotional development beyond the first year. In this chapter, I briefly summarize what we know about the content and coordination of mother-infant play from two months through the middle of the first year and review the influence of maternal depression on mother-infant play during this period. The effects of depression on play during the first half year can inform our understanding of normal mother-infant play and, from the perspective of developmental psychopathology, suggest mechanisms through which individual differences in mother-infant play may mediate developmental outcomes.

Recent research (Cohn and Elmore 1988; Cohn and Tronick 1988, 1987) supports a model of dyadic interaction initially pro-

Preparation of this manuscript was supported in part by National Institute of Mental Health Grant MH40867 and NSF Grant 8919711.

posed by Brazelton and colleagues (Brazelton, Koslowski, and Main 1974). During mother-infant play, maternal positive affective expression (e.g., smile, exaggerated "play face," or animated vocal expression) frames the baby's positive affective expression (e.g., interest or smile) as the baby cycles from attention to and away from the mother. The dyadic sequence begins with the mother passively watching her baby while the baby's attention is directed away from her. The mother then elicits her baby's attention by showing positive affect; the baby responds with neutral affective expressions; the baby then becomes positive in affective expression; and a dyadic state of positive engagement is achieved. This shared positive dyadic state is terminated when the baby becomes neutral in expression and turns his or her attention away from the mother while she remains positive.

In this model, two key functional features of the mother's (or other caregiver's) behavior are its affective quality and its temporal relationship to the infant's behavior. The mothers' positive affect (Cohn and Tronick 1987) and responsiveness (Cohn and Elmore 1988) are critical to infant attention and affect. Infants match their mother's level of affective expression (Cohn and Tronick 1987; Tronick and Cohn 1989), and this matching is achieved through a process of bidirectional influence (Cohn and Tronick 1988; Symons and Moran 1987). Mother and baby respond contingently to changes in each other's behavior. Thus, both the quality and the timing of the mother's affect influence the infant's response during normal interactions. Factors that influence either of these features are likely to have profound effects on social play between mothers and infants.

Constricted or negative affect and diminished responsiveness are characteristic features of depression. Affective expression may be sad, depressed, flat, angry, or irritable. The normal timing of affective expressions may also be altered. They may be either slowed down and delayed (psycho-motor retardation) or speeded up and frenetic (mania or hypomania). These emotional states may be relatively stable and traitlike (e.g., as in dysthymia); or they may be labile, alternating, for instance, between sad and angry. Because depression is likely to distort both the quality and the timing of affective expression, maternal depression is likely to affect adversely interactions with infants and young children.

Simulated Depression and Mother-Infant Play

Using an experimental simulation of maternal depression, two studies have tested the hypothesis that sad or withdrawn affective

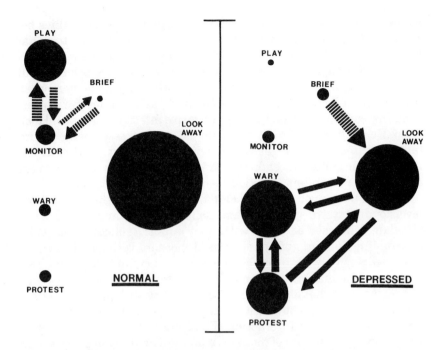

Figure 9.1. State transition diagram for normal and simulated depressed conditions. The relative proportion of time spent in each state is indicated by the size of the circle representing that state. Arrows represent transition probabilities among states. The thickness of arrows represents the size of transition probabilities. Striped arrows indicate those transition probabilities for which conditional and unconditional probabilities significantly differ, $p < .05$. Only transition probabilities greater than 0.20 are depicted (from Cohn and Tronick 1983).

expression during face-to-face play leads to negative affect in infants. With Ed Tronick (Cohn and Tronick 1983), I instructed mothers of three–month-old infants to simulate depression or behave normally while interacting with their infant. In the simulated depression condition, mothers' affect was either sad or flat. Infants responded dramatically to this perturbation.

Figure 9.1, from Cohn and Tronick (1983), shows the difference in infants' behavior between the simulated depressed and normal interactions. The size of the circles represents the proportion of time that infants spent in each affective state. The arrows represent the probability of transitions among states.

In the simulated depressed condition, the proportion of positive affect (denoted by *play*) was far less than in the normal interaction. Extreme reductions in the mother's positive affect resulted in extreme reductions in the positive affect of the baby. When babies became positive, they did so only briefly (*brief positive*). Note, too, that the organization as well as the distribution of infant's behavior was affected. Not only were infants more negative and less positive, but they also organized their behavior differently. They no longer cycled between neutral (denoted by *monitor*) and positive affective expression. Instead, they cycled between negative affective states and *look away*. Even after mothers again resumed nondepressed behavior, infants remained more negative and withdrawn. Thus, in this experimental manipulation, sad, flat affect depressed both concurrent and subsequent infant affective response.

In a follow-up study, Field (1984) instructed mothers with high levels of depressive symptoms and nondepressed control mothers to simulate depressed behavior with their infant. Replicating the original findings, infants of nondepressed mothers responded to simulated depression with increased negative affect, and they remained more negative and less responsive even after their mother resumed nondepressed behavior. Infants of mothers with high levels of depressive symptoms showed little change between the normal and simulated depressed interaction. Field interpreted this finding as suggesting that infants of mothers who were actually depressed saw little change between their mother's normal behavior and a situation in which she was instructed to act sad and withdrawn. Affective expressions other than sad or constricted affect have yet to be studied experimentally.

In the simulated depression experiments, maternal affect and responsiveness were dampened. However, it is possible that depression might differentially affect one or the other aspect of the mother's behavior. For instance, clinically depressed mothers might successfully "simulate" positive affect, but have greater difficulty in coordinating the timing of their expressions. Ekman (1984) has emphasized the role of false smiles in adult interactions, but little attention has been paid to the temporal organization of disingenuous affective expression.

Perturbations in the Timing of Mother-Infant Play

To test whether the timing as well as the quality of maternal affect influences infant behavior, Marquita Elmore and I (Cohn and Elmore 1988) instructed mothers of three–month-old babies to become still-faced for five seconds contingent on their infant becoming positive. This perturbation of the usual relation between mothers' and infants' affect tests how closely infants monitor the temporal relationship between their own and their mother's affect.

Consistent with previous research (Cohn and Tronick 1987; Kaye and Fogel 1980), mothers were almost always in a positive state when their infant became positive. But when mothers briefly became still-faced contingent on infants' positive expression, the infants became less likely to cycle between positive and neutral expression and more likely to turn away. This study found that babies are sensitive to the reciprocity of their mother's affective behavior. However, the mismatches (cf. Tronick and Cohn 1989) between mothers' and infants' affect in this manipulation were relatively long (five seconds) and were defined primarily in terms of facial expression of affect. Timing violations of shorter duration and in other modalities might have less effect. The durations of maternal vocalizations are much briefer than those of maternal facial expressions, and infants may be more sensitive to their mother's latency to respond vocally.

In view of the strong experimental evidence that infants are sensitive to depressed maternal affective expression, it is crucial to learn whether mothers who are actually depressed show similar distortions of affective expression and timing while playing with their babies. The answer depends in part on how depression is defined.

Diagnostic Issues

Most research on infants younger than a year (Bettes 1988; Cohn, Matias, Tronick, Lyons-Ruth, and Connell 1986; Field 1984; Field et al. 1988) has used self-report measures of depressive symptoms rather than a standard clinical interview to diagnose depression. Typical instruments are the Center for Epidemiologic Studies Depression Scale (CES-D) (Radloff 1977) and the Beck Depression Inventory (BDI) (Beck, Ward, Mendelson, et al. 1969). These are Likert-type scales that include items about mood and cognitive and vegetative symptoms associated with depression. High scores suggest greater severity and are considered diagnostic for screening purposes. Self-report measures in the postpartum period, however, over-diagnose depression and fail to identify some women who meet formal diagnostic criteria (Campbell and Cohn 1991). Elevated levels of depressive symptoms may index a range of psychiatric disorders, and not just depression (Garrison and Earls 1986).

Depression also is often confounded with other risk factors, such as poverty and child abuse or neglect. Some epidemiologic evidence suggests that parental depression in the absence of multiple risk factors is of little consequence to social and emotional development (Robins 1974; Rutter et al. 1974; for review, see Rutter and Garmezy 1983). Thus, findings from studies that assess depression through self-report instruments or that confound depression with other risk factors cannot support strong inferences about the influence of depression. It is important, therefore, to make careful distinctions with respect to diagnosis of depression and presence of other risk factors.

High Levels of Depressive Symptoms Co-Occurring with Multiple Other Risk Factors

Using the BDI to assess depression in women of low SES, Field has conducted a series of studies that suggest depressed mothers and their infants show fewer positive and more negative facial expressions and vocalize less than nondepressed mothers and infants (Field 1984). Depressed mother-infant pairs were more likely to share negative affect, whereas nondepressed were more likely to share positive affect (Field, Healy, Goldstein, and Guthertz 1990). Infants of depressed mothers were also more likely to respond with increased negative and less positive affective expressions during interactions with a nondepressed female stranger (Field, Healy, Goldstein, Perry, and Bendell 1988). These studies by Field and colleagues suggest that negative affect is more common in interactions between depressed versus nondepressed mothers and infants in multiproblem families.

Individual Differences.

Depression is a highly variable disorder, and it is likely that its influence on mother-infant play is not uniform. To investigate this possibility, my colleagues and I (Cohn et al. 1986; Cohn and Tronick 1989) studied individual differences in mother-infant play in multiproblem families. Subjects were thirteen mothers and their six– to seven–month-old infants. The mothers had moderate to severe levels of depressive symptoms, as assessed with the CES-D, and high rates of factors associated with risk of childhood behavior disorder, such as child neglect, substance abuse, and low SES (Rutter and Garmezy 1983).

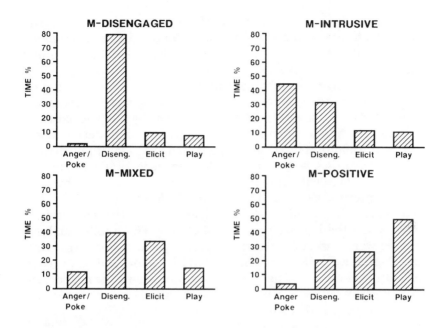

Figure 9.2.   Individual differences among mothers in the percentage of time spent in behavioral states during face-to-face interaction with their babies (from Cohn and Tronick 1989).

With few exceptions, the mothers in this study all showed at least some negative affect. Variation among mothers in type of negative affect shown, however, was pronounced, requiring that the group be broken down into subgroups (Figure 9.2).

At the extreme of disengagement, two mothers (M-Disengaged) showed a pattern similar to some clinical descriptions of depressed mothers (Weissman and Paykel 1974) and what Cohn and Tronick (1983) and also Field (1984) had modeled in the simulated depression studies. These mothers were disengaged more than 75 percent of the time. They slouched back in their chairs, often turned away, and spoke in an expressionless voice. They were responsive only to active infant distress.

At the other extreme was the largest group (M-Intrusive): six mothers with high proportions of angry or intrusive behaviors, such as rough handling, poking at their babies, and speaking in an angry tone. Two others (M-Mixed) also showed *anger/poke,* although less so, together with some *play* and much *elicit* (attempts to get the baby's attention). A small group of three mothers (M-Positive) showed high rates of positive expression, comparable to those found among nondepressed mothers (Cohn and Tronick 1987; Kaye and Fogel 1980).

These individual differences among mothers had striking effects on their babies (Figure 9.3). Infants of disengaged mothers had the highest proportions of *protest,* which suggests that the most distressing behavior for infants may be the pattern of maternal disengagement. Infants of intrusive mothers had the highest proportions of *look away,* which is consistent with previous work indicating that increases in maternal intensity are unsuccessful in reestablishing mutual interaction when infants are looking away (Cohn and Tronick 1987; Kaye and Fogel 1980). The infants of the most positive mothers had the highest proportions of *play.* These individual differences were unrelated to any particular combination of risk factors. Depressive symptoms and other risk factors did not predict maladaptive interaction patterns in a simple one-to-one fashion. Infants' affective behavior was specific to the affective quality and reciprocity of mothers' behavior.

High Levels of Depressive Symptoms Occurring in the Absence of Other Risk Factors

The studies reviewed above suggest that depression impacts on mothers and infants in low-SES, multiproblem families. Even subclinical levels of depression may significantly influence mother's interactive behavior. Using the BDI to assess depression in middleclass mothers, Bettes (1988) studied the timing and acoustic contours of mothers' vocalizations to three–month-old infants. The mothers she studied had subclinical to mild depression according to the BDI. Depressed mothers were slower to respond to their infant's vocalizations and were less likely to use the expanded intonation contours that are typical of infant-directed speech. Depressed mothers also used vocal utterances and pauses of more variable duration. Predictable utterance and pause durations and exaggerated contours are believed to promote dyadic interaction. Although differences in vocal behavior between depressed and nondepressed mothers in this study were striking, no differences in infant behavior were found. One reason may be the low levels of depression, or that measurements of infant behavior were limited to vocal utterances

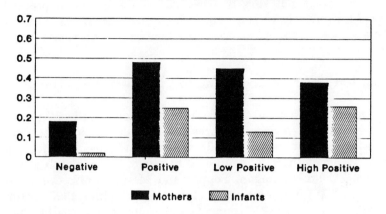

coeffs > .25, p < .05

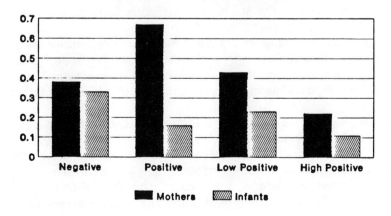

coeffs > .25, p < .05

Figure 9.3.   Individual differences among babies in the percentage of time spent in behavioral states during face-to-face interaction with their mothers (from Cohn and Tronick 1989).

and pauses and measures of mothers' behavior were limited to the vocal expression. It is possible that maternal facial expression, in particular, did not vary between depressed and nondepressed groups. Alternatively, the influence of depression on infant behavior in the absence of multiple risk factors may be less pervasive.

Depression Assessed According to Diagnostic Criteria

The studies reviewed in the preceding sections used self-report symptom ratings to assess depression and depression often co-occurred with other risk factors. To determine the specific effects of depression on mothers' and infants' behavior, my research group (Campbell, Cohn, Flanagan, Popper and Meyers 1992; Campbell and Cohn 1991; Cohn, Matias, Campbell and Hopkins 1990; Cohn, Campbell, and Ross 1991) conducts screening interviews by telephone at six to eight weeks postpartum with married, primiparous mothers of full-term, healthy singletons. Mothers who screen positive for depression on an abbreviated diagnostic interview (see Cohn et al. 1990 for details) and nondepressed control mothers are then interviewed at home, using a more extensive semistructured psychiatric interview (SADS-L) (Endicott and Spitzer 1978). Mothers' responses and interviewer ratings are scored according to Research Diagnostic Criteria (RDC) (Spitzer, Endicott, and Robins 1978). RDC for depression are dysphoric mood lasting two or more weeks and at least three of eight symptoms of depression (e.g., loss of interest, or sleep disorder not associated with nighttime feedings). For inclusion in the study, subjects must meet RDC for depression or be nondepressed, control subjects.

We also obtain from each mother a self-report depression measure. How a woman feels may differ from how she is perceived through the lens of a psychiatric interview and diagnostic criteria. The CES-D is administered independently of the psychiatric interview.

What follows are preliminary findings from the first sixty-eight mothers and infants that have been studied. Twenty-seven mothers met RDC and also had CES-D scores above sixteen. These women were both clinically depressed, as determined by psychiatric interview and diagnostic criteria, and reported subjective feelings of acute distress. Ten women met RDC only. Thirty-one mothers were nondepressed, control subjects. Women were excluded from the study if they had clinically significant CES-D scores without meet-

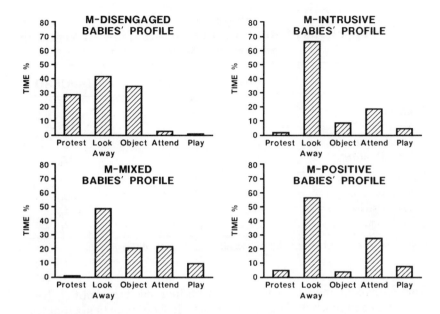

Figure 9.4.   Stability coefficients for percentage of time mothers' and babies' spent in affective states.

ing RDC for depression. By defining subgroups of depressed mothers, the study can determine whether diagnostic criteria alone, or diagnostic criteria together with high levels of self-reported distress, are crucial mediating factors of mothers' and infants' affect.

At two, four, and six months structured face-to-face interactions were videotaped in the families' home as part of a longer assessment. Videotapes were later coded using affect descriptors on a one-second time base by staff blind to mothers' diagnosis and CES-D score. The principal descriptors for mothers are *high positive* (exaggerated facial expressions, e.g., mock surprise), *low positive* (smile), and *negative* (sad, angry, or harsh responses, poking, and also disengagement, e.g., leaning back and away from the interaction). We have not yet examined variation in the type of negative affect shown. For infants, *high positive* refers to smiles and *low positive* refers to facial expressions of interest or excitement.

Mothers' behavior during face-to-face interaction showed moderate stability (Figure 9.4). The test-retest correlation between a two- and four-month composite for positive affect (high and low positive) during the structured face-to-face interaction approached .5;

Table 9.1
Mean Proportions of Mothers' and Infants' Time in Negative and Positive States

	Control	RDC	RDC/CESD
Mothers			
Negative	—	1	3
Low Positive	72	75	72
High Positive	40_a	56_a	22_b
Babies			
Negative	16_a	14_a	39_b
Low Positive	45_a	43_a	24_b
High Positive	25_{ab}	41_a	17_b

Note: Row means with dissimilar subscripts significantly differ, $p < .05$

from four to six months, this correlation increased to about .7. Negative affect in mothers became more stable from four to six months. The change appears due to increasing negativity in some depressed mothers. Infant behavior was less stable but also showed an increase in stability for negative affect.

These stability coefficients are much larger than those reported in some other microanalytic research (e.g., Bakeman and Brown 1980). One reason may be the wide range of affect sampled in depressed and nondepressed subjects.

Table 9.1 shows the mean proportion of time that mothers and babies were in positive and negative affective states at two months. Mothers who met psychiatric criteria and reported high levels of subjective distress (denoted as RDC/CES-D mothers) differed from both mothers who met RDC-only and control subjects. The RDC/CES-D had a narrower range of positive affect (lower percentages of high positive/exaggerated expressions). These data support Stern's early speculation (1977) that depressed mothers are less able to play with their own behavior. The proportion of negative affect at two months in RDC/CES-D mothers, while not significant, signaled an important developmental trend. With development, incidence of negative rather than positive affect more consistently discriminated depressed from nondepressed mothers.

At two months, infants of RDC/CES-D mothers differed from other infants on most measures. They were less positive and more negative than other infants. At four and six months, however, differences in infant behavior related to initial depression were not found. One reason may be that about half of the women who were depressed at two months were no longer depressed by six months. The course of depressive episodes may be an important factor that influences mothers' and infants' behavior.

To assess mother-infant reciprocity, we conducted two sets of analyses. First, correlations were computed for the distributions of mother and infant negative and positive affect. This analysis indicates whether mother-infant pairs match affective level over time. Second, time-series analyses were conducted to assess synchrony and mutual influence (Cohn and Tronick 1988; Cohn et al. 1990). At each age, the durations of mothers' and infants' positive affect were moderately correlated (e.g., $r = .61$ at two months). Moment-to-moment synchrony, or coherence, increased from two to four months, but was unrelated to diagnostic status. In the analyses so far, no differences in mutual influence or synchrony related to depression were found (cf. Field et al. 1990).

To assess the infant's capacity to cope with an interpersonal stressor, mothers were asked to sit en face and maintain a still-face expression for three minutes. This assessment was repeated at two, four, and six months, and findings were aggregated across age. We tabulated the frequency of infant attempts to elicit the mother to change her expression. Like Field, we found that infants of depressed mothers were less likely to positively elicit the mother. This difference occurred in the RDC/CES-D group only.

RDC/CES-D infants were also less likely to change affect expression during the still-face manipulation. They would become upset or sober and then remain so for the duration of the episode. One interpretation is that infants of depressed mothers found the still-face stressful, but were less resourceful at coping with this stress. They seemed to lack a sense of their own effectance. An alternative interpretation is that for infants of depressed mothers the still-face represents less of a change from the mother's normal expression and so is less stressful than for infants of nondepressed mothers (Field et al. 1988). However, what distinguished depressed from nondepressed mothers during structured face-to-face interactions after two months was negative, not positive, expression, and even then the absolute amount of negative expression in this context was low. Thus, this alternative explanation seems less compelling. Rather, the still-face situation was equally stressful, but the infants of RDC/CES-D depressed mothers were less able to cope with the stress of a nonresponsive partner.

Summary and Discussion

Mother-infant play is characterized by positive affect sharing and mutual responsiveness. In normative studies, infants cycle between neutral and positive expression while their mothers remain positive. A naturally occurring variation of this pattern may occur when mothers are depressed.

Experimental studies suggest that infants of nondepressed mothers have a dramatic reaction to simulated depression. They become wary; they try to positively elicit their mother to change; and, when unsuccessful, they become increasingly negative and unresponsive (Cohn and Tronick 1983). This increased negative affect and lack of responsiveness then carries over into situations in which the mother is no longer acting depressed. These data suggest that were the mothers to behave continually with depressed affect, the infant's affect would come to resemble the mother's. Indeed, in the study by Field (1984), this seemed to be the case. Infants of mothers with high levels of depressive symptoms were more negative and less responsive than infants of nondepressed mothers, and their behavior varied little between simulated depressed and 'normal' interactions.

Depressed affect may include anger and irritation and result in highly intrusive behavior. The experimental study of "simulated" depression has so far been restricted to sad and flat affective expression. Cohn and Tronick (1989) speculated that restricted maternal affect and lack of responsiveness led to increased infant distress, whereas maternal anger and intrusiveness led to increased avoidance. In the absence of further experimental studies, it is not known whether variation in the type of negative affect mothers show will lead to qualitative differences in infant response.

Infants also have dramatic reactions to violations of the temporal relationship between their own and their mothers' positive affect. Cohn and Elmore (1988) found that when mothers sobered in response to their infant's becoming affectively positive, the infant's response was to sober and look away. Inappropriate timing of affective displays is a likely concomitant of maternal depression. Bettes (1988), for instance, found that in mothers with mild to moderate levels of depressive symptoms, vocal utterances were more variable and turns were of longer duration than in nondepressed mothers. The primary focus to date has been on the affective aspects of depression. Temporal aspects may be equally important to infant behavior and development.

With few exceptions, research about the influence of maternal depression during the first year has tended to ignore diagnostic criteria and to confound depression with other risk factors. Results from these studies suggest that depressed mothers and their babies are more negative and less positive than nondepressed mother-infant pairs. In the study by Cohn (Cohn et al. 1986; Cohn and Tronick 1989), negative affect was characteristic of almost all of the depressed mothers, although there were substantial individual differences in how negative affect was expressed. In families that have fewer risk factors, however, the influence of depression appears moderated. Bettes (1988), for instance, found consistent effects in mothers' vocal behavior but no differences in infant behavior related to depression. More recent research (Cohn et al. 1990) has also found more moderate effects on maternal behavior in mothers whose focal problem is depression in the absence of other risk factors.

Another important factor may be the infant's age. Over the age range from two through six months, negative affect in mothers appears to increase steadily even in the absence of other risk factors (Cohn et al. 1990). Reasons for this increase are unclear. Older infants may require more active social engagement, which a mother who is depressed finds difficult to manage. Older infants are also more demanding of autonomy. Alternatively, the effect may be related to changes in the phenomenology of depression over time, which may be unrelated to the demands of parenting an older infant.

The most important factor influencing mother's and infant's behavior, however, may be the mother's own subjective feelings of distress. Mother's self-reported level of subjective distress was a central factor in mediating mothers' and infants' affect through six months (Cohn et al. 1990). A mother's experience of her own distress was more important than her diagnostic status alone. On most measures, women who met RDC without having high levels of subjective distress were indistinguishable from nondepressed controls. Mothers who met criteria and had higher subjective distress clearly differed on almost all measures at two months, and continued to be more negative through six months. Negativity in fact increased over this time period. Thus, in mothers with high levels of initial symptoms, the continuing effect of depression may be more evident in negative rather than positive affect expression.

A central finding across studies was that mothers and infants matched each other's level of affective expression. At each age,

mothers' and infants' affect distributions were moderately correlated. Initial time-series analyses showed no difference in reciprocity related to depression. However, when we consider the very
sizable stability of maternal affect over time, and the increasing
stability of infant negative affect, it is clear that maternal affect is
potentially more influential in determining infant response. The
mother's affect is a consistent environment within which the infant
develops. Spitz (1965) emphasized the cumulative nature of affective exchanges in shaping infant personality. That phenomenon is
clearly evident in this context. Maternal subjective distress is manifest in affective behavior and exerts a strong negative bias on the
infant's social and emotional development.

References

Bakeman, R., and Brown, J. (1980). Early interaction: Consequences for so-
    cial and mental development at three years. *Child Development* 51:
    437–47.

Beck, A. T., Ward, C. H., Mendelson, M., Mock, J. E., and Erbaugh, J. H.
    (1961). An inventory for measuring depression. Archives of General
    Psychiatry, *4*, 561–571.

Bettes, B. (1988). Maternal depression and motherese: Temporal and into-
    national contours. *Child Development* 59:1089–96.

Brazelton, T. B.; Koslowski, B.; and Main, M. (1974). The origins of reciproc-
    ity: The early mother-infant interaction. In M. Lewis and L. A.
    Rosenblum (eds.), 49–76. *The Effect of the Infant on its Caregiver.*
    New York: Wiley.

Campbell, S. B., and Cohn, J. F. (1991). Prevalence and correlates of post-
    partum depression in first-time mothers. *Abnormal Psychology* 100:
    594–99.

Campbell, S. B.; Cohn, J. F.; Flanagan, C.; Popper, S.; and Meyers, T. (1992).
    The course and correlates of postpartum depression during the tran-
    sition to parenthood. *Development and Psychopathology* 4:29–47.

Cohn, J. F.; Campbell, S. B; and Ross, S. (1991). Infant response in the still-
    face paradigm at 6 months predicts avoidant and secure attachment
    at 12 months. *Development and Psychopathology* 3:367–76.

Cohn, J. F., and Elmore, E. (1988). Effect of contingent changes in mothers'
    affective expression on the organization of behavior in 3-month-old
    infants. *Infant Behavior and Development* 11:493–505.

Cohn, J. F.; Matias, R.; Campbell, S. B.; and Hopkins, J. (1990). Face-to-face interactions of postpartum depressed mother-infant pairs at 2 months. *Developmental Psychology* 26:15–23.

Cohn, J. F.; Matias, R.; Tronick, E. Z.; Lyons-Ruth, K.; and Connell, D. (1986). Face-to-face interactions, spontaneous and structured, of mothers with depressive symptoms. In T. Field and E. Z. Tronick (eds.), *Maternal Depression and Child Development,* New Directions for Child Development, No. 34, San Francisco: Jossey-Bass.

Cohn J. F., and Tronick E. Z. (1983). Three-month-old infants' reaction to simulated maternal depression. *Child Development* 54:185–93.

Cohn, J. F., and Tronick, E. Z. (1987). Mother-infant interaction: The sequence of dyadic states at 3, 6, and 9 months. *Developmental Psychology* 23:68–77.

Cohn, J. F., and Tronick E. Z. (1988). Mother-infant interaction: Influence is bidirectional and unrelated to periodic cycles in either partner's behavior. *Developmental Psychology* 24:386–392.

Cohn, J. F., and Tronick, E. Z. (1989). Specificity of infants' response to mothers' affective behavior. *Journal of the American Academy of Child and Adolescent Psychiatry* 28:242–48.

Ekman, P. (1984). Expression and the nature of emotion. In K. R. Scherer and P. Ekman (eds.), *Approaches to Emotion.* Hillsdale, N.J.: Erlbaum.

Endicott, J., and Spitzer, R. L. (1978). A diagnostic interview: The Schedule for Affective Disorders and Schizophrenia. *Archives of General Psychiatry* 35:837–44.

Field, T. (1984). Early interactions between infants and their postpartum depressed mothers. *Infant Behavior and Development* 7:527–32.

Field, T.; Sandberg, D.; Garcia, R.; Vega-Lahr, N.; Goldstein, S.; and Guy, L. (1985). Pregnancy problems, postpartum depression, and early mother-infant interactions. *Developmental Psychology* 21:1152–56.

Field, T.; Healy, B.; Goldstein, S.; Perry, S.; Debra, B.; Schanberg, S.; Zimmerman, E. A.; and Kuhn, C. (1988). Infants of "depressed" mothers show depressed behavior even with nondepressed adults. *Child Development* 59:1569–1579.

Field, T.; Healy, B.; Goldstein, S.; and Guthertz, M. (1990). Behavior-state matching and synchrony in mother-infant interactions of nondepressed versus depressed dyads. *Developmental Psychology* 26:7–14.

Garrison, W. T., and Earls, F. J. (1986). Epidemiologic perspectives on maternal depression and the young child. In T. M. Field and E. Z.

Tronick (eds.), *Maternal Depression and Child Development*. San Francisco: Jossey-Bass.

Kaye, K., and Fogel, A. (1980). The temporal structure of face-to-face communication between mothers and infants. *Developmental Psychology* 16:454–64.

Radloff, L. S. (1977). The CES-D Scale: A self-report depression scale for research in the general population. *Applied Psychological Measurement* 3:385–401.

Robins, L. (1974). *Deviant Children Grown Up*. New York: Krieger.

Rutter, M., and Garmezy, N. (1983). Developmental psychopathology. In M. N. Haith, J. J. Campos, and P. H. Mussen (series ed.), *Handbook of Child Psychology: Vol. 2*. New York: Wiley.

Rutter, M.; Yule, B.; Quinton, D.; Rowland, O.; Yule, W.; and Berger, M. (1974). Attainment and adjustment in two geographical areas: III. *British Journal of Psychiatry* 123:520–33.

Spitz, R. (1965). *The First Year of Life*. New York: International Universities Press.

Spitzer, R. S.; Endicott, J.; and Robins, E. (1978). Research diagnostic criteria: Rationale and reliability. *Archives of General Psychiatry* 36: 773–82.

Stern, D. (1977). *The First Relationship*. Cambridge: Harvard.

Symons, D. K. and Moran, G. (1987). The behavioral dynamics of mutual responsiveness in early face-to-face mother-infant interactions. *Child Development* 58:1488–1495.

Tronick, E. Z., and Cohn, J. F. (1989). Infant-mother face-to-face interaction: Age and gender differences in coordination and miscoordination. *Child Development* 59:85–92.

Weissman, M. M., and Paykel, E. S. (1974). *The Depressed Woman: A Study in Social Relationships*. Chicago: University of Chicago.

PART III

Cross-Cultural Perspectives

CHAPTER 10

Peekaboo across Cultures: How Mothers and Infants Play with Voices, Faces, and Expectations

Anne Fernald and Daniela K. O'Neill

Introduction

A young mother catches her nine–month-old infant's gaze, smiles at him, and brings her hands slowly up and together to cover her eyes. "Uphi? Uphi?" ("Where? Where?") she asks brightly, with high rising pitch. The baby stares transfixed at his mother's hands, a small smile of anticipation beginning to spread on his face as the suspense builds over three seconds. "Na-a-a-a-a-n *ku!*" ("Here!") exclaims the mother, uncovering her eyes on the "*ku!*" and grinning broadly at her son, who shows his pleasure with hearty laughter. The language is Xhosa, a Bantu click language, and the scene is a mud-walled hut in a rural village in the Ciskei homeland of South Africa. Worlds away in a Tokyo apartment, a Japanese mother plays out the same little drama with her twelve–month-old daughter. She covers her eyes with a cloth, then chants "Inai inai *ba!*" as she pulls the cloth away to reveal her face to the delighted child. The words and the vocal melody of the game are different in Xhosa and Japanese, but the rhythm, dynamics, and shared pleasure in the inevitable outcome are fundamentally similar.

The peekaboo game as played by American mothers and infants has been studied from a variety of theoretical and empirical perspectives. Observers with a psychoanalytical bent have speculated that playing peekaboo helps the infant to master anxiety aroused when the mother disappears (e.g., Call and Marschak 1966; Kleeman 1967). Experimental psychologists have manipulated the degree of response uncertainty and contingency within the peekaboo game in order to study the development of attention and learning in infancy (Charlesworth 1966; Millar 1988; Parrot and Gleitman 1989). Other psychologists interested in early social development have focused on the power of the peekaboo game to elicit smiling and laughter (Sroufe and Waters 1976; Washburn 1929), and on infants' responsiveness to peekaboo as a possible precursor to humor (e.g., Schulz 1976). Peekaboo has also been considered as a prototypical social routine which may facilitate language acquisition, by giving preverbal infants valuable experience with complex rule structures and role reversability (Bruner and Sherwood 1976; Ratner and Bruner 1978).

It is often simply asserted that some version of the peekaboo game is "universal" (e.g., Bruner and Sherwood 1976; Kleeman 1967), although no evidence is cited to support this claim. Given the impressive range of developmental angles from which peekaboo has been studied, there is surprisingly little cross-cultural data available on this and other highly engaging mother-infant games. Occasional references to games resembling peekaboo are found in anthropological reports of mother-infant interaction in non-Western cultures (e.g., Martini and Kirkpatrick 1981), although the actions and vocalizations involved in these games are rarely specified. Our goal in this chapter is to explore the common features of peekaboo across a number of diverse cultures. We will start by describing and comparing the gestures and vocalizations accompanying the peekaboo game in seventeen cultures, based on new observational and interview data. We will then review previous observational and experimental research findings on peekaboo from the literature on American and European mothers and infants, in order to understand why the peekaboo game looks and sounds so similar across cultures, and why, for both mothers and infants, this game is a source of universal delight.

Peekaboo Vocalizations in American English

Figure 10.1 shows pitch contours derived from vocalizations recorded during three rounds of an American mother's peekaboo game with her eleven–month-old son. In the first round of their familiar routine, the mother covers the infant's head with a diaper, asking "Where's Donnie?" (Figure 10.1a). As the baby eagerly snatches the cloth off his head, his mother exclaims *"There* he is!" Her *"There"* is vividly marked with pitch and a big smile, coinciding with the in-

fant's triumphant removal of the diaper. After three repetitions of
the game in this format, mother and infant turn their attention to
a picture book, returning to peekaboo ten minutes later. This time
the mother initiates the game by holding up the book in front of her
face. From behind the book she summons the infant's attention by
chanting "p-e-e-e-e-k a-a-a-a-a" in a low voice, drawing out the vow-
els dramatically (Figure 10.1b). Donnie looks intently at the book,
his eyes bright with expectation. When his mother pops out from
her hiding place with a high-pitched "*boo!*" Donnie squeals with
laughter and waves his arms. After two repetitions of this version of
the game, the baby pulls the book onto his lap and starts fiddling
with the plastic spiral binding. His mother attempts to keep the
game going, covering her face now with her hands and peeking out
between her fingers to monitor Donnie's attention. "Hey!" she calls,
to alert him. His attention lingers on the book in his lap for a second
before he looks up. His mother waits until she sees his eyes through
her fingers, then drops her hands abruptly with a jaunty "*Peek*a-
boo!" (Figure 10.1c). This time Donnie smiles cheerfully but doesn't
laugh, returning to poking his finger into the spiral binding of the
book. His mother follows this shift in attention, pointing to the duck
on the book's cover, and for now the game is over.

The three vocal routines shown in Figure 10.1, all typical variants used in the American English peekaboo game, are similar yet
different in revealing ways. All three follow the same basic format:
the mother gives an alert call to summon the infant's attention, followed by a high-pitched release call to accompany her reappearance
after hiding. However, the words and pitch patterns differ to some
extent across the three examples. In Figure 10.1a, the alert call consists of a stylized intonation pattern, "Where's Donnie?" which is
very much "part of" the game for this mother and infant. After covering the baby's face, the mother sets the stage for their reunion by
using this highly stereotyped question vocalization. Similarly in
Figure 10.1b, the first two syllables of "peekaboo" are drawn out and
dramatically emphasized in a stereotyped manner. This type of
alert call not only recruits the baby's attention, but also enhances
the build-up of tension as well as the predictability of the sequence
of events. Having played this game hundreds of times before, the infant knows that "p-e-e-e-e-k a-a-a-a-a" will soon be followed by
"*boo!*" and his mother's smile.

The alert call shown in Figure 10.1c differs from the first two in
that it is not a stereotyped vocal pattern. The mother's lively "Hey!"
is simply an attention-getting device, not typically part of the game

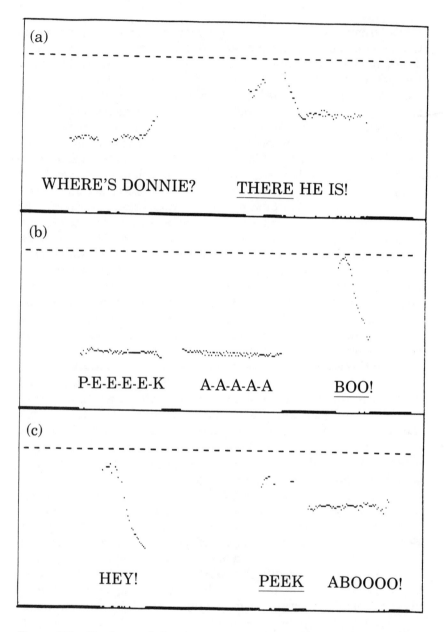

Figure 10.1. Fundamental frequency (F_o) contours from vocalizations recorded during three rounds of an American mother's peekaboo game with her eleven–month-old son.

for this particular pair. In this case the baby's interest in the game was waning and the mother had not established eye contact with the infant before hiding. While the elongated and suspenseful "p-e-e-e-e-k" shown in Figure 10.1b is used as part of the build-up, the short, high-pitched *"peek"* shown in Figure 10.1c is the high point of the release call which marks the mother's reappearance. The variability in these three examples shows that while stereotyped in its overall structure, the peekaboo game is quite flexible in format. The mother varies, within limits, the gestures, words, and melodies, as well as the tempo and dynamics of the game, in order to make each repetition of the familiar routine engaging and slightly different from the last, and to accommodate the fluctuating attention of the infant.

A Cross-Cultural Comparison of Peekaboo Vocalizations

The release calls used by mothers playing peekaboo with infants in five other cultures are shown in Figure 10.2. These vocalizations (as well as those shown in Figure 10.1) were recorded in conjunction with a large-scale study of the prosodic characteristics of speech to infants in German, French, Italian, Japanese, and British and American English (Fernald et al. 1989). The subjects in this study were middle-class, monolingual mothers of infants from ten to fourteen months of age, five in each language group, recorded playing with their infants during hour-long observation sessions in the family home. High-quality samples of spontaneous speech were acoustically analyzed using a Visipitch machine (Kay Elemetrics) to extract fundamental frequency (F_o), the acoustic correlate of pitch.

The release calls of the peekaboo game in all of these languages are distinctive acoustic signals. When the mother's face suddenly reappears, she marks this climactic moment in the game with a stereotyped vocalization that is either unusually high in pitch or dramatically elongated, or both. In the Italian and Japanese examples in Figure 10.2, the low-pitched alert call is an integral part of the vocal routine, leading up to the high-pitched release. In German, too, the alert call "ku kuck" is stereotyped, anticipating the release on *"da!"*, although in the German game the alert call is high in pitch, while the release is typically low and elongated. The French peekaboo vocalizations resemble those in British and American English, with considerable variability in the format of the alert, followed by a sudden high-pitched release on "cou cou!" However, note

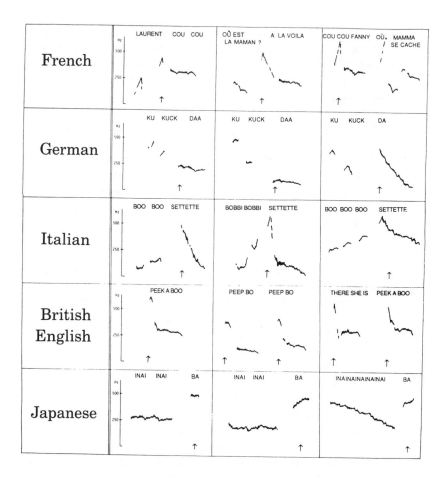

Figure 10.2. Cross-cultural comparison of F_0-contours from the release calls of peekaboo vocal routines in five languages. Examples are shown from three different mothers interacting with ten– to 14–month-old infants in each language, recorded during naturalistic observations. (Arrows indicate the point in the vocalization when the mother reappears after hiding.)

that even in those vocal routines that include a relatively stereotyped alert call, there is room for variation. Italian mothers alternate between "boo boo" and "bobbi bobbi," for example. And in Japanese, where the standard format for the alert call is "inai inai," with each repetition clearly enunciated, mothers also sometimes produce long strings of "inai"s run together rapidly and descending in pitch from high to low over the sequence, as a particularly invigorating variant of the alert.

To supplement our observational data on the peekaboo game in five European cultures and Japan, we collected additional comparative data on hiding-game vocalizations by recording interviews with mothers from several other cultures. The subjects in this informal study were all foreign visitors to the United States who were either mothers or other women experienced with infants. Each was asked whether there was a hiding game like peekaboo in her culture, and how it was played. Subjects were audiorecorded as they described the game and demonstrated the characteristic vocalizations involved, specifying at what points in the vocal pattern the hiding and reappearance occurred. The F_o-contours from the release calls recorded during these demonstrations are shown in Figure 10.3. The one exception is the Xhosa peekaboo vocalization, which was recorded during extensive field observations of ten mother-infant dyads in South Africa (Fernald and Eisen 1993).

Two common types of prosodic pattern characterize the peekaboo release calls illustrated in Figure 10.3. The first type, shown in the Malaysian, Greek, and Hindi examples, consists of a high, rising pitch contour, abrupt in onset, to mark the mother's reappearance. The three subjects reporting this type of vocal pattern all claimed that there was no stereotyped alert call that was integral to the peekaboo routine in their cultures, although the mother might call the baby's name or vocalize in other salient ways to engage the infant's attention prior to the release call. The second and more prevalent type of prosodic pattern found in the vocalizations illustrated in Figure 10.3 is similar to the pitch patterns in the European and Japanese examples shown in Figure 10.2. These release calls consist of bi- or tri-syllabic vocalizations, generally with high pitch on the first syllable and exaggerated vowel lengthening on the final syllable. In some cases, subjects reported that the mother's reappearance should coincide with the high initial syllable, as shown in the Persian, Russian, and Portugese examples. In other languages, the reappearance was said to coincide with the emphatic final syllable of the release call, as shown in the Tamil example. It is likely, of course, that in all these languages considerable flexibility is possible in the timing of the mother's reappearance relative to the high and low points of the pitch pattern, just as we found in the American English vocal routines shown in Figure 10.1. The examples illustrated in Figure 10.3 probably represent one popular version of the peekaboo call from each culture, rather than invariant vocal routines.

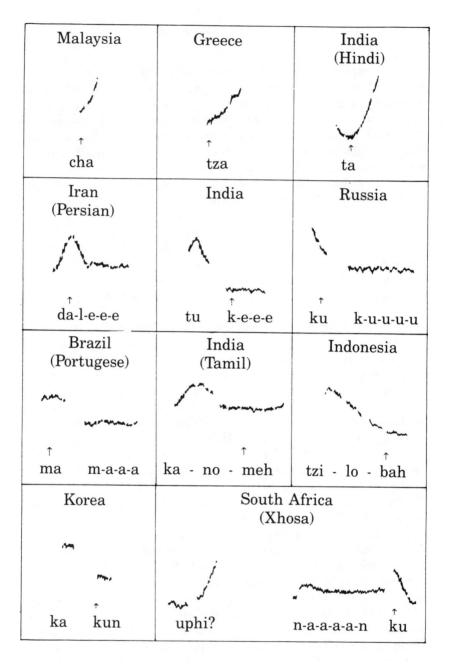

Figure 10.3. Cross-cultural comparison of F_o-contours from the release calls of peekaboo vocal routines in eleven languages, based on recordings made during interviews. (Arrows indicate the point in the vocalization when the mother reappears after hiding.)

All of the examples of peekaboo vocalizations from the diverse range of Western and non-Western cultures represented in Figures 10.1–10.3 have one critical feature in common: The point in the sequence when the mother reappears is an exhilirating moment, marked by exaggerated and relatively stereotyped vocal and facial gestures. Both within and between cultures, however, several different acoustic cues are used to highlight this culminating moment. A pitch peak signals the mother's return in the majority of the release calls shown in Figures 10.1–10.3, although in some cases, such as German and Tamil, the reappearance is timed to coincide with the low, final note in the sequence. Here the low note is made especially salient through vowel elongation and increased intensity. Variation in vowel quality is another acoustic cue employed to highlight the reunion. In the South African mother's routine, for example, the sustained vowel of "N-a-a-a-a-n" had a rough and gravelly quality, a kind of playful growling sound used several times by this mother, to her infant's repeated delight.

The "lyrics" of the peekaboo routine are another variable feature of the game. In some languages, for example, Japanese, Korean, and Italian, the standard release call consists of nonsense sounds, while in other languages the words are meaningful. For example, "kanomeh" in Tamil (Figure 10.3) means "where are you," and "da" in German means "there." In Brazilian Portugese, a mother playing peekaboo sings "Ma m-a-a-a" (Figure 10.3), while the father's call is "Pa p-a-a-a." As shown in Figure 10.1, American English release calls alternate between nonsense syllables ("peek-aboo") and meaningful words ("there you are"). However, while the lyrics differ in these two American English examples, the melody stays the same. It may well be the case that in other languages too there is semantic variation in the peekaboo release call, perceptually unified through the imposition of a common, stereotyped intonation contour.

Universal Features of Mother-Infant Games

Is the peekaboo game indeed "universal"? This question can be interpreted in different ways, and must in any case be approached with caution, for two reasons. First, although the data presented here reveal that mothers play hiding games with infants in a number of different cultures, and that these games are very similar in form, our sample is obviously small. Cultures vary considerably in the extent to which social interaction with infants is viewed as valuable and appropriate. Among the Gusii (Dixon et al. 1977) and the Navajo (Callaghan 1981), for example, mothers spend very little time in face-to-face contact with their infants and talk to them infrequently. Social games like peekaboo are perhaps less likely to be present in the caregiving repertoires of such cultures. Second, even if a traditional form of peekaboo is available in the culture, it may not be practiced extensively. Even in European cultures where peekaboo is widespread, there are notable differences in the frequency of play both between and within groups. In a study of early face-to-face interaction among British and American middle- and working-class mother-infant dyads (Field and Pawlby 1980), differences related both to culture and to socioeconomic status were evident. American mothers played more social games such as peekaboo with their infants than did British mothers, although in both cultures middle-class mothers were more likely than working-class mothers to engage their infants in social games. In another study investigating cultural differences in the frequency of game playing, Snow, de Blauw, and Van Roosmalen (1979) found that peekaboo was a popular activity in their sample of British mothers of six–month-old infants, while Dutch mothers were less likely to play the equivalent Dutch game "Kiekeboe" with infants of the same age.

Although we cannot conclude on the basis of the available data that mother-infant hiding games are universal across cultures, the striking similarities among the peekaboo routines described here suggests that wherever such games *are* found, they will share common structural features and dynamics. As we will argue in later sections, the peekaboo game is effective because it exploits perceptual, attentional, and affective predispositions of the young infant, and because it both engages and accommodates the developing cognitive capabilities of the child. Since such characteristics are common to all human infants in the first year of life, it seems likely that games which engage and appeal to infants in this early period will have universal design features with relatively minor cultural modifications.

A comparative study of mother-infant games in different ethnic groups within the United States offers some valuable insights into features of games that are common across cultures. Van Hoorn (1987) observed immigrant mothers from China (n = 20), the Philipines (n = 37), and Mexico (n = 47), as well as forty-eight U.S. mothers of European descent. These subjects were observed during home visits as they played games with infants ranging in age from one to eighteen months, and were also interviewed about the types of infant games popular in their culture. Of the 450 games demonstrated or described by the mothers in this study, about 80 percent were traditional games learned from others. Such games invariably involved motor actions such as clapping, swinging, tickling, rocking, and disappearance/reappearance, usually accompanied by words coordinated with the relatively stereotyped action patterns. Mothers typically spoke or sung the words rhythmically, to highlight and entrain the movements in the behavior sequence, as in peekaboo and pat-a-cake. The exaggerated use of repetitive and rhythmic vocal emphasis appeared to help maintain both motoric and affective synchrony between mother and infant during the game. Van Hoorn also observed that mothers conveyed their own pleasure in the game by using exaggerated facial expressions as well as distinctive positive vocalizations, and by maintaining eye contact with the infant as they played together.

What is it about games consisting of exaggerated vocal routines rhythmically timed to accompany simple, repetitive motor activities that is so captivating for young infants? Why do infants enjoy playing these games over and over again, if their rhythms are so familiar and their outcomes so predictable? These questions will be addressed in the following sections, using the peekaboo game as an example. Although almost all of the research on peekaboo is based on the American English version of the game, we can draw on this literature for insights into the widespread appeal of peekaboo and other social games played by mothers and infants across cultures.

How the Peekaboo Game Develops Over the First Year

Disappearance and reappearance are central to the peekaboo game in all its forms. But when mothers play peekaboo with their infants at the age of four, eight, and twelve months, and well into the second year, they are not repeating the same routine over and over again. The nature of the game changes dramatically over the first year, as the infant develops from being a relatively passive observer to becoming an active initiator and innovator in the game. In the earliest versions of peekaboo, the infant is an enraptured spectator, smiling in response to the mother's antics. Gradually the infant comes to predict what will happen next in the familiar sequence, smiling now in anticipation of the climactic reappearance of the mother's face.

And by the end of the first year, the child begins to take the lead, initiating the game, embellishing the moves, and alternating with the mother in the roles of actor and audience.

Beginning when the infant is about three to five months old, the mother introduces an early form of peekaboo simply by moving her face in and out of the infant's view in various ways. She may present her full face to the infant, look to the side or down, and then, with an exaggerated expression present her face again (Stern 1977). Or, she may present her face up close to get the baby's attention, pull her head back about three feet, and then "loom" toward the infant until their faces almost touch. This looming is accompanied by an arousing vocalization such as "Ahhhh boo!" similar to the release calls shown in Figure 10.1 (Bruner and Sherwood 1976; Snow et al. 1979; Stern 1977), and elicits smiling and laughter in very young infants (Washburn 1929).

At about five to eight months, this early looming routine is replaced by the more prototypical version of the peekaboo game, consisting of three steps in a relatively fixed order: (1) establishing mutual attention; (2) hiding; and (3) uncovering and reappearance (Bruner 1975; Bruner and Sherwood 1976; Greenfield 1972; Ratner and Bruner 1978). In these first games of peekaboo proper, as in the looming version of the game, the mother is completely in charge, initiating all three steps in the sequence. To establish mutual attention, the mother uses an alert call, usually during a period of face-to-face interaction. If an object, and not the mother's face, is being hidden, she vocalizes to orient the infant to the object or the hiding instrument. If the mother is hiding herself, she generally hides only her face or eyes and not her whole body, often continuing to vocalize while hiding to maintain the infant's attention (Ross and Kay 1980). The mother may incorporate variation into the game at this stage by changing who or what is hidden, or the nature of the hiding instrument, for example by covering the infant's head with a cloth. The rate of disappearance and the duration of hiding are also sometimes varied by the mother, although only to a limited extent—probably constrained by the infant's short attention span at this age (Bruner and Sherwood 1976; Greenfield 1972). The step of uncovering and reappearance is marked by a release call, after which the mother reappears either quickly or slowly (Ratner and Bruner 1978).

Between eight or nine months and fifteen months, the game of peekaboo changes again, as the infant begins to initiate the steps in the game and assumes the role of agent as well as observer in the hiding and reappearance. One of the most striking developments during this period is in infants' increasing ability to reverse roles towards the end of the first year (Bruner 1975; Bruner and Sherwood 1976; Golinkoff 1983; Gustafson, Green, and West 1979; Rubin and Wolf 1979). While their participation in the game has been mainly passive up to this point, infants gradually begin to take a more active role around the age of eight months, trying to produce the appearance and reappearance effects on their own (Kleeman 1967; Ross and Kay 1980). In a series of detailed observations of the development of peekaboo in one mother-infant pair, Ratner and Bruner (1978) reported that the mother initiated the hiding in 100 percent of the games observed when the infant was between six and eleven months of age, while the infant Richard initiated the hiding in 78 percent of the games observed at fourteen to fifteen months. Another change in the game occurred as Richard became more actively mobile and began hiding himself behind the sofa, reappearing on his own with a smile.

This trend from passive to active participation is not limited only to peekaboo. Observational studies of several mother-infant games show that as infants get older, they more frequently use newly acquired behaviors such as pointing or showing a toy to initiate games with the mother (Green, Gustafson, and West 1980; Gustafson, Green, and West 1979). With four–month-old infants, mothers primarily play games which engage the infant's attention and involve physical stimulation. However, when their infants are eight months old, mothers engage them more in games involving motoric roles that the infants can readily initiate and maintain by themselves (Crawley et al. 1978). These changes in the content and dynamics of peekaboo and other mother-infant games over the first year of life reflect developmental changes in the infant's perceptual, cognitive, and motor abilities. To accommodate these developmental changes, the mother sensitively modifies the nature of the game as well as the roles both she and the infant play.

Faces and Voices as Visual and Auditory Stimuli in the Peekaboo Game

One reason peekaboo is such a captivating game is that faces and voices are particularly compelling stimuli for young infants. Faces are interesting even to the newborn, not yet because of any social significance, but because as visual stimuli they are high in contrast, rich in contours, and have other visual features which young infants find especially attractive (Fantz and Nevis 1967). By three months of age, infants prefer to look at faces over other equally complex visual stimuli (Dannemiller and Stephens 1988), and they scan the internal features of faces, rather than the external contours which captured their attention as newborns (Haith, Bergman, and Moore 1977). There is also evidence that 3–month-old infants can distinguish the mother's face from unfamiliar female faces (Maurer and Barrera 1981). Looming visual stimuli, in general, have a powerful effect on infants at this age, causing them to raise their arms and move their heads backwards (Bower, Broughton, and Moore 1970). Thus by three to four months of age, when the earliest form of the peekaboo game first appears in the repertoire of mother-infant play routines, infants find the looming face of the mother to be a highly engaging event.

As a form of acoustic stimulation, the exaggerated high-pitched vocal melody which accompanies the peekaboo game is also well designed to capture infants' attention. Several studies have shown that infants prefer to listen to the special infant-directed speech style known as "motherese," characterized by elevated pitch and highly modulated intonation contours (Cooper and Aslin 1990; Fernald 1985; Werker and McLeod 1989), in contrast to the relatively flat intonation of adult-directed speech. The exaggerated pitch contours alone, even without linguistic content, are sufficient to elicit this listening preference for motherese speech in four–month-old infants (Fernald and Kuhl 1987). Further evidence for infants' special attentiveness to motherese speech comes from a study of heart-rate response to infant- and adult-directed pitch contours, showing that four–month-old infants respond with greater cardiac orienting to exaggerated intonation (Fernald and Clarkson 1993).

Infants not only pay more attention to exaggerated pitch contours, they also respond with more positive emotion. Wolff (1963) observed that a high-pitched voice is the most effective elicitor of smiling in very young infants. Two recent studies have found that when listening to highly modulated infant-directed speech, four– to five–month-old infants smile more than when listening to adult-directed speech (Fernald in press; Werker and McLeod 1989). When adults listen to content-filtered speech addressed either to infants or adults, they are able to identify the speaker's communicative intent, for example, praise versus prohibition, much more reliably in infant-directed speech (Fernald 1989). This finding suggests that motherese pitch contours may be more distinctive and informative for infants as well. Indeed five–month-old infants respond with more appropriate affect when listening to infant-directed speech than when listening to adult-directed speech, smiling more to praise vocalizations and showing more negative affect to prohibition vocalizations even in completely unfamiliar languages (Fernald in press). Thus it seems likely that the vocal melody in itself, independent of semantic content, is the dimension of infant-directed speech which affects infants' emotions. The fact that infants at this age are able to recognize melodies which have been transposed into a different frequency range (Trehub, Bull, and Thorpe 1984) is further evidence that pitch contour information is accessible to infants. These findings on early auditory processing abilities and preferences suggest that the high-pitched, prosodically exaggerated vocalizations which accompany the peekaboo game are prominent and appealing auditory stimuli for young infants. Moreover, the stereotyped intonation contours of the "peekaboo" melody may in themselves be salient to infants, easily recognizable across variations in semantic content (Fernald 1984; 1992).

Although the visual and auditory components of the peekaboo routine are each compelling stimuli on their own, the combination is even more effective. Auditory stimulation recruits visual attention in young infants (Haith 1980), and when a face is accompanied by a voice, two–month-old infants scan the eyes even more intently than when viewing the face in silence (Haith, Bergman, and Moore 1977). Peekaboo can be played without vocalization, and eight–month-old infants often smile to the silent reappearance of a face (Sroufe and Wunsch 1972). However, in a study of peekaboo with a four–month-old infant, Greenfield (1972) found that vocalization was critical in eliciting a smile the first time the game was played in a new location. Although the infant eventually smiled to the face alone, and the role of vocalization declined over trials, the voice was essential to the success of the game in unfamiliar settings. Games with older infants, including peekaboo, continue to have a strong vocal component accompanying the action. In a study of thirty-six games played by mothers with twelve–month-old infants, Ross and Kay (1980) found that fifteen of the games involved a stereotyped vocalization, repeated on 95 percent of the adult turns. Eleven other games also included a central auditory element, often nonvocal, and in the ten remaining games mothers verbalized on 64 percent of the turns. Thus mothers tend to combine auditory stimulation with visual, tactile, and vestibular stimulation when playing games with infants throughout the first year.

One obvious motivation for combining auditory with other forms of stimulation in mother-infant games is that dynamic, multimodal stimulation is much more likely to elicit laughter and smiling in young infants than are visual stimuli alone (Sroufe and Waters 1976). However, Greenfield (1972) suggests another important reason, with special relevance to the peekaboo game. Auditory signals can contribute "informational redundancy" by virtue of two critical design features: First, sounds can help the infant in *spatial* localization, guiding visual attention to the mother's face. And second, sounds can mark and enhance the *temporal* organization of a multimodal event, by imposing "points of articulation" on the continuous flow of visual and other stimuli (Greenfield 1972, p. 296). Thus the alert call in the peekaboo game (see figure 10.1) not only summons the infant's attention to the mother's disappearance, but also gives the infant important information about *where* and *when* to expect the next move in the familiar sequence. The release call which accompanies the mother's reappearance then marks the climax of the game, adding acoustic emphasis to an already exciting visual event.

The Role of Expectations in the Peekaboo Game

In the earliest games of peekaboo, the three–month-old infant responds directly to the sights and sounds of the mother's playful looming approach. The young infant's pleasure in the game is based on immediate sensory stimulation, not yet influenced by anticipation of things to come. Bruner and Sherwood distinguish this early form of interaction from later rule-governed versions of the game:

> . . . at the outset, peekaboo is not a game in the sense of it being governed by rules and conventions that are in any respect arbitrary. It is, rather, an exploitation by the mother of very strong, preadapted response tendencies in the infant, an exploitation that is rewarded by the child's responsiveness and pleasure (1976, p. 60).

Increasingly, however, the child's pleasure in the game is mediated by expectations about what will happen next, and when and where it will happen. As the infant develops the cognitive competencies needed to predict future events and to compare them to past events, the peekaboo game takes on new dimensions.

The ability to form expectations, and to recognize and appreciate new variations on old familiar themes, begins to develop early in the first year of life. By the time infants are three months old, they can form simple expectations about where an event will occur in a regular spatiotemporal sequence (Haith, Hazan, and Goodman 1988). Over the next year, infants become able to make increasingly complex predictions about the reappearance of objects that have disappeared (Gopnik 1984). Four–month-old infants understand that objects do not cease to exist when out of sight, although they are unable to act upon this understanding except to register their surprise when their expectations are not met (Baillargeon 1987). One month later, infants predict that an object will reappear when they turn away from it and then turn back towards it, and that an object will reappear after moving behind a screen (Bower, Broughton, and Moore 1971; Charlesworth 1966). By nine months of age, infants begin to search actively for objects that have disappeared, lifting a cloth or looking into a container in their attempts to find a hidden toy (Piaget 1954).

Observational studies of peekaboo suggest that mothers intuitively respect the initial limitations and gradual developments in the infant's grasp of object permanence over the first year. In the looming version of the game played with three–month-old infants, the mother's face is kept continually in the infant's view, and the arousing event consists of her approach from a distance. It is typically not until the infant is about five months old that the mother starts to "disappear" before the infant's eyes during the peekaboo game. And it is not until five to seven months of age that infants first show *anticipatory* looking and smiling during the alert call prior to the mother's reappearance (Charlesworth 1966; Greenfield 1972; Ratner and Bruner 1978). Early games of peekaboo, with their structured format and limited variation, may provide the infant with a forum to test, or to play with, some of these developing notions about the existence, disappearance, and reappearance of objects. Towards the end of the first year, however, the mother lets the infant take the lead, as the child begins to search actively for her when she hides and initiates the uncovering to make her reappear (Bruner and Sherwood 1976; Gustafson et al. 1979).

Infants also begin early to form expectations about more complex social situations, as well as about objects. By four months of age, infants know something about particular face-voice relationships, expecting the mother's face, and not the face of another person, to accompany the mother's voice (Spelke and Cortelyou 1981). Young infants also react with negative affect and gaze aversion if the mother interrupts her normal interactive behaviors and assumes a still face (Fogel et al. 1982; Tronick et al. 1978). As they grow older, infants reveal more elaborate expectations about the rules governing social interactions. Ross and Lollis (1987) observed nine- to eighteen–month-old infants in a situation in which the adult playing with them suddenly discontinued her involvement in the game for fifteen seconds. Even nine–month-old infants attempted to keep the interaction going by vocalizing, repeating their own turn, looking repeatedly at the adult, and touching the adult, with older infants using more sophisticated strategies. It is also around this age that infants begin to show signs of having mastered the various steps involved in peekaboo, and of making moves to engage their mothers more fully in the game. One eleven–month-old infant observed by Bruner and Sherwood (1976) stayed hidden and did not uncover her face until the mother said "boo!" showing an awareness of the turn-taking structure of the game. Another fourteen–month-old infant struggled to coordinate his own actions of hiding and reappearance with vocalizations approximating those he had heard his mother use when playing peekaboo. Both of these examples reflect the presence of complex and highly structured expectations developed by the infant in the course of many repetitions of the game.

One way in which infants learn to form expectations is through experiencing contingencies between their own behaviors and subsequent events. Research has shown that infants are sensitive to contingencies very early in life, responding more vigorously when their own behavior makes something interesting happen. For example, two–month-old infants increase their response rates when their leg movements make a mobile rotate (Watson 1972), or when their arm movements trigger an audiovisual display (Alessandri, Sullivan, and Lewis 1990). By three months of age, infants still remember associations between their own behavior and interesting environmental consequences when tested two weeks later (Enright et al. 1983). It is interesting to note that three–month-old infants seem to display an attentional preference for *moderate* contingency over perfect contingency. In an experimental paradigm involving mobiles, infants learned more slowly when the contingency was either low *or* perfect, with the fastest learning occurring in a situation of moderate contingency (Watson 1979). Watson (1985) concludes that this bias may result because infants experience moderate levels of contingency more often than perfect contingencies in their normal interactions with the world.

A study with older infants suggests that the appreciation of contingencies may change with age, as infants' sense of control and self-efficacy come to play a larger role. Millar (1988) used the peekaboo game in an experiment investigating seven– and ten–month-old infants' affective responses to contingency and noncontingency. In Millar's paradigm, the mother appeared from behind a curtained window, remaining for two seconds before the curtain closed again. In the contingent condition, she reappeared whenever the infant pulled a lever; in the noncontingent condition, she reappeared at intervals independent of the infant's behavior. The results showed that seven–month-old infants displayed more positive affect in the noncontingent condition, that is, when the mother always appeared unexpectedly, while ten–month-old infants smiled more when they controlled the mother's reappearance. Millar suggests that smiling in the younger infants may not yet be dependent on the infant's sense of being in control of the situation. For the ten–month-old infants, however, noncontingent events may elicit less positive affect because such events signal lack of control to infants at this age.

Two other studies have used experimental analogues of the peekaboo game to investigate infants' responses to violations of expectation. Charlesworth (1966) varied the location in which an inanimate face reappeared, while Parrot and Gleitman (1989) varied both the location and the identity of a person reappearing from behind a screen. In Charlesworth's study, five– to nineteen–month-old infants were shown a terrycloth face which appeared from behind a screen at two different locations, accompanied by a tape-recorded voice saying "ah . . . peekaboo." Three experimental conditions varied in the degree of uncertainty as to where the face would appear on each trial. Charlesworth found that even five–month-old infants persisted longest in the condition of highest uncertainty, when the side on which the face would reappear was unpredictable. Infants played the game for fewer trials when the face always appeared on the same side, although the greatest amount of anticipatory looking was observed in this condition. These results suggest that although infants were able to anticipate the location of the face more often in conditions where the face always reappeared in the same place, they persisted in playing the game longer in conditions where there was most uncertainty. However, infants apparently found it reinforcing when an anticipatory look was confirmed by the reappearance of the face. If a confirmed anticipatory look occurred on one trial, there was a significantly greater probability that an anticipatory look would occur on the following trial. It would appear from these findings that infants like to have their expectations in the peekaboo game confirmed, but only if there is some kind of challenge involved. When the game becomes too predictable, infants quickly lose interest.

The findings of the Parrot and Gleitman (1989) study suggest, however, that persistence in playing the game may not be the most appropriate index of infants' engagement. These authors investigated infants' affective responses to violations of expectations about the location and the identity of the person reappearing in the peekaboo game. Six to eight month olds participated in a game which included occasional "trick" trials, where one adult hid and another adult "reappeared" in his or her place, or where the location at which the adult had previously reappeared was suddenly switched. Infants raised their eyebrows more, and smiled less, after both types of trick reappearance, leading Parrott and Gleitman to conclude that infants' enjoyment of the game is generally enhanced by conformity to their expectations.

What can we infer from these diverse findings about how infants' expectations influence their pleasure and engagement in the peekaboo game? The results of these studies are unfortunately difficult to interpret given the particular manipulations used. For example, the negative affect displayed by infants in Parrott and Gleitman's (1989) study does not seem surprising, since a change of identity occurred. In playing peekaboo with a six- or eight–month-old infant, the mother might vary slightly the location at which she reappears, although it is not usually until and child is mobile that variability in location becomes a regular feature of the game. More likely, the mother will vary the duration of hiding or the timing of her reappearance. She will never, however, reappear with a different face. Indeed, the experimental studies as a whole do not seem to capture what Stern (1977) and Bruner (Bruner and Sherwood 1976; Ratner and Bruner 1978) describe as the most fascinating feature of the peekaboo game—the manner in which a mother plays with the *timing* of its constituent features. Both Bruner's and Stern's observations suggest that up until twelve months, the timing of mother's reappearance is the most critical and captivating source of variation in the game. However, no studies to date have described in detail how mothers time their reappearance in relation to alert calls and to the duration of hiding, nor how this temporal variability influences infants' persistence and pleasure in playing the game.

Changing Sources of Delight in the Peekaboo Game

Changes in the structure and dynamics of the peekaboo game over the first year of life can be partly understood in terms of the infant's developing perceptual and cognitive abilities, as suggested in the preceding sections. However, these perceptual and cognitive developments are intimately linked to changes in the infant's affective response tendencies over the first year, and it is through affect that the infant shows delight in the game and shares this pleasure with the mother. Research showing that infants smile and laugh for different reasons at different ages offers further insights into the nature of early mother-infant games such as peekaboo.

The first elicited smiles appearing at around one month of age are generally referred to as "social" smiles, because they occur most frequently in response to faces and voices (Wolff 1963). In this early period, smiling derives primarily from *stimulation* per se, rather than from the content of the stimulus. Increasingly, however, smiling is influenced by the infant's *cognitive engagement,* and the infant smiles more readily to "meaningful" stimuli than to stimuli that are merely dynamic and interesting (Sroufe and Wunsch 1972). The development of laughter follows a similar progression from stimulation-produced arousal to cognitively produced arousal. Laughter first occurs in the fourth month in response to vigorous multimodal stimulation, and intense tactile and auditory stimulation remain the most potent means of eliciting laughter in infants up to six months of age. By eight months, however, infants begin to laugh at more subtle visual events involving social stimuli, such as the mother crawling on the floor or shaking her hair (Sroufe and Waters 1976). Such events amuse the infant not because of any preemptory sensory qualities, but because they are *discrepant* from expectations the infant has developed about how the mother usually behaves. By the end of the first year, infants laugh most in situations which include some obvious element of cognitive incongruity, and laugh in *anticipation* of arousing events within familiar routines. At this age, infants also laugh heartily during their own attempts to reproduce an incongruous situation. For example, Sroufe and Waters (1976) observed a twelve–month-old infant laughing as his mother appeared with a cloth in her mouth, then laughing even harder as he pulled it out and tried to stuff it back in again. Summarizing this developmental progression, Sroufe and Waters describe the infant's gradual transformation from passive recipient to active participant:

> . . . in the development of both smiling and laughter, the infant's progress is from response to intrusive stimulation and to stimulation mediated by active attention, toward smiling and laughing in

response to stimulus content, and finally toward an ever more active involvement in producing the stimulus itself (1976, p. 179).

This same progression is mirrored in the changing nature of the peekaboo game over the first year. At first the infant is a passive spectator, delighted by the immediate stimulation provided by the mother's looming face and melodic voice. As the infant matures and gains experience with the game, however, expectations come increasingly into play, and the infant begins to take pleasure in subtle variations in the game. As Bruner and Sherwood (1976) point out, the basic rules of appearance and disappearance hold constant, but the potential sources of variation within the standard format are endless: Who or what is hidden; what kind of mask is used; who initiates the uncovering; what vocalizations are used; and how they are timed in relation to the disappearance and reappearance—all of these features of the game can be modified in fascinating ways. And through such minor variations, the mother plays with the expectations of the infant, introducing suspense and playful tension into the familiar routine. For the ten–month-old infant, the mother's face and voice in and of themselves are no longer the primary source of delight in the peekaboo game. Rather the child's pleasure at this age is strongly influenced by how and when and where the mother disappears and reappears. The how and when and where can now be anticipated, which is exciting for the infant, but they are never completely predictable, which makes the game even more exciting. Bruner and Sherwood acknowledge the impressive skill of the mother in maintaining this balance between novelty and predictability, "knowing how to keep the child in an anticipatory mood, neither too sure of outcome nor too upset by a wide range of possibilities" (1976, p. 61). By the end of the first year, the child's pleasure derives more and more from active participation and agency. The cognitive challenge of the peekaboo game has been transformed from that of *predicting* the reappearance of the mother in a routine that incorporates increasing variability to that of *initiating* the hiding and reappearance and making these exciting events happen in the first place.

Conclusions

The peekaboo game is widespread across cultures, a source of great pleasure for both mothers and infants. Mothers play the game because it is so effective in eliciting infants' attention and in making them smile and laugh, as long as the game is skillfully modified over time and adapted to the developing abilities and interests of the child. Infants play the game because it engages them perceptually, cognitively, and emotionally, presenting compelling challenges that change continually as the infant changes over the first year. Shultz (1976) has made the interesting observation that mother-infant games often center around potentially threatening actions and events. Watching the mother disappear, being tickled, or being chased, among the most popular activities in infant games across cultures (Van Hoorn 1987), are all events that under other circumstances could be perceived as intrusive and terrifying to an adult. Perhaps the deep and universal appeal of peekaboo is also related to this potential emotional ambiguity in its central theme, as Shultz suggests, as well as to the cognitive challenges the game presents to the developing infant. In any case, cross-cultural research on universals of mother-infant games is a virtually unexplored source of insight into central issues in early human development. The peekaboo game is a microcosm in which we can observe both extraordinary changes in the infant's capacities and dispositions over the first year of life, as well as the parental skills and intuitions which so successfully use play as a means of accommodating and encouraging these developmental changes.

References

Allesandri, S. M.; Sullivan, M. W.; and Lewis, M. (1990). Violation of expectancy and frustration in early infancy. *Developmental Psychology* 26(5):738–44.

Baillargeon, R. (1987). Object permanence in 3 ½- and 4 ½-month old infants. *Developmental Psychology* 23:655–64.

Bower, T. G. R.; Broughton, J. M.; and Moore, M. K. (1970). Infant responses to approaching objects: An indicator of response to distal variables. *Perception and Psychophysics* 9:192–96.

Bower, T. G. R.; Broughton, J. M.; and Moore, M. K. (1971). Development of the object concept as manifested by changes in the tracking behavior of infants between 7 and 20 weeks of age. *Journal of Experimental Child Psychology* 11:182–92.

Bruner, J. S. (1975). The ontogenesis of speech acts. *Journal of Child Language* 2:1–19.

Bruner, J. S., and Sherwood, V. (1976). Early rule struture: The case of "peekaboo." In J. S. Bruner; A. Jolly; and K. Sylva (eds.), *Play: Its Role in Evolution and Development.* Harmondsworth: Penguin.

Call, J. D., and Marshack, M. (1966). Styles and games in infancy. *Journal of the American Academy of Child Psychiatry* 5(1): 193–210.

Callaghan, J. W. (1981). A comparison of Anglo, Hopi, and Navajo mothers and infants. In T. M. Field, A. M. Sostek, R. Vietze, and P. H. Leiderman (eds.), *Culture and Early Interactions.* Hillsdale, N.J.: Lawrence Erlbaum.

Charlesworth, W. R. (1966). Persistence of orienting and attending behavior in infants as a function of stimulus-locus uncertainty. *Child Development* 37(3): 473–90.

Cooper, R. P., and Aslin, R. N. (1990). Preference for infant-directed speech in the first month after birth. *Child Development* 61:1584–95.

Crawley, S. B.; Rogers, P. P.; Friedman, S.; Iacobbo, M.; Criticos, A.; Ricardson, L.; and Thompson, M. A. (1978). Developmental changes in the structure of mother-infant play. *Child Development* 14(1): 30–36.

Dannemillar, J. L., and Stephens, B. R. (1988). A critical test of infant pattern preference. *Child Development* 59:210–16.

Dixon, S.; Tronick, E.; Keefer, C.; and Brazelton, T. B. (1981). Mother-infant interaction among the Gusii of Kenya. In Field, Sostek, Vietze, and Leiderman (eds.), *Culture and Early Interactions.*

Enright, M. K.; Rovee-Collier, C. K.; Fagan, J. W.; and Caniglia, K. (1983). The effects of distributed training on retention of operant conditioning in human infants. *Journal of Experimental Child Psychology* 36: 512–524.

Fantz, R. L., and Nevis, S. (1967). Pattern preferences and perceptual-cognitive development in early infancy. *Merrill-Palmer Quarterly* 13: 77–108.

Fernald, A. (1984). The perceptual and affective salience of mothers' speech to infants. in L. Feagans, C. Garvey, and R. Golinkoff (eds.), *The origins and growth of communication,* New Brunswick: Ablex.

Fernald, A. (1985). Four-month-old infants prefer to listen to motherese. *Infant Behavior and Development* 8:181–95.

Fernald, A. (1989). Intonation and communicative intent in mother's speech to infants: Is melody the message? *Child Development* 60: 1497–1510.

Fernald, A. (1992). Maternal vocalisations to infants as biologically relevant signals: An evolutionary perspective. In J. H. Barkow, L.

Cosmides, and J. Tooby (Eds.), *The adapted mind: Evolutionary psychology and the generation of culture.* Oxford: Oxford University Press.

Fernald, A. (in press). Approval and disapproval: infant responsiveness to vocal affect in familiar and unfamiliar languages. *Child Development.*

Fernald, A., and Clarkson, M. (1993). Infant cardiac orienting to infant-directed vocalizations. Manuscript submitted for publication.

Fernald, A., and Eisen, J. (1993). Prosodic modifications in the infant-directed speech of rural Xhosa-speaking mothers in rural South Africa. Manuscript submitted for publication.

Fernald, A., and Kuhl. P. K. (1987). Acoustic determinants of infant preference for motherese. *Infant Behavior and Development* 10:279–93.

Fernald, A.; Taeschner, T.; Dunn, J.; Pepousek, M.; Boysson-Bardies, B.; and Fukui, I. (1989). A cross-language study of prosodic modifications in mothers' and fathers' speech to preverbal infants. *Journal of Child Language* 16:477–501.

Field, T., and Pawlby, S. (1980). Early face-to-face interactions of British and American working- and middle-class mother-infant dyads. *Child Development* 51:250–53.

Fogel, A.; Diamond, G. R.; Langhorst, B. H.; and Demos, V. (1982). Affective and cognitive aspects of the 2-month-olds' participation in face-to-face interaction with the mother. In E. Z. Tronick (ed.), *Social Interchange in Infancy: Affect, Cognition and Communication.* Baltimore: University Park Press.

Golinkoff, R. M. (1983). *Infant Social Cognition: Self, People, and Objects.* Hillsdale, N.J.: Lawrence Erlbaum.

Gopnik, A. (1984). The acquisition of *gone* and the development of the object concept. *Journal of Child Language* 11:273–92.

Green, J. A.; Gustafson, G. E.; and West, M. J. (1980). Effects of infant development on mother-infant interactions. *Child Development* 51:199–207.

Greenfield, P. M. (1972). Playing peekaboo with a four-month-old: A study of the role of speech and nonspeech sounds in the formation of a visual schema. *The Journal of Psychology* 82:287–98.

Gustafson, G. E.; Green, J. A.; and West, M. J. (1979). The infant's changing role in mother-infant games: The growth of social skills. *Infant Behavior and Development* 2:301–8.

Haith, M. M. (1980). *Rules That Infants Look By.* Hillsdale, N.J.: Lawrence Erlbaum.

Haith, M. M.; Bergman, T.; and Moore, M. J. (1977). Eye contact and face scanning in early infancy. *Science* 198:853–55.

Haith, M. M.; Hazan, C.; and Goodman, G. S. (1988). Expectation and anticipation of dynamic visual events by 3.5-month-old babies. *Child Development* 59:476–79.

Kleeman, J. A. (1967). The peek-a-boo game. In H. Hartman and M. Kris (ed.), *The Psychoanalytic Study of the Child*. New York: International Universities Press.

Martini, M., and Kirkpatrick, J. (1981). Early interactions in the Marquesas Islands. In T. M. Field, A. Sostek, P. Vietze, and A. H. Leiderman (eds.), *Culture and Early Interactions*.

Maurer, D., and Barrera, M. (1981). Infants' perception of natural and distorted arrangements of a schematic face. *Child Development* 52: 196–202.

Millar, W. S. (1988). Smiling, vocal, and attentive behavior during social contingency learning in seven- and ten-month-old infants. *Merrill-Palmer Quarterly* 34(3): 301–25.

Parrott, W. G., and Gleitman, H. (1989). Infant's expectations in play: The joy of peekaboo. *Cognition and Emotion* 3(4): 291–311.

Piaget, J. (1954). *The Construction of Reality in the Child*. New York: Ballantine

Ratner, N., and Bruner, J. (1978). Games, social exchange and the acquisition of language. *Journal of Child Language* 5:391–401.

Ross, H. S., and Kay, D. A. (1980). The origins of social games. *New Directions for Child Development* 9: 17–31.

Ross, H. S., and Lollis, S. P. (1987). Communication within infant social games. *Developmental Psychology* 23(2): 241–48.

Rubin, S., and Wolf, D. (1979). The development of maybe: The evolution of social roles into narrative roles. *New Directions for Child Development* 6:15–28.

Shultz, T. R. (1976). A cognitive-developmental analysis of humour. In A. J. Chapman and H. C. Foot (eds.), *Humour and Laughter: Theory, Research, and Applications*. London: John Wiley and Sons.

Snow, C.; de Blauw, A.; and Van Roosmalen, C. (1979). Talking and playing with babies: The role of ideologies in child-rearing. In M. Bullowa (ed.), *Before speech: The Beginning of Interpersonal Communication*. Cambridge, Eng.: Cambridge University Press.

Spelke, E., and Cortelyou, A. (1981). Perceptual aspects of social knowing: Looking and listening infancy. In M. E. Lamb and L. R. Sherrod (eds.), 61–84. *Infant Social Cognition: Empirical and Theoretical Considerations.* Hillsdale, N.J.: Lawrence Erlbaum.

Sroufe, L. A., and Waters, E. (1976). The ontogenesis of smiling and laughter: A perspective on the organization of development in infancy. *Psychological Review* 83(3): 173–89.

Sroufe, A., and Wunsch, J. P. (1972). The development of laughter in the first year of life. *Child Development* 43:1326–44.

Stern, D. (1977). *The First Relationship.* Cambridge: Harvard University Press.

Trehub, S. E.; Bull, D.; and Thorpe, L. (1984). Infants' perception of melodies: The role of melodic contour. *Child Development* 55:821–30.

Tronick, E.; Als, H.; Adamson, L.; Wise, S.; and Brazelton, T. B. (1978). The infant's response to entrapment between contradictory messages in face-to-face interaction. *Journal of Academy of Child Psychiatry* 17: 1–13.

Van Hoorn, J. (1987). Games that babies and mothers play. In P. Monighan-Nourot, B. Scales, J. Van Hoorn, and M. Almy (eds.), *Looking at Children's Play.* New York: Teachers College Press.

Washburn, R. W. (1929). A study of smiling and laughing in the first year of life. *Genetic Psychology Monographs* 6:397–535.

Watson, J. S. (1972). Smiling, cooing, and "the game." *Merril-Palmer Quarterly* 18(4): 323–39.

Watson, J.S. (1979). Perception of contingency as a determinant of social responsiveness. In E. Thoman (ed.), *The Origins of Social Responsiveness.* Hillsdale, N.J.: Erlbaum.

Watson, J. S. (1985). Contingency perception in early social development. In T. M. Field and N. A. Fox (eds.), *Social Perception in Infants.* Norwood, N.J.: Ablex.

Werker, J. F., and McLeod, P. J. (1989). Infant preference for both male and female infant-directed talk: A developmental study of attentional and affective responsiveness. *Canandian Journal of Psychology* 43: 230–46.

Wolff, P. H. (1963). Observations on the early development of smiling. In B. M. Foss (ed.), *Determinants of Infant Behavior.* London: Methuen.

CHAPTER 11

Gentle Play Partners: Mother-Child and Father-Child Play in New Delhi, India

Jaipaul L. Roopnarine, Frank H. Hooper, Mohammad Ahmeduzzaman, and Brad Pollack

Researchers have long recognized the need to broaden our understanding of parent-child relations. Since the 1960s, there has been a growing body of research on early patterns of socialization in diverse cultural settings (see Roopnarine and Carter 1992). The growing data base on patterns of socialization in other cultures should help us to tease out the cultural relevance and adaptive value of particular parent-child behavioral tendencies and simultaneously allow us to reflect on parent-child social activities in our own North American society (see Lamb 1987; Roopnarine, Lu, and Ahmeduzzaman 1989). It is our belief that whatever the mechanisms and processes, parents in all cultures socialize their children toward achieving instrumental and social competency. These processes and mechanisms have been shaped and reshaped over many generations to facilitate adaptation.

In this chapter, we hope to shed some light on adult-infant play in a society with a very lengthy history. While the major focus of the chapter is on early patterns of play between parents and infants in New Delhi, India, we provide some preliminary information on infant games, and play and infant stimulation. In the latter part of the chapter, we discuss the importance of rough play in the devel-

The research reported herein was supported by grants from the National Science Foundation through the Committee on the International Exchange of Scholars and from the Indian Government.

opment of attachment to fathers. Before we launch into a discussion of these topics, however, it is appropriate that we take a brief look at some factors that are central to life in India.

Family Structure and Socialization

There are three major defining characteristics of life across India: family solidarity, kinship structure, and its hierarchical organization; caste; and the religious belief structure. Despite subcultural practices and linguistic diversity, these three factors form the core values in the socialization of children in India. In a larger sense, they are the basis for the formation of interpersonal relationships, are integral in guiding parent-child relations and attending practices, and they define the boundaries of human social relationships. Below, we examine briefly each factor's role in interpersonal functioning in the family.

Kinship Structure

Early accounts of family structure point to the pervasiveness of patriarchy within the Indian family. With very few exceptions, throughout much of India's recent history men have accorded themselves extreme power whereas women have assumed more subordinate roles. This type of arrangement is seen in the economic and social responsibilities delegated to and assumed by sons and older males in the family. By contrast, women are expected to be subservient. They are expected to display total loyalty, *pativarata*, to their husbands and often wield little or no influence in family decisions and economic issues. For the Indian woman, it is the mother-in-law who reigns supreme over domestic activities. A woman's status is vastly improved, however, if she gives birth to male offspring, and under certain circumstances eldest daughter-in-laws can gain control over domestic issues. In general, however, men are the liaisons to the outside world.

The joint family system remains the major context for the socialization of children. Today, family structure ranges from the large joint family which is comprised of three or more generations to the nuclear family with dependents. Whereas the number of such nuclear families is increasing in urban areas in India, most families function in the manner that extended families do. The nuclear families' presence appears to be so only in structural terms because both nonfamilial and familial members are central to the functioning of most families in India. Family boundaries are permeable and flexible. As a consequence Indian children are in constant contact with numerous adults and children. Life is never dull within the confines of an Indian family; people are always visiting and meddling in family affairs (cf. Ross 1967).

Indian mothers and other women in the household can be characterized as indulgent. The mother's role as caregiver is close and physical. Babies are always in close proximity to the mother; they are carried on the hip, massaged daily, and are constantly cuddled, crooned, and talked to (Kakar 1978). This physical intensity continues way beyond the infancy period. The mother is a caregiver who is always accessible, and she follows rather than leads a child's inclinations.

By contrast, Indian men are still reluctant to embrace childcare roles (see Roopnarine et al. 1989; Roopnarine and Hossain 1992). The Indian father appears dominant and at times stern. His role as chief authority figure can instill fear in children and may serve to distance him from primary caregiving and socialization roles. Nevertheless, he dictates the patterns of certain childhood practices.

Caste

The patriarchical nature of Hindu society is intimately tied to the caste system. There are numerous castes in India; they define the boundaries of human social relationships, occupational choices, marriage partners, and a multitude of other aspects of life in India (Kakar 1978). Irrespective of size and prevailing practices, each member is expected to participate in the defining social order of the caste. Historically, the *panchayat,* the caste council, was a dominant establishment that discerned the worthwhileness of caste membership and a member's inclusion or exclusion in caste activities. Although the government of India has been vigorously working to eradicate the caste system, the fact is the caste system remains central in the formation of social relationships in India. Its exclusionary practices are demeaning and self-serving.

Religious Belief Structures

The religious belief structures of Hindus are also strongly interwoven into the hierarchical structure of life in India. Life is dominated by rituals and religious practices. While religious practices vary among subcultural groups, they generally serve to guide Hindus toward an understanding of the self and the formation of interpersonal relationships. These belief structures form the basis for defining and framing ideological notions about the world. Through serious devotion, Hindus strive to achieve a balance in understanding between the spiritual and physical world.

Two concepts, *Dharma* and *Karma,* are central to existential notions about life in India. *Dharma* refers to the interdependent and complementary nature of roles and responsibilities, whereas *Karma* directs the cycles of birth and death through which a person regresses or progresses depending on past deeds (Kakar 1978). These concepts offer validity to one's fortunes or woes in life and are taken very seriously in the formation of interpersonal relationships.

Religious concepts are portrayed in daily practice or through the personification of epics. Some epics convey messages of loyalty, fidelity, and family solidarity. The messages serve as reminders of "good" and "evil" and allow Hindus to tie in experiences in the immediate environment with those of their cultural and religious past.

This all too brief introduction to a historically complex culture suggests that, for the most part, the focal context for the socialization of children remains the joint family. The hierarchical social organization of families, however, ensures that rigid boundaries are maintained in relationship formation and social interactions. These latter are formed in accord with caste distinctions and religious practices which are also at the core of family socialization practices.

Mother-Infant Games in Different Regions in India

The importance of parent-infant play and "co-playing" with children has been addressed by numerous researchers. More specifically, the games adults engage in with infants have been viewed as focused interactions that contain repetition, temporal regularities, and are often of intrinsic interest to both parent and infant (Stern 1974, 1977). The games may involve visual, auditory, and tactile stimulation, limb or large body movements, and special objects (see Rubin, Fein, and Vandenburg 1983 for a review). During bouts of play, infants may coo, smile, and laugh (Sroufe and Wunsche 1972). These early games expose the infant to the structural elements of language and therefore provide the social milieu for learning language (Ratner and Bruner 1978); they arouse the infant which may encourage exploration (Power and Parke 1982); and they provide the context within which the infant is provided an opportunity to acquire control of social stimuli including the basic child-caretaker social relationship itself (Watson 1972; Watson and Ramey 1972).

These events are best viewed in the larger context of life span developmental theory. To merely assume that "the child is father to the man," of course, suggests banality. Yet the demonstration of developmental precursors is particularly important in furthering our understanding of the infancy period. As Lipsitt has stated, "I have always thought that infancy must be a practice period, a time of preparation, an opportunity to experience the pleasures of sensation without fear of appreciable censure, and an arena in which the models of life's later battles are rehearsed. This preparatory aspect of infancy is seen especially well in the play behavior of infants (e.g., peek-a-boo games, reciprocal face looming) and in early manifestations of approach-avoidance conflict. It is probably aided by an immature nervous system which at once is altered by and alters experience, and which matures as it experiences . . . " (Lipsitt 1982, pp. 41–42). Play behaviors and infant games, in particular, fit well in the confines of general "Action Theory" whether as presented by Piaget (1963), Bruner (1973), or the Soviet writers (e.g., Vygotsky 1962). The most general developmental event (in terms of the life span implications) concerns *intentionality* (Vedeler 1987). The infant's growing awareness of means-ends relationships underlies all later goal-directed behavior. And it is precisely the pleasurable play situations which often explicitly demonstrate these special contingency relations most directly (e.g., Mandler 1990; Watson 1972). In so far as intentional communicative acts are concerned, the shared concrete social context between infant and caretaker leads to eventual language acquisition (Harding 1982; Meacham 1984) as well as symbolic functioning in its most general sense (Furth 1983; Werner and Kaplan 1963).

Against this backdrop, we discuss infant games found in different regions of India. Developmental psychologists in India (e.g., Anandalakshmy 1989; Sharma 1989) have argued that these early games reflect the depth of maternal involvement and, perhaps, because of their high tactile content provide and encourage a sense of security and abiding trust between parent and infant. The games are described in *Children's Games* (Muralidharan, Khosla, Mian, and Kavar 1981). They reflect both traditional and contemporary games.

Regardless of whether it is in Maharashtra, Bengal, Gujarat, Andra Pradesh, Punjab, or Kerala, infant games involve a good deal of touching and movement. In most cases, the child is seated on the parent's lap or held on the hip while the mother recites the games and goes through the physical motions with the child. During other games, the infant is placed opposite the mother on the floor or ground. For example, in a traditional mother-infant game played in Maharastra, the baby is on the mother's lap while the mother sings. The mother traces a half-circle in the air and later completing the circle puts a teeka on

> Adgule madgule
> Sonyache kadbule
> Rupyacha vala
> Tanhya bala
> Teet lava

> "Adgule madgule*
> Golden kadbule**
> Silver ring
> Little baby
> I put on teet***"

   * Rhyming sounds with no specific meaning
  ** A salty delicacy round in shape
 *** Black teka' put on the child's face to ward off evil spirits.

the baby's forehead. A Gujrati game also ends up by placing a dot on the baby's forehead. In a Bengali game, the mother sits in the sun and places the baby on her outstretched legs; the mother recites the lines of a song while massaging the baby with oil. By the last line, she lifts the baby by the legs and then drops it lightly. In yet other games played in Punjab the child is rocked on the feet while the mother sings, and in Maharastra the baby rocks back and forth to the rhythm of the song.

> Dol bai dol ga
> Halu vealu dol ga
> Bhara Bhara dol ga
> Dol bai dol ga
> Jai tura tol ga.

> "Rock baby, rock,
> Swiftly, swiftly rock,
> Rock baby rock
> Be careful, you are going off balance."

What is striking about infant games in India is the rich use of language in the form of songs. The content of the songs reflect religious figures, convey cultural child-rearing practices (e.g., the teeka is placed to ward off evil spirits), kinship relationships, marriage, and an assortment of other culture-specific and environmentally relevant events/objects. The tactile nature of infant games bodes well with the emphasis on close physical contact during infancy. In other words, the zeitgeist of early parent-infant interplay is characterized by physical closeness.

Massage as a Context for Play

As noted above, a few of the mother-infant games occur within the context of massage. Indian infants are massaged daily. During massages, the caregiver plays, coos, and sings to the infant. Whereas the massage affects circulation and the resilience and contractability of the muscles (Tur 1980), it also provides the context for meaningful stimulation. In a country where most parents cannot afford to buy toys for infants, finger games and songs during massage provide infants with early stimulation that is necessary for adequate later development. It is not unusual to see homeless individuals massaging, oiling, and playing with babies on the pavements. The importance of the stimulation provided during massage, while not fully explored, may influence the formation of parent-child attachments and the development of a range of cognitive and social skills as stressed in the action theories briefly mentioned earlier.

Play and Early Stimulation

Because of India's staggering health and malnutrition problems and their implication for early social and cognitive development, Indian researchers have begun to implement early intervention programs whose main goal is to introduce play as a major factor in stimulating development. The assumption behind these programs is that a large number of children are not provided with the opportunity for optimal development at home. Lack of employment, migration, poor literacy skills, and general bleak economic outlook can have a depressive impact on parent-child relations. Moreover, nonstructured close physical contact with adults and siblings, itself, may not be sufficient in providing developmentally appropriate stimulation for infants.

By and large, early intervention studies of India have focused on nutritional status, maternal attributes, and the relationship of these variables to infants' performances on scales of early development. For example, Misra (1977) found good concordance between the kind of maternal interaction and performance on the Casati Lezine Scale and Bayley Scales of Infant Development. Infants who performed well on these scales had mothers who would label and point to objects, had playthings within reach of infants, imitated infants, and played peekaboo games with them. Infants who had low scores had mothers who held them for most of the day and rarely played with or vocalized to them.

In a large scale study of 512 infants Anandalakshmy (1979) examined further the contribution of maternal social interaction and cognitive stimulation and encouragement of exploration to infant development. Infants were observed during play with their mothers and cognitive and motor development were assessed using the Bayley Scales of Infant Development. Again, it was found that infants who had low MDI scores had mothers who did not encourage play and engaged in little interaction with them. This tendency was noticeable even when the home environment appeared to be adequately furnished with objects and materials. In general, upper socioeconomic status families provided more cognitive stimulation to infants than lower socioeconomic status families. This discrepancy was attributed to the genuine lack of awareness of the importance of play for infant development among lower socioeconomic status mothers.

In subsequent work, a subsample of fifty-nine infants from the original 512 were included in a play intervention program geared to boost cognitive functioning. The infants had low MDI scores initially. Twenty-nine of the infants were provided with maternal stimulation in the form of verbal and social interaction and were exposed to ample play materials in the home setting during ten play sessions over the course of a month. While there were increases in cognitive functioning in the experimental group, the overall gains were not significantly different from those in the control group. Nonetheless, Anandalakshmy (1985) argued that the play stimulation provided opportunities for exploration and aroused interest in exploration and play activities. Furthermore, it encouraged general responsiveness to adults.

In a play intervention study conducted in Haryana, infants were exposed to intense maternal interaction and mother-child play activities that tapped into gross and fine motor skills and block building over a ten–month period (Patri 1988). At the end of the intervention period, experimental group children showed significant gains in IQ when compared with control group children.

In sum, Indian psychologists are beginning to assess the impact of maternal stimulation and mother-child play for cognitive and social development during infancy. Thus far, preliminary results have shown the positive value of play during parent-child interactions. With this is mind, Indian investigators (e.g., Muralidharan 1988) are now introducing culturally appropriate materials and experiences into early intervention efforts. Likewise, assessment tools are becoming more culturally relevant. This is similar to a number of recent efforts to achieve a nonstereotypic approach to minority populations in the United States designed to yield a degree of cultural validity (cf. Eckensberger 1973) for studies of economically deprived infants (e.g., Coll 1990) as well as older school-aged children (e.g., Slaughter-Defoe, Nakagawa, Takanishi, and Johnson 1990).

Attachment and Play

A few researchers (e.g., Stern 1977) argue that the early exchanges during parent-infant play can facilitate the development of attachment relationships. More recently, Lamb (1985) has argued that the highly stimulating bouts of interactions that occur during rough play may provide one avenue for the development of father-infant attachment. Whereas the formation of attachment to the mother develops as result of her intense daily involvement with the baby, the father-child attachment develops in the context of less frequent but physically more stimulating interactions. This argument was formulated on the basis of results presented in a number of studies conducted in the United States (see Belsky 1979; Lamb 1976, 1985). Fathers are more likely to engage in vigorous play with infants than are mothers (see Lamb 1985).

Data from other cultures, however, have led researchers to question the role rough play assumes in the development of affective saliency with fathers (see Hewlett 1987). Data from four cultures bring this issue to the forefront of our discussion. In a semistructured interview study, Lu (1987) asked Malaysian mothers and fathers residing in Kuching, Sarawak, to describe the play activities they engaged in with their one–year-old infants. What was striking about the parents' assessments was that they rarely reported engaging in physical play with their children. A similar trend was observed among the Aka pygmies of Central Africa. Aka mothers and fathers showed almost no inclination to engage in rough play with young children (Hewlett 1987). The Aka father appeared quite intimate and displayed a good deal of close physical contact with young children. In the same vein, Roopnarine et al. (1990) found that among middle-income Indian families in New Delhi, fathers and mothers were more likely to display affection than to play or feed infants while holding them. Bouts of play between parents and infants rarely involved rough stimulating activities. And, in Italian families in a small city north of Rome, familial and nonfamilial women, not fathers, were observed to engage in rough play with infants (New and Benigni 1987).

The above-mentioned findings would suggest that rough play may be culture specific and that its importance in the development of attachment uniquely to the father or other male figures in other cultures is yet to be determined. Perhaps in some cultures a didactic nonphysical social context may provide the basis for the development of affective bonds to fathers. In the rest of this chapter, we present data that would provide some support for the above contentions. The more important general issue may lie with the principle of alternate paths to similar developmental goals and outcomes (cf. Werner 1937). *Consistent* social interaction patterns involving a variety of activities which are pleasurable and intrinsically arousing to the infant probably provide the essential developmental context for much subsequent cognitive and socioemotional development.

An Illustrative Study

Two issues guided our observations and interviews regarding patterns of adult-infant play. First, judging from the data presented on father-child play in other cultures, the notion that rough play is critical for the development of father-child attachment may need modification (Hewlett 1987). Father-infant play in the United States appears quite different from father-infant play in Kuching, India, and Africa. Thus, while father-infant rough play may be important for understanding the development of attachment in American families, its particular relevance for the development of attachment to fathers in other cultures appears questionable. From a theoretical standpoint, then, we need to reevaluate this perspective within the context of attachment theory.

Second, much has been written about the importance of early parent-child play. In India, researchers have long recognized the need for cognitive and social stimulation while parents are holding their infants. As some have argued, holding the baby may be the initial step toward early stimulation but that alone certainly falls short of providing a prerequisite basis for charting optimal growth (See Anandalakshmy 1985). Unless parents realize the value of play, they may not be inclined to implement it as a part of parenting responsibilities. There is some evidence to suggest that lower socioeconomic status Indian mothers, in particular, do not seem to understand the value of play (cf. Anandalakshmy 1985). Indeed, it would be of value to assess the reasons why Indian parents engage in certain modes of play with infants.

The present data are based on semistructured interviews and home observations conducted on thirty-four dual-earner families that lived in small joint family units. The data are from that portion of the study that dealt with parent-child play and parental beliefs about the value of play with infants. Additional data on this study are presented elsewhere (Roopnarine and Hossain 1992). Each family was observed for two thirty-minute sessions and interviewed regarding a range of parent-child activities in their homes. Observations focused on *rough* (tossing, roughhousing) and *minor physical play* (tickling, bouncing on lap), *object-mediated play,* and "*peekaboo*" games. During interviews parents were asked why they engaged in different play activities with infants. The data presented below center on gender-of-parent and gender-of-infant differences during play; the reasons for engaging in play with infants; and the predominant mode of play during social interaction with infants.

Focal Population and Sample

Our data were gathered in thirteen colonies in New Delhi, India. New Delhi, the capital of India, is a sprawling metropolis with about 6.2 million people. The city which is located in North Central India is made up of individuals from every state and region of India. Its diversity in linguistic and subcultural groups is due in part to the city's economic growth. Four-fifths of the population is Hindu; Moslems constitute the largest minority, followed by smaller number of Jains, Christians, and Buddhists. Hindi is the most common language spoken, although most individuals speak some English. New Delhi is a modern city with a large civil servant work force.

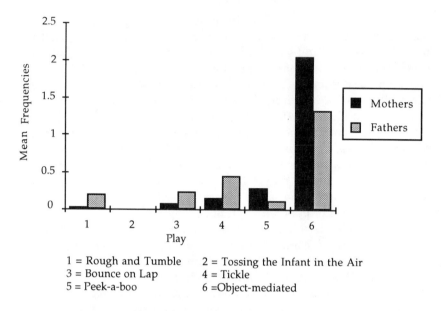

1 = Rough and Tumble   2 = Tossing the Infant in the Air
3 = Bounce on Lap   4 = Tickle
5 = Peek-a-boo   6 =Object-mediated

Figuire 11.1.   Mean frequencies of play participation between parents and infants.

The thirty-four families observed and interviewed were from middle- to upper-middle income backgrounds. Both spouses had at least a bachelor's degree. Mothers and fathers were primarily employed as doctors, civil servants, teachers, legal advocates, and business personnel. The couples were married for an average of 4.79 years. The mean age of the husbands was 32 years, while the mean age of mothers was 29 years. Their infants were within two weeks of their first birthdays. There were sixteen boys and eighteen girls.

Play Findings

As figure 1 demonstrates, mothers and fathers engaged in low levels of play interactions with their infants. Mothers and fathers did not differ on the mean frequencies of participation in any of the categories of minor physical, rough physical play or peek-a-boo with infants. However, mothers were more likely to engage in object-mediated play with infants than were fathers ($p<.05$). There were no gender-of-infant differences on any of the play measures.

Figure 11.2 represents the reasons parents offered for engaging in different play activities with infants. As can be seen from this figure, both mothers and fathers played with infants for enjoyment

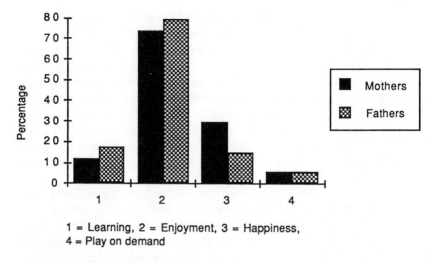

1 = Learning, 2 = Enjoyment, 3 = Happiness,
4 = Play on demand

Figure 11.2.   Reasons for parental play.

and to make the infant happy. In contrast, perhaps, with many sur-
veys in the United States, few parents emphasized learning or the
acquisition and refinement of skills as major reasons for playing
with infants.

Discussion

It is clear from these data that Indian fathers are not rough,
vigorous play partners. Our observations substantiate the findings
of earlier work on father-infant play in India (Roopnarine et al.
1990). The frequency of rough play in general was quite low—on the
average of less than one incident per one hour period of observation.
Were individuals other than parents engaging in rough play with
infants? Relatives did not engage in a single incident of rough play
and siblings were rarely observed to engage in rough play with infants. In other data (Roopnarine and Hossain 1992) presented on
these families, fathers and mothers did not differ on the number of
times they picked up the infant or on the duration of time they held
the infants. Similarly, infants showed no significant tendency to
touch or approach mothers more than fathers. Thus, in the context
of attachment theory, infants appeared to be attached to both mothers and fathers if we consider approach and touch as behaviors that
may be indicative of attachments per se. Moreover, the lack of significant differences between mothers and fathers in holding infants

would also suggest that perhaps these fathers were accessible to infants in social activities other than through rough play.

We failed to detect any differential treatment of infants by parents during play. This was contrary to our expectations. Religious doctrines and cultural prescription bemoan the birth of daughters and boys are accorded greater importance in India than girls. Besides, data from other cultures point to the differential treatment of boys and girls by parents. Our surmise is that urban-educated Indians may have come to recognize the need to treat boys and girls similarly and hence this egalitarian view may reflect changes that are occurring in the basic family socialization patterns.

Finally, mothers and fathers emphasized the pleasurable aspects of playing with infants. They rarely mentioned learning as a major component of play with infants. Does this mean, then, that these parents are not aware of the value of play for infant social and cognitive development? Recall that we mentioned earlier that holding alone was not sufficient to provide early infant stimulation. The fact is Indian infants are frequently held by a variety of familial and nonfamilial figures. While the degree of social interaction with babies may vary a good deal from adult to adult, the comfort and happiness of the baby appear paramount. Moreover, parents did mention engaging in a wide range of play activities beyond those that we observed. In all likelihood, then, while they did not articulate the cognitive values of play experiences they most certainly recognized the contribution of play to the baby's general social disposition and comfort.

Conclusion

We can view our contentions and results in terms of two levels of analysis, broadly from the perspective of general cross-cultural psychology, and more specifically, in light of the particular Indian child/parent interactions. The former, cross-cultural psychology " . . . *attempts to ascertain the different expressions of behavior that occur as a consequence of the interaction of the individual with his specific cultural environment*" (Eckensberger 1973, pp. 44). This definition serves to direct our attention toward the general issue of cultural relevance and such concepts as cultural, interpretive, population, ecological, and construct validity (cf. Washington and McLoyd 1982). The same formal task relevance issue is found in any life span assessment investigation with widely disparate age samples (Hooper 1976). Thus, despite any preconceptions and reservations we may have regarding child-rearing practices and associated parental attitudes in Western technical societies like the United States, we must judge these comparative results on their own merits *within* the culture in question. In short, the infant/parent play practices we observed in Indian families are obviously functionally appropriate for the India culture subsample assessed. As we have tried to show, these practices are a natural consequence of the beliefs, mores, and role relationships, as reflected in the family structure, the caste system, and the religious beliefs of modern India.

Concerning the particular mother/child and father/child play patterns we may conclude that rough stimulating play may not be as central to the development of attachment to fathers when we consider a wider range of cultures other than those found in the industrialized West. This whole perspective on the contribution of rough play for the development of attachment needs rethinking. Perhaps a cultural-ecological approach to the development of attachment to the father would bring us closer toward developing theories of father-child relationships (See Ogbu 1985). It is the very issue of underlying approaches to socialization that is at the crux of the matter not necessarily the end product. People in all cultures socialize their children to adapt to the challenges of the immediate culture. To observe how they go about doing this and the ability of psychologists to capture these disparate but sometimes similar approaches to socialization would require a good deal of creative energy.

References

Anandalakshmy, S. (1979) Recent research on the young child. *The Indian Journal of Social Work,* 40, 295–309.

Anandalakshmy, S. (1982). *Cognitive Competence in Infancy.* ICSSR Research Abstract Quarterly 14(1–2).

Anandalakshmy, S. (1985). Child development paper from the proceedings of the Lady Irwin Conference on Children. Lady Irwin College, New Delhi, India.

Anandalakshmy, S. (1989) Infant stimulation: Documentation of research in India. New Delhi, India: Lady Irwin College.

Belsky, J. (1979). Mother-father-infant interaction: A naturalistic observation study. *Developmental Psychology* 15:601–7.

Bruner, J. S. (1973). Competence in infants. In J. S. Bruner (ed.), *Beyond the Information Given*. New York: Norton.

Coll, C. T. G. (1990). Developmental outcome of minority infants: A process-oriented look into our beginnings. *Child Development* 61:270–89.

Eckensberger, L. H. (1973). Methodological issues of cross-cultural research in developmental psychology. In J. R. Nesselroade and H. W. Reese (eds.), *Life-Span Developmental Psychology: Methodological Issues*. New York: Academic.

Furth, H. G. (1983). Symbol formation: Where Freud and Piaget meet. *Human Development* 26:26–41.

Harding, C. G. (1982). Development of the intention to communicate. *Human Development* 25:140–51.

Hewlett, B. S. (1987). Patterns of paternal holding among Aka pygmies. In M. Lamb (ed.), *The Father's Role: Cross-Cultural Perspectives*. Hillsdale, N.J.: Erlbaum.

Hooper, F. H. (1976). Life-span analyses of Piagetian concept tasks: The search for non-trivial qualitative change. In K. F. Riegel and J. A. Meacham (eds.), *The Developing Individual in a Changing World*. Vol. 1, *Historical and Cultural Issues*, 219–32. Chicago, Aldine.

Kakar, S. (1978). *The Inner World: A Psychoanalytical Study of Childhood and Society in India*. New Delhi, India: Oxford University Press.

Lamb, M. E. (1976). Interactions between 8-month-old children and their fathers and mothers. In M. Lamb (ed.), *The Role of the Father in Child Development*. New York: Wiley.

Lamb, M. E. (1985). Observational studies of father-child relationships in humans. In D. Taub (ed.), *Primate Paternalism*. New York: Van Nostrand Reinhold.

Lamb, M. E. (1987). *The Father's Roles: Cross-Cultural Perspectives*. New Jersey: Erlbaum Associates Publishers.

Lipsett, L. P. (1982). Infancy and life-span development. *Human Development* 25:41–47.

Lu, M. (1987). Maternal and paternal assessments of their activities with their infants in Kuching, Malaysia. Unpublished master's thesis, Syracuse University.

Mandler, J. M. (1990). A new perspective on cognitive development in infancy. *American Scientist* 78:236–43.

Meacham, J. A. (1984). The social basis of intentional action. *Human Development* 27:119–24.

Misra, N. (1977). Cognitive and motor development of infants (6–12 months): Nutritional and socioeconomic status correlates. Unpublished master's dissertation, University of Delhi, India.

Muralidharan, R. (1988). Unpublished work cited in S. Anandalakshmy (ed.), *Infant Stimulation: Documentation of Research in Delhi.* Department of Child Development, Lady Irwin College, New Delhi.

Muralidharan, R.; Khosla, R.; Mian, G. M.; and Kavar, B. (1981). *Children's Games.* New Delhi: National Council of Educational Research and Training.

New, R., and Benigni, L. (1987). Italian fathers and infants: Cultural constraints on paternal behavior. In M. Lamb (ed.), *The Father's Role: Cross-Cultural Perspectives.* Hillsdale, N.J.: Erlbaum.

Ogbu, J. (1985). A cultural ecology of the compentence among inner-city Blacks. In M. B. Spencer, G. K. Brookins, and W. R. Allen (eds.), *Beginnings: The Social and Affective Development of Black Children.* Hillsdale, N.J.: Erlbaum.

Patri, V. (1988). An intervention programme of early stimulation in a group of disadvantaged children. Unpublished research report, New Delhi.

Piaget, J. (1963). *The Origins of Intelligence in Children.* New York: Norton.

Power, T., and Parke, R. (1982). Play as a context for early learning: Lab and home analyses. In I. Sigel and L. Laosa (eds.), *Families as Learning Environments for Children.* New York: Plenum Press.

Ratner, N., and Bruner, J. S. (1978). Games, social exchange, and the acquisition of language. *Journal of Child Language* 5:391–402.

Roopnarine, J. L., and Hossain, Z. (1992). Parent-child interaction patterns in urban Indian families in New Delhi: Are they changing? In J. Roopnarine and B. Carter (eds.), *Parent-Child Relations in Diverse Cultures.* Norwood, N.J.: Ablex.

Roopnarine, J. L.; Lu, M.; and Ahmeduzzaman, M. (1989). Parental reports of early patterns of caregiving in India and Malaysia. *Early Child Development and Care* 50:109–20.

Roopnarine, J. L., and Carter, B. (1992). *Parent-Child Relations in Diverse Cultures.* Norwood, N.J.: Ablex.

Roopnarine, J. L.; Talukder, E.; Jain, D.; Joshi, P.; and Srivastav, P. (1990). Characteristics of holding, patterns of play, and social behaviors between parents and infants in New Delhi, India. *Developmental Psychology* 26:667–673.

Ross, A. D. (1967). *The Hindu Family in Its Urban Setting.* Toronto: University of Toronto Press.

Rubin, K.; Fein, G. G.; and Vandenburg, B. (1983). Play. In P. H. Mussen (ed.), *Handbook of Child Psychology.* Vol. 4, *Socialization, Personality and Social Development,* 393–474. New York: Wiley.

Sharma, N. (1989). *Infant Stimulation: Documentation of Research in India.* Department of Child Development, Lady Irwin College, New Delhi, India.

Slaughter-Defoe, D. T.; Nakagawa, K.; Takanishi, R.; and Johnson, D. J. (1990). Toward cultural/ecological perspectives on schooling and achievement in African and Asian-American children. *Child Development* 61:363–83.

Sroufe, L. A., and Wunsche, J. P. (1972). The development of laughter in the first year of life. *Child Development* 43:1326–44.

Stern, D. N. (1974). Mother and infant play: The dyadic interaction involving facial, vocal, and gaze behaviors. In M. Lewis and L. Rosenblum (eds.), *The Effect of the Infant on Its Caregiver.* New York: Wiley, 1974.

Stern, D. N. (1977). *The First Relationship.* Cambridge: Harvard University press.

Tur, A. (1980). *Know Your Child.* Moscow.

Vedeler, D. (1987). Infant intentionality and the attribution of intentions to infants. *Human Development* 30:1–17.

Vygotsky, L. S. (1962). *Thought and Language.* Cambridge: MIT Press.

Washington, E. D., and McLoyd, V. C. (1982). The external validity of research involving American minorities. *Human Development* 25: 324–39.

Watson, J. S. (1972). Smiling, cooing, and "the game". *Merrill-Palmer Quarterly* 4:323–39.

Watson, J. S., and Ramey, C. T. (1972). Reactions to response-contingent stimulation in early infancy. *Merrill-Palmer Quarterly* 18:219–27.

Werner, H. (1937). Process and achievement: A basic product of education and developmental psychology. *Harvard Education Review* 7: 353–68.

Werner, H., and Kaplan, B. (1963). *Symbol Formation.* New York: Wiley.

CHAPTER 12

"Mother, Older Sibling and Me": The Overlapping Roles of Caregivers and Companions in the Social World of Two– to Three–Year-Olds in Ngeca, Kenya

Carolyn Pope Edwards and Beatrice B. Whiting

In recent years, our increasing knowledge of young children's active participation coconstructing their learning environments has led to growing sophistication in examining socialization within the context of the multiple and embedded relationships of ongoing family life. This chapter compares the overlapping roles of mothers and adjacent older siblings as social partners for young children aged two to three growing up in the periurban community of Ngeca, Kenya.[1] The siblings, although usually only two years older than the focal children, provide stimulation that is cognitively and emotionally complex, rich, and challenging. This stimulation provides an important supplement to the mothers' more restricted (and less playful) style of interaction. Because mothers and adjacent siblings are the two most frequent social partners of Ngeca toddlers, their interaction with them needs to be studied of a piece. Only when seen jointly can we understand how mothers and siblings together influence young children's emerging behavioral expectancies, concepts of self and others, and social and moral knowledge.

Anthropologists have long noted the importance worldwide of children as partners and caregivers of their younger siblings (Konner 1975; Mead 1928; Read 1960; Whiting and Whiting 1975). Barry

This research was funded by grants from the National Institute of Mental Health (to Beatrice Whiting) and the Carnegie Foundation (to the Child Development Research Unit). We thank Tom Weisner for comments on an earlier draft of the paper.

and Paxson (1971) systematically surveyed the ethnographic literature and rated 186 societies at all levels of economic complexity in
terms of who were reported to be young children's principal companions and caretakers. They found that adults were reported to be
the most frequent caretakers during infancy, but during the postinfancy period of early childhood, other children took over as principal companions and caretakers in the majority of societies.

Yet only in recent years have researchers begun to investigate
the many questions and hypotheses about sibling influence suggested by Weisner and Gallimore (1977) in their now classic review.
For example, detailed descriptions from several parts of the world
compare parents with siblings in terms of their language dialogues
with young children (Harkness 1975; Heath 1983; Watson-Gegeo
and Gegeo 1989), scaffolding of play (Dunn and Dale 1984; Farver,
Chapter 14, this volume; Zukow 1989), literacy-related behavior
(Weisner, Gallimore, and Jordon 1988), and overall profiles of nurturance, training, control, and sociable interaction (Wenger 1983,
1989; Whiting and Edwards 1988). The findings confirm that parents and siblings are important coactors in socializing young children and guiding their participation into culturally meaningful
activities (Rogoff, Mistry, Goncu, and Mosier 1991; Weisner 1989b).
For example, with respect to cognitive and linguistic stimulation,
Zapotec (Mexican) and Embu (Kenyan) siblings engage toddlers in
interactions that are sustained, elaborate, well-matched to the toddlers' developmental level, and facilitative of mature responses by
the toddlers (Sigman et al. 1988; Zukow 1989).

For the East African context, the comparative roles of mothers
and older siblings as caretakers and companions of young children
are especially interesting because of the cultural ideals surrounding maternal behavior. Cultures differ in their perceptions of the
maternal role and the ideal patterns for mother-child interaction.
LeVine (1990) has studied mother-infant interaction among the
Gusii in Western Kenya and argues that in any community the cultural model of the mother-infant relationship is influenced by (1)
wider codes of communicative conduct prevailing in the community;
(2) prevalent folk beliefs about the nature of the infant as a conversational partner; and (3) parental goals or models of a "good child."
In the case of the Gusii, the wider codes of communication are organized around respect (*obosiku*) and restraint (*ensoni*) norms that
apply to persons of adjacent generations (indeed, the cultures of
many sub-Saharan agricultural peoples emphasize age and sex hi-
erarchies and social distance between persons differing in age and

sex; LeVine 1973). In addition, Gusii folk beliefs do not portray infants as potential conversational partners. Finally, the models of virtue that guide Gusii mothers in their socialization of their children are toward obedient, respectful children who are attentive to adult commands without being socially intrusive and attention-seeking. In comparison with mothers in other societies, Gusii mothers engage in less purely sociable interaction with their young children, and they begin training children at an earlier age (two- to three-years-old) in appropriate social behavior and work habits (Whiting and Edwards 1988).

From many studies, a distinctive picture has emerged of East African mothers' interactions with toddlers. In general these mothers (1) attend closely to children's physical needs and survival; (2) provide much physical closeness and responsiveness to kinesthetic cues; (3) conceptualize the maternal role primarily in terms of responsive nurturance and training; and (4) are sociable and talkative without conferring conversational peer status on the toddler or scaffolding object play (Blount 1972; Harkness 1975; Sigman et al. 1988; Weisner 1989a; Wenger 1983, 1989; Whiting and Edwards 1988).

East African mothers leave the role of "playmate" to others in the family, especially siblings. For example, Sigman and colleagues (1988), who have studied an Embu-speaking community geographically and culturally proximate to Ngeca, summarize the character and importance of siblings' interaction with toddlers as follows: "The influence of siblings and peers appears to be quite important for the Embu toddlers' development. Older sisters were frequently the caregivers who listened to and talked to their younger sibling. Furthermore, those toddlers most involved in sustained social interaction developed the most rapidly, and social interactions almost always involved other children rather than adults" (p. 1259).

This study investigates the patterns of social interaction for toddlers (Margaret Mead called them "knee children") and their mothers and adjacent older siblings in Ngeca, a community of 7,000 studied by Beatrice Whiting in 1968–70 and 1972–73. Because the data base is large, this analysis involves a much more precise comparison than in the previous studies of East African children. Behavioral rate (rather than proportion) scores are used; and for the analysis, a repeated-measures design is used to statistically compare mothers' and siblings' behavior to (and from) focal children, allowing for more confident generalizations.

While the role of the Kenyan child nurse (ideally aged five to ten years, the infant's "skip one" older sibling) has been well characterized, the role of the adjacent older sibling has not received much attention. In Ngeca, however, mothers and adjacent older siblings (usually aged four to five years) were the most frequent social partners of young children just past infancy. Fathers had little involvement in the care of infants and young children. Infants spent much of the day carried by the mother or a child nurse; while toddlers (weaned from the back and breast) were commonly left in the care and company of older siblings during times when mothers were out of the homestead.

Significant shifts appeared to be occurring, however, in the age of the toddlers' sibling caregivers and companions (Wenger 1976). In 1968 when the study began, child nurses aged six to ten were usually the ones found home during late morning and early afternoon when mothers were off working in their gardens. By 1972 this had changed: almost all five– to ten–year-olds were now in nursery or primary school. Although mothers considered children under five years old too young to be consistently nurturant and reliable, and moreover held a cultural belief that adjacent siblings are inherently rivalrous, nevertheless many were forced to use children as young as four to look after younger siblings when temporarily out of the homestead. The knee children were very responsive to the social overtures from their adjacent older siblings and trailed after them continually. The older siblings, in turn, often engaged their followers in sociability, either because they were ignored by their school-aged siblings or those children were off doing chores or at school.

Wenger (1976) analyzed the Ngeca observations and compared the behavior of children aged three to four, five to seven, and eight to ten, to two–year-old partners. She found that with increasing age, children were significantly more nurturant and prosocially commanding toward two–year-olds, and less sociable, aggressive, and egoistically dominant, suggesting that in accord with the Ngeca mothers' folk beliefs, children over five more closely approximated the Ngeca maternal profile and were (in cultural terms) more mature caregivers for toddlers. The same age differences in behavior by older children were replicated by Wenger (1983 1989) in her study of two– to three–year-old Giriama-speaking children from Coastal Kenya, and by Whiting and Edwards (1988) in their analysis of data from four Kenyan communities. Whiting and Edwards (1988) concluded:

> Children who are close in age [age four to five] to knee children
> treat them as companions more than as individuals to be trained;

they play with, tease, and nurture them. In contrast, children in
the older age group [age eight to twelve] behave more like social-
izers who are responsible for the safety and training of their
younger siblings [two to three] (p. 192).

The present analysis provides a focused comparison of Ngeca mothers and adjacent older siblings in their interaction with two– to
three–year-olds and confirms that four– to five–year-olds interact
in a mix of positive and negative modes with their toddler-followers
and a combination of nurturing and companion roles.

Since our data were collected, a host of studies from the United
States, Great Britain, and Canada have addressed early sibling relationships. Using home or laboratory observations, all of the studies find that young siblings interact a great deal, with a marked
assymetry of older and younger child's roles (Lamb and Sutton-
Smith 1982). Older siblings are more likely to initiate prosocial and
agonistic behaviors, while the younger siblings follow, observe, and
imitate more often (Lamb 1978a, 1978b; Abramovitch, Corter, and
Lando 1979; Abramovitch, Corter, and Pepler 1980; Pepler, Abramovitch, and Corter 1981; Teti, Gibbs, and Bond 1989). The relationship of young sibling dyads has been characterized as a mix of adult
and peer systems (Pepler, Corter and Abramovitch 1982).

The researchers have been particularly interested in the effect
of various sibling characteristics on their interaction. Some studies
find same-sex pairs to engage in more positive and less negative interaction than mixed-sex pairs (Dunn and Kendrick 1981). Other
studies, however, do not find consistent or enduring sex-relationship
effects (Lamb 1978b; Abramovitch, Corter, Pepler, and Stanhope
1986). Examining simply the sex of the older sibling, some but not
all studies report differences: older girl siblings have been found to
be more prosocial (Abramovitch, Corter and Pepler 1980), directive
(Lamb 1978b), and less physically aggressive (Abramovitch, Corter,
and Lando 1979) than older boy siblings. Similarly, there have been
conflicting findings regarding the length of the age interval between siblings. The studies by Dunn, Abramovitch and their respective colleagues do not find birth-spacing differences in sibling
interaction; but Teti, Gibbs, and Bond (1989) report pronounced differences, with widely spaced pairs showing more frequent, lengthy,
and complex bouts of social interaction than do closely spaced pairs.

For this study, then, the central issue concerns the nature of
mother versus adjacent sibling interaction with Ngeca knee children. Given that the mothers' behavior to knee children can be ex-

pected to center on nurturing and training (rather than scoffolding play), will the adjacent older siblings mirror this pattern, or instead assert a complementary pattern centered on object play (like that described in the North American and British studies)? Because mothers and adjacent older siblings are the most frequent social partners of knee children in Ngeca, what they do with them is surely of great importance in understanding early behavioral development. In addition, the sex composition and age interval of the sibling dyads will be examined as factors in the interaction.

Subjects and Community

The focal subjects of this report (seventeen girls, fourteen boys) were part of a larger sample of 104 children aged two to ten years old observed in thirty-six households by the research team of the Child Development Research Unit, University of Nairobi. For this analysis, focal children included all those two– to three–year-olds with interacts recorded toward both mother and adjacent older sibling. They lived in twenty-one different household compounds, five of which were polygynous (with cowives in residence) and half of which included three generations. Of the thirty-one children, three were second-borns, seven were third-borns, eight were fourth-borns, four were fifth-borns, and nine were sixth to twelfth in the birth order. The group of adjacent older siblings (twenty girls, eleven boys) were on average 23.5 months older than the focal subjects.

These children lived in Ngeca sublocation in the Central Province of Kenya, twenty miles northwest of the capital city, Nairobi. Beatrice Whiting directed behavioral observation of children there in 1968–70 and 1972–73. Behavioral and ethnographic data on Ngeca have been presented by B. Whiting (1977), Wenger (1976), Cox (1977), Leiderman and Leiderman (1977), Worthman and J. Whiting (1987), Edwards and B. Whiting (1980), and B. Whiting and Edwards (1988).

Ngeca and the surrounding areas became inhabited by the Southern Kikuyu at the turn of the century. The Kikuyu are part of the Bantu language family and the most populous ethnic group in Kenya; their traditional culture is described in the classic ethnographies by Jomo Kenyatta (1938) and Louis B. Leakey (1977); for contemporary description see Davison (1989).

Ngeca is composed of nine sections: the towns of Ngeca and Kabuka and seven farm communities. The densely settled town of Ngeca includes the site of the former Emergency Village where

Kikuyu from outside were resettled by colonial authorities during the Mau Mau Rebellion. At the time of our study, the town center consisted of a central marketplace, post office, hotel (serving as a men's gathering spot), gas station, public water pump, and assorted small shops. At one end were the bus station, chief's office, and primary school; at the other were a Protestant church and high school. Surrounding the towns were seven country sections composed of farm homesteads—each section predominately occupied by members of one *mbari,* or patrilineage tracing their descent to a recognized founder.

For the larger observational study, forty-two households were selected from both town and farm sections. Of those, twenty-one (six town, fifteen from two of the farm sections) figure in this report. The town families lived in rectangular houses of daub-and-wattle or wooden construction with tin roofs and rain barrels, laid out on quarter-acre lots in a grid pattern. Those in the farming sections lived on homesteads ranging in size from 1 to 25 acres, with an average of 5.7 acres. The largest homesteads were headed by a polygynous man and extended to include his married sons and their families. Traditionally each of the cowives had her own hut. Traditional style huts were round, daub-and-wattle constructions with thatched roofs; but by 1968 many huts were built in the modern, rectangular, wooden frame style. On all homesteads each woman was allotted a garden in which to grow food for her husband and children. Each of the farm sections was dominated by homesteads composed of people related through the male line, members of the same lineage. Thus, even those children living in single-family homesteads had cousins living next door. A map of the homestead of one of the large sublineages is found in Whiting and Edwards (1988, p. 23), showing separate huts for the senior man, his wives, adolescent boys, and adolescent girls. In such a homestead, the child grew up surrounded by playmates—siblings, half-siblings, and cousins; as many as thirty-six people might live on the same homestead (Whiting and Edwards 1988, figure 2.14, p. 37).

Land pressure in Ngeca was intense, due not only to the resettlement during the Mau Mau years but also the high fertility rate of the Kikuyu. Mothers in our present sample had an average of five living children. Traditionally the Kikuyu in the Ngeca area had been farmers with sheep, goats, and cattle, but by 1968 few families could make a living on their decreasing acreage. In seventeen of the twenty-one households involved in this report, fathers had some form of wage employment to supplement their farms.

The employment available to the fathers depended on their level of schooling at the time when they first secured employment. All but three of the men in our sample had some primary schooling, and twelve had completed eight or more years of school. Several had further training equipping them to work as drivers, electricians, photographers, telephone repairmen, clerks, or teachers. Some of the older men with two or three years of schooling were retired railroad and power linemen. The men with the poorest paying jobs were farm laborers and domestic servants. Until 1973 when the roads were improved so that they were passable in all seasons, the men working at a distance from Ngeca came home only on weekends, or but once or twice a month if they worked in the Rift Valley.

The mothers in our sample ranged in age from twenty-six to forty-nine. Because girls had not been sent to school until at least a decade later than boys, the oldest women in our sample to attend primary school were born in 1938. Nine of the eleven mothers born in the 1940s had at least four years of schooling; four of them had completed primary school and three others had additional training.

The work load of these mothers was very heavy. The majority carried water from the town pump or nearby stream. Most did their cooking over open fires, using wood that they had collected and carried. They were the principal gardeners, responsible for raising maize, beans, and other vegetables for family consumption, selling any surplus in the local market. With the exception of the three women who were employed as a teacher and as secretaries, they put in an average of four hours of work a day in their gardens. A typical Ngeca mother's day is described by Whiting and Edwards (1988, pp. 99–101). Their children were required to help according to their assessed capabilities.

Within the community, economic differences existed. A typical family of least wealth had little or no farming land and no cash income, no livestock, and carried water from the river or town pump. In contrast, a typical family of greatest wealth had a large farm or cash income, livestock, house with glass windows and wood or cement floor, and a water tap in the yard.

Observation Methods and Sample Protocols

The observation methods are fully described in Whiting (1980) and Whiting and Edwards (1988). The focal children were observed in their homes or yards as they freely interacted with family members, neighbors, and visitors. Each child was observed on three or more separate days (sometimes over a period of months) for a timed period of 15 or 30 minutes (providing a total of 45–300 minutes of observation per child). The observers were Kikuyu secondary or college students trained to record the focal child's behavior in written running sentences. The observer attempted to follow the eyes of the focal child and identify wherever possible not only the focal child's behavior but also the instigating social event that preceded it and any subsequent response by the social partner. Before an observation was begun, a record was made of the date, time, exact location, identity of persons present in the vicinity, and activities in progress. The observer then kept a rough record of passing time and recorded when people entered or left the interactional space. Observations were limited to the daylight hours and distributed over the periods of the day.

To provide a sense of the data as well as of Ngeca household life and flow of events, we present three sample observations from one of our town households. The focal child of the observation is three–year-old Muthoni, seen interacting with her mother, grandmother, older sisters Wambui and Loise, and others. The observations have been fleshed out in full sentences for readability, but are otherwise as recorded in the field protocol. Notice how Muthoni's interactions with her mother and nine–year-old sister center on giving and receiving care. The mother feeds Muthoni tea, pats her affectionately, instructs the nine–year-old to care for Muthoni on two occasions, and commands five–year-old Wambui to return a potato she had snatched from Muthoni. In contrast, Muthoni's interactions with Wambui are a complex mix of play with household objects, seeking and offering of sociability, verbal and physical teasing, help and support, and dominance. More will be said about these contrasts later.

> Observation (1): Persons present in the homestead include Muthoni (girl, aged 3); mother; paternal grandmother (living on adjacent plot); aunt; three older sisters aged 11, 9, and 5; and two neighbor children aged 5 and 3. As the observation begins at 9:45 a.m., Muthoni is standing in the kitchen fiddling with a corn cob. Her aunt asks, "How are you?" She replies, "Okay." She throws the maize cob up in the air, counting, "One, two, three."
>
> Her mother tells her to bring a cup, and Muthoni complies, asking whether mother wants another one, too. Mother says no, pouring Muthoni some tea. Muthoni drinks it and holds the cup upside down, banging on the bottom to drain the last drop.

Her mother asks her to fetch more tea leaves from the table. She does so, then says she wants to urinate, and mother asks Loise (9-year-old sister) to take her. Loise takes Muthoni out to the yard and talks with her as she does her toileting. Returning to the kitchen, Muthoni watches a male visitor talking to the grandmother. She goes to stand near her mother, who pats her affectionately. She pretends to be a mother pouring tea from the pot (now empty). Loise commands her to stop playing with it, and she does for a moment, then resumes. She watches her mother cleaning a lid.

Muthoni sees Wambui (her next-older sister, aged 5) playing with a piece of corn cob and asks for it; but Wambui ignores her, even when she begins to whine for it. The grandmother and aunt intervene to tell Wambui to give Muthoni the cob. Wambui gives it up, and Muthoni begins to play with it, covering it with green corn husks. She throws a husk at Wambui in a playful, teasing way.

Muthoni notices a woman visitor arriving and runs to lie on her mother's lap. She throws the corn husks away and fiddles with the cob, standing beside her mother, then climbing on her lap. Her mother asks her to move away as she needs to blow the fire. Muthoni moves away and begins to tease Wambui about a white object on her head; Wambui brushes it off. Muthoni climbs on her mother's back. She pulls at a piece of corn husk that Wambui has stuck on her own mouth. Wambui threatens to hit her, and Muthoni stops. (End of 30-minute observation).

Observation (2): Present in the observation are mother, sisters Loise and Wambui, and neighbor child (aged 8). The observation begins at 3:15 in the afternoon, in the yard. Muthoni is standing near where her mother is at work in the garden. She picks up a small potato that her mother has dug up and whines when Wambui snatches it from her hand. Mother commands Wambui to give it back. Muthoni holds it for awhile, then drops it.

She stands holding her hands together behind her back, looking at the ground. She hooks one hand into the sash of her dress to pretend it is a pocket. The hand gets stuck and she cries. Mother asks Loise to carry her—that perhaps she is feeling sleepy. Loise picks her up (her hand still under the belt of her sash) and holds her on her lap. She sleeps on Loise's lap until Loise takes her to bed. (End of 15-minute observation).

Observation (3): Present in the observation are the grandmother and Wambui. The mother is out of the homestead working. The observation begins at 10:00 a.m. inside the grandmother's hut, where Muthoni is sitting on a small chair drinking porridge. Her grandmother asks her to finish it all, but she ignores her. The old lady takes the bowl and places it on the table. Muthoni goes outside. Grandmother asks her to take the small chair outside and sit on it.

Muthoni is sitting on the chair, and Wambui takes hold of her dress and responsibly comments, "Look at the porridge on your dress!," then playfully tells her to lick it up. Wambui tries (playfully), then Wambui asks her, "Shall I wipe it off?" Muthoni says, "Yes," so Wambui wipes the porridge.

Wambui sticks a piece of plastic to her face, and Muthoni imitates her. Wambui tells Muthoni to turn around so she can stick the plastic on her face properly. They play for some moments, trying to get the plastic positioned but it keeps falling off. Wambui calls her little sister, "Kinono" (a corruption of "Muthoni").

Their play continues as Muthoni stands on the small chair, then follows Wambui to sit behind the blankets hanging on the line. She peeps around to see the observer, laughs, then follows Wambui again around the blankets. She stands next to her, holding her arms behind her back, and watches Wambui tie a string around a dry orange peel. She stands stretching apart her legs as far as they will go, then sits down to play with a piece of string. Wambui says, "Move closer, so I can show you what I am doing."

Muthoni fiddles with a dry corn husk. Wambui teasingly and playfully tells her that she could be bitten by a lizard, but Muthoni ignores her. Wambui now shows her what she has made, a piece of round metal tied at the end of a string. She asks Muthoni if she wants one made for her, and Muthoni says, "Yes." While Wambui is looking for another piece of metal, Muthoni takes Wambui's plaything and tries swinging it. The metal flies off the string. Wambui, upset at this, tells Muthoni she will not make her one because she spoiled hers (Wambui's), but Muthoni ignores her. Wambui repairs her plaything and teasingly calls Muthoni, "You bad Kinono." Muthoni takes it as a joke and repeats it after Wambui, who is amused.

Muthoni sits with her feet together, squeezing a clod of earth between her feet. Wambui takes the piece of earth, saying it belongs to her. Muthoni starts to cry, and Wambui gives it back. Muthoni picks some dry mucus out of her nose and eats it. Wambui teases her about it, but Muthoni ignores. (End of 30-minute observation).

Behavior records were coded while still fresh in the observer's mind. Each social event (act) for which the focal child was either the initiator or recipient was coded according to category and identity of persons involved. The social act code (Whiting 1980; Whiting and Edwards 1988) contains seventy-five categories (collapsed for this analysis to twenty-five) defined in terms of the actor's judged intention and the resources given or received. Social behaviors coded in this system include nurturance, prosocial responsibility, dependence, dominance, aggression, sociability, imitation, and watching. These categories were applied in terms of the local interpretations given to social events. The coders (cultural insiders) were instructed to take into account facial expressions, body language, and implicit assumptions about communication when interpreting, for example, whether a mother's assignment of a task was intended to comfort the child (nurturance), terminate interaction (egoistic dominance), or simply get a job executed (prosocial command). The Kikuyu interpretations did not necessarily fit with North American assumptions about the meaning of social events, and behaviors co-occurred in ways we might find surprising, as Weisner (1989a) shows concerning support-giving, aggression, teasing, and dominance among the Abaluyia of Western Kenya.

From the coded protocols, four sets of twenty-five behavior scores were derived for every focal child: (1) mother-to-child scores; (2) sibling-to-child scores; (3) child-to-mother scores; (4) child-to-sibling scores. The behavior scores were calculated as frequencies (rates): the number of acts of a given type, divided by the total number of minutes (X100) that the mother or sibling was observed in the presence of the focal child. In all cases, there were at least five acts for each focal child in the mother-to-child and sibling-to-child sets.

Findings

Rate scores comparing mothers' behavior to older siblings' are presented in Table 12.1. The mothers were much more likely than the four– to five–year-old siblings to *offer food or basic caretaking* or *help, attention, comfort, or approval* to knee children and more likely to use authority to shape children's behavior through *commanding chores, commanding etiquette or hygiene,* and *scolding or reprimanding.* They rarely engaged in play or purely sociable interaction with the two– to three–year-olds, rather, most of their interaction was "business" of the nurturant or prosocially dominant types. The adjacent siblings, in contrast, were significantly more likely than mothers to engage in various kinds of playful and sociable as well as aggressive interaction. They were more likely to

Table 12.1

Frequency (Rate) Scores[a] of Behaviors of Mothers and Adjacent Older Siblings to Focal Children ($N = 31$), and T-test of Difference Between Mothers' and Siblings' Scores

Behavior	Mo→Ch	Sib→Ch	t of Difference[b]
Behaviors Mothers Scored Higher than Siblings			
Scolds, criticizes, or reprimands behavior	4.5	0.9	+5.29***
Offers help, attention, comfort or approval	2.8	0.8	+3.38**
Commands economic or housekeeping chore	2.6	0.0	+3.90***
Commands etiquette or hygiene behavior	2.4	0.2	+2.63*
Offers food or basic caretaking	1.7	0.3	+4.97***
Commands task related to child care	1.4	0.0	+2.40*
Exchanges information or teaches	1.1	0.6	+1.64
Playfully teases (verbally)	1.0	0.8	+0.46
Terminates interaction	0.9	0.7	+0.61
Offers affection or entertainment	0.1	0.1	+0.03
Behaviors Siblings Scored Higher than Mothers			
Clearly seeks sociability	0.8	1.9	−2.21*
Dominates or grabs object	0.2	1.8	−2.87**
Insults or derogates (verbal aggression)	0.0	1.7	−2.84**
Playfully teases (physically)	0.2	1.5	−3.79***
Seeks material resources (food, drink, or object)	0.1	0.9	−3.69***
Seeks attention or approval	0.0	0.8	−1.72
Plays with or runs around with	0.0	0.8	−4.40***
Miscellaneous sociability (chats, greets, etc.)	0.4	0.6	−1.00
Sits with; follows after	0.1	0.6	−3.05**
Seeks help or comfort	0.1	0.2	−0.47

(continued)

Table 12.1   (continued)

Behavior	Mo→Ch	Sib→Ch	t of Difference[b]
Behaviors Siblings Scored Higher than Mothers (continued)			
Assaults or beats (physical aggression)	0.1	0.2	−0.85
Watches (5-second interval)	0.0	0.2	−2.68*
Seeks permission	0.0	0.1	−1.39
Competes with	0.0	0.1	−1.92
Imitates	0.0	0.0	—

Note: a. Frequency scores are number of acts of a given type per minute, X100.

b. The *t*-test performed was the repeated measures *t*-test (heterogeneous variances). Significance tests are two-tailed.

*p < .05.   **p < .01.   ***p < .001.

clearly *seek sociability, physically tease, sit with or follow after, watch, play or run around with, seek material resources, dominate or grab an object,* and *insult or derogate.*

We designated all behaviors which mothers did more frequently than siblings (positive *t*-score) as "mother role" behaviors, and all those that siblings did more frequently (negative *t*-score) as "peer role" behaviors, then added up the behaviors of each type for the mother-to-child and sibling-to-child columns. For the mothers, 90 percent of their acts were of the "mother role" type, versus 10 percent of the "peer role" type. For the siblings, 73 percent of their acts were of the "peer role" type and 27 percent of the "mother role" type. This suggests that siblings mixed both "mother" and "peer" behaviors into their acts to knee children, while mothers remained almost exclusively within the maternal role.

In a second analysis, mothers and siblings were compared with respect to "negative" or agonistic modes of behavior to knee children. The following five behaviors were classified as clearly negative: *scolds or reprimands, terminates interaction, dominates or grabs object, insults or derogates,* and *assaults or beats.* Twenty-eight percent of the mothers' behavior, versus 34 percent of the siblings' was of this clearly negative type. The siblings can be characterized as somewhat more agonistic than were mothers to the knee children.

Table 12.2 presents the rate scores (and *t*-tests) for the reciprocal behaviors of the focal children to their mothers versus their older siblings. All behaviors which went significantly more toward mothers than siblings are dependency behaviors: *seeking material resources, attention or approval, help or comfort,* and *permission*. We designated all behaviors which children directed more to mothers than siblings (positive *t*-score) as "dependent-child role" behaviors, and all behaviors which children directed more to siblings (negative *t*-score) as "peer role" behaviors, then added up the behaviors of each type for the child-to-mother and child-to-sibling columns. A total of 83 percent of children's behavior to mothers was of the "dependent-child role" type, and only 17 percent of the "peer role" type. In contrast, 59 percent of their behavior to siblings was of the "peer role" type and 41 percent of the "dependent-child role" type. Thus, in a way parallel to the findings for the reciprocal older-to-younger behavior, the knee children acted toward their mothers in a predominately "dependent-child" way, but combined "peer" and "dependent-child" roles in their behavior toward adjacent older siblings aged four to five.

In terms of "negative" behavior, only 1 percent of knee children's behavior to mothers was clearly negative, versus 16 percent of their behavior to older siblings. The knee children were less negative to their elders than their elders were to them, in accord with their relative status. Moreover, knee children were much less negative to mothers than they were to older siblings.

Effects of Birth-Spacing and Sex Composition on Sibling Interaction.

Following Murphy (1937) and Wenger (1976), we expected that the longer the age interval between siblings, the more likely the older siblings would be to show various "mother role" behaviors (especially nurturance). The shorter the interval, the more they would show the "peer role" behaviors (especially aggression). The age interval between each of the sibling pairs was measured in terms of number of months between the children's respective births. We then tested the hypotheses with a correlation analysis, and found several significant correlations between the behavior scores and the age interval. For older-to-younger scores, the length of the interval was negatively correlated with *assaulting or beating* ($r(30) = -0.36$, $p < .05$), and positively correlated with *imitating* ($r(30) = 0.41$, $p < .05$) and *watching* ($r(30) = 0.39$, $p < .05$). These findings suggest that the

Table 12.2
Frequency (Rate) Scores[a] of Behaviors of Focal Children (N = 23) to Mothers and Adjacent Older Siblings, and T-test of Difference Between Scores to Mother and Sibling

Behavior	Ch—Mo	Ch—Sib	t of Difference[b]
Behaviors Children Directed			
More to Mothers			
Sits with; follows after	3.4	2.2	+1.48
Seeks material resources (food, drink, or object)	2.0	0.9	+2.25*
Seeks attention or approval	1.5	0.4	+2.60*
Seeks help or comfort	1.3	0.3	+2.89**
Seeks permission	1.1	0.1	+2.72*
Exchanges information or inquires	1.1	0.3	+1.97
Watches (5-second interval)	0.9	0.5	+1.11
Behaviors Children Directed			
More to Siblings			
Clearly seeks sociability	1.0	1.2	−0.33
Playfully teases (physically)	0.1	1.1	−3.03**
Insults or derogates (verbal aggression)	0.0	1.1	−2.97**
Miscellaneous sociability (chats, greets, etc.)	0.7	0.9	−0.80
Imitates	0.4	0.6	−1.21
Plays with or runs around with	0.0	0.6	−2.99**
Dominates or grabs object	0.0	0.3	−2.20*
Playfully teases (verbally)	0.0	0.3	−2.03
Terminates interaction	0.1	0.2	−0.85
Offers help, attention, comfort or approval	0.0	0.2	−1.87
Assaults or beats (physical aggression)	0.0	0.1	−2.14*
Competes with	0.0	0.1	−0.73
Offers food or basic caretaking	0.0	0.1	−0.75
Scolds, criticizes, or reprimands behavior	0.0	0.1	−1.04
Offers affection or entertainment	0.0	0.0	—

(continued)

Table 12.2 (continued)

Behavior	Ch—Mo	Ch—Sib	t of Difference[b]
Behaviors Children Directed More to Siblings (continued)			
Commands economic or housekeeping chore	0.0	0.0	—
Commands task related to child care	0.0	0.0	—
Commands etiquette or hygiene behavior	0.0	0.0	—

Note: a. Frequency scores are number of acts of a given type per minute, X100.

b. The *t*-test performed was the repeated measures *t*-test (heterogeneous variances). Significance tests are two-tailed.

*$p < .05$.   **$p < .01$.   ***$p < .001$.

longer the age interval, the greater the older child's interest (indicated by watching and imitating) and the less the physical aggression (measured by assaulting). For the reciprocal younger-to-older behavior, the length of the age interval was significantly correlated with *clearly seeking sociability* ($r(22) = 0.43, p < .05$) by the younger child. Again, this is suggestive of a more positive relationship for the sibling pairs with the larger age intervals. These findings represent a considerable refinement of the data reported by Wenger (1976). Using aggregate behavior categories, she compared the behavior of three– to four–, five– to seven–, and eight– to twelve–year-old Ngeca siblings to two–year-olds, and found that five– to seven–year-olds were significantly more nurturant and less dominant-aggressive and sociable than were three– to four–year-olds.

Interestingly, the Ngeca mothers themselves have a folk belief concerning the closeness of sibling relationships but it centers on sibling-adjacency rather than length of birth spacing. The Kikuyu believe that adjacent siblings are inherent rivals; therefore no child should be expected to serve as nurse to his or her immediate follower. Wenger (1976) attempted to test this Ngeca belief by comparing the profile of interaction of "adjacent" versus "skip-one" older siblings, controlling for age. With very few pairs to compare, the data were in the direction of the hypothesis, with the "skip-one" five– to seven–year-old siblings being both more nurturant and less aggressive than five– to seven–year-old "adjacent" siblings. Further research on the effects of birth order and spacing on sibling relationships is clearly needed.

Sex composition effects were examined by means of analyses of variance using sibling sex and knee-child sex as the independent variables. (Note: For these analyses, tests were done only for behaviors which comprised at least 1 percent of all social acts). The dyad frequencies were as follows: ten girl/girl; four boy/boy; seven older boy/younger girl; ten older girl/younger boy). Using the older-to-younger scores, we found that older brothers more than sisters *insulted* knee children $(F(1,27)= 4.51, p <.05)$. Further, older brother/younger brother dyads were particularly characterized by the behavior of *terminating interaction* $(F(1,27)$'s for sex-of-actor main effect $= 5.89$, sex-of-recipient main effect $= 6.13$, and interaction $= 8.79, p <.01$ for each).

Using younger-to-older scores, we found that older brothers were the recipients of more *scolding and reprimanding* than older sisters $(F(1,22 = 4.17, p = .06)$. Furthermore, younger brother/ older sister dyads were highest in *clearly seeking sociability* $(F(1,22)$'s for sex-of-actor main effect $= 23.99, p <.001$, sex-of-recipient main effect $= 8.26, p <.01$, and interaction $= 11.55, p <.01$. Younger sister/older sister dyads were especially high in the *seeking of help or comfort* $(F(1,22)$'s for sex-of-actor main effect $= 11.34$, for sex-of-recipient main effect $= 13.81$, and for interaction $= 7.20, p <.01$ for each).

Together, these sex composition findings suggest that older brothers were more agonistic (verbally insulting and terminating of interaction) than older sisters. Perhaps as a result, younger siblings attacked them verbally in an overtly prosocial manner (scolds, criticizes, reprimands) and went to older sisters for sociability, help, and comfort. The older sisters were *not* more likely to offer help and comfort and attention than the older brothers, yet the younger children sought sociability, help, and comfort from them, suggesting that knee children in Ngeca saw females as the appropriate sources of nurturance even if they were but two years older!

Discussion

This study has examined the interaction patterns of knee children with mothers and preschool-aged siblings in an East African community. The mothers' behavior with their two– to three–year-olds was, as has been reported in other studies, focused on nurturing and training. The low level of playfulness on the Ngeca mothers' part derived from two interrelated factors: (1) their desire to socialize the toddlers away from an attachment on themselves deemed appropriate during infancy but not early childhood (cf. Edwards 1989); and (2) their heavy economic and household responsibilities which kept them extremely busy and required them to train their children early into habits of cooperation and helpfulness (Whiting and Edwards 1988; Whiting and Whiting 1975).

In contrast, the four– to five–year-old siblings, one up in the birth order from the focal children, engaged in many of the same kinds of "mother role" behaviors that their mothers did; for example, they scolded and reprimanded and offered help or comfort, attention, material resources, and information. When offering nurturance, their caretaking style seemed closely patterned after the mothers', although often they themselves had caused the very distress they were now trying to comfort or alleviate. Certainly, they did "mother role" behaviors less frequently than did mothers; and they engaged in many "peer" behaviors rarely seen in mothers, such as clearly seeking sociability, teasing physically, playing and running around with, insulting, dominating or grabbing, sitting with or following after, watching, and seeking material resources.

These "peer behaviors" seemed different in two respects from those reported for North American and British preschool-aged siblings. First, the play was not nearly so often focused on symbolic play with toys (of which the Ngeca children had few or none) but instead revolved around natural and household objects, other human beings (often the family baby), physical chasing and horseplay, and idle sociability while mutually engaged in tasks. In a parallel way, Bakeman, Adamson, Konner, and Barr (1990) have found that among the !Kung San of Botswana (another culture with few or no toys for children), infants' exploration of objects was largely ignored by both nurturing caregivers and entertaining playmates; rather, people communicated with infants more about interpersonal than referential aspects of experience.

Second, the behavior of Ngeca older siblings involved a continuous blend of behaviors with counterposed intentions: nurturance, sociability, and dominance/aggression. Weisner (1989a) identified this pattern for the Abaluhia of Western Kenya; it is a distinct cultural style that confronts the toddler with cognitive and emotional challenge. For instance, in observation (3) of Muthoni and Wambui quoted above, the five–year-old teases her toddler sister about porridge on her dress, then wipes it off; lets her play with her string toy, but calls her, "Bad Kinono" when it comes apart; takes her dirt clod, then returns it when the child cries; corrects her hygiene, but in an insulting way. On another occasion, the girls study an insect together and Wambui says Muthoni will have to be responsible for "herding" and "milking" it. Another time, Wambui repeatedly teases Muthoni about a lizard coming to attack and bite her (Muthoni ignores her); then the girls chase each other with sticks. On yet another day, Wambui notices urine glistening on Muthoni's legs and reprimands her by telling her she looks as if she is wearing a "pair of stockings." Likewise, in other families, older siblings engaged knee children in sustained, provocative, and testing bouts that served to guide them to learn culturally valued modes of skillful social interaction. From these experiences, we believe, toddlers received valuable opportunities to learn to deal with grabbing, snatching, hitting, and teasing. The lessons in teasing seem particularly important. Teasing is frequent in Kikuyu culture, and children must learn to be able to discriminate what is real or true from what is not real or not true. They must learn not only to take teasing without offense but also give back as good as given. Muthoni seemed to be learning these lessons well, as in the case of the lizard that was not really attacking her. Moreover, in confronting older sibling's dominance, Ngeca toddlers have a chance to learn that different techniques of persuasion work for adult versus child partners. Crying and whining may get the mother to intervene, but on those occasions when the adult is not present, the toddler must learn to fight back, outwit, or better yet, deflect the sibling's behavior into playfulness. The toddler thereby is stimulated to cognitively discriminate between different kinds of social situations and to develop a rich repertory of behavioral responses.

The mothers (and grandmothers), meanwhile, maintained a watchful eye and intervened only when essential to nurture, train, assign, or protect.

In initiating interaction with their mothers and siblings, the knee children, in turn, displayed toward both groups various "dependent-child role" behaviors. They sought proximity, attention, help, and material resources; though they sought these more frequently from their mothers. They were also much less negative and agonistic to mothers than to siblings and obviously preferred their mothers when in a great state of need. Nevertheless, they were being effectively socialized to look to a wider social world for help and fun and give up an infantile kind of attachment exclusively focused on their mother. Far from avoiding their adjacent siblings, they followed and imitated them, accepted their nurturance, and attempted to hold their own against their dominance, teasing, and aggression. Often, as with Muthoni, they managed to keep the interaction going by accepting or ignoring dominance or returning a provocation in a playful spirit.

What about effects of age and sex composition of the sibling dyads? We found that the shorter the age interval, the greater the physical aggression and the less the imitation and watching by the older sibling and seeking of sociability by the younger sibling. The findings suggested that too short a birth interval may have had an adverse effect on the closeness of the sibling relationship. Given the parallel, more extensive findings by Teti, Gibbs, and Bond's (1989) for Vermont children, the influence of age interval on early sibling relations appears to deserve a renewed look.

In addition, there were sex effects. Older brothers in Ngeca were more aggressive and terminating of interaction than sisters; while older sisters were more frequently sought for sociability, help, and comfort. These patterns are reminiscent of Wenger's (1983, 1989) findings for children in Kaloleni, a rural Giriama-speaking community in the Coastal Province of Kenya with clearly defined gender roles for adults and children. Wenger found that both children and adults directed more prosocial commands to girls than to boys, even when the child targets were as young as age two to three; and already by age five to eight, girls had begun to show more nurturance and prosocial responsibility (and less dominance and ego-oriented behavior) than did boys to their two- to three–year-old siblings. Thus, children appeared to be shaping their younger siblings toward acquiring gender-appropriate behavior.

In past papers, also, we have theorized about how siblings in Kenyan families play a prominent role in one another's sex-role socialization (Edwards 1992; Whiting and Edwards 1988). The present study extends that conclusion and suggests that in the realm of play—through introducing their younger siblings to the richness, provocation, and excitement of social exchange as enjoyed by the Kikuyu—Ngeca children close of an age are key partners with mothers in helping toddlers learn to interpret complex communicative events and become skillful protagonists in the family drama and their own growth.

References

Abramovitch, R.; Corter, C.; and Lando, B. (1979). Sibling interaction in the home. *Child Development* 50:997–1003.

Abramovitch, R.; Corter, C.; and Pepler, D. J. (1980). Observations of mixed-sex dyads. *Child Development* 51:1268–71.

Abramovitch, R.; Corter, C.; Pepler, D. J.; and Stanhope, L. (1986). Sibling and peer interaction: A final follow-up and a comparison. *Child Development* 57:217–29.

Bakeman, R.; Adamson, L. B.; Konner, M.; and Barr, R. G. (1990). !Kung infancy: The social context of object exploration. *Child Development* 61: 794–809.

Barry, H., III, and Paxson, L. M. (1971). Infancy and early childhood: Cross-cultural codes 2. *Ethnology* 10:466–508.

Blount, B. G. (1972). Parental speech and language acquisition: Some Luo and Samoan examples. *Anthropological Linguistics* 14:119–30.

Cox, F. with N. Mberia. (1977). *Aging in a Changing Village Society: A Kenyan Experience*. Washington, D.C.: American Federation on Aging.

Davison, J. (1989). *Voices From Mutira: Lives of Rural Kikuyu Women*. Boulder, Colorado: Lynne Rienner Publishers.

Dunn, J. (1983). Sibling relationships in early childhood. *Child Development* 54:787–811.

Dunn, J., and Dale, N. (1984). I a Daddy: Two-year-olds' collaboration in joint pretend with sibling and with mother. In I. Bretherington (ed.), *Symbolic Play*. New York: Academic.

Dunn, J., and Kendrick, C. (1981). Social behavior of young siblings in the family context: Differences between same-sex and different-sex dyads. *Child Development* 52:1265–73.

Edwards, C. P. (1989). The transition from infancy to early childhood: A difficult transition and a difficult theory. In V. R. Bricker and G. Gossen (eds.), *Ethnographic Encounters in Southern Mesoamerica: Essays in Honor of Evon Zartman Vogt, Jr.* Albany: SUNY Press.

Edwards, C. P. (1992). Behavioral sex differences in children of diverse cultures: The case of nurturance to infants. In M. E. Pereira and L. A. Fairbanks (eds.), *Juveniles—Comparative Socio-Ecology*. New York: Oxford University Press.

Edwards, C. P., and Whiting, B. B. (1980). Differential socialization of girls and boys in light of cross-cultural research. In C. Super and S. Harkness (eds.), *Anthropological Perspectives on Child Development*. San Francisco: Jossey-Bass.

Harkness, S. (1975). Child language socialization in a Kipsigis community in Kenya. Ph.D. diss., Harvard University.

Heath, S. B. (1983). *Ways with Words: Language, Life, and Work in Communities and Classrooms.* Cambridge, Eng.: Cambridge University Press.

Kenyatta, J. (1953). *Facing Mount Kenya, The Tribal Life of the Kikuyu.* London: Secker and Warburg.

Konner, M. (1975). Relations among infants and juveniles in comparative perspective. In M. Lewis and L. A. Rosenblum (eds.), *Friendship and Peer Relations.* New York: Wiley.

Lamb, M. E. (1978a). Interaction between eighteen-month-olds and their preschool-aged siblings. *Child Development* 49:51–59.

Lamb, M. E. (1978b). The development of sibling relationships in infancy: A longitudinal study. *Child Development* 49:1189–96.

Lamb, M. E., and Sutton-Smith, B. (eds.). (1982). *Sibling Relationships: Their Nature and Significance across the Life Span.* Hillsdale, N.J.: Erlbaum.

Leakey, L. S. B. (1977). *The Southern Kikuyu Before 1903.* London: Routledge and Kegan Paul.

Leiderman, P. H., and Leiderman, G. F. (1977). Economic change and infant care in an East African agricultural community. In P. H. Leiderman, S. R. Tulkin, and A. Rosenfeld (eds.), *Culture and Infancy.* New York: Academic.

LeVine, R. A. (1973). Patterns of personality in Africa. *Ethos* 1:123–52.

LeVine, R. A. (1990). Infant environments in psychoanalysis: A cross-cultural view. In J. W. Stigler, R. A. Shweder, and G. Herdt (eds.), *Cultural Psychology: Essays on Comparative Human Development.* New York: Cambridge University Press.

Mead, M. (1928). *Coming of Age in Samoa.* New York: Morrow.

Murphy, L. (1937). *Social Behavior and Child Personality.* New York: Columbia University Press.

Pepler, D.; Abramovitch, R.; and Corter, C. (1981). Sibling interaction in the home: A longitudinal study. *Child Development* 52:1344–47.

Pepler, D.; Corter, C.; and Abramovitch, R. (1982). Social relations among children: Siblings and peers. In K. Rubin and H. Ross (eds.), *Peer Relationships and Social Skills In Childhood.* New York: Springer-Verlag.

Read, M. (1960). *Children of Their Fathers: Growing up Among the Ngoni of Nyasaland.* New Haven, Conn.: Yale University.

Rogoff, B.; Mistry, J.; Goncu, A.; and Mosier, C. (1991). Cultural variation in the role relations of toddlers and their families. In M. Bornstein (ed.), *Cultural Approaches to Parenting*. Hillsdale, N.J.: Erlbaum.

Sigman, M.; Neumann, C.; Carter, E.; Cattle, D. J.; D'Souza, S. D.; and Bwibo, N. (1988). Home interactions and the development of Embu toddlers in Kenya. *Child Development* 59:1251–61.

Teti, D. M.; Gibbs, E. D.; and Bond, L. A. (1989). Sibling interaction, birth spacing, and intellectual/linguistic development. In P. G. Zukow (ed.), 117–42. *Sibling Interaction across Cultures*. New York: Springer-Verlag.

Watson-Gegeo, K. A., and Gegeo, D. W. (1989). The role of sibling interaction in child socialization. In P. G. Zukow (ed.), *Sibling Interaction across Cultures*. New York: Springer-Verlag.

Weisner, T. S. (1989a). Cultural and universal aspects of social support for children: Evidence from the Abaluyia of Kenya. In D. Belle (ed.), *Children's Social Networks and Social Supports*. New York: John Wiley.

Weisner, T. S. (1989b). Comparing sibling relationships across cultures. In P. G. Zukow (ed.), *Sibling Interaction across Cultures*.

Weisner, T. S., and Gallimore, R. (1977). My brother's keeper: Child and sibling caretaking. *Current Anthropology* 18:169–90.

Weisner, T. S.; Gallimore, R.; and Jordon, C. (1988). Unpackaging cultural effects on classroom learning: Native Hawaiian peer assistance and child-generated activity. *Anthropology and Education Quarterly* 19(4).

Wenger, M. (1976). Child-toddler interaction in an East African community. Unpublished qualifying paper, Harvard Graduate School of Education, Cambridge, Mass.

Wenger, M. (1983). Gender role socialization in an East African community: Social interaction between 2- to 3-year-olds and older children in social ecological perspective. Ed.D. diss., Harvard Graduate School of Education.

Wenger, M. (1989). Work, play, and social relationships among children in a Giriama community. In D. Belle (ed.), *Children's Social Networks and Social Supports*. New York: John Wiley.

Whiting, B. B. (1977). Changing life styles in Kenya. *Daedalus* 106:211–25.

Whiting, B. B. (1980). Culture and social behavior: A model for the development of social behavior. *Ethos* 8:95–116.

Whiting, B. B. (n.d.) *Social Change: Family Life Styles in Ngeca, Kenya, 1968–1973.*

Whiting, B. B., and Edwards, C. P. (1988). *Children of Different Worlds: The Formation of Social Behavior.* Cambridge: Harvard University Press.

Whiting, B. B., and Whiting, J. W. M. (1975). *Children of Six Cultures: A Psychocultural Analysis.* Cambridge: Harvard University Press.

Worthman, C. M., and Whiting, J. W. M. (1987). Social change in adolescent sexual behavior, mate selection, and premarital pregnancy rates in a Kikuyu community. *Ethos* 15:145–65.

Zukow, P. G. (1989). Siblings as effective socializing agents: Evidence from Central Mexico. In P. G. Zukow (ed.), *Sibling Interaction across Cultures.*

CHAPTER 13

Persistence of Play and Feeding Interaction Differences in Three Miami Cultures

Tiffany M. Field

The three Miami cultures that have been most frequently compared for child-rearing differences are the Cuban immigrants, the Haitian immigrants, and the native southern blacks. These groups are probably compared because they are the low socioeconomic status groups that present themselves to the University of Miami Medical School hospitals and clinics. In an earlier study of mother-infant interaction patterns in black and Hispanic (Cuban, Puerto Rican, and South American) samples a number of differences were noted between the adult mothers of these cultures (Field and Widmayer 1981). For example, the Cuban mothers generally indulged their infants as well as talked to them almost excessively. In contrast, the black mothers frequently expressed concerns about not spoiling their infants by giving them too much attention and talked very little to their infants. Thus, the face-to-face interactions of Cuban mothers and their infants were more effective than those of black mother-infant dyads, in part because the Cuban mothers and infants were more attentive and responsive to each other and engaged in more verbal interaction.

Although we had expected that the differences between Latin cultures and American cultures (given that socioeconomic status was similar) would dissipate following the process of acculturation,

This research was supported by NIMH Research Scientist Development Award #MH00331 and NIMH Basic Research grant #MH40779. Reprint requests can be sent to Tiffany Field, University of Miami Medical School, Mailman Center for Child Development, P.O. Box 016820, Miami, Fl. 33101.

dramatic differences remain. We attributed these persistent cultural differences to the relative isolation of these groups in separate geographical areas where strong cultural bonds and persistence of the native language were characteristic. We argued that for "real" acculturation to occur, cultural and group identity would have to be subsumed by or become secondary to their life-style or living conditions as represented by socioeconomic status. Socioeconomic status would then become a more critical independent variable than one's cultural group membership. An example of this phenomenon was a comparison between the Florida Seminole and Miccosukee Indians who at one time belonged to the same tribe. The Miccosukee wished to remain separatist (from the American culture) while the Seminoles wanted to become more assimilated. The distinguishing identity or characteristic of the Miccosukees today is that they are still a separate Indian tribe affected only peripherally by Anglo-American mores. Although the Seminoles also constitute a tribe, they are commonly identified as part of a lower SES group living in southern Florida (Lefley 1979). This observation was somewhat disconcerting given that different cultural groups are often lumped together with native Americans as a lower SES group.

If differences among groups do not tend to dissipate following immigration, ethnic groups cannot be lumped together with native Americans as a lower SES group. Researchers would then be mixing apples and oranges in their studies of lower SES groups, which may in part explain some of the inconsistencies in the literature. An example of this problem comes from our own SES comparisons of early interactions that by necessity of numbers were a comparison between black lower SES and white middle SES (because our geographic location at the time featured too small a black middle SES and too small a white lower SES sample) (See Field 1979). The most dramatic difference noted in this comparison was a small amount of mother talk in the lower SES group, suggesting that lower SES mothers are less talkative. However, a subsequent comparison of white middle and lower SES groups in the United States and England (Field and Pawlby 1980) suggested that although the lower SES British mothers talked less than the middle SES mothers, they talked, indeed, a great deal. Thus, our earlier observation of minimal maternal vocalization appeared to have been an ethnic more than an SES group difference.

Thus, in that earlier study (Field and Widmayer 1981) we concluded that strong cultural/ethnic differences persisted following immigration possibly because the groups were not "acculturated" in the true sense of the word but remained relatively isolated in their own neighborhoods where they continued to practice their native languages. The question arises whether these cultural/ethnic differences may disappear as groups attempt to become more acculturated and even more so as groups become increasingly removed from immigration status, that is, second generation ethnic groups. Although there are clearly dramatic differences between cultures that are geographically remote, for example, Japanese living in Japan versus Americans living in the United States (Caudill 1962), these differences may gradually disappear as the Japanese move to Hawaii and then even more so to California. There may be a gradient, as there is for coronary heart disease with the Japanese becoming increasingly like Americans in their interaction styles as they move from Japan to Hawaii to California. Then, depending on whether they continue to identify with their own group by isolating themselves in separate areas or acculturate themselves into an inner-city or suburban neighborhood, they may share varying degrees of similarity to the local interaction patterns. In the latter case we would expect that "real" acculturation would occur and their cultural group identity would be subsumed by or become secondary to their life-style or living conditions as manifested by socioeconomic status.

To illustrate the persistence of cultural differences in mother-infant interactions, we will draw examples from research we have conducted on Haitian/black American differences despite the earnest attempts of Haitians to acculturate. Haitians are a group of people who have seriously attempted to model themselves after black Americans who live in the same neighborhoods. In the example we will use, Haitian mothers who have been reared to believe in breast feeding which is the most common practice in their own country, for example, turn to bottle feeding in Miami because, as they know, bottle feeding is more "modern." It would appear that this "modern" practice was adopted from the southern blacks living in Miami. However, as will be seen, despite both Haitians' and southern blacks' bottle-feeding their infants, there remains a critical difference in the feeding interaction. This difference relates to the southern black mothers holding their infants in a cradled face-to-face position while the Haitian black mothers hold their infants in an upright, infant's back to the mother's chest, facing away position.

To address the question of whether cultural differences in mother-infant interaction patterns disappear over time and generations (with the second generation being more assimilated and therefore more similar), we will provide an example from a study comparing second generation Cuban and American black teenage mothers and their infants. As in the previous example we will see that significant cultural differences remain despite superficial similarities. In this case we would have expected greater similarities given that both these groups of mothers grew up in the Miami area. However, other factors which may prevail in specific cultures but are not necessarily culture-specific, such as whether the mothers live in a nuclear extended family and whether the mothers are primary or secondary caregivers, would appear to confound the cross-cultural comparison.

In brief, in this chapter we will first provide a general description of the three different cultural groups, the southern blacks, the Haitians, and the Cubans and the methodologies we use to compare these groups. Second, we will present the comparison of the Haitian and black American mother-infant dyads' interactions as an example of cultural persistence despite attempts to acculturate. And, finally, we will review the study comparing second-generation Cuban mother-infant dyads with similar SES native black mother-infant dyads. This example is presented as evidence that culture-specific child-rearing patterns persist despite the group being second-generation, namely the mothers being reared themselves in this culture.

Historical Background of the Three Lower SES Miami Cultures

The three cultures included here, the southern American black, the Haitian immigrant, and the Cuban-American come from a lower SES inner-city neighborhood surrounding the University of Miami Medical School complex in the Miami civic center. Most of the participants of this study lived within a twenty-block radius of the hospital/civic center complex although each group was somewhat segregated from the others by living area. Most of the families were supported by unskilled laborers and most of the housing was substandard with relatively high crowding indexes. In many families grandparents with their children and their children's children live together in a small two- or three-bedroom house (in the case of the black families), or next door to parents, aunts, uncles, brothers, sisters, and other family members (in the case of the Cuban-Americans). Despite their poverty, all three of these groups showed considerable interest in their children. Other similarities are that each group is highly religious to the point of believing in spiritualism and the banishing of evil spirits (Weidman 1978). Finally, they share language barriers, with the Haitians speaking a very exotic language (Creole), the second-generation Cuban-Americans continuing to speak Spanish, and the southern blacks speaking a dialect (black English) that is still difficult for nonblack natives to comprehend. Despite these similarities these groups come from markedly different backgrounds.

Southern Black

The geographic origins of the southern black native of Miami are complex; some have moved there from Georgia or the Carolinas and others have intermarried with the Bahamians who have lived in Miami since the mid 1700s. The majority of blacks in Miami have lived there for several generations. Black people are at a particular disadvantage in Miami given that large numbers of lower SES Hispanic groups compete for employment. Even when employment is obtained, most black women live alone in order to remain on public assistance.

The children, particularly during the infancy stage, are doted on much like playthings. The infants' clothes and food are given highest priority. However, most black women believe the children are easily spoiled by too much attention including being held, carried, and praised. Thus the infants are often unattended for long periods of time and are forced to be autonomous at a much earlier age than the average. In this culture teenage pregnancy is tolerated but the teenage mother fast becomes disinterested in the baby leaving much of the baby's care to the grandmother. As the children grow up they are exposed to rigorous physical discipline including shaking and spanking, often with belts and switches (Harrington 1962).

Haitian Immigrants

The fact that the Haitians are also black is only a superficial similarity. Ethnically, the southern black and the Haitian black are from different African peoples. Culturally, the groups differ in many ways including their language and the predominant culture in which they are raised. The Haitians, for example, come from a French colonial culture but they were not an ethnic minority in their own country, while the southern black became an ethnic cultural minority when they arrived in the United States. The fact that both groups are poor is also superficial given that poverty has many facets. For example, while the southern black American mothers

are eligible for Aid to Dependent Children and other sources of welfare, those resources are not extended to Haitian mothers. On the
other hand, the Haitian laborer has experienced more success on
the Miami job force than the southern black American laborer.
Thus, while both groups are poor, the difference in their source of
income has considerable sociological and psychological implications.

Very little is known about the child-rearing patterns of the Haitian immigrants except those reported by the anthropologist Weidman (1978) who conducted an extensive household survey in the
neighborhoods of these low SES Miami groups. Large numbers of
Haitian women have become pregnant in the last decade to insure
their right to remain in the United States. These women infrequently seek prenatal care because of their concern about their
alien status and cultural prohibitions concerning male physicians
(Weidman 1978). Thus they often present themselves in labor in the
emergency room of the local county hospital. The hospital staff
rarely speak Creole and therefore have difficulty communicating
with these women. The Haitian mothers have reported that they
feel people are hostile towards them particularly in the hospital
and well baby clinics and therefore they go there infrequently and
only when their infants are very sick (Charles 1980). Thus, very little is known about the early child-rearing patterns of the Haitians.

Cuban-Americans

The lower SES Cuban-Americans tend to isolate themselves in
urban areas where the usually find at least skilled labor. They continue to speak Spanish and insist that their children speak Spanish
exclusively. Teenage pregnancy (prior to marriage) is not accepted
among Cubans of the lower SES groups leading to the problem of an
extremely high incidence of elective abortions despite their being
contrary to their religious beliefs (Scott 1979). Cuban infants and
children of the lower SES groups are the center of the household,
receiving everyone's attention including parents, grandparents,
aunts, and uncles. They appear to enjoy being carried everywhere
and rocked a great deal, are scolded infrequently, and are seldom
physically punished.

Haitian Immigrant and Southern Black
Mother-Infant Interactions

Although immigrant groups may fully intend to become acculturated in their child-rearing patterns, the following comparison illus-

trates the difficulty of acculturation. As part of a major study on the heritability of blood pressure in native and American black adults and their twin offspring, we videotaped the feeding and face-to-face interactions of Haitian and southern black American mother-infant dyads (Field, Widmayer, Adler, and DeCubas 1989). In an earlier study on the feeding and face-to-face interactions of the southern black mother-infant dyads living in Miami we noted significantly inferior interaction patterns in this group (Field and Widmayer 1981). In this study the interaction patterns of the southern black mother and her infant were compared to Latin groups of equivalent socioeconomic status including Puerto Rican, Cuban, and heterogeneous South American group. Almost uniformly, the black mothers and their infants were rank ordered lowest on face-to-face and feeding interaction ratings. The black mothers showed less infantized behavior, contingent responsivity, game playing, and talking to their infants during their face-to-face interactions. The infants themselves showed fewer positive facial expressions and greater fussiness than the other groups of infants. Similarly, the black mothers showed a more depressed/anxious state, less activity, and more frequent head aversion during their feeding of the infants. The infants in turn showed more frequent squirming and received lower summary ratings on the feeding interactions. These inferior ratings emerged despite the fact that the groups of mothers who were of similar age, education, parenting, and SES (including lifestyle and living conditions), and lived in the same neighborhood for a number of years.

The interactions of Haitian mother-infant dyads are generally noted to be positive (Weidman 1978). However, a disproportionate number of Haitian infants are failure-to-thrive, suggesting that this problem may derive from disturbed infant feeding practices of Haitian mothers (Weidman 1978). Although the majority of Haitian mothers living in Haiti reportedly breast-feed their infants, the female Haitian immigrants do not. The women suggest that they do not breast-feed because they are very anxious to be assimilated into American culture and feel that nursing their infants is "less modern" (Charles 1980). They appear to model their behavior after their black American neighbors, who also bottle-feed their infants. Anecdotal reports by well baby clinic staff and informal observations by Weidman (1978) suggest that the feeding interactions of Haitian mothers and their infants are quite different from those observed among southern black Americans. The mothers typically do not cradle their infants and often position them almost upright and facing outward on their laps. The mothers rarely look at their infants during the feeding but rather appear to "stare off into space," looking indifferent and often anxious and depressed. Often the bottle is held parallel to the infant's stomach preventing the milk from successfully reaching the infant. Squirming by the infant and other signs of frustration at failing to find the nipple as well as cessation of sucking are often unnoticed or unresponded to by the mother. These behaviors were almost invariably observed in the mother-infant dyads of our study (Field, Widmayer, Adler, and DeCubas 1989).

In this study the Haitian and native black American twin infants were matched on gestational age and birth weight and happened to have had similar Ponderal Index (Index of Intrauterine Growth Deprivation) at birth. Their mothers were primiparous and of low socioeconomic status and the majority were living in father-absent, extended-family households. Although most of the black American group received welfare assistance and the Haitian group received incomes as laborers, there was virtually no difference in their income. The mothers and infants were seen at the neonatal stage and then at the follow-up clinic when the infants were four and twelve months. At four months mothers and infants were videotaped during a three-minute feeding interaction and a three-minute face-to-face play interaction. For the feeding interaction, the infant was placed in the mother's lap. One camera was focused on the face and torso of the infant and the other on the torso and face of the mother. The behaviors of the mothers and infants were subsequently rated on the feeding interaction scale of the Interaction Rating Scale (Field 1980). For the mother-infant face-to-face play interaction the infant was placed in a semireclining infant seat on a table and the mother was seated approximately fifteen inches from the infant in a face-to-face position. The mothers were simply asked to play with their infants as they would if they were at home. The videotaped images were mixed using a split screen generator and the mothers' and infants' behaviors were rated on the Interaction Rating Scale for face-to-face interactions (Field 1980). At twelve months growth measures were again taken and the infants were administered the Bayley Scales of Infant Development.

At four months there were no differences between groups on the weight of the infant or Ponderal Index Score. However a number of differences were noted on the feeding and face-to-face interaction rating scales. For the feeding interaction ratings the Haitian mothers received lower ratings on positioning of the infant for feeding (i.e., cradling of the infant) and the Haitian mothers looked more depressed, and showed more head aversion and less gazing at the

Table 13.1
Feeding Interaction Ratings

Infants			Groups		
	Haitian		Black Americans		F ratio & p level
State	2.3	(.5)	2.4	(.5)	N.S.
Physical Activity	2.2	(.6)	2.6	(.7)	4.37[1]
Head Orientation	1.6	(.5)	2.2	(.6)	8.03[2]
Gaze Behavior	1.5	(.4)	2.1	(.4)	5.19[1]
Persistence in Feeding	1.7	(.5)	1.9	(.5)	N.S.
Mother					
Feeding position	1.9	(.4)	2.4	(.5)	6.11[1]
State	2.1	(.6)	2.5	(.6)	4.92[1]
Physical Activity	1.7	(.4)	1.9	(.4)	N.S.
Head Orientation	1.8	(.4)	2.3	(.5)	5.86[1]
Gaze Behavior	1.7	(.4)	2.2	(.4)	5.23[1]
Contingent Vocalization	1.9	(.4)	2.3	(.5)	6.19[1]
Timing Bottle Removal	2.5	(.7)	2.6	(.6)	N.S.
Burping	2.4	(.7)	2.5	(.7)	N.S.
Persistence of Feeding	2.1	(.5)	2.3	(.6)	N.S.

1. $p < .05$ (df = 1, 38)

2. $p < .01$

infant and less frequent contingent vocalization during the feedings. The Haitian infants, in turn, showed less optimal activity level for feeding (i.e., they engaged in more squirming) and they showed more head aversion and less gaze at their mothers (see Table 13.1). The face-to-face interaction ratings of the Haitian mothers and infants, in contrast, were superior to those of the black American mothers and infants. The Haitian mothers were more sensitive to the gaze aversion of their infants (respecting their need for silence and ceasing activity when the infant gaze averted), they talked more and showed more animated facial expressions, and their behavior was more infantized (e.g., they showed more exaggerated facial expressions). They were also more contingently responsive to their infants' behaviors and they engaged in more infantlike games, (e.g. peekaboo and pat-a-cake). The Haitian infants also showed more optimal activity level, more head orientation towards their

Table 13.2
Face-To-Face Interaction Ratings

Infants		Groups		
		Haitian	Black Americans	Effect & p level
State		2.1 (.6)	2.0 (.6)	N.S.
Physical Activity		2.6 (.7)	1.9 (.6)	8.11^2
Head Orientation		2.4 (.6)	1.9 (.5)	7.48^2
Gaze Behavior		2.4 (.7)	1.8 (.6)	7.16^2
Facial Expressions		2.3 (.6)	1.8 (.6)	6.35^1
Fussiness		2.8 (.7)	2.4 (.7)	5.92^1
Vocalizations		2.2 (.5)	1.7 (.5)	6.27^1
Mother				
State		2.5 (.4)	2.2 (.5)	N.S.
Physical Activity		2.4 (.5)	2.2 (.5)	N.S.
Head Orientation		2.6 (.3)	2.5 (.3)	N.S.
Gaze Behavior		2.6 (.2)	2.4 (.3)	N.S.
Silence during Gaze Aversion		2.4 (.7)	1.7 (.6)	8.79^2
Facial Expressions		2.5 (.7)	2.1 (.7)	4.13^1
Vocalizations		2.3 (.6)	1.9 (.5)	4.35^1
Infantized Behavior		2.3 (.7)	1.8 (.5)	7.41^2
Contingent Responsivity		2.5 (.7)	2.0 (.6)	6.98^1
Game Playing		1.8 (.7)	1.3 (.7)	7.62^2

1. $p < .05$ (df = 1,38)

2. $p < .01$

mothers, and more gaze at their mothers in addition to being more vocal and more facially expressive and less fussy during face-to-face interactions with their mothers (see Table 13.2). Thus, the black American mothers appeared to have more optimal feeding interactions than the Haitian mothers and the Haitian more optimal face-to-face interactions.

Although there were no group differences at twelve months on the weight of the infants or the Ponderal Index, the Haitian infants showed a trend toward small weight for length. The analysis of the Bayley Scale scores also suggested significantly poorer performance on the part of the Haitian than the black American infants. On the

Bayley Mental Scale the mean score for the Haitian infants was 97 and the mean score for the black Americans was 117, and on the motor scale the Haitian infants averaged 107 and the black American infants 117.

Even the face-to-face interaction behavior noted in the Haitian mothers appeared to be an attempt to acculturate and do like American mothers do with their infants. They appeared to be more anxious to please the interaction observers than were the black mothers and thus presented more animated, affectionate behavior during the face-to-face interactions. This performance behavior, however, seemed to be inconsistent with the behavior noted in the clinic waiting room. During the waiting period they showed little if any face-to-face interaction behavior, typically placing their infants on their laps facing outward. Thus the optimal face-to-face interaction behavior of the Haitian mothers may have been unique to the laboratory situation and not characteristic of their typical behavior with their infants. Similarly, their efforts to bottle-feed their infants appeared to be an attempt to acculturate. Yet, their feeding interactions were awkward. Their four–month–old infants were frequently placed in an upright sitting position on the mother's lap with the infants faced outward. The Haitian mothers typically looked directly ahead instead of at the baby and rarely monitored the infant's sucking behavior. Several of the mothers held the bottle upright, making it more difficult for the infant to suck, and the sounds of "sucking air" were audible on the videotape. Similar types of feedings have been observed in the films of Berggren and Berggren who filmed older infants and young children on the island of Haiti (Berggren and Berggren 1980). In several of their film clips the mothers placed food in front of the children and did not sit with them or monitor their eating. Eating may be a less important social event in that culture and thus Haitian mothers may have a more passive attitude toward monitoring their children's eating behavior. This practice may in turn contribute to infant malnutrition on Haiti and a higher incidence of failure to thrive in the Haitian infants of Miami. While the difficult feeding interactions and the lower Bayley scores suggest the possible need for intervention, any interventions will require sensitivity to this cultural difference of lesser sociability surrounding eating. Thus, functional adaptations may occur as immigrant groups attempt to acculturate themselves, but additional modeling and some instruction may be necessary for the adoption of new practices.

Mother-Infant Interactions among Second-Generation Cuban-Americans

Even when the time for acculturation is more prolonged and the women have been born and reared in this country, child-rearing practices often persist. In a recent comparison between Cuban and black teenage mother-infant dyads the data yielded behaviors that were consistent with those we reported earlier for adult mothers and infants of the same cultures (Field et al. 1989). In this study 164 infants born to a representative sample of black and Cuban-American teenage mothers were observed during interactions with their mothers and were given developmental assessments when they were twelve, eighteen, and twenty-four months of age.

With respect to maternal background, the Cuban teenage mothers reported having a superior social support system, such as more closeness, more stable friends, more relatives on whom they could depend, and more stable living situations. On the other hand, the black teenage mothers reported having greater child-care support and generally felt they had better care for their child than the Cuban teenage mothers. The black teenage mothers also responded more positively than the Cuban mothers on questions regarding their upbringing including feeling that their own childhood was happy and that they had been "disciplined alright."

On the Caldwell Home Inventory the Cuban teenage mothers were rated superior to those of black teenage mothers on all dimensions including emotional and verbal responsivity of the mother, avoidance of restriction and punishment, maternal involvement with the child, and opportunity for variety in daily routines. Similarly on the Jerusalem Childrearing Questionnaire the Cuban teenage mothers were noted to have more knowledge of developmental milestones that the black mothers. The black mothers expected their infants to engage in activities such as first steps, feeding self, and toilet training three to six months earlier. Very much like the comparison of adult Cuban and black mothers from our earlier study (Field and Widmayer 1981), the Cuban teenage mothers touched, looked at, talked to, smiled at, and laughed at their infants more frequently than the black teenage mothers did. In addition, they played with their infants, demonstrated toys, and read to their infants more frequently. The black teenage mothers directed their infants' play and ignored their infants more frequently than the Cuban teenage mothers. The infants of Cuban teenage mothers, like their mothers, engaged in more interactive behaviors including vocalizing, smiling, and laughing. They also examined toys and fussed more frequently than the infants of black teenage mothers (see Table 13.3). Despite the early advantage of being born to a Cuban mother, the stimulation of both groups of mothers and the performance of both groups of infants decreased over the second year of life. These decreases occurred irrespective of ethnic group; they also occurred regardless of family constellation (nuclear or extended) and caregiving arrangement (primary versus secondary caregiver). Even though the Cuban mother-infant dyad may have been advantaged by typically living in a nuclear family and being a secondary caregiver during the early months, these confounding factors did not make a difference as the child became older.

This cross-cultural comparison between Cuban and black teenage mother-infant dyads yielded data that are consistent with those reported for adult mothers and infants of the same cultures (Field and Widmayer 1981). Although the teenage mothers in this study were generally less stimulating than the adult mothers in the Field and Widmayer study, the cultural differences for teenage mothers were very similar to the cultural differences for adult mothers. The data from the Jerusalem Childrearing Survey, the Caldwell Home Inventory, and the mother-infant play interactions suggest that the Cuban teenage mothers, like their adult counterparts, are more "indulgent" and provide more social stimulation for their infants. Black teenage and adult mothers, in contrast, behave in a more restrictive/punitive and less stimulating way, consistent with their fears of "spoiling the child" and their expectations for earlier autonomy of their offspring.

The behaviors of both groups of mothers appeared to reflect the child-rearing attitudes and expectations generally held by their cultures. Although the socioeconomic status of the Cuban and black mothers was roughly equivalent, the greater social support felt by the Cuban mothers may have contributed to their being more involved with their infants; they may have had more emotional energy to interact with them. Because mothers who show more affective and interactive behavior generally have infants who are more responsive (Field 1980), it is then not surprising that the Cuban infants were also more sociable. Greater fussiness of the Cuban infants may relate to their having been more aroused, probably because of the excessive amounts of verbal stimulation from their mothers. The problem of overstimulation may have also contributed to the declines of infant Bayley scores across the two year period. Overstimulation by the Cuban teenage mothers may have nega-

Table 13.3
Means for Variables which Reliably (p < .05) Differentiated Cuban and Black Samples.

Variables	Blacks (N = 112)	Cubans (N = 52)
Maternal Background Interview		
Social Support System	4.9	5.8
Childcare Support	2.9	1.8
Own Childhood	2.9	2.3
Caldwell Home Inventory		
Emotional & Verbal Responsivity	6.8	8.1
Avoidance Restriction & Punishment	5.0	6.3
Organization of Environment	4.9	6.3
Provision Appropriate Play Materials	4.8	5.6
Maternal Involvement with Child	3.3	5.8
Opportunities Variety in Daily Routines	2.5	4.1
Jerusalem Childrearing Questionnaire (In Months Development Expected)		
Infant Knows Mother	3.5	2.4
First Steps	9.6	11.0
Obedience	10.6	14.1
Feeding Self	13.9	20.1
Toilet Training	14.3	17.3
Watching T.V.	11.2	5.0
Mother Talking to Infant	4.1	2.5
Mother Telling Stories	12.8	8.8
Mother-Infant Play Interactions (In Percent Time Behavior Observed)		
Mother—Touching	17.9	38.1
Looking	71.9	95.0
Talking	70.2	82.0
Smiling	13.2	34.1
Laughing	6.5	12.0
Playing	56.2	81.0
Demonstrating Toys	15.8	48.6
Reading	1.3	4.8
Directing	52.2	25.6
Ignoring	6.1	.9
Infant— Looking	31.6	47.3
Vocalizing	16.4	34.1
Smiling	6.6	14.7
Laughing	2.6	12.8
Examining Toys	22.5	38.8
Fussing	10.2	23.9

*Standard deviations can be obtained from the authors.

tively affected infant development in ways very similar to the effects of low levels of stimulation provided by the black teenage mothers. Thus, while the two groups of mothers behaved very differently, the overstimulation by the Cuban mothers and the understimulation by the black mothers may have had similar negative effects on later infant performance on the Bayley Mental Scale.

The considerable cultural differences noted between the second generation Cuban-American mothers and the native black American mothers are somewhat surprising given that these women were raised in the same neighborhoods by low SES parents and attended the same schools. However, it would appear that the differences noted between the first generation Cuban-American adult mothers and native black American mothers in the Field and Widmayer (1981) study may have persisted in this second-generation sample. As has been suggested before, the qualitative differences in the mother-child relationship may have far more impact on the child's subsequent child-rearing attitudes and behaviors than any other variable including living in the same neighborhood and attending the same schools. Child-rearing attitudes and behaviors may be transmitted across generations in a culturally specific way such that Haitians, no matter whether they are breast-feeding or bottle-feeding, do not view eating as a social experience, and the Cuban mother, whether in Cuba or the United States, whether first or second generation, may spoil her children and overstimulate them just as the native black American mothers may be continually concerned about spoiling their children and may more often leave them to their own devices. Although all of the groups in the comparisons reviewed in this chapter were low SES cultures from similar neighborhoods in the city of Miami, the "culture" variable appears to have persisted despite the active attempts of the Haitians to become acculturated and the changing society of the Cuban-Americans as they become second-generation or more removed from their original immigration. The modeling of child-rearing attitudes and behaviors by one's parents may have stronger effects than modeling by other more socially desirable social groups. Thus, it should not be assumed that as immigrant groups attempt to acculturate themselves and with the passing of generations that significant cultural differences in child-rearing attitudes and behaviors will disappear. They appear to have a strong base in generation-to-generation transmission. Although it would be difficult not to compare those attitudes and behaviors to American middle-class attitudes and behaviors we observed in our mother-infant interaction studies, it would be important to look for a variation within these cultural groups as contrasted to the models each of those groups provides for their young women. Perhaps this can happen as more data are collected on these new American cultures.

References

Berggren, W., and Berggren, G. (1980). High infant and child mortality rates in rural Haiti. Paper presented at the Society for the Development of Infants and Parents, Boston, Mass.

Caudill, W. (1962). Patterns of emotion in modern Japan, In R. J. Smith and R. K. Beardsley (eds.), *Japanese Culture, Its Development and Characteristics*. Chicago: Aldine.

Charles, D. (1980). The Haitian community. Paper presented at the University of Miami, Miami, Fla.

Field, T. (1979). Interaction patterns of preterm and term infants. In T. Field, A. Sostek, S. Goldberg, and H. H. Shuman (eds.), *Infants Born at Risk*. New York: Spectrum.

Field, T. (1980). Interactions of preterm and term infants with their lower and middle class teenage and adult mothers. In T. Field, S. Goldberg, D. Stern, and A. Sostek (eds.), *High-Risk Infants and Children: Adult and Peer Interactions*. New York: Academic Press.

Field, T., and Pawlby, S. (1980). Early face-to-face interactions of British and American working- and middle-class mother-infant dyads. *Child Development* 51:250–53.

Field T., and Widmayer, S. (1981). Mother-infant interactions among lower SES Black, Cuban, Puerto Rican and South American immigrants. In T. Field, A. Sostek, P. Vietze, and A. H. Leiderman (eds.), *Culture and Early Interactions*. Hillsdale, N.J.: Lawrence Erlbaum Associates.

Field, T., and Widmayer, S. (1982). Motherhood. In B. Wellman (ed.), *Handbook of Developmental Psychology*. New York: Prentice Hall.

Field, T.; Widmayer, S.; Adler, S.; and Decubas, M. (1989). Teenage parenting in different cultures, family constellations and caregiving environments: Effects on infant development. *Infant Mental Health Journal*. 11:58–74.

Harrington, M. (1962). *The Other America: Poverty in the United States*. New York: Penguin Books.

Lefley, H. (1979). Personal communication.

Scott, K. (1979). Personal communication.

Weidman, H. H. (1978). *Miami Health Ecology Project Report.* Vol. 1. Miami, Fla.: University of Miami.

CHAPTER 14

Cultural Differences In Scaffolding Pretend Play: A Comparison of American and Mexican Mother-Child and Sibling-Child Pairs

Jo Ann M. Farver

This study compares the pretend play behavior of mother-child and sibling-child pairs in the United States and Mexico. The primary objective is to understand how adult and sibling participation differs culturally and how their participation influences children's play.

Research with Western populations influenced by the work of Vygotsky (1978) suggests that mothers and older siblings scaffold or structure young children's emerging pretend play by arranging play situations, providing props and suggestions, and coordinating the interaction (Miller and Garvey 1984; O'Connell and Bretherton 1984; Bruner 1975; Slade 1987; Dunn and Wooding 1977; Deloache and Plaetzer 1985; Sachs 1980; Seidner 1985). By collaborating with older, more skilled partners young children are able to extend their level of pretend play expertise.

In a study of mother-child play Miller and Garvey (1984) found that mothers structured their children's play by offering teaching directions. They also provided encouragement and support for their children in performing nurturing play themes with dolls or other toys, and in engaging in family role play.

This study was supported by the University of California, Los Angeles Chicano Studies Program and Organization of American States, Washington, D.C. The author gratefully thanks the American and Mexican families who participated in this research. Additional thanks is also extended to Mexican assistants Victor Guererro, Patricia Rodriguez, Evelyn Aron, and the Menzie Family.

Similarly, O'Connell and Bretherton's (1984) research showed that children displayed a greater diversity of pretend play behavior with mothers than when playing alone. This diversity was attributed to the mothers' use of explicit guidance in structuring play.

Dunn and Dale's (1984) comparison of mother- and sibling-child play highlighted the importance of sibling partners in the development of young children's pretend play. They noted several important differences in behaviors of the two partners. Like mothers, older siblings created the context of play and suggested complex pretend. In contrast to the mothers, older siblings provided models for younger children to observe and imitate. Siblings also tended to orchestrate play activities by setting up the play and inviting the younger child to join in. Younger partners were expected to coordinate their role actions and to comply with the older siblings' directions. Recognizable pretend themes in sibling play included everyday routines and household activities as well as more dramatic fantasy themes involving travel to distant places, and environmental dangers such as monsters, crashing vehicles, and similar accidents.

Although these patterns of mother- and sibling-child play may be characteristic of contemporary Western societies, there is little existing research to support their generalizability to other cultures. Pretend play with mothers and siblings may be very different in cultures where mothers are not available and willing play partners, or where siblings are engaged in caretaking of young children. Cultural variations in household composition (i.e., nuclear or extended family households) and childrearing practices (maternal or sibling caretaking), can be expected to shape who is available to play (Whiting and Whiting 1975), the nature of their social interaction with the child (Whiting 1980; Whiting and Edwards 1988), and their pretend play behavior.

The American and Mexican communities compared in the present study provide two very different contexts to examine Western models of mother-child and sibling-child play, and to compare the influence of different partners on the nature of children's pretend play. The American and Mexican social environments differ most significantly in the amount of time mothers and siblings spend in direct interaction with young children, and in the nature of their interactions. For example, American mothers often spend time directly organizing children's play activities by providing objects and ideas for play as well as engaging in the play itself. In contrast, Mexican mothers rarely involve themselves in children's play activity. Mexican children are infrequent adult companions, and most interaction with parents takes place in shared work activity rather than child-centered play.

Young Mexican children's play interactions are more common with mixed-age companions and siblings, and often take place in the context of sibling caretaking. Growing up in an extended family household provides a Mexican child with a variety of play companions. In contrast, young American children who are raised in relatively socially isolated nuclear families must rely on mothers and older siblings for play.

Based on these differences in play partner availability and childrearing practices, it was expected that the pretend play of mother-child and sibling-child pairs would be different in the two cultures. More specifically, it was predicted that Mexican siblings would be more skilled in scaffolding the play of young children than their American counterparts. Mexican siblings would use behaviors facilitative of pretend play (i.e., join, comment on, and suggest pretend play), more often than American siblings; and Mexican sibling pairs would engage in more complex social pretend play than American sibling pairs.

The second hypothesis predicted that the play of Mexican sibling dyads would be similar to American mother-child dyads. Mexican siblings would use scaffolding behaviors similar to American mothers; there would be corresponding frequencies of shared positive affect in Mexican sibling pairs and American mother-child pairs, and they would enact similar play themes.

Method

Subjects

The subjects were forty children and their mothers and older siblings—twenty American and twenty Mexican, ten from each culture at twenty-four (M = 26), and thirty-six (M = 39) months, half girls and half boys. Criteria for selection was parent willingness to participate in the study and that the child was at least a second-born. The target child will be referred to as "the child" and the older sibling as "the sibling."

The American Setting

The American families came from the economically depressed, white working-class community in northern California. Fathers were employed in construction, or as truck drivers, store clerks, and similar occupations. Few mothers worked outside the home. Nuclear family households contained two to five children (M = 2.70) ranging in age from six months to twelve years. In the majority of families the sibling was the firstborn (age: 4.5 to 7 years; M = 5.5 years), and the child was the secondborn. The exceptions were three families that had children younger than the target child and four families that had additional older siblings. These extra children were not included in the study.

The Mexican Setting

The Mexican participants were traditional Spanish-speaking Mestizos living in a small town on the Pacific Coast about 1700 miles south of the U.S. border. The socioeconomic status of the Mexican families can be equated with American workingclass. Fathers were employed as automobile mechanics, iron workers, or in construction. Mothers worked in their homes caring for children, and they earned money selling produce from gardens, eggs from their chickens, cooked food, or soft drinks. All families had modestly furnished homes, access to medical care, and education for their children.

The typical extended family household included both parents, their children, and a variety of relatives, for example, paternal siblings and their children, or widowed grandparents. Mexican families had two to six children (M = 3.3) ranging in age from eight months to thirteen years. In only four of the families the older sibling was the firstborn, and the target child the secondborn. Eight families had children younger than the target child and eight had additional older siblings. The siblings ranged in age from 3.5 to 7 years (M = 5.1 years). Like the American sample, the additional siblings were not included in the study.

Procedure

The study incorporated both qualitative and quantitative research methods. In the Mexican setting, the qualitative data collection began first and continued throughout the fieldwork period. The intent was to ethnographically describe the Mexican community with regard to family life, socialization practices, and the characteristics of the settings children typically inhabited. In the American setting, qualitative data was collected during observations of participants in their homes and through informal interviews and conversations.

In the quantitative procedure mother-child and sibling-child pairs of both cultures were videotaped as they played with a bag of wooden shapes suggestive of pretend play in their home, free from distractions for about twenty minutes. The order of the play sessions with the two partners was counterbalanced.

The wooden shapes approximated real objects and included humanlike figures, different sizes of arched structures (suggesting houses, bridges, churches), animal and tree figures, a wooden train connected by magnets, flat rectangular pieces, and square blocks. The purpose of the shapes was to provide suggestions for pretense without introducing "toys" from the American culture to the Mexican and vice versa. Since the shapes were novel in Mexico, and by maternal report very different from toys and blocks in the American homes, children in both cultures were allowed to examine and play with the shapes for fifteen minutes prior to beginning the formal data collection.

Coding Procedure and Measures

Videotapes were fully transcribed. The transcriptions were segmented into play episodes. An episode began when either partner touched an object or verbally interacted with the partner in the immediate environment. An episode ended when participants were no longer involved in play (e.g., either partner's attention was directed away for more than thirty seconds, or either partner moved away), or the theme of the play changed. The use of a new object constituted a change in theme, unless the objects were used in relationship to each other. For example, placing an animal shape on top of a tall stack of blocks was considered related to the ongoing theme of "stacking blocks." Sustained attention to or introduction of another shape into play signaled the beginning of a new episode.

All episodes containing pretend play were isolated. Pretend play was defined as instances in which "the child transformed activities from their real objective and objects from their real counterparts" (McCune-Nicholich 1981, p. 786). Pretend play episodes were coded for level of social pretend play complexity displayed by the dyads, maternal and sibling play behaviors, frequency of shared positive affect, and thematic content.

Complexity of Partners Joint Involvement in Social Pretend Play

A coding scheme developed by Howes, Unger and Seidner (1989) was used to rate the joint involvement of mother-child and sibling-child pairs in social pretend play. Five successive levels of increasingly complex pretend play were rated:

1. Pretend in the Presence of Partner was coded when one partner performed a pretend act while making eye contact (e.g., A feeds self and B ignores); or while engaging in parallel social play and making eye contact, both partners perform unrelated pretend acts (e.g., A feeds self and B puts self to sleep).

2. Parallel Social Pretend was coded when partners engaged in parallel social play with eye contact and each partner performed a similar pretend act (e.g., both partners push dolls in baby carriages).

3. Simple Social Pretend Play was coded when partners engaged in simple social or complementary and reciprocal play, and both performed parallel pretend acts (e.g., A and B push baby carriages; A smiles at B; B offers A her doll).

4. Scripted Social Pretend was coded as in simple social pretend (above), but partners shared a common script for pretend actions (e.g., partners have a tea party. They pour "tea" and "drink" from cups while smiling and talking.)

5. Cooperative Social Pretend was coded as in scripted social pretend (above) but partners assume complementary social roles (e.g., mother-baby, doctor-patient).

Frequencies of play level complexity were averaged across episodes to yield one mean score for each mother-child and sibling-child pair.

Behaviors Used to Scaffold Play

The following categories of scaffolding behaviors were derived from the qualitative observations of mother-child and sibling-child interaction in the two cultures. These behaviors were judged to be the most characteristic of both partners in the two cultures and were coded by episode.

Join Play was coded when partners became engaged in the child's play activity without being explicitly recruited or invited to play.

Comment on Play was coded when partners described or explained their own or the child's play activity, named or labeled the play shapes.

Suggest Symbolic Play was coded for partners' verbal suggestions for pretend play with the shapes. This category included suggestions such as "let's make a farm. This could be a fence for the animals"; or role assignments such as "You be the little girl and I'll be the mommy."

Teach was coded when the partners gave explicit instructions regarding the use of the shapes in play. This category also included setting up a model for the child to copy.

Direct Play was defined as any verbal behavior used to control or influence the child's behavior. Directives included commands, requests, and corrections of the child's behavior.

Reject Play was coded for sibling-child play only. (No mother in either culture displayed this behavior.) Reject play was coded when the older sibling refused or ignored the child's suggestions for play, refused to share the shapes, or prohibited the child from taking part in the play. For example, the sibling moves the shapes out of the child's reach and says "mine."

Shared Positive Affect was coded for episodes in which the child and the partner laughed and/or smiled at each other while engaging in joint pretend play.

Thematic Content

Four pretend play themes were coded for each episode using a scale adopted from Rosenberg (1985). A theme was defined as "a plan or logical temporal order of events, that was identifiable either by the participants' explicit comments on the plan or by an obvious relation between actions" (Dunn and Dale 1984, p. 137).

1. Family Relations included the setting up of a family structure, identifying play shapes as family members, or acting out family roles.

2. Caretaking or Nurturance included helping or caring for another person, figure, or animal, and the enactment of fireman, doctor, or nurse roles.

3. Affiliation included adultlike activity such as going to a cocktail party, driving to distant cities, or grocery shopping.

4. Danger in the Environment included aggressive behaviors such as crashing cars, killing, chasing, and disasters such as storms or accidents.

Reliability

Reliability was established between the author and a bicultural, bilingual assistant using 20 percent of the videotapes. The assistant was unaware of the research hypotheses. Agreement on identification of episodes, coding the complexity of dyadic involvement in social pretend play, shared positive affect, determining and coding maternal, and sibling behaviors ranged from .85 to .94 (median = .90). Reliability was reestablished on additional randomly selected tapes midway through the coding procedure.

Results

Complexity of Partners' Joint Involvement in Social Pretend Play

Age and cultural differences in the complexity of the partners' involvement in social pretend play were examined using a 2 (age group) × 2 (culture) repeated measures MANOVA with partner as the repeated factor. Table 14.1 shows a significant interaction for age, culture, and partner ($F(1,36) = 4.84$, $p < .03$). Thirty-six-month-old American children experienced more social pretend play complexity with mothers and Mexican children experienced more with siblings.

Sibling Scaffolding Behaviors

The six behaviors siblings used to scaffold play were compared using a 2 (age group) × 2 (culture) ANOVA. Significant main effects for age and culture are shown in Table 14.2.

American siblings directed ($F(1,36) = 4.01$, $p = .05$), taught ($F(1,36) = 4.58$, $p = .03$), and rejected ($F(1,36) = 7.55$, $p = .009$) their younger partners' play more often than Mexican siblings. In contrast, Mexican siblings joined ($F(1,36) = 5.13$, $p = .03$), suggested symbolic play ($F(1,36) = 3.91$, $p = .05$), and commented on ($F(1,36) = 5.83$, $p = .02$) their younger partners' play more often than American siblings.

Siblings in both cultures joined their thirty-six-month-old partners more often than twenty-four-month-old partners ($F(1,36) = 9.25$, $p = .004$).

Frequency of Shared Positive Affect

The frequency of shared positive affect was examined in a 2 (age group) × 2 (culture) repeated measure MANOVA with partner

Table 14.1
Complexity of Social Pretend Play by
Age, Culture and Partner[a]

Partner	Age			
Culture	24		36	
	M	SD	M	SD
Mother				
USA	2.70	(.48)	3.00	(.32)
Mex	2.80	(.42)	2.50	(.52)
Sibling				
USA	2.40	(.51)	2.60	(.69)
Mex	2.50	(.52)	2.90	(.31)

	F	Significance
age	1.10	.32
culture	.25	.61
partner	3.10	.08
age × culture	1.01	.32
age × partner	1.74	.19
culture × partner	.77	.38
age × cult × part	4.84	.03*

[a]Mean Level of Play

as the repeated factor. Significant main effects for partner and the interaction of culture and partner; age and partner are displayed in Table 14.3.

Shared positive affect was most frequent with mothers than with siblings in both cultures ($F(1,36) = 33.09$, $p = .000$). There was more shared positive affect with American mother-child and Mexican sibling-child dyads than with Mexican mother-child dyads and American sibling-child dyads ($F(1,36) = 6.03$, $p = .01$).

Shared positive affect was higher among twenty-four-month-old mother-child dyads than with the thirty-six-month-old mother-child and sibling-child dyads ($F(1,36) = 10.87$, $p = .002$).

Themes in Pretend Play

The frequency of the four pretend play themes were examined in a 2 (age group) × 2 (culture) repeated measure MANOVA with

Jo Ann M. Farver

Table 14.2
Sibling Scaffolding Behaviors by Age and Culture

Behavior Culture	Age				F	F	F
	24		36		Cult	Age	AXC
	M	**SD**	**M**	**SD**			
Join Play							
USA	.70	(.67)	1.80	(2.74)	5.13*	9.25**	2.61
Mex	1.20	(2.14)	4.80	(3.35)			
Comment							
USA	5.40.	(4.69)	3.80	(3.85)	5.83*	1.87	.04
Mex	10.10	(6.29)	14.00	(12.98)			
Suggest Symbolic Play							
USA	10.80	(8.33)	13.30	(5.10)	3.91*	1.26	.07
Mex	15.80	(8.76)	19.90	(13.09)			
Teach							
USA	5.10	(7.86)	3.30	(3.40)	4.58**	.61	.24
Mex	.90	(1.10)	.50	(.84)			
Direct							
USA	5.80	(5.32)	7.70	(6.70)	4.01*	1.55	.02
Mex	2.10	(3.41)	4.50	(5.79)			
Reject Play							
USA	9.10	(8.04)	4.30	(4.39)	7.55**	2.84	1.72
Mex	2.60	(2.36)	2.00	(3.59)			

partner as the repeated factor. Significant main effects for age, and the interaction of culture and partner; culture and age are displayed in Table 14.4.

Themes of nurturance ($F(1,36) = 3.83$, p. = .05), affiliation ($F(1,36) = 7.80$, p = .000), and danger in the environment ($F(1,36) = 5.04$, p = .03) were more frequent among thirty-six-month-olds in the two cultures and with both partners.

Family role themes were highest with Mexican thirty-six-month-olds and American twenty-four-month-olds ($F(1,36) = 3.80$, p = .05). Nurturing themes were most common with American mother-child and Mexican-sibling pairs ($F(1,36) = 5.96$, p = .02).

Table 14.3
Frequency of Shared Positive Affect by Age, Culture and Partner

Partner Culture	Age			
	24		36	
	M	SD	M	SD
Mother				
USA	8.20	(3.64)	8.20	(4.44)
Mex	7.70	(4.13)	4.60	(4.85)
Sibling				
USA	1.00	(1.88)	2.70	(3.68)
Mex	.90	(1.01)	6.30	(4.47)

	F	Significance
Age	1.25	.270
culture	.03	.860
partner	33.09	.000***
age × culture	.03	.860
age × culture	10.87	.002***
culture × partner	6.03	.010*
age × cult × part	4.83	.030*

Comparison of American Mothers and Mexican Sibling Play Behaviors

American mothers' and Mexican siblings' play behaviors were compared using a univariate analysis of variance test. Results displayed in Table 14.5 showed no significant differences between cultures for the proportion of join, suggest symbolic play, and comment on play.

Discussion

The results of the current study revealed three interesting cultural differences in the pretend play of mother-child and sibling-child pairs: (1) Older siblings scaffolded play very differently in the two cultures; (2) American children experienced higher pretend play

Table 14.4
Frequency of Pretend Play Themes by Age, Culture and Partner

Partner Culture	24 M	24 SD	36 M	36 SD	F AGE	F CULT	F PART	F CXA	F CXP	F AXP	F CXAXP
Family Roles											
Mother											
USA	2.30	(2.94)	1.60	(1.17)	.38	.00	1.83	3.80*	1.06	.66	1.06
Mex	.50	(1.26)	2.50	(1.71)							
Sibling											
USA	1.10	(1.91)	.60	(1.07)							
Mex	1.20	(2.82)	1.50	(2.41)							
Nurturance											
Mother											
USA	.80	(1.22)	2.30	(2.35)	3.83*	.82	.08	.82	5.96*	.00	2.49
Mex	.50	(1.08)	.30	(.48)							
Sibling											
USA	.40	(.69)	.80	(1.31)							
Mex	.70	(1.25)	1.60	(2.50)							

Affiliation

					F	F	F	F	F	F	F
Mother					7.80*	4.59*	.24	1.52	3.10	.84	.04
USA	1.20	(1.61)	2.50	(2.27)							
Mex	.30	(.94)	.50	(.84)							
Sibling											
USA	.50	(1.58)	2.30	(2.11)							
Mex	.70	(1.70)	1.70	(1.70)							

Danger in the Environment

					F	F	F	F	F	F	F
Mother					5.04*	.17	2.47	.17	2.11	2.11	2.11
USA	.20	(.42)	1.00	(1.33)							
Mex	.20	(.42)	.10	(.31)							
Sibling											
USA	.30	(.67)	1.10	(1.59)							
Mex	.30	(.48)	1.50	(2.75)							

Table 14.5
The Proportion of American Mothers and Mexican Siblings
Use of Scaffolding Behaviors in Play

	American Mother	Mexican Sibling	
	%	%	
Join Play	.12	.11	*
Suggest Symbolic Play	.30	.37	*
Comment on Play	.22	.21	*

Proportions were calculated by dividing the frequency of the individual behaviors by the total frequency of all behaviors for each partner.

* groups do not differ

complexity with their mothers; whereas Mexican children experienced more complex pretend play with their older siblings; and (3) Mexican sibling-child play resembled American mother-child play.

These three interrelated findings suggest that these Mexican older siblings developed the skill of scaffolding play with young children to a greater extent than the American siblings; and in using the skill, they played a role similar to American mothers in constructing play. The use of siblings as caregivers for young children, and the nature of the sibling relationship in the Mexican culture seems to foster the development of this skill. For example, research conducted in traditional cultures similar to Mexico suggests that in societies where siblings are regularly responsible for child care, children develop prosocial and nurturant behavior very early in life (Weisner and Gallimore 1977; Whiting and Whiting 1975).

Sibling caretaking may also provide opportunities for older Mexican children to develop skills in directing play with younger siblings, and younger children may begin to acquire skills and knowledge by participating in play activities with more competent partners.

In American culture children experience playing with both mothers and siblings. However, the nature of American sibling relationships tended to be conflictual and this discord was apparent in their play behavior. American siblings used teaching strategies in scaffolding play and were frequently very directive. They rejected their younger partner's suggestions and often prohibited them from playing. In the sequence below, Aaron age 5.5 years, and her brother Eric aged 3 years, had just finished bashing each other with stuffed animals when the following play began:

E: Ok, play! Let's play western town. I get the horse!
A: Yeah! uh, NO! I have it!
E: No! I have it!

(Mother instructs A to give E the horse.)
(The two children begin to silently set up the pieces.)

E: (talks to himself while holding a human figure on the horse and moving it in the air.)
   Not that way thisa way thisa way! Oh cowboy!
   whoa whoa.
A: (Reaches over and takes one of the other horses lying near E.)
E: Gimme it! (He screams!)
A: You gotta gimme the horse E!
E: Gimme it!
A: You gotta gimme the horse!
E: (Cries) She took it away from me!
   She took it away from me! (He appeals to the observer.)
A: See E. (A shows E the horse.)
E: Gimme it!
A: It's all gone! (Puts it behind her back)
E: No!
A: Why do you wanna see it? Huh?
E: (Stares silently.)
A: (Throws the horse to E.) Well, stand it up then! (demonstrates.)
   See? (Then takes one of the figures lying next to E.)
E: A taked the yellow one away from me! (Cries)
A: No, I have the the blue one!
E: Then you'll have two and I'll have only one!

In contrast, Mexican children rarely experienced playing with their mothers and instead spent more time interacting within groups of mixed-age children and siblings. Mexican siblings were far more tolerant of the younger children's behavior; they were more willing to share, and displayed more cooperative attitudes than American children. This prosocial orientation was reflected in their scaffolding behaviors. Mexican siblings joined their partner's play activity, kept the younger child informed by commenting about the objects or the play itself, and made frequent suggestions for pretend play. The example below was typical of Mexican sibling play:

> Roberto (three years) and his sister Sylvia (five years) are playing with the shapes:
>
> R: Look! Look! Look! (Holds the train pieces for S to see.)
> S: (Looks and continues to put the animal shapes on her train.)
> R: (Watches S while holding a piece of the train, then pushes his train piece.)
>   Beep! Beep! Beep Beep! Rrrrruunnnnnn!
> S: Beep Beep
> R: Rrrrrruuuunnn
> S: (Puts an animal piece on her train like R.)
>   Rrunnnnn! Beep beep!
>   Runnnnnruuun!
>   Here's the street. Ruunnnnruuuunnnn!
> R: Ay! (His train comes apart.)
> S: Here. Let me help you. Let me fix it.
> R: (Gives S his pieces.)

The similarity of American mothers' and Mexican siblings' play with regard to their scaffolding behaviors, their frequency of shared positive affect, and nurturing themes in play may be explained by the roles they took in constructing play.

Fundamental to an apparent "motherly" attitude displayed by the Mexican siblings in play and in daily interaction is the emotional bond which is formed with siblings when the mother's attention is diverted to a new infant and the child joins the sibling group. In two classic accounts of Mexican family life Diaz-Guerrero (1955) and Ramirez and Parres (1957) describe the strong mother-child bond that continues until the birth of the subsequent child. Young infants are the object of attention and their mothers indulge their every need. However, with the birth of the next sibling, the young child joins sibling group and the symbiotic relationship with the mother ends. Siblings become responsible for the young child's socialization and are the main source of the younger child's emotional involvement as well. Therefore, in the context of early interaction older Mexican siblings are gaining knowledge not only about caregiving, but also about how to guide young children's learning and play.

The results of this study demonstrate that siblings can be important facilitators of young childrens' early pretend. This study also illustrates the importance of context when examining childrens' play behavior. It is quite possible that researchers who have argued that children in traditional cultures or American ethnic groups do not engage in pretend play may have overlooked the contexts where play more typically occurs.

References

Bruner, J. (1975). The ontogensis of speech acts. *Journal of Child Language* 2:1–19.

Diaz-Guerrero, R. (1955). Neurosis and the Mexican family structure. *American Journal of Psychiatry* 12:411–417.

Deloache, J. and Plaetzer, B. (1985). Tea for two. Paper presented at the Biennial Meeting of the Society for Research in Child Development, Toronto, Canada.

Dunn, J. and Dale, N. (1984). I a daddy: Two year-olds' collaboration in joint pretend play with sibling and with mother. In I. Bretherton (ed.), *Symbolic Play,* New York: Academic.

Dunn, J. and Wooding, C. (1977). Play in the home: Its implications for learning. In B. Tizard and D. Harvey (eds.), *Biology of Play,* Suffolk: Lavenham Press.

Howes, C., Unger, O. and, Seidner, L. (1989). Social pretend play in toddlers: Parallel with social play and solitary pretend. *Child Development* 60:77–84.

McCune-Nicolich, L. (1981). Towards symbolic functioning: Structure of early pretend games and potential parallels with language. *Child Development* 52:785–797.

Miller, C., and Garvey, C. (1984). Mother-baby role play. In I. Bretherton (ed.), *Symbolic Play,* New York: Academic.

O'Connell B. and Bretherton, I. (1984). Toddler's play alone and with mothers. In I. Bretherton (ed.), *Symbolic Play,* New York: Academic.

Ramirez, M., and Parres, R. (1957). Some dynamic patterns in the organization of the Mexican family. *International Journal of Social Psychiatry* 3:18–21.

Rosenberg, D. (1985). Fantasy play and socio-emotional development. Paper presented at the Society for Research in Child Development, Toronto, Canada.

Sachs, J. (1980). The role of adult-child play in language development. In K. Rubin (ed.), *Children's Play,* San Francisco: Jossey-Bass.

Seidner, L. (1985). Mothers and toddlers: Partners in early pretend. Paper presented at the Biennial Meeting of the Society for Research in Child Development, Toronto, Canada.

Slade, A. (1987). A longitudinal study of maternal involvement and symbolic play. *Child Development* 58:367–375.

Vygotsky, L. 1978. *Mind in Society*. M. Cole (ed.), Cambridge: Harvard Press.

Weisner, T., and Gallimore, R. (1977). My brother's keeper: Child and sibling caretaking. *Current Anthropology* 18:169–90.

Whiting, B. (1980). Culture and social behavior: A model for the development of social behavior. *Ethos*. 8:95–116.

Whiting, B. and Edwards, C. P. (1988). *Children of different worlds: The formation of social behavior*. Cambridge: Harvard Press.

Whiting, B. and Whiting, J. W. M. (1975). *Children of Six Cultures*. Cambridge: Harvard Press.

CHAPTER 15

The Cultural Context of Mother-Infant Play in the Newborn Period

J. Kevin Nugent, Sheila Greene, Dorit Wieczoreck-Deering, Kathleen M. Mazor, John Hendler, and Cynthia Bombardier

In general, parents view their infants as individuals with subjective experiences, social sensibilities, and a sense of self that is present and developing from the very beginning. This view makes varied sequences of interactional play possible, even at the earliest stage of the mother-infant relationship (Brazelton and Cramer 1990; Stern 1985). Parents attribute intention and motives as well as authorship of action to their infants, and by the end of the first month, periods of play for up to fifteen minutes are possible as mothers smile at, sing and talk to, touch, soothe, and generally respond to the social behaviors of their young infants (Brazelton and Cramer 1990).

This early exploratory parent-infant interactional mode of play constitutes the first stage in the development of more complex forms of play that emerge and develop over the course of infancy and early childhood (Belsky and Most 1981). This study examines the nature of early mother-infant play in a sample of primiparous mothers and their newborn infants. In order to examine the nature

The authors would like to thank Marie-Therese Joy, Ann Rath, Dr. Paul O'Mahony of Trinity College, Dr. John Stronge, Master of the National Maternity Hospital, and all the women and infants who participated in this study. Special thanks to Kathleen Neff for her editorial assistance. The Dublin Child Development Study has been funded by grants from the Fogarty Foundation; National Institutes of Health, Washington, D.C.; and the Department of Health and Social Welfare, Dublin, Ireland.

and degree of variability in early mother-infant play, we compared the interaction patterns of a sample of single and married first-time Irish mothers during the first month of their infant's life. Since there is some evidence to suggest that single mothers may be at risk for interactional failure with their infants (Field 1981), this study was designed to test the validity of this hypothesis in a different cultural setting. Thus, we had the opportunity to examine the range of variability in early mother-infant play forms and to study the degree to which the play of the single mother-infant pairs might differ qualitatively from that of the married mother-infant pairs.

Much of what we know about early mother-infant play in single mothers is embedded in the studies of the effects of adolescent pregnancy. The data on the effects of pregnancy on the early interactions of adolescent and single mothers and their infants appear to be consistent across several studies, indicating that young mothers are generally less responsive to their infants and spend less time talking and looking at them than older mothers do (Field 1981; Osofsky and Culp 1986; McAnarney, Lawrence, and Aten, 1979; Roosa, Fitzgerald, and Carlson 1982). LeVine, Garcia-Coll, and Oh (1985) found that during face-to-face interactions with eight-month-old infants, nonadolescent mothers showed more positive affect toward their infants. Culp, Appelbaum, Osofsky, and Levy (1988) studied mother-infant interaction patterns during the newborn period in a sample of adolescent mothers, 90 percent of whom were single, and showed that adolescent mothers vocalized less to their infants than did the primiparous, nonadolescent mothers, although the authors pointed out that the adolescent mothers exhibited a far more variable pattern of behaviors than did the nonadolescent mothers.

In addition, there is a general consensus in the literature that infants born to unmarried mothers are at increased risk for negative developmental outcome (Baldwin 1981; Garfinkel and McLanahan 1986; McAnarney and Thiebe 1981). Moreover, as those infants get older they tend to exhibit more behavioral disorders and perform less well in school (Hetherington, Camara, and Featherman 1983). Since marital status and age are confounded in most studies of unmarried mothers it is very difficult to establish a direct relationship between marital status and mother-infant adaptation. It is now recognized that the children of unmarried mothers are more susceptible to poor developmental outcome, not because of the mother's marital status per se but because of a combination of prenatal and obstetric risk factors and the neonate's exposure to a less than optimal caregiving environment.

Brooks-Gunn and Furstenberg (1986) in their review of this area of research point out that the majority of the studies on adolescent parenting tend to confound age, marital status, race, and SES, by focusing on black unmarried teenagers, especially those living in disadvantaged, urban neighborhoods. This research focus tends to limit our knowledge about other groups of adolescent mothers; it also reinforces the stereotype of the modal adolescent mother (Brooks-Gunn and Furstenberg 1986). In their study of adolescent and unmarried mothers in Puerto Rico, Lester, Garcia-Coll, and Sepkoski (1983) demonstrated that in their sample neither age nor marital status was related to newborn outcome. They argued for the importance of examining the effects of mothers' marital status within the context of the traditions and values of the culture under study. From this point of view, it can be argued that the comparative cultural approach to the study of unmarried mothers may yield a very different risk matrix based on the hypothesis that the combination and hierarchical organization of the predictor variables will vary across cultures, reflecting the range of variability in reproductive and child-rearing contexts in different cultural settings.

In this chapter, data will be presented from the Dublin Child Development Study, comparing the quality of mother-infant play in a sample of primiparous single and married working-class mothers in Ireland. The goal of this study, then, is not only to examine the degree to which unmarried mothers in Ireland are at risk for interactional dysfunction, but also to discover the specific components of the reproductive and child-rearing context in Ireland that may influence the quality of mother-infant play from the very beginning.

Over the last decade it has been widely recognized that there is a need to document the degree of variability in the patterns of early social behavior in different cultural settings, with a view of better understanding what is context-specific and what are the universal processes in the ontogeny of the parent-child relationship (Brazelton 1972; Eibl-Eibesfeldt 1983; Konner 1977; Valsiner 1989; Levine, Caron, and New 1980; Nugent Lester, and Brazelton 1989). In an attempt to understand the origins of early social relations, many researchers have presented evidence from an expanding range of cultures on the nature of the earliest interactions between mothers and their young infants (e.g., Chisholm 1989; Dixon, Tronick, Keefer, and Brazelton 1981; Field and Widmayer 1981; Grossmann and Grossmann 1991; Winn, Tronick, and Morelli 1989; Landers 1989). On the basis of these findings, there has been a conceptual shift in the study of the relationship between biology, culture, and infant development. The traditional unidirectional focus on the parents' socialization practices and on the age/sex/kinship identities of the child's potential interactors (e.g., Caudill and Weinstein 1969; Whiting and Whiting 1975) as the exclusive predictors of interpersonal behavior has given way to a more dialectical approach that emphasizes the role of the infant and the caregiving environment as active participants in the socialization process. From this cultural-ecological perspective, the infant can no longer be viewed as a passive recipient of cultural messages, as many researchers assumed in the past. The socialization process itself is viewed as an active reconstruction process in which the developing child reconstructs the cultural messages of the parents (Chisholm 1989; Valsiner 1989) and the infant is viewed as an active partner in social interaction from the very beginning (Brazelton 1984; Stern 1985; Tronick and Gianino 1986; Valsiner 1989). In sum, infant socialization takes place in a particular cultural niche where the points of pressure and flexibility in mutual adaptation will be patterned by both the niche and the infant him- or herself (Super and Harkness 1982). The earliest forms of mother-infant play provide a powerful example of the transactional nature of the process.

A Cultural-Ecological Perspective

In every culture, the child's immediate cultural niche is the family. The family can be described as an organized social context, where kinship ties and residence are shared. Whether it is an intergenerational social unit or a nuclear unit, the family structure provides the social resources to help organize the infant's niche in terms of providing the nurturance and stimulation necessary for the infant's growth and successful adaptation (Valsiner 1989). Within the family it is the social relationships between marriage partners together with the composition of the family households that make up the core elements of the cultural-ecological niche, within which child development takes place. This niche is an integrated unit, such that no aspect of that niche is independent from the others. When any of the core elements of the niche are missing then the socialization process itself may be at risk and the infant's development may be compromised (Garbarino 1982).

While the historical record demonstrates that family types as the basic parameters that organize family life are adaptive inventions that have emerged over the course of human history and make it possible for individuals to live and develop under a variety of conditions, there is evidence to suggest that infants in Western societies born into a nuclear family where there is no father present may be at risk for a less optimal developmental outcome. In Ireland and in most Western societies, where the nuclear family is the modal family structure, the case of the single mother family represents a special adaptive challenge for society in general and for both the child and parent in particular. In contemporary Irish society, childhood socialization tends to take place in a neolocal nuclear family setting, where after marriage husbands and wives establish a common household in a place where the parents of neither partner lived. In recent years, however, a significant number of children are being born to unmarried mothers and brought up in father-absent households.

From a cultural-ecological perspective, the question to be addressed is, how successful can the child's adaptation be in such a setting or how flexible can individual psychological adaptation be across contexts? Can the emotional support of the joint or extended family network compensate for missing elements in the family of the unmarried mother in such settings? The goal of this study is to examine the degree to which unmarried marital status is a risk factor in terms of family functioning, specifically in terms of the quality of the early mother-infant relationship in Irish society.

In order to understand the degree to which pregnancy out of wedlock and being a single mother affect the quality of early mother-infant play, the phenomenon was examined from a cultural-ecological viewpoint, within the historical and cultural context of Irish society.

Historical and Cultural Context of Out-of-Wedlock Births

While there has been a consistent decrease in the birth rate in the Republic of Ireland over the last decade (Trost 1989), the number of babies born to single mothers continues to rise. The dramatic nature of this trend can best be understood when we examine the percentage of out-of-wedlock births recorded in Ireland since the beginning of the twentieth century. The average percentage of births to unmarried mothers in the first half of this century was below 2 percent. In 1960 the figure stood at 1.6 percent, and while the percentage began to gradually rise in the next decade, by 1975 3.7 percent of the total number of newborns in Ireland were born to unmarried mothers. The 1980s witnessed an even sharper increase in the number of infants born to single mothers, so that by 1985 the percentage had risen to 8.5 percent, and by 1990 the percentage of babies born to unmarried mothers had reached 14 percent of the total number of infants born in Ireland (Central Statistics Office). Greene, Joy, Nugent, and O'Mahoney (1989) presented data to show that with the increase in sexual activity among unmarried people, poor access to contraception, and lack of information on contraception seemed to be the important factors contributing to the increase in out-of-wedlock births in Ireland in recent times. Moreover, it was pointed out that because 95 percent of the population of the Republic of Ireland is Catholic and artificial birth control and sexual activity outside of marriage are contrary to church teaching, for the unmarried pregnant mother in Ireland the general societal disapproval is compounded by the moral disapproval of the church.

There is evidence to suggest that at least since the middle of the last century, attitudes towards unmarried mothers in Ireland have been overwhelmingly negative and birth outside of marriage has not been culturally sanctioned. Testimony given before the Poor Inquiry Commissioners in the mid-1800s suggests that unmarried mothers were often treated as social outcasts, condemned by the church, shunned by former acquaintances, and in some cases driven to begging or prostitution (Connolly 1985). MacGreill, in his comprehensive study of Irish attitudes in recent times, presents evidence to suggest that although attitudes towards unmarried mothers are becoming more tolerant, they still remain predominantly negative (MacGreill 1977). In an earlier report on the Dublin

Table 15.1
Sample Characteristics (n = 108)

	Married Mothers		Unmarried Mothers	
	(n = 74)		(n = 34)	
	mean	S.D.	mean	S.D.
Age	25.4	3.15	21.1	2.3
Educational level				
Primary (7 years)		25%		35%
Junior Level (10 years)		21%		29%
Senior Level (15 years)		40%		29%
College (18 up)		14%		6%

Child Development Study, we presented corroborative data which suggest that attitudes towards pregnancy outside of marriage are still predominantly negative. These data show that single mothers received little positive support from their immediate family members during pregnancy (Nugent, Greene, O'Mahoney, and Hourihane 1989).

The purpose of this study, then, is to examine the degree to which unmarried mothers in an Irish context are at risk for interactional failure with their young infants. To do this we examined the earliest examples of mother-infant play.

Methods

Subjects

Subjects in this study were participants in the Dublin Child Development Study, a longitudinal study of first-time Irish mothers and their infants and families. Two hundred primiparous mothers were first interviewed at the antenatal clinic at the National Maternity Hospital, Dublin, during the beginning of their final trimester of pregnancy. One hundred of the mothers were married, and one hundred were single. One hundred and eight of these mothers and their newborn infants were later observed in their home settings at three weeks after delivery and were the subjects for this study. Of these, seventy-four of the mothers were married, and thirty-four were single. The average age of the mothers in this sample was twenty four (m = 24.1, range, 17–32 years). The average education level was at the secondary school junior level or about three years of post primary schooling. The mothers came predominantly from working-class Dublin families, identified with the use of the social-class index of the Irish Medico-Social Research Board. The sample cannot therefore be considered representative of the population of Ireland as a whole.

Procedures and Measures

Three sets of measures were included. The first set was collected during the beginning of the final trimester of pregnancy, the second during the first three days of the infant's life in the hospital, and the third during a home visit at three weeks postpartum. During the prenatal interview, demographic and maternal psychosocial data sets were collected. The demographic set included information on mothers' marital status, age, and education levels. The maternal psychosocial set included data collected on the social support network of the mothers, specifically as the mothers' perceptions of the degree to which the support met their needs. In addition, mothers' emotional status in terms of the degree of depressive symptomatology was measured using the Center for Epidemiological Studies Depression Scale (CES-D) (Radloff 1977). The CES-D is widely used in epidemiologic studies and has been validated against standardized psychiatric interviews. It discriminates between depressed and nondepressed people, with a false-positive rate of six percent and a false-negative rate of 36.4 percent (Myers and Weissman 1980).

The infant data set included information on the infant's medical status; the information was collected from the hospital medical records during the immediate postnatal period. Only infants who were born by vaginal delivery at term with birth weights above 2,500 grams were selected for this study. Exclusion criteria were as follows: gestational age below thirty eight weeks, Apgar scores lower than eight at one minute and nine at five minutes, and infants with any congenital anomalies.

The infant data set also included measures of the infant's behavior gathered through the administration of the Neonatal Behavioral Assessment Scale in the hospital on the third day of life and in the infant's home at three weeks of age (Brazelton 1984). The individual scores were compiled into seven cluster scores following Lester, Als, and Brazelton's (1982) scheme, and the Orientation, Range of State, and Regulation of State clusters were used in the subsequent analysis. A mean score over the two examinations was computed by combining the three-day cluster score and the three-week score as a way of measuring neonatal adaptation over the first month.

The third set of data was based on the home observations. At three weeks, observations of mother-infant play were carried out under fully naturalistic conditions in the home. Observations lasted for a period of about fifteen minutes and were conducted by a female observer. A continuous fifteen-second time-sampling procedure developed by Belsky, Taylor, and Rovine (1984) was used to gather information on the mother-infant relationship. Information was gathered on the frequency of occurrence of a specific set of maternal, infant, and dyadic behaviors. The individual scores were then reduced to the four categories described by Belsky and his colleagues by summing the frequencies of individual behaviors: *Re-*

ciprocal Interaction, which measures the nature and extent of synchronous and contingent interaction between mother and infant (this included such items as maternal vocalization, stimulate/arouse, maternal positive affect, infant respond/explore, infant vocalization, etc.); *Noninvolvement,* which measures the degree to which the mother was not attending to her infant during the context of the interaction; *Distress,* which captures the amount of infant fussing and the mother's response to her infant's distress; and *Basic Care,* which scores the degree to which the mother was involved in looking after the baby's basic needs during the observation period. Two additional summary scales were added: *Mother-Initiated Interactions* and *Infant-Initiated Interactions,* which were coded to assess the degree to which the infant and the mother took the lead in the interactions.

Results

Demographic Measures

In comparing single and married mothers on the variables that made up the demographic set, t-tests revealed that the single mothers were younger than the married mothers (21.1 years versus 25.4 years, $F = 1.77$, $p < .07$). The unmarried mothers also had lower education levels than married mothers, though only 13 percent of all the mothers in the sample had attended a third level educational institution. Sixty-four percent of the unmarried mothers had ten years or less of formal education, while forty-six percent of the married mothers had the same amount of education. Fifty-five percent of the married mothers and thirty-five percent of the unmarried mothers had twelve years or more of formal education.

Psychosocial Measures

Single mothers reported that they had less adequate social support during pregnancy than married mothers ($F = 2.28$, $p > .04$). On the Maternal Depression Scale the single mothers as a group scored just below the cutoff point of sixteen, which is one standard deviation above the mean ($m = 15.79$, S.D. $= 10.86$). (The cutoff point of sixteen has been used to clinically differentiate between depressed and nondepressed people.) The CES-D scores for the single mothers were higher than those of the married mothers ($m = 15.79$, SD $= 10.6$ versus $m = 13.47$, SD $= 10.6$). In sum, the

comparisons of the prenatal psychosocial profiles of the married
and unmarried mothers reveal that the single mothers felt more
isolated during pregnancy and showed more depressive symptomatology than the married mothers.

Newborn Behavior

There were no differences in birth weight between infants of
unmarried and married mothers (3486 versus 3483 gms). On comparisons of newborn neurobehavioral status as measured by the
Brazelton Scale, there were also no differences on the three selected
cluster scores, the Orientation, Range of State, and State Regulation clusters, at either three days or three weeks between infants of
single and married mothers.

Mother-Infant Play Measures

Comparisons of single and married mothers on the Mother-
Infant Interaction Scale revealed no differences on any of the six
dimensions. While the Reciprocal Interaction, Relief of Distress,
Mother-Initiated, and Infant-Initiated Behavior dimension scores
were all higher for the single mothers, and married mothers scored
higher on the Noninvolvement and Basic Care clusters, none of
these differences reached significance. In a comparison of individual
items on the Reciprocal Interaction dimension, single mothers were
more likely to stimulate their infants ($F = 1.79$, $p < .10$), to look at
them ($F = 1.72$, $p < .10$), and their infants, perhaps as a consequence, showed more positive affect during the interaction than the
infants of the married mothers ($F = 8.86$, $p < .0001$). There was
more evidence of mutual gaze among the married mother-infant dyads than the unmarried mother-infant dyads ($F = 2.6$, $p < .003$). In
the Basic Care dimension, the scores of the unmarried mothers
were higher on the Maternal Caregiving item ($F = 1.75$, $p < .05$).

In order to better understand the relative contributions of the
different demographic, psychosocial, and infant variables to differences in mother-infant play, stepwise multiple regression was performed. Maternal age, maternal education, maternal depression
during pregnancy, maternal perceptions of social support, and newborn behavior as measured by the Brazelton Scale clusters were entered into the regression to see which variables predicted the
quality of mother-infant interaction. There were no significant relationships between any of the variables and the Reciprocal Interaction dimension score. Table 15.2 summarizes the results that

Table 15.2
Results of Multiple Regression Analysis Predicting Mother-Infant Interaction Scale Dimension

Mother-Infant Interaction Dimension	Predictor Variable	R2	F	P
Response to Stress	Mother's Education	.10	10.7	.002
Response to Stress	NBAS Orientation	.17	9.5	.0002
Noninvolvement	NBAS Range of State	.08	8.56	.004
Infant-Initiated Interactions	NBAS Orientation	.07	7.5	.007

were statistically significant. The table shows that there was a significant independent relationship between both the infants' social interactive capacities and the mothers' education levels and the Distress dimension of the Mother-Infant Interaction Scale, which measures the infant's distress and the mother's responsivity to these stress signals. Together these variables contributed to 17 percent of the variance in outcome (R square = .17, p = < .001). In addition, the table shows that the contribution of the infant's behavioral repertoire as measured by State Organization on the Brazelton Scale was the best predictor of maternal noninvolvement in mother-infant interaction (R square = .11, p = < .002). The Brazelton Orientation scores also predicted the number of infant-initiated behaviors during the interaction observation (R square = .07, p = < .007). No relationship was found between the selected variables and outcome on the Basic Care or Reciprocal Interaction summary variables.

In all the analyses, neither marital status nor maternal age, nor the mother's rating of her social support or maternal depression during pregnancy played a role in predicting the quality of reciprocal interaction between mothers and infants during the first month of life.

Discussion

This study shows that while studies of the cultural ecological niche of the newborn infant can extend our understanding of the effects of the cultural environment on early mother-infant play patterns, they also challenge our conceptions of the meaning of psychosocial risk and suggest that what constitutes risk status in one setting may not in another. Definitions of risk are inevitably cultural constructions by virtue of the fact that they are derived from specific circumscribed empirical data sets that often have limited application across cultural settings. The existing literature on adolescent and single parenting, therefore, because the studies are in the main based on a relatively narrow range of adolescent unmarried mothers as Brooks-Gunn and Furstenberg (1986) point out, tells us little about the effects of the mother's marital status or her age on the quality of the mother-infant relationship in different cultural settings.

However, the results of this study suggest that unmarried mothers are not necessarily at risk for interactional failure and that we have to examine a range of competing biological and cultural variables before we can attribute these apparent deficits to the mother's age or marital status. In this comparison of mother-infant play in an Irish sample of primiparous working-class mothers, we found few differences between the interaction scores of single and married mothers and their infants. The differences we did find showed that it was the unmarried mothers who tended to stimulate their infants more and spend more time looking at their infants than the married mothers. These findings are all the more surprising since the single mothers in the sample demonstrated the established characteristics of mothers who are considered to be at risk for interactional failure. They were not only younger and less well educated than the married mothers; they were also more depressed and felt more isolated throughout pregnancy than the married mothers. An examination of the psychosocial profile of these first-time Irish mothers showed that in this Dublin sample, unmarried mothers had an emotionally stressful pregnancy, insofar as they had little support from their families and friends and were more depressed than their married counterparts during pregnancy (Greene, Nugent, Weiczoreck-Deering, O'Mahony, and Graham 1991; Nugent, Greene, O'Mahony, and Hourihane 1989). Even so, the interaction patterns of the unmarried mother-infant dyads were generally indistinguishable from those of the married mothers in the sample at three weeks postpartum, and in some aspects the unmarried mother-infant pairs showed higher levels of reciprocal interaction than those seen in the married mother-infant dyads.

To better understand the possible reasons for this unexpected finding, we proceeded to examine the role of the other demographic and infant variables to see if they had played a moderating role in leading to this outcome. We first decided to map mothers' patterns of depressive symptomatology from the third trimester of pregnancy to the three-week postpartum point. Surprisingly, we found that although unmarried mothers were more depressed during pregnancy, there were no longer any differences between the depression levels of married and single mothers at three weeks, at the time of our assessment of mother-infant interaction (18.82 versus 12.98 during pregnancy and 11.39 versus 12.04 on the CES-D at three weeks). As we suggested in a previous report (Greene et al. 1991), the relative disappearance of depressive symptomatology in unmarried mothers may be due to the fact that the cultural rejection experienced by the unmarried mothers during pregnancy was replaced by a general cultural acceptance of mother and infant, which characterizes Irish societal attitudes to babies and their mothers. This shift in the mothers' psychological profiles may in turn have contributed to the apparent absence of differences between married and unmarried interaction patterns in the postnatal period. (This finding suggests that prenatal measures of depression have little relevance for assessing the effects of current levels of maternal depression on outcome and also highlights the need for documenting patterns of maternal depression over time (Greene et al. 1991).)

A central goal of this study was to understand the process of mother-infant play during the first month of life and to examine the role of both infant and mother in the regulation of interpersonal relations at the beginning of life. These results suggest that the infant has a dominant role in shaping the early patterns of mother-infant relations in the newborn period. The primary finding of the research reported in this chapter is that the major determinant of differences in mother-infant interaction patterns during the newborn period were due not to the mother's marital status or her age but, rather, to the characteristics of her infant. Furthermore, the degree of depressive symptomatology during pregnancy was not related to mother-infant interaction patterns, nor was the perceived adequacy of the degree of social support mothers received during pregnancy predictive of differences in mother-infant play. Specifically, it was a combination of the baby's social responsiveness, as assessed by the orientation items of the Brazelton Scale over the first three weeks and the mother's educational level that predicted the mother's ability to respond to the infant's distress signals during her interactions with her infant. This suggests that mothers who had higher education levels and whose infants were alert and responsive were better able to read and decipher the infants' signs of stress, and were better able to console their infants when they were aroused or crying. While it is difficult to identify the psychological mechanisms by which the mother's education level can contribute to her ability to better respond to her infant, it may be that if this higher education level involves having more knowledge about child development, then this may be an explanatory factor, as Field (1981) and de Lissovey (1973) suggest in their studies of interaction patterns in adolescent mothers and their infants. However, it is also clear that the infant's own social responsivity and perhaps the clarity of his/her communication cues and thus the degree to which the infant was able to elicit maternal caregiving made an independent contribution to the positive reciprocal outcome. It may be that even for these mothers, whose pregnancy had been emotionally stressful, the newborn infant acted as a catalyst in eliciting responsive caregiving from the mother. This could also help explain the absence of depressive symptomatology in the unmarried mothers after the baby was born. Nugent and Brazelton (1989) have argued that not only is the newborn period a time when both infants and parents are in a state of heightened readiness for exploratory interaction and mutual exchange but also that the infant can be seen to provide a powerful motive for positive change in the mother. From a bio-evolutionary perspective the human infant is beautifully designed to elicit from the caregiving environment all the stimulation necessary for his or her species-specific adaptation. Fraiberg has also pointed out that the newborn infant can mobilize the positive adaptive tendencies in the new mother and that "the birth of the infant stands for the renewal of the self; his birth can be experienced as a psychological rebirth for his parents" (Fraiberg 1980, p. 54).

Another intriguing finding is that infants who demonstrated good state organization over the first three weeks of life, that is, who were not irritable or liable and had well-organized sleep-arousal patterns, tended to have mothers who were less involved with their infants. While no causal relationship can be inferred between the degree to which the infants were easy or placid and the lower involvement level of their mothers, this finding suggests that "easy" or so-called placid babies may tend to elicit less involvement from caregivers. It may be as McKim (1987) points out, that a more fretful baby presents more of a challenge to parents than a placid one. Horowitz, Linn, and Buddin (1983) also found that infants whose behavior was variable tended to receive more stimulation from their caregivers, while Nugent (1991) in a study of father-infant involvement concluded that a certain degree of unpredictability and variability in state behavior may elicit more involvement in parental caregiving. From this point of view, the data reported here suggest that the so-called easy baby may lead to less involvement from the mother and as a behavioral phenotype may be less adaptive in achieving the infant's developmental goal of eliciting and receiving the kind of stimulation necessary for promoting his or her successful adaptation. An alternative explanation is that the mothers of these infants were reading their infant's cues accurately and were responding appropriately to their baby's well-organized sleep-wake states. The mothers did not need to be attentive to their infants, so that their apparent noninvolvement may not imply inadequate or inappropriate caregiving, and the infant's behavior in turn is not necessarily maladaptive.

While it has been well established that both mothers and infants contribute to reciprocal play interactions, as Tronick and Gianino (1986), Brazelton et al. (1974), and Belsky and colleagues (1984) have demonstrated, the question of whether mothers exercise relatively greater power and influence in the dyadic relationship as it emerges at the beginning of life is difficult to answer. This is a particularly important question for researchers and clinicians who wish to understand the origins of social play. It is also important for those who wish to understand the meaning of psychosocial risk and the degree to which unmarried mothers are at risk for interactional failure with their infants. Belsky, Taylor, and Rovine (1984) point out that the infant's influence as a controlling agent in the interaction seems to be stronger at the beginning and then seems to decrease over time. The data reported in this chapter can be interpreted to confirm the tilting of the interactional power balance in favor of the infant at least in this early stage of its emergence and development. It supports the notion of the child as an active agent in the regulation of interpersonal relations from the very beginning, as Brazelton, Tronick, and others have argued (e.g., Brazelton 1984; Tronick and Gianino 1986). The infant's behavior can influence outcome even in an environment of established psychosocial risk. This has important implications for intervention work with infants of at-risk mothers or infants born into high-risk settings, in that the contribution of the infant may serve to counterbalance the risk present in the microsystem itself. Since

the child seems to play an active role in the regulation of interpersonal relations, it may be that infant-centered but family-
focused interventions with a responsive infant may help to mitigate
the risk status of the relatively sparse ecological niche of the unmarried mother.

In sum, an important finding in this study of primiparous
working-class Irish mothers is that neither mothers' marital status
nor their age was predictive of interactional difficulties in the newborn period. Moreover, although the unmarried mothers reported
having little emotional support from their families and friends and
reported feeling very depressed during pregnancy, they were able to
respond positively to their infants in the newborn period. The quality of their play interactions with their infants was generally indistinguishable from that of the married mothers; in fact, they tended
to provide more stimulation to their infants than did the married
mothers. In addition, their infants showed more positive affect during mother-infant play than did the infants of the married mothers.
The infant's active role in the emerging mother-infant relationship
seemed to be able to moderate the effects of what potentially may
have been an environment of risk. These results demonstrate the
difficulty in assuming the validity of specific risk factors across settings and suggest that definitions of risk must include measurements of the infant's contribution and must be context-specific in
order to be able to provide appropriate guidelines for both clinicians
and policymakers who are attempting to meet the needs of infants
and their families in at-risk settings.

References

Als, H.; Lester, B. M.; and Brazelton, T. B. (1982). Regional obstetric anes-
thesia and newborn behavior: A re-analysis for synergistic effects.
Child Development, 53:687–92.

Baldwin, W. (1981). Adolescent pregnancy and childbearing: An overview.
Seminars on Perinatology 5:1–8.

Belskey, J., and Most, R. K. (1981). From exploration to play: A cross-
sectional study of infant play behavior. *Developmental Psychology*
17:630–39.

Belsky, J.; Taylor, D. G.; and Rovine, M. (1984). The Pennsylvania infant and
family development project, II: The development of reciprocal interaction in the mother-infant interaction dyad. *Child Development* 55:
706–17.

Brazelton, T. B. (1972). Implications of infant development among the Mayan Indians of Mexico. *Human Development* 15:90–111.

Brazelton, T. B. (1984). *Neonatal Behavioral Assessment Scale.* 2d ed. Clinics in Developmental Medicine, No. 50. London: William Heinemann Medical Books; Philadelphia: J. B. Lippincott.

Brazelton, T. B., and Cramer, B. G. (1990). *The Earliest Relationship.* Reading, Mass.: Addison-Wesley.

Brazelton, T. B.; Koslowski, B.; and Main, M. (1979). The origins of reciprocity: The early infant-mother interaction. In M. Lewis and L. A. Rosenblum (eds.). *The Effects of the Infant on the Caregiver.* New York: Wiley and Sons.

Brazelton, T. B.; Yogman, M. W.; Als, H.; and Tronick, E. Z. (1979). The infant as a focus for family reciprocity. In M. Lewis and L. Rosenblum (eds.), *Social Network of the Developing Child.* New York: John Wiley.

Brooks-Gunn, J., and Furstenburg, F. F. (1986). The children of adolescent mothers: Physical, academic, and psychological outcomes. *Developmental Review* 6:224–51.

Caudill, W., and Weinstein, H. (1969). Maternal care and infant behavior in Japan and America. *Psychiatry* 32:12–43.

Chisholm, J. (1989). Biology, culture, and the development of temperament. In *The Cultural Context of Infancy.* Vol. 1. *See* Nugent, Lester, and Brazelton 1989.

Connolly, S. J. (1985). Marriage in pre-famine Ireland. In A. Cosgrove (ed.), *Marriage in Ireland.* Dublin: College Press.

Culp, R. E.; Appelbaum, M. I.; Osofsky, J. D.; and Levy, J. D. (1988). Adolescent and older mothers: Comparisons between prenatal and maternal variables and newborn interaction measures. *Infant Behavior and Development* 11:353–62.

de Lissovey, V. (1973 July–August). Child care by adolescent parents. *Children Today:* 22–25.

Dixon, S.; Tronick, E.; Keefer, C.; and Brazelton, T. B. (1981). Mother-infant interaction among the Gusii of Kenya. In T. Field, A. Sostek, P. Vietze, and P. H. Liederman (eds.), *Culture and Early Interactions.* Hillsdale, N.J.: Lawrence Erlbaum Associates.

Eibl-Eibesfeldt, I. (1983). Patterns of parent-child interaction in a cross-cultural perspective. In A. Oliverio and M. Zapella (eds.), *The Behavior of Human Infants.* New York: Plenum.

Field, T. (1981). Early development of preterm offspring of teenage mothers. In K. Scott, T. Field, and E. Robertson (eds.), *Teenage Parents and Their Offspring.* New York: Grune and Stratton.

Field, T., and Widmayer, S. (1981). Mother-infant interactions among lower SES Black, Puerto Rican, and South American immigrants. In Field, Sostek, Vietze, and Liederman (eds.), *Culture and Early Interactions.*

Fraiberg, S. (1980). *Clinical Studies in Infant Mental Health: The First Year of Life.* New York: Basic Books.

Garbarino, J. (1982). Sociocultural risk: Dangers to competence. In C. B. Kopp and J. B. Crakow (eds.), *The Child: Development in Social Context.* Reading, Mass.: Addison-Wesley.

Garfinkel, I., and McLanahan, S. (1986). *Single Mothers and Their Children.* Washington, D.C.: The Urban Institute Press.

Greene, S. M.; Joy, M. T.; Nugent, J. K.; and O'Mahony, P. (1989). Contraceptive practices of married and single first-time mothers. *Journal of Biosocial Science* 21:379–85.

Greene, S.; Nugent, J. K.; Wieczoreck-Deering, D.; O'Mahony, P.; and Graham, R. (1991). Patterns of depressive symptomatology in a sample of first-time mothers. *Irish Journal of Psychology* 12(2): 263–75.

Grossman, K., and Grossman, K. (1991). Newborn behavior: The quality of early parenting and later toddler-parent relationships in a group of German infants. In *The Cultural Context of Infancy.* vol. 2. *See* Nugent, Lester, and Brazelton 1989.

Hetherington, M.; Camara, K.; and Featherman, D. L. (1983). Achievement and intellectual functioning of children in one-parent households. In J. Soence (ed.), *Achievement and Achievement Motives.* San Francisco: W. H. Freeman.

Horowitz, F. D.; Linn, P.; and Buddin, B. (1983). Neonatal assessment: Evaluating the potential for plasticity. In T. B. Brazelton and B. M. Lester (eds.), *New Approaches to Developmental Screening for Infants.* New York: Elsevier.

Konner, M. (1977). Infancy among the Kalahari San. In P. H. Liederman, S. R. Tulken, and A. Rosenfeld (eds.), *Culture and Infancy: Variations in the Human Experience.* New York: Academic.

Landers, C. (1989). A psychobiological study of infant development in South India. *See* Nugent, Lester, and Brazelton 1989.

Lester, B. M.; Garcia-Coll, C.; and Sepkoski, C. (1983). A cross-cultural study of teenage pregnancy and neonatal behavior. In T. Field and A. Sostek (eds.), *Infants Born at Risk.* New York: Grune and Stratton.

Levine, L.; Garcia-Coll, C.; and Oh, W. (1985). Determinants of mother-infant interaction in adolescent mothers. *Pediatrics* 75:1–23.

L. W. (1980). New Knowledge about the infant from current re-arch: Implications from psychoanalysis. *Journal of American Psy-oanalytic Association* 28:181–98.

. (1985). *The Interpersonal World of the Infant.* New York: Basic.

. M., and Harkness, S. (1982). The infant's niche in rural Kenya d metropolitan America. In L. L. Adler (ed.), *Cross-Cultural Re-irch at Issue.* New York: Academic Press.

E. Z., and Gianino, A. (1986). The transmission of maternal distur-nce to the infant. In E. Z. Tronick and T. M. Field (eds.), *Maternal pression and Infant Disturbance,* New Directions for Child Devel-ment. San Francisco: Jossey-Bass.

(1989). Family models in Northern Europe. Presented at the NESCO/CNR Conference, "Changing Family Patterns and Gender les in Europe," Rome, May 1989.

J. (1989). *Human Development and Culture.* Lexington, Mass.: xington Books.

B. B. and Whiting, J. W. (1975). *Children of Six Cultures.* Cam-dge, Mass.: Harvard University Press.

Tronick, E. Z.; and Morelli, G. (1989). The infant and the group: A k at Efe caretaking practices in Zaire. In *The Cultural Context of ancy.* Vol. 1. See Nugent, Lester, and Brazelton 1989.

LeVine, R. A.; Caron, J.; and New, R. (1980). Anthro
opment. *New Directions for Child Developme*

MacGreill, M. (1977). *Prejudice and Tolerance in Ire*
Industrial Relations.

McAnarney, E. R. and Thiebe, H. A. (1981). Adolesc
have learned in a decade and what remains
in Perinatology 5(1):91–103.

McAnarney, E. R.; Lawrence, R.; and Aten, M. (19
hood: A preliminary report of adolescent m
Pediatric Research 13:328–35.

McKim, M. K. (1987). Transition to what? New
first year. *Family Relations* 36:22–25.

Myers, J. K. and Weissman, M. M. (1980). Use of s
to detect depression in a community samp
Psychiatry 137(9):1081–83.

Nugent, J. K. (1991). Cultural and psychological i
role in infant development. *Journal of M*
53(2):475–85.

Nugent, J. K., and Brazelton, T. B. (1989). Preven
fants and families: The NBAS model. *Infa*
10(2):84–99.

Nugent, J. K.; Greene, S.; O'Mahony, P.; Houriha
mothers and the transition to parenthoo
sented at the WHO/CNR conference, "Cha
Gender Roles in Europe," Rome, May 198

Nugent, J. K.; Lester, B. M.; and Brazelton, T. B.
text of Infancy, vol. 1. Norwood, N.J.: Able

Osofsky, J.; Culp, A. (1986, April). Adolescent
tionship between prenatal factors and pa
presented at the International Conferer
Angeles.

Radloff, L. S. (1977). The CES-D. Scale: A self-
research in the general population. *Appl*
ment 1:385–401.

Richardson, V. (1991). Decision-making by unr
Journal of Psychology 12(2):165–81.

Roosa, M.; Fitzgerald, H.; and Carlson, N. (198
and older mothers: A systems analysis.
Family 44:367–77.

Contributors

Mohammad Ahmeduzzaman, Department of Human Environmental Studies, Central Michigan University, Mount Pleasant, MI 48859

Marjorie Beeghly, Harvard Medical School and Child Development Unit, Children's Hospital, 300 Longwood Ave., Boston, Mass. 02115

Maxine Biben, Laboratory of Comparative Ethology, National Institute of Child Health and Human Development, National Institutes of Health, Building 112, Room 205, Bethesda, Md. 20892

Cynthia Bombardier, Department of Human Development, University of Massachusetts at Amherst, Amherst, Mass. 01003

Virginia Burks, Department of Psychology, Box 86, Peabody Hall, Vanderbilt University, Nashville, Tenn. 37215

James Carson, Department of Psychology, University of California-Riverside, Riverside, Calif. 92521

Jeffrey F. Cohn, Department of Psychology, University of Pittsburgh, 604 Engineering Hall, 4015 O'Hara St., Pittsburgh, Pa. 15260

Carolyn Edwards, Department of Family Studies, Funkhouser Building, University of Kentucky, Lexington, Ky. 40506-0054

Jo Ann Farver, Department of Psychology, University of Southern California, SGM 501, Los Angeles, Calif. 90089

Anne Fernald, Department of Psychology, Jordan Hall, Bldg. 420, Stanford University, Stanford, Calif. 94305-2130

387

Tiffany Field, University of Miami Medical School, Mailman Center for Child Development, P. O. Box 016820, Miami, Fla. 33101

Alan Fogel, Department of Psychology, University of Utah, Salt Lake City, Utah 84112

Sheila Greene, Department of Psychology, Trinity College, Dublin, Republic of Ireland

John Hendler, Department of Human Development, University of Massachusetts, Amherst, Mass. 01003

Frank H. Hooper, College of Human Development, Department of Child and Family Studies, 201 Slocum Hall, Syracuse University, Syracuse, N.Y. 13244-1250

Jeanne Karns, Department of Psychology, Indiana University, Bloomington, Ind. 47405

Phyllis Levenstein, Verbal Interaction Project, Inc., Center for Mother-Child Home Program, 3268 Island Road, Wantagh, N.Y. 11793

Kevin MacDonald, Department of Psychology, California State University Long Beach, Long Beach, Calif. 90840

Kathleen M. Mazor, School of Education, University of Massachusetts, Amherst, Mass. 01003

J. Kevin Nugent, Children's Hospital, Child Development Unit, Harvard Medical School, 300 Longwood Ave., Boston, Mass. 02115; and Department of Social Services, School of Education, University of Massachusetts, Amherst, Mass. 01003

Evangeline Nwokah, Department of Child Development and Family Studies, Purdue University, West LaFayette, Ind. 47907

John O'Hara, Verbal Interaction Project, Inc., Center for Mother-Child Home Program, 3268 Island Road, Wantagh, N.Y. 11793

Daniela K. O'Neill, Department of Psychology, Jordan Hall, Bldg. 420, Stanford University, Stanford, Calif. 94305-2130

Jaak Panksepp, Department of Psychology, Bowling Green State University, Bowling Green, Ohio 43403

Ross Parke, Department of Psychology, University of California-Riverside, Riverside, Calif. 92521

Brad Pollack, College of Human Development, Department of Child and Family Studies, 210 Slocum Hall, University of Syracuse, Syracuse, N.Y. 13244-1250

Jaipaul Roopnarine, College of Human Development, Department of Child and Family Studies, 201 Slocum Hall, Syracuse University, Syracuse, N.Y. 13244-1250

Stephen Suomi, Laboratory of Comparative Ethology, National Institute of Child Health and Human Development, National Institutes of Health, Building T-18 (NIHAC), Room 1, Bethesda, Md. 20892

Brian Sutton-Smith, Graduate School of Education, University of Pennsylvania, Philadelphia, Pa. 19104

Dorit Wieczoreck-Deering, Department of Psychology, Trinity College, Dublin, Republic of Ireland

Beatrice Whiting, Harvard Graduate School of Education, Cambridge, Mass. 02138